Children Who Resist Postseparation Parental Contact

American Psychology-Law Society Series

Children Who Resist Postseparation Parental Contact

A Differential Approach for Legal and Mental Health Professionals

Barbara Jo Fidler

Nicholas Bala

Michael A. Saini

OXFORD
UNIVERSITY PRESS

OXFORD
UNIVERSITY PRESS

Oxford University Press is a department of the University of Oxford.
It furthers the University's objective of excellence in research, scholarship, and
education by publishing worldwide.

Oxford   New York
Auckland   Cape Town   Dar es Salaam   Hong Kong   Karachi
Kuala Lumpur   Madrid   Melbourne   Mexico City   Nairobi
New Delhi   Shanghai   Taipei   Toronto

With offices in
Argentina   Austria   Brazil   Chile   Czech Republic   France   Greece
Guatemala   Hungary   Italy   Japan   Poland   Portugal   Singapore
South Korea   Switzerland   Thailand   Turkey   Ukraine   Vietnam

Oxford is a registered trade mark of Oxford University Press in the UK
and certain other countries.

Published in the United States of America by
Oxford University Press
198 Madison Avenue, New York, NY 10016

Library of Congress Cataloging-in-Publication Data

Fidler, Barbara Jo, 1956–
Children who resist postseparation parental contact: a differential approach
    for legal and mental health professionals/Barbara Jo Fidler, Nicholas Bala,
    Michael A. Saini.—1st ed.
p. cm.—(American psychology-law society book series)
Includes bibliographical references and index.
ISBN 978-0-19-989549-6
1. Children of divorced parents—Psychology.   2. Children of separated parents—Psychology.
    3. Separation anxiety in children.   4. Divorced people—Counseling of.
    5. Alienation (Social psychology)   I. Bala, Nicholas C.   II. Saini, Michael A.   III. Title.
HQ777.5.F43 2012
362.82'943—dc23
2011050786

Printed in the United States of America on acid-free paper

Contents

Series Foreword

This book series is sponsored by the American Psychology-Law Society (APLS). APLS is an interdisciplinary organization devoted to scholarship, practice, and public service in psychology and law. Its goals include advancing the contributions of psychology to the understanding of law and legal institutions through basic and applied research; promoting the education of psychologists in matters of law and the education of legal personnel in matters of psychology; and informing the psychological and legal communities and the general public of current research, educational, and service activities in the field of psychology and law. APLS membership includes psychologists from the academic, research, and clinical practice communities as well as members of the legal community. Research and practice are represented in both the civil and criminal legal arenas. APLS has chosen Oxford University Press as a strategic partner because of its commitment to scholarship, quality, and the international dissemination of ideas. These strengths will help APLS reach its goal of educating the psychology and legal professions and the general public about important developments in psychology and law. The focus of the book series reflects the diversity of the field of psychology and law, as we will publish books on a broad range of topics.

In the latest book in the series, *Children Who Resist Postseparation Parental Contact: A Differential Approach for Legal and Mental Health Professionals*, Barbara Fidler, Nicholas Bala, and Michael A. Saini, a multidisciplinary team consisting of a psychologist, a law professor, and a professor of social work, provide a comprehensive overview of the literature and law on alienation and resistance to contact with a parent after separation and divorce. Rich descriptions from qualitative interviews with 37 leading international experts from a variety of professions and disciplines, including mental health professionals, advocates, lawyers, judges, and scholars, are interwoven throughout, providing a breadth of perspectives that is rarely compiled in one volume. The use of legal decisions and clinical cases serves to illustrate the ways in which issues related to parental alienation play out in real life and demonstrates the interplay between the clinical issues and the legal decisions.

Fidler, Bala, and Saini begin by discussing the prevalence of alienation and the increase in the number of alienation cases seen in recent years. The definition and debate surrounding the psychological implications of alienation as a "syndrome," and the risk factors and indicators involved in alienation, are considered. Issues involved in the evaluation of alienation and assessment tools developed to assist in these evaluations are reviewed, as are the prognosis and long-term consequences of untreated alienation. Prevention strategies, intervention techniques, and legal responses to alienation are presented. The authors conclude with a synopsis of the most relevant issues and provide recommendations for practice, policy, and research. Throughout the volume, qualitative interview data and legal decisions and cases allow the reader to gain a rich understanding of both the clinical and legal implications of the issues related to alienation and for the various parties involved.

Children Who Resist Postseparation Parental Contact presents a detailed description of the multitude of issues—clinical and legal—involved in parental alienation and from a variety of perspectives, both international and interdisciplinary. Scholars, clinicians, policymakers, legal professionals, and practitioners will undoubtedly find that this book will shape the future of family law and clinical practice in this area.

Patricia A. Zapf
Series Editor

Preface

Since 1976, when Judith Wallerstein and Joan Kelly first coined the term "unholy alliance" to describe the relationship between an aligned parent and children who reject the other parent, there has been controversy about why children resist or refuse to have contact with a parent after separation. Richard Gardner's conceptualization of "parental alienation syndrome" (PAS) in the 1980s advanced the study of this question by popularizing the concept of "parental alienation," though his work was and remains highly controversial, including debate over whether this should be characterized as a "syndrome." By the start of the millennium, the use of the concept of "parental alienation" became more common among legal and mental health professionals, and parents going through high-conflict separations have increasingly become aware of and started to use, and sometimes misuse, the concept. Despite its now widespread usage, controversy about the definition and use of the term "alienation" has persisted. Some claim that the primary cause of children to resist or refuse contact with a parent after separation is the behaviors and attitudes of the alienating parent, while others argue that this is usually due to acts of abuse, neglect, or poor parenting by the rejected parent. Polarized advocacy groups have become involved in the debate, with feminist groups tending to dismiss alienation claims and emphasizing concerns about violence and abuse, while groups representing "alienated parents," including fathers' rights groups, argue that alienation is inevitably caused by the attitude and conduct of custodial parents (usually mothers). There is also significant controversy in the professional literature about how to respond to alienation, with some arguing for a change in custody when severe alienation exists and others arguing for a more cautious response.

There is growing interest and concern about alienation among the public, parents, advocacy groups, professionals, the courts, and governments. This heightened concern is due in part to the growing frustrations of parents with the apparent inability of the courts and other agencies to deal effectively with these cases. The courts, in turn, often struggle with the complexity of the mental health and developmental issues in these cases. Further, there has been an increase in media interest and public advocacy about the issue of alienation, often focusing on the most extreme cases. While some of the public commentary is biased or ill informed, there is a clear need for improvements in how the justice system and mental health professionals respond to high-conflict cases where alienation or abuse allegations are made.

The study of alienation is both complicated (e.g., distinguishing between alienation and abuse) and complex (e.g., understanding cases that involve both alienation and abuse). While there are some important emerging areas of consensus, there remain some significant areas of disagreement in the field. Although the term "alienation" is widely used, there is no single definition that is widely accepted. While exploring the language and definitional controversies, for the purposes of this book we have relied on the widely used definition of Kelly and Johnston (2001). We use the term "alienation" to describe when a child resists or rejects a parent, and this reaction is disproportionate to the child's actual experience (current or previous) with that parent and involves, in part, alienating strategies and behaviors on the part of the favored parent, in situations where previously the child had a positive relationship with the rejected parent. While the rejected parent may have some parenting limitations, as expected of any parent, these do not deter the child from having a good relationship with the parent prior to the separation, and in the absence of the favored parent's alienating behavior, these parental limitations would not be cause for a child to reject the parent.

"Alienation" is distinguished from more common strained parent–child relationships or contact problems primarily related to developmental factors, such as age or gender preferences, or time-limited, expected reactions to the separation or divorce (e.g., anger or upset at one parent, reaction to new partner), or parental conflict. Importantly, "alienation" is also distinguished from cases in which there is a "justified rejection" (or "realistic estrangement"[1]) of a parent primarily due to abuse, neglect, or significantly compromised parenting. In high-conflict cases it is common for both parents to engage in alienating behaviors; however, not all children become alienated by alienating parental behavior. It is clear that any assessment of a family requires consideration of the conduct of both of the parents, and often other adults like grandparents or stepparents, the child's temperament, development and adjustment, and the

---

[1] The term "realistic estrangement" is used by some writers. We prefer to avoid this term as it can be confusing because the word "estrangement" has a broader range of meaning and connotations.

broader sociolegal context. While there is controversy over many aspects of alienation, it is clear that these cases are presenting themselves with increasing frequency in the family justice system.

As alienation is a multidimensional concept, there is an assortment of risk factors and indicators that are related to the occurrence of alienation. Of these, the parents' mental health and the child's level of involvement in the parents' dispute stand out as significant markers to consider when assessing the presence of alienation. The assessment and accurate measurement of alienation is an emerging area of research. To date, several decision trees have been created, and there is a growing interest is developing diagnostic tools capable of distinguishing a child's justified rejection of a parent from alienation. We also offer a differential approach for identifying the nature, severity, frequency, and impact of alienating behaviors based on our review of this emerging literature. There are also a growing number of prevention and intervention strategies developed that range from educating parents and children about the pitfalls of high conflict and alienation to more intensive interventions in severe cases of alienation. The courts have also been actively involved in redressing the negative consequences of alienation, and judges are increasingly willing to differentially address the most severe cases, which in some cases involves removing a child from the custodial or favored parent.

By focusing on alienation as a complex problem, this book provides a comprehensive approach for the early identification of alienation and for intervening to resolve the negative consequences of alienation. By highlighting the need for early identification of families at risk of high conflict and parent–child contact problems, irrespective of the cause, we emphasize the value of differential responses to screen and identify cases of alienation and abuse. Once cases are screened and identified, a differential response to intervention can occur based on the severity, nature, and frequency of the parent–child contact problem, to link families to particular interventions, such as educational, therapeutic, and/or legal. There needs to be a comprehensive strategy that involves multiple stakeholders from various fields of practice working together to conduct better research, develop more effective programs, and foster wider collaboration to help deal with this growing problem.

This book is written by a multidisciplinary team: a psychologist, a law professor, and a professor of social work. The purpose of the book is to help professionals, students, and policymakers better understand the complexity of alienation and resistance to contact with a parent, and to propose strategies to effectively respond to these cases. Although it is not intended to be a "parenting" or "self-help" guide for those involved in these cases, concerned members of the public and parents will also find the book useful in helping to discern the complexity of these issues and in considering options for consideration.

We provide a critical and empirically based review of literature and law on alienation and resistance to contact with a parent after separation and divorce. The research team also surveyed all reported Canadian cases to the end of 2009 plus cases during the first 8 months of 2010 that deal with parental alienation, and Australian cases to the middle of 2011. Leading cases and selected legal literature from other jurisdictions are also discussed. The book interweaves our review of the growing body of social science and legal literature, our experiences as clinicians and teachers, and our conversations with 37 leading international experts from a number of disciplines and professions. We make transparent the distinctions about the status of knowledge claims that are based on clinical inferences.

The qualitative interviews provide a rich picture of the range of perspectives of scholars, mental health professionals, advocates, lawyers, and judges. We undertook these interviews to explore the perceptions of leaders in the family justice field; to learn how they define, assess, and respond to cases of alienation and resistance to contact; to learn about their experiences of what works and does not work for these children and families; and to explore their views on the current controversies and debates.

The book starts with a summary of the historical development of the concept of alienation and discusses the causes, dynamics, and differentiation of various types of parent–child contact problems. We explore the definitional controversies, including the ongoing debate over whether alienation is a "syndrome." The book critically reviews the social science literature with respect to prevalence, risk factors, indicators, assessment, and measurement to form a conceptual integration of the confluence of multiple factors that are more precisely relevant to the etiology, maintenance, and prognosis of parent alienation and alienated children. We include detailed consideration of the developing literature on the short- and long-term impact of alienation. Legal and clinical strategies for early intervention and the prevention of alignments and alienation, both from a societal and individual case perspective, are discussed. We discuss the rights of children and the role of their wishes and preferences in legal proceedings. The book also considers legal and clinical strategies and interventions that are based on the level and nature of the problem, and concludes with recommendations for practice, research, and policy.

This book discusses a set of complex, interdisciplinary topics that can be the subject of lifelong study. Although there are many references to jurisprudence, legislation, and social science literature, this book does not purport to be a comprehensive review of all literature and law. In particular, while lawyers, judges, and law students should find this text valuable, we caution that this book does not purport to comprehensively state the law of any jurisdiction. Courts around the world face similar challenges and have often taken similar approaches to these problems. We discuss common themes reflected in the jurisprudence and legislation of English-speaking countries. Not surprisingly, given the fact that we are all Canadians, we have drawn quite extensively on legal examples from our own country, but there are also many references to cases and statutes from the United States, England, and Australia. For most issues related to alienation and postseparation resistance to contact, there are common legal themes and judicial approaches, and the specific jurisdiction in which an illustrative case example is decided may not be very significant. There are, however, also issues for which there are very different approaches in different jurisdictions, such as whether alienation of children should result in a reduction of child or spousal support; for these issues we attempt to explore the variation between jurisdictions. This book should not be relied upon for detailed legal information about the law of any jurisdiction, which may in any event change after completion of this manuscript. Those with specific legal problems should get appropriate legal advice about the law in their jurisdiction.

Barbara Jo Fidler
Nicholas Bala
Michael A. Saini
January 2012

Acknowledgments

We extend our utmost appreciation to the 37 experts, including judges, lawyers, mental health professionals, academics, policy advisors, and advocates who gave their time to participate in our interviews and share their expertise and insight.

We also wish to thank the research assistants who worked on this project during 2010 and 2011: Max Laskin and Alex Fidler Wener, graduates of the Desautels Faculty of Management, McGill University; Marlo Drago, graduate of York University; Christine Ashborne, J.D. 2011, at the Faculty of Law, Queen's University; and Shely Polak and Emnet Yadeta, graduate students at the Factor-Inwentash Faculty of Social Work, University of Toronto.

As we were writing this book, we presented highlights of the many complex issues raised in this manuscript to interdisciplinary professionals at professional education programs, and we are grateful for the many helpful, and sometimes challenging, comments made by members of these audiences and colleagues. Some members of the writing team have also continued to work with children and parents involved in these complex cases, and we are grateful for what we have learned from working with them and hope that we have also served them well.

About the Authors

Barbara Jo Fidler is a registered psychologist and accredited mediator practicing in Ontario, Canada. She maintains a private practice and is a founding member of Family Solutions, a team devoted to working with separated and divorced families. She provides consultation, reunification intervention, mediation, arbitration, parenting coordination, expert court testimony, and custody assessment reviews. Her practice also includes marital/couple, individual (child, adolescents, and adult), and family counseling. Dr. Fidler provides training and supervision for child custody assessments, parenting coordination, mediation, and other special topics relating to high-conflict families. She is on the faculty of the Professional LL.M. (family law specialization) Program at Osgoode Hall Law School, York University, Toronto, and is on the editorial board of the *Family Court Review*. She has been actively involved in the development and training of parenting coordination services and was appointed to the AFCC Task Force charged with developing guidelines and standards of practice for parenting coordination. She is President of AFCC Ontario (2011–2012) and a member of the High Conflict Forum in Toronto. Dr. Fidler is a frequent presenter to the judiciary, family bar, and mental health professionals on high-conflict families and related topics. She has published in the areas of parenting plans and residential schedules, alienation, and parenting coordination.

Nicholas Bala has been a Professor at the Faculty of Law at Queen's University in Kingston, Canada since 1980. Since 2006 he has also been the Academic Director of the Professional LL.M. (family law specialization) Program at

Osgoode Hall Law School in Toronto. Most of his teaching and research has been in the area of family and children's law, with research focusing on issues related to parental rights and responsibilities after divorce, spousal abuse, young offenders, child witnesses, and child abuse. Much of his research work is interdisciplinary, and he has undertaken collaborative projects with psychologists, social workers, health professionals, and professionals. Professor Bala has published extensively; this is the 17th book that he has written or coauthored. His work has been cited by all levels of court in Canada, including the Supreme Court of Canada, and has been cited by courts in the United Kingdom, Australia and the United States. He frequently presents at academic conferences and professional education programs for judges, lawyers, psychologists, social workers, doctors, child welfare workers, youth probation officers, and teachers.

Michael A. Saini is an Assistant Professor at the Factor-Inwentash Faculty of Social Work at the University of Toronto. His interests focus on research, policy, and practice with children and families involved with child welfare, family law, and alternative dispute programs. He has conducted research to explore high-conflict divorce and separation, parenting competency after divorce, the intersection of child welfare and custody disputes, and child protection mediation as an alternative to legal disputes within the child welfare context. He has published in the areas of high-conflict divorce, custody evaluations, judicial decisions of joint custody, and parenting after divorce and separation. Professor Saini is an editorial board member for the *Family Court Review* and the *Journal of Child Custody* and a member of the Association of Family and Conciliation Courts. For the past 12 years, he has been conducting custody evaluations and assisting children's counsel for the Office of the Children's Lawyer, Ministry of the Attorney General of Ontario. He is also the course director of "Foundations for Conducting Custody Evaluations," a 48-hour workshop with Continuing Education at the University of Toronto.

Children Who Resist Postseparation Parental Contact

1

Introduction

After separation or divorce, children may resist or reject contact with a parent[1] for many reasons. For example, there may be developmental factors such as separation anxiety for infants and toddlers, affinities with one parent as a result of age, a gender preference, or similar interests, or alignments in response to parental conflict and loyalty binds. Children may refuse or resist contact with one parent due to the conduct or influence of a favored parent, or due to the abuse, neglect, or otherwise compromised parenting of a rejected parent. Each of these different types of complicated, strained, parent–child problems is the result of the complex interaction of many factors, including the social and legal contexts.

We explore the language and definitional controversies more fully in the next chapter. Kelly and Johnston (2001) use the term "alienation" to refer to a situation "where the child's rejection or resistance of a parent is disproportionate to the child's actual experiences with that parent and the parental separation." In other words, the child's reaction is inconsistent with the child's own actual observable experience and involves to some extent alienating strategies and behaviors on the part of the favored parent (or perhaps other family members or siblings). Previously, the child had a good, reasonably good, or excellent relationship with the rejected parent. "Alienation" is distinguished from

---

[1] The label used to identify the child's time with the nonresidential parent or a parent's legal right to time with his or her children may vary across jurisdictions. For example, "visits" or "visitation" is commonly used in the United States, "access" in Canada, and "contact" in Australia and England. "Parenting time" is another term used in the social science and legal literature.

parent–child contact problems primarily related to developmental reasons or time-limited, expected reactions to the separation or divorce (e.g., anger or upset at one parent, reaction to new partner), or parental conflict. Importantly, "alienation" is distinguished from cases of "justified rejection" where the child's resistance or rejection is justified on the basis of abuse, neglect, or significantly compromised parenting. In this circumstance, the child's rejection or resistance is considered adaptive and a reasonable coping mechanism. Conversely, the term "alienation" refers to a situation "where the child's rejection or resistance of a parent is disproportionate to the child's actual experiences with that parent and the parental separation" (Kelly & Johnston, 2001).

Although there is some overlap between situations of alienation and high-conflict divorce, it is important to note that not all high-conflict cases involve alienation or resistance to parent contact (Birnbaum & Bala, 2010a). Not all children exposed to conflict become alienated (Johnston, Walters, & Olesen, 2005b). Although it is common in high-conflict cases for one or both parents to engage in alienating parental behavior, not all children take sides in high-conflict separations, as many of them remain stuck in the middle of the conflict. Even in the face of a parent attempting to undermine his or her child's relationship with the other parent, many children struggle to remain on good terms with both parents. Alienation cases are a subset of high-conflict cases, characterized by the child's resistance to contact with a parent. A child whose relationship with one parent is compromised due to alienation faces risks to development and emotional well-being (Johnston, Roseby, & Kuehnle, 2009; Johnston, Walters, & Olesen, 2005c). Irrespective of the cause, when cases of resistance to contact arise, both parents and the children must be assessed to determine the various precipitating, perpetuating, and protective factors that in turn will inform the appropriate clinical, legal, and judicial responses.

Alienation is a complicated and complex problem that poses significant challenges for both the courts and for legal and mental health professionals. These cases have received much public and professional attention in recent years. As it will be discussed in this book, there are an increasing number of cases in the courts (Bala, Hunt, & McCarney, 2010). With this increase and growing awareness of the problem by parents and professionals, there is also a heightened controversy in the academic literature and popular media on how best to identify, assess, and respond to children resisting a parent after separation.

As with so many issues in family law, there are polarized, strongly gendered narratives about alienation. Some men's rights activists claim that mothers alienate children from their fathers to seek revenge for separation, asserting that many mothers make false and malicious allegations of abuse to further the alienation of the children. Some of these groups also complain that the courts are gender biased against fathers when dealing with child custody matters generally, and especially when addressing alienation.

Some feminists dismiss all, or most, alienation claims as fabricated by male perpetrators of intimate partner violence, often by abusive fathers, to exert control over the victimized mother by sabotaging the mother–child relationship. These advocates assert that allegations of alienation are often attempts by male perpetrators of violence to maintain contact with the other parent and their children, who justifiably resist or refuse contact with them. This is, in effect, a continuation of the intimate partner abuse. While there is some validity to both of these highly gendered narratives, each has very significant limitations. In our view, neither is especially helpful as a guiding narrative for improving the lives of children. The reality of these cases is often highly complex and generally not adequately captured by either of these relatively simplistic explanations. Both mothers and fathers have been found to alienate their children from the other parent, and in high-conflict separations men and women are probably equally likely to engage in alienating parental behavior.

Clinical experience and research have shown that abusive men may try to alienate their children from their victim mothers. These fathers may allege alienation by the victim mothers as a smoke screen to their own abusive and alienating behavior and claim that it is the mother's behavior that has alienated the children from them. Rightly, mothers whose partners are abusive attempt to protect their children. However, there are other women consciously or unconsciously motivated by vengeance, or due to personality disorders or mental illness, who alienate their children from fathers with whom the child had at least an adequate relationship, and in many cases a good and loving relationship. A subset of these women make repeated false allegations of sexual abuse, some intentionally and more unintentionally, truly believing that abuse occurred. These mothers cannot be reassured that abuse did not occur, even after multiple and thorough investigations where the abuse remains unsubstantiated.

The existence of alienation is not equivalent to a denial that child abuse and intimate partner violence are serious and widespread problems. What is concerning is that the feminist advocates who, in the name of helping women, deny that alienation exists, do a great disservice to not only the many mothers who are unjustifiably alienated from their children, often by abusive men, but more importantly to the children. We question the existence of a double standard that appears to be adopted by some feminist commentators—alienation by protective mothers does not exist, but alienation, although labeled differently, by abusive or violent fathers does. Similarly, fathers' rights and "parental alienation *syndrome*" groups do a disservice to children and rejected parents if they portray all rejected parents as "victims," and resist scrutiny of the conduct of these parents. There are clearly cases where abuse, neglect, and dysfunctional parenting may justify a child's resistance to contact with a parent.

These narrow and polarizing perspectives mirror the inflexible all-or-nothing thinking observed in alienated children and their parents. This is not an either/or proposition; there are abused children who justifiably resist contact *and* there are alienated children. The reality that some cases are misidentified as alienation when they are not does not detract from the significance of the problem of alienation. Courts, professionals, and scholars need to move beyond extreme and simplistic analyses. It can be very challenging to properly understand the dynamics of an individual family where allegations of abuse or alienation are present, and for judges, lawyers, and mental health professionals to make decisions or offer opinions that truly promote the best interests of the children. It can also be very difficult for parents to gain an objective understanding of their situation and respond in a way that will minimize harm to their children. We maintain that the too often strongly gendered polemics on alienation and abuse are polarizing and need to be replaced with a more nuanced and balanced discussion that recognizes the complexity of the issues so that the needs of children and families can be better met.

There is a growing awareness by parents, the courts, and legal and mental health practitioners that there are significant gaps in services to meet the needs of these families and children. There is a need for improvements in the justice system to more effectively respond to children resisting or refusing to have contact with a parent after separation and divorce, especially when alienation or abuse allegations are made. There is also a need for more psychological research on alienation, its nature and effects, and which types of intervention are most appropriate for different types of cases, including the long-term effects of variation of custody.

1.1 The Prevalence of Alienation

Although there is no research on population-based rates of alienation, alienation cases are a subgroup of families involved in more extreme forms of high-conflict separation or divorce. Based on longitudinal data of over 1,400 families and over 2,500 children in the United States, Hetherington and Kelly (2002) concluded that approximately 20% of parental relationships remained conflictual 6 years after separation. More conservative estimates of conflict, based primarily on litigation rates, suggest that approximately 10% of families remain stuck in "high conflict" (Hetherington, Stanley-Hagan, & Anderson, 1989; Maccoby & Mnookin, 1992; Mnookin & Kornhauser, 1979). But, we do not know how many of these high-conflict entrenched litigation cases would be considered alienation cases.

Janet Johnston notes that there is significant overlap between alienation and high-conflict cases, and that there are:

> all these developmentally expectable reactions that you have to
> sort out—whether they have appropriate attachment, whether
> they have separation anxiety, gender identifications, whether it is a
> teenager whose negativity is due to their separation-individuation

and they're going through a stage, whether it is due to high-conflict divorce and anger and hurt over the parents leaving, loyalty binds and guilt about being in the middle of a conflict, being worried and sympathetic about the left behind parent, or being simply influenced by an older sibling to reject a parent.[2]

The onset of alienation does not necessarily start after the dissolution of the parents' union. In some cases alienation starts only years after separation, while in others, factors that contribute to children's resistance to contact can be present before the parents decide to separate. As Joan Kelly notes:

> ...it has certainly been observed that sometimes in high-conflict marriages children are encouraged by a parent to take sides, to support them, to be hostile to the other parent, and to be triangulated into the marital or partner dispute. And so, therefore, sometimes the conditions for alienation are laid down in the marriage and get exacerbated as a result of situations of separation and the parents' reaction to that separation.[3]

Bernet (2010) estimates that 1% of all children and adolescents in the United States experience parental alienation, although the basis for this estimation is unclear, and it does not appear to be based on population-based empirical evidence. Based on the review of the literature and interviews with professionals, the prevalence rate is most likely found within the subsample of the 10% of known high-conflict cases, but clearly more research is needed to document the etiology and occurrence of alienation at the population level.

1.2 Prevalence of Alienation in Community Samples

In general, alienation is more likely to occur in highly conflicted, custody-disputing families rather than in community samples of separated parents with no involvement with the courts. There are a number of studies that have used community samples of children and parents to study alienation (Johnston, 1993, 2003; Johnston et al., 2005b; Racusin & Copans, 1994), but all of these community samples had involvement with the courts or other court-based services.

1.2.1 Court-Based Prevalence of Alienation

Estimates of the presence of alienation in *custody-disputing samples* range from 11% to 60% , depending on the sampling strategy, sample setting, definitions

---

[2] Interview, May 10, 2010, Janet Johnston, sociologist, clinical social worker, and researcher in the field of family law.
[3] Interview, April 21, 2010, Joan Kelly, psychologist and researcher in the field of family law.

used to establish the presence of alienation and the methods for data collection. At the low end of the range, some studies have found between 11% and 15% of children whose parents are involved in litigation are rejecting or resisting contact with one parent while remaining aligned with the other parent (Johnston, 1993, 2003; Johnston et al., 2005b; Racusin & Copans, 1994; Wallerstein & Kelly, 1980). At the high end of the range, a 12-year longitudinal study commissioned by the Family Law Section of the American Bar Association of over a 1,000 divorces found that alienation, as defined by "programming of a child" against another parent, was present in over half (60%) of all court cases (Steinberger, 2006a). This high occurrence of alienation may in part be due to the vague, broad definition of alienation used in this study. More conservative estimates of alienation within court samples report that approximately 20% of these litigated cases have alienation issues (Johnston, 1993, 2003; Johnston, Walters, & Olesen, 2005a).

Bow, Gould, and Flens (2009) conducted a national Internet search to locate e-mail addresses of professionals involved in child custody cases, including child custody evaluators, family attorneys, family court judges, court-ordered therapists, parenting coordinators/special masters, mediators, researchers, consultants, and advocates. A survey of 448 of these professionals found that the mean reported presence of alienation was 26% of cases handled by the professional. Of those, 47% were considered mild alienation, 32% were moderate, and 21% were severe.

Severe cases of alienation also vary across studies, which may be influenced by how authors conceptualize and operationalize the severity continuum of alienation, and by the samples included to distinguish levels of severity. The prevalence of severe cases of alienation ranges from 6% (Johnston et al., 2005a), 11% (Wallerstein & Kelly, 1980), and 15% (Johnston, 2003), to 27% (Johnston, Lee, Olesen, & Walters, 2005). Based on a study of 80 highly conflicted separated families involved in custody evaluations, Johnston and Campbell (1988) found approximately 37% of children between 7 and 14 years of age had experienced alienation. Of these alienated children, 16% completely refused contact with the noncustodial parent. It should be noted that this sample consisted of high-conflict families, which provides further evidence that not all high-conflict cases involve alienation.

Differences in the rates of prevalence of alienation in these studies are based on multiple factors, including: how "alienation" is conceptualized and operationalized, how it is measured, the various ways of sampling for cases involving alienation, different sample settings, and the methodologies used in these studies (e.g., surveys of professionals, court case analysis, interviews with participants directly or indirectly involved with the courts).

1.2.2 Prevalence of Alienation by Gender of the Favored Parent

Gardner originally suggested in the 1980s that 85% to 90% of his alienation cases involved the mother as the alienating parent (quoted in Bow et al., 2009), but he later modified this to suggest that due to the increase in father involvement in parenting, both mothers and fathers were involved in alienating behaviors approximately equally (Gardner, 2002b). As stated earlier, children can be alienated from either their mother or their father (Bala et al., 2010), although most "successful" alienation is perpetrated by the parent with custody or primary care of children (most commonly the mother), as it is difficult (though not impossible) for a parent with limited contact with a child to alienate a child from the primary caregiver.

Bow et al. (2009) reported that the 448 mental health and legal respondents in their study indicated that mothers (66%) were more frequently the alienating parent. Likewise, of the 84 out of 416 court cases with custody and parent contact issues identified as alienation, Deidre Rand and Randy Rand (2006) found that 49 of the cases (58%) involved an alienating mother, 31 (37%) involved an alienating father, and 4 cases involved other relatives. While mothers were significantly more often the alienating parent, mothers much more frequently had sole custody of the children (84%), or were the primary resident parent in joint legal custody cases (13%).

Braver, Coatsworth, and Peralta (2006) surveyed 86 university students whose parents had separated and both of their parents. The mothers reported that fathers alienated significantly more, while the fathers reported that mothers alienated significantly more. The adult children however, did not report a significant difference between their mothers and fathers in their alienating behaviors.

1.2.3 Prevalence of Alienation by Age and Gender of the Child

Research consistently indicates that boys and girls experience alienation in about equal numbers (Baker, 2010; Bow et al., 2009; Kelly & Johnston, 2001). Bow et al. (2009), for example, found that the mental health practitioners surveyed indicated the presence of alienation slightly more (53%) for girls. Baker (2010) surveyed 253 full-time and part-time staff working in a large child welfare agency in New York and found that 73 respondents (29% of the sample) indicated that there was no association between gender and parental alienation.

Kelly and Johnston (2001) reported that adolescents are more likely to become alienated from a parent than younger children. Richard Warshak also notes that "older children are more likely to have the intellectual capacity to understand long-term consequences, but at the same time…. are very much subjected to great external influence."[4] Although children from ages of 1 through 17 years have become alienated, one American study found that the mean, mode, and median of onset was at 10 years of age (Bow et al., 2009), suggesting that preadolescence is the most common developmental phase for the onset of alienation.

---

[4] Interview, April 15, 2010, Clinical Professor of Psychology, University of Texas Southwestern Medical Center.

1.3 Increase in the Number of Alienation Cases[5]

There has been a very significant increase over the past decades in cases explicitly raising "parental alienation" issues in the Canadian courts. In a study of reported Canadian court decisions, Bala et al. (2010) searched for court cases involving alienation (see Figure 1.1.). There were no reported Canadian cases prior to 1989 that used the term "parental alienation." The authors found 175 cases between 1989 and 2008 where the court made a finding about whether or not alienation occurred. They found that there were 40 decisions between 1989 and 1998 about alienation, with 24 of those cases where the judge decided that alienation had occurred. Between 1999 and 2008, there was a very substantial increase in the number of cases raising a claim of parental alienation, with the courts finding alienation in 82 out of 135 cases. In 2009, there were 57 cases, with alienation found in 31 cases. It is impossible to determine the extent to which the increase in reported use of the concept of "alienation" merely reflects greater awareness and use of the concept by parents, lawyers, and mental health professionals, and the extent to which there may be an actual increase in the occurrence of alienation, likely due to greater paternal involvement in postseparation parenting. It is likely there are elements of both. It is notable that the rate of substantiation of alienation remained essentially unchanged, at 60% of court cases in the 1989 to 1998 period, and 61% in the decade from 1999 to 2008, suggesting that the increase in cases does not reflect an increase in unsubstantiated claims being made.

In surveys of reported court decisions in the United Kingdom and Australia that dealt with "parental alienation," there were similar trends; almost no decisions prior to 2000, and significant increases starting around 2005 (Bala, 2011, 2012).

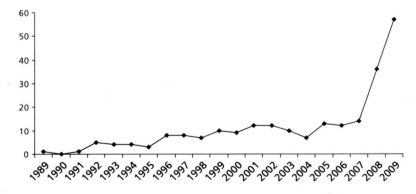

Figure 1.1 Reported Court Cases in Canada per Year With PA Claimed

---

[5] Statistical data in this section of the chapter is for 1989–2009. The 1989–2008 data appears in Bala et al. (2010) and was updated to include 2009 by the authors.

In recent years, judges seem to have a more sophisticated understanding of the dynamics of these cases. Although Canadian courts continue to use the concept of "parental alienation," starting in 2003 there were a number of reported cases where judges discussed whether this is a "syndrome," generally accepting that mental health professionals, not the judiciary, must resolve this controversy.[6]

In order to be alienated by one parent, a child must identify very closely with that parent. This close identification generally only occurs if the child is living primarily or exclusively with that parent. In this study (see Figure 1.2.), the alienating parent had sole custody of the child(ren) in 111 cases (81%), and joint or shared custody in 20 cases (15%). Alienation was found by the court to be the result of the conduct and attitude of a parent who only had contact rights in only 6 out of the 137 cases of parental alienation (4%). Thus, in terms of the cases where alienation was found, differences in gender are reflective of custody and childcare arrangements rather than a maternal predisposition to alienate children.

1.3.1 Cases Where Alienation Claim Was Not Substantiated

It is important to consider not only those cases in which the court found alienation, but also those in which the claim was rejected. In the Canadian study, this amounts to a total of 95 cases of the 232 cases (41%) (Bala et al., 2010). In some cases, the judge's reasons for rejecting a claim of alienation are clear. However, judges often give vague or multiple reasons when rejecting a claim, so the classification of such decisions was not always an easy exercise. A classification scheme was created with the following categories, which broadly reflect the mental health literature:

- justified rejection due to abuse or violence,

- justified rejection due to significant parenting limitations,

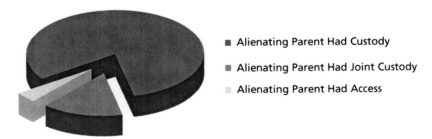

- Alienating Parent Had Custody

- Alienating Parent Had Joint Custody

- Alienating Parent Had Access

Figure 1.2 Alienating Parent's Degree of Control (Canadian Case Law Study)

---

[6] See, e.g., *A.J.C. v. R.C.*, [2003] B.C.J. 664 Bennett J. (B.C.S.C.).

- child disengaged but not rejecting the other parent, and
- insufficient evidence to substantiate the claim of alienation.

The first two categories were the clearest in the case law, as they involved a judicial finding of abuse or violence, or were reflected in judicial commentary about inadequate parenting. These are also the cases that most clearly fit into the reasonably well-defined situation of "justified rejection," where there is a clear rejection of one parent by the child. It should, however, be appreciated that the classification of cases is based on the researchers' assessment of the reasons of the judge, and very few cases used terminology like "justified rejection," "disengagement," or "estrangement."

In 30 of the 95 cases (32%) where the court did not find alienation, the case was classified as "justified rejection" (the conduct or inadequate parenting of the rejected parent or of a new partner was the primary cause of the child's rejection of the parent). In 6 of these cases, the court found that the rejection was due to abusive behavior by the rejected parent toward the child or partner; the father was the estranged parent in 5 of these cases, and the mother was the estranged parent in 1 case. In 32 of the 95 cases (34%) where claims of alienation were rejected, the court focused on the inadequate parenting of the rejected parent. These included cases where the rejected parent displayed a lack of warmth or interest in the child or showed insensitivity to the child's needs. In some cases, the child's rejection of the parent was due to the parent's drug addiction or violent temper, or the animosity or temper of a stepparent. In a number of the "justified rejection" cases, the child revealed that the parent who was claiming alienation was in fact trying to control the child or turn the child against the other parent.

In 20 of the 95 cases (21%), the court rejected the claim of "alienation," with its connotation that the conduct of the "alienating parent" was responsible for the failure of the child to regularly see the noncustodial parent, and instead concluded that the lack of contact was a reflection of the child's independent decision making. These cases typically involved the child's interests changing as he or she grew older, with the child wanting to spend more time with peers or involved in various activities; sometimes, the child seemed to be reacting to the stress of a high-conflict separation by aligning with one parent. In some of these cases, tension between the child and a stepparent or stepsiblings was a factor.

In 37 of the 95 cases (39%), the court rejected the claim of "alienation" as the cause of the breakdown in the relationship between the rejected parent and child. In some of these cases, the concern of the parent making the claim was the infrequency of contact, rather than a complete breakdown in the parent–child relationship. These were classified as cases of "insufficient evidence to establish alienation."

In 72 out of the 95 cases (76%) in which the court rejected a claim of "parental alienation," it was the father who made an unsubstantiated claim against the mother, while mothers made unsubstantiated claims in only

22 cases (23%). Thus, fathers made three times as many unsubstantiated claims of alienation as mothers. This gender difference in the making of unfounded claims of alienation, however, largely reflects the fact that most founded and unfounded allegations were made by nonresidential parents, who were mainly fathers.

1.4 Summary

The actual number of alienation cases at a population level remains unknown, in part because the concept is relatively new. There is disagreement about definitions and language, and there are no formal mechanisms for measuring or tracking it (Baker, 2005a; Turkat, 2002). Although a number of studies have suggested estimates of alienation, there continues to be no reliable statistics to suggest the exact percentage of children who experience alienation after separation and divorce. Current estimates vary depending on the definitions of alienation, sample settings, and study designs.

It is, however, clear that the number of reported court cases in Australia, Canada, and the United Kingdom has increased in the past two decades (Bala, 2011, 2012; Bala et al., 2010), and interviews with experts suggest that there have been similar increases in other jurisdictions. Whether that increase reflects more understanding, recognition, and reporting of the phenomenon, or an actual increase in its incidence, is unknown.

Further, while precise figures are unknown and may well vary over time or location, it seems that among high-conflict cases, which take up much of the time and resources in family courts, the proportion of cases raising issues of alienation or resistance to contact is perhaps in the range of one fifth to one half of these high-conflict cases. The number of severe alienation cases is relatively small in comparison with the total number of parental separations, but as will be discussed in subsequent chapters, the impact is far reaching with potentially devastating consequences for children and parents, and burdens for the justice system.

2

Definitions and Debates

In this chapter we provide an overview of the historical context relating to alienation, beginning with Richard Gardner's introduction of parental alienation syndrome (1985, 1998b), followed by a discussion of Kelly and Johnston's (2001) reformulated model and further developments in the field. Next, we discuss the need for differentiating alienation from other types of parent–child contact problems, including justified rejection, and the challenges in making this distinction. We conclude this chapter by discussing the current debate about whether alienation is a diagnosis or "syndrome."

2.1 Historical Context

There is a range of overlapping concepts and terminology used for what in this book will be referred to as "alienation." The terms in the literature include: "parental alienation syndrome" (Burrill, 2006b; Gardner, 1985), the "alienated child" or "child alienation" (Kelly & Johnston, 2001), "pathological alignments" and "visitation refusal" (Johnston, 1993; Johnston & Campbell, 1988; Wallerstein & Kelly, 1980), "parental alienation" (Baker, 2005a; Darnall, 1998; Garrity & Baris, 1994), "visitation interference" and "divorce-related malicious mother syndrome" (Turkat, 1999), "pathological" or "irrational alienation" (Warshak, 2003a), "threatened mother syndrome" (Klass & Klass, 2005), and "toxic parent" (Cartwright, 1993). The lack of consistency in language poses significant challenges for the identification of the problem, choosing appropriate interventions, and attempts in researching this phenomenon. In this chapter, we discuss these concepts with the goal of establishing consistent terminology.

2.1.1 History of Recognition of Parental Alienation

Becoming alienated from one parent because of the other parent's influence is not a new phenomenon. Starting in the late 19th century, at the beginning of the modern divorce, American judges were expressing concern about cases in which one parent "poisoned the mind" of a child against the other parent. In 1949, psychoanalyst Wilhelm Reich (Reich, 1949) wrote in his book, *Character Analysis*, that certain personality types among divorced parents defend themselves from narcissist injury by fighting for custody of the child and defaming their former partner to rob the other parent of the pleasure of the child.

Wallerstein and Kelly (1980) referred to an "unholy alliance between a narcissistically enraged parent and a particularly vulnerable older child, who together waged battle in efforts to hurt and punish the other parent." Ten years later, Wallerstein and Blakeslee (1989) used the term "Medea syndrome" to describe a parent who seeks revenge on a former spouse by destroying the child's relationship with that parent. Others have described "pathological alignments" and "visitation refusal" (Johnston, 1993; Johnston & Campbell, 1988) and "pathological alienation" or "irrational alienation" (Warshak, 2001, 2003a, 2010b).

In 1985, the late American psychiatrist, Richard Gardner, introduced the term "parental alienation syndrome" (PAS), defining it as:

> [A] disorder that arises primarily in the context of child custody disputes. Its primary manifestation is the child's campaign of denigration against a parent, a campaign that has no justification. It results from the *combination* of a programming (brainwashing) parent's indoctrination and the child's own contribution to the vilification of the target[1] parent. When true parental abuse and/or neglect are present, the child's animosity may be justified, and so the parental alienation syndrome explanation for the child's hostility is not applicable. (p. 61)

Gardner reserved the term "PAS" for the child's rejection of a parent that would not otherwise occur without the influence of the alienating parent's behavior. He used the more general term "parental alienation" for situations where the rejection was due to other reasons, such as violence, abuse or neglect, developmental affinities, or alignments.

Gardner proposed that a diagnosis of "parental alienation syndrome" (PAS) is dependent on eight behavioral factors identified in the child:

1) a campaign of denigration,
2) weak, frivolous, or absurd rationalizations for the deprecation,
3) lack of ambivalence by the child toward the rejected parent,

---

[1] The term "target parent" is used by some when referring to the rejected or alienated parent.

4) the "independent thinker" phenomenon (child claims these are his or her own, and not the alienating parent's beliefs),

5) reflexive support of the alienating parent in the parental conflict,

6) child's absence of guilt over cruelty to, or exploitation of, the alienated parent,

7) presence of scenarios and descriptions borrowed from the favored parent, and

8) the spread of rejection to extended family and friends of the alienated parent.

Additional considerations noted by Gardner include the child and parents' behavior during transitions and the parenting time, the child's attachment with the favored parent, and the nature of the attachment or relationship with the rejected parent before the alienation. This latter consideration is one of the key factors in differentiating different types of parent–child contact problems; alienation is *not* used to describe a situation where the rejected parent was largely absent from the child's life before separation. Gardner proposed that PAS is determined by the extent to which the efforts of the favored parent have been successfully manifested in the *child*, and not by the parent's efforts alone. Gardner further argued that PAS is a diagnosable disorder that can vary in nature, intensity, and frequency of alienating behaviors. He proposed different treatment and judicial interventions depending on the degree: mild, moderate, or severe forms of alienation.

2.1.2 A Response to Gardner: The Reformulated Model of Kelly and Johnston (2001, 2004)

Gardner's formulation of PAS has been controversial. In 2001, Kelly and Johnston (2001) provided a reformulated, systems-based,[2] multifactor model to explain why some children resist contact with one parent and become aligned with the other parent. Figure 2.1, taken from Kelly and Johnston (2001), illustrates the interacting factors that may be involved:

1) the alienating behavior of the aligned parent,

2) the rejected parent's inept parenting and counterrejecting behavior (before or after rejection),

3) domestic violence/abuse and child abuse/neglect,

4) chronic litigation that typically includes "tribal warfare" (involvement of family, friends, new partners, remarriage),

5) sibling dynamics and pressures,

---

[2] Systems refers to the intrapsychic (within the individual), to the interaction between and among family members, and to the external sources, like extended family, lawyers, and the broader community like church, school, and extracurriculars.

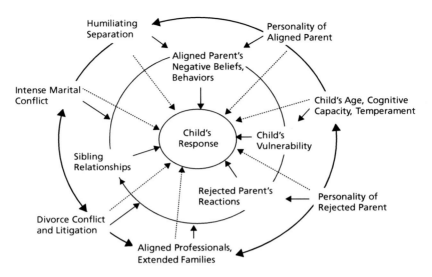

Figure 2.1 Model of Factors Predicting Child Alienation (Kelly & Johnston, 2001)

6) a vulnerable child (dependent, anxious, fearful, emotionally troubled, and with poor coping and reality testing), and

7) developmental factors (e.g., age-appropriate separation anxiety, response to conflict consistent with the cognitive development of children aged 8 to 15).

While many parents embroiled in high-conflict disputes over child custody and contact engage in undermining and indoctrinating behaviors, also referred to as alienating behavior or strategies, only some of their children become alienated (Johnston, 1993; Johnston, Walters, & Olesen, 2005c). Thus, in the reformulated model depicted above, the behavior of the favored parent is one of a number of interacting factors, and not necessarily the primary component in understanding the parent–child relationship problem. In this model, a child's perception and degree of internalization of the favored parent's alienating strategies or behaviors also play a significant role as to whether these behaviors are defined as "alienating" to the child. Others, including extended family, siblings, or aligned professionals, may be involved. Further, even when this parent's conduct is a contributing factor, Kelly and Johnston note that the other factors may be equally important for understanding the child's resistance or refusal.

Kelly and Johnston (2001) proposed that the term "alienated child" is preferable to "parental alienation" because the former focuses more on the child and is less blaming of the favored parent. They defined an alienated child as one who "freely and persistently expresses unreasonable negative feelings and beliefs (such as anger, hatred, rejection, and/or fear) toward a parent that are disproportionate to their actual experience of that parent" (p. 251).

Kelly and Johnston's reformulated model and subsequent developments of this model (Drozd & Olesen, 2004, 2010; Friedlander & Walters, 2010) require the various types of rejection or resistance (e.g., normal developmental preferences or affinities, alignments due to parental separation or high conflict, or justified rejection due to child abuse/neglect or violence) to be differentiated based on the reasonableness or objectivity of the child's reaction (Gardner 2002b; Warshak, 2000, 2001).

More recently, Johnston notes that their initial definition of child alienation is problematic, to the extent that in some cases it may become difficult, if not impossible, to determine what constitutes a reasonable, justified, or proportionate reaction on the part of the child. She proposes moving from the concept of the "alienated child" to a more general definition with a focus on what the alienating parent is doing. She stated:

> I prefer to put the word "alienation" into what a parent does; the parent engages in alienating behaviors. A parent who engages in alienating behaviors, which are observable and measurable, is conducting parent alienation upon a child; the child may or may not be able to resist or manage or succumb [to the alienating parenting behaviors]. I prefer to keep the term alienation for what a parent does, which I think is emotionally abusive.[3]

In commenting on the multiple causes, Johnston explains that the alienating parent behavior has "the potential for turning the child to become negative and resistant [toward the other parent]. It can be a sufficient cause for a child to become alienated, but it is not a necessary and sufficient cause."

2.2 The Difficulty in Defining Alienation

Adding to the complexity in defining alienation, there are many factors that may contribute to parent–child relationship problems after separation. The presence of alienation, for example, should be distinguished from other circumstances that may contribute to these strained relationships, including time-limited expected reactions to the separation, such as anger or upset, a child's affinity toward a parent, reactions to parental conflict, rejection of a parent due to the presence of child neglect or abuse, significantly compromised parenting or exposure to domestic violence. In some of these situations, the child's affinity and alignment to one parent over another may be adaptive for the child. In other situations, the presence of alienation may interact with other factors contributing to parent–child problems.

---

[3] Interview, May 10, 2010.

Warshak (2001) identified three components that must be present for a bona fide identification of what is frequently referred to as "parental alienation":

1) a persistent, not occasional, rejection or denigration of a parent that reaches the level of a "relentless campaign,"
2) an unjustified (unreasonable) or irrational rejection by the child, and
3) rejection by a child that is at least a *partial* result of the alienating parent's influence [emphasis added].

Initially, Warshak (2003a, 2006) suggested that the concept of "pathological alienation" might address some of the controversy related to differentiating a bona fide alienation from an "estrangement" that is justified or expected given circumstances of neglect, abuse, or domestic violence. He defined "pathological alienation" as:

"a disturbance in which children, usually in the context of sharing a parent's negative attitudes, suffer unreasonable aversion to a person, or persons, with whom they formerly enjoyed normal relations or with whom they would normally develop affectionate relations" (2006, p. 361).

More recently, Warshak (2010b) questioned his previous use of a label that included "pathological," because of its association with the medical model.[4] His definition not only considers the role of the child but also explicitly identifies the role of the alienating parent, a necessary component of the problem. Importantly, Warshak's definition further identifies two critical aspects:

1) a *change* from a previously good relationship where the child shared a warm and healthy attachment, or would have been expected to develop a good relationship; and
2) the possibility that the aversion may also be *applied to others* (such as other family members), and not only to parents.

---

[4] The term "irrational" has been used more recently by Warshak and others to replace the use of "pathological" to describe "alienation" (Fidler, Bala, Birnbaum, & Kavassalis, 2008; Warshak, 2010a). Concerns have been expressed about the inclusion of the term "irrational," when describing alienation. By definition, "irrational" means "illogical" or "unreasonable" and thus defines what is meant by alienation as it is differentiated from a justified (realistic, reasonable) rejection (estrangement), which is when a child has a good reason to resist or reject a parent due to abuse, neglect, or domestic violence. To address the concern and avoid confusion, in this book we follow the now common practice of not including "irrational" in the label and instead refer to "child alienation" or "alienation" as the preferred term.

The recognition that a child once had a positive relationship with the now rejected parent, notwithstanding in some cases personality or parenting flaws, is of particular relevance for accurate assessment and for delivering effective interventions. Children can establish a positive relationship with a parent or others having had little actual time together. However, the term "alienation" is *not* meant to include situations where the child's relationship with the rejected parent was never established or was interrupted for a significant time because the parent was physically absent or largely uninvolved. In these circumstances, the child has a proportionate or reasonable response, and the best term to use would be "justified rejection." Although cases when a parent has been physically absent or uninvolved can fit within this definition, labeling a child's rejection as justified can become contentious, especially if the involved parent seems to be undermining efforts of the absent parent to establish or reestablish a relationship with the child.

Confusion arises when using the terms "alienation" or "alienated," and "estrangement" or "estranged," when communicating with the public and the legal profession, given that these terms have different meanings in the professional and academic literature, but similar meanings in ordinary parlance (Drozd, interview, June 23, 2010; Warshak, 2010a). The *Oxford Dictionary* defines the term "alienation" as "the act of estranging or state of estrangement in feeling or affection." As Warshak points out (interview, April 15, 2010; Warshak, 2010a), this definition of "alienation" addresses only the withdrawal of emotion and does not necessarily imply a physical separation and, further, does not address the basis for the emotional distance, rational or irrational. Warshak notes the distinction made by both *Black's Law Dictionary* and the *Merriam-Webster Dictionary* between alienation and estrangement: the physical separation of the parent and child is what distinguishes estrangement from alienation; an alienated child may show contempt and withdraw affection from a parent but still be in contact with that parent, whereas an estranged child is physically apart from the parent in addition to being emotionally separated. Warshak (2010a), adopting suggestions by Mark Otis, proposes one of three terms—"disillusioned," "alienated," or "estranged"—to differentiate resistance or refusal to having contact with one parent:

> Disillusioned children have misgivings about one or both parents, remained involved with parents, do not join in a campaign of denigration, and interact cooperatively in many contexts, but remain discontented, resentful, aloof or reserved. Alienated children show contempt and withdraw affection while still in contact with the parent (often not by choice). Estranged children are physically apart from a parent in addition to the emotional separation that characterizes alienation. (Warshak, 2010a, p.72)

In an attempt to provide a manageable framework, Carter and his colleagues (Carter, interview, June 16, 2010; Carter, Haave, & Vandersteen, 2009a,

2009b) have identified the "four alternative A's" of resistance to parent contact:

1) "alienation" (either deliberate or accidental behavior of a parent or another family member, such as a grandparent or sibling),
2) "alignment" (child's response to high conflict that does not involve actual rejection),
3) "attachment" (age- or gender-appropriate affinity, separation anxiety), and
4) "appropriate" (justified rejection or realistic estrangement).

Attachment theory has recently been discussed in the alienation literature within a systemic framework to further inform assessment protocols and tools and intervention/treatment for the full gamut of parent–child contact problems. For example, Garber (2007, 2011) writes about concepts and language commonly used by family therapists, such as "triangulation," "parentification," "adultification," "infantilization," and "overburdened child."[5]

Lawyer and social worker Bill Eddy (2010; interview, April 29, 2010) offers a theory of alienation called "1000 little bricks," based on three "cultures of blame" and the little behaviors (bricks) children absorb from them. These three cultures are:

1) a family culture of blame apparent in high-conflict families,
2) a family court culture of blame inherent in the adversarial system, and
3) society's increasing culture of blame of individuals for complex problems as reflected in our media.

Eddy explains that each of these three cultures of blame separately and in combination teaches children maladaptive behaviors, including all-or-nothing thinking, unmanaged emotions, and extreme behaviors. He writes: "When these three cultures reinforce each other, it is a perfect storm which can build alienation. This is in contrast to what cultures are supposed to do by protecting children and building their resilience for the future." (p. 39). Resilience, he maintains, requires children to be taught flexible thinking, managed emotions, and moderate behavior.[6]

Psychologist and researcher Douglas Darnall (1997, 1998) differentiates "parental alienation syndrome" (PAS) from "parental alienation" (PA), noting that "PAS" focuses on the *child's* reaction while "PA," his preferred term, focuses on the *alienating parent's* behavior. Unlike some others, who criticize Gardner's apparent emphasis on the conduct of the alienating parent's role in

---

[5] We discuss parent–child and family dynamics further in Chapter 3, which elaborates on the associated risk factors and indicators, and in Chapter 7, which discusses psychoeducational and clinical interventions.

[6] Eddy has developed an early court intervention called New Ways for Families to assist parents and their children to develop these skills. We discuss this program more fully in Chapter 7.

the child's resistance or refusal, at the exclusion of other factors, Baker and Darnall (2006) argue that while Gardner focused on the child's role as manifest in the eight previously noted symptoms, they stress the alienating parent's behavior in their conceptualizations. Darnall maintains that the conscious *or* unconscious behavior of the parent could evoke rejecting behavior in the child, but he acknowledged that some children are not affected by a parent's alienating behavior.

Darnall identifies three types of alienators:

1) *Naïve alienators* recognize the value of the child's relationship with the other parent and genuinely strive to develop or maintain that relationship prior to or after the separation. Occasionally, though, they say or do something that communicates to the child that the other parent is flawed or has done something wrong.
2) *Active alienators* know that what they are doing is wrong but, intermittently in an effort to cope with the separation and the associated hurt and anger, exhibit alienating behaviors or strategies as a result of their own emotional vulnerability or poor impulse control.
3) *Obsessed alienators* are distinguished from active alienators by their persistence in wanting to destroy the target (rejected) parent and the child's relationship with that parent, rarely showing self-control or insight into any of their own contributions. They lack empathy, are unwilling to forgive, and have a strong need to be in control. The most severe examples of this type include cases of false allegations of abuse where the alienating parent professes to be protecting the child. This parent cannot be convinced otherwise, even when there is evidence to the contrary; those, including professionals and the court, who do not agree with them are dismissed by them as wrong or biased. These parents are not motivated to seek help to restore the child's relationship with the other parent. The alienating behaviors are intentional, although their actions may be direct, indirect, or a result of protective behaviors based on genuine beliefs. Mental illness or personality disorders are likely contributors to the alienating parent's irrational thinking.

Psychiatrist William Bernet also distinguishes "parental alienation" from "parental alienation syndrome" (PAS) (Bernet, 2010).[7] He writes that the former refers to the "child's strong alliance with one parent and rejection of a relationship with the other parent without legitimate justification." He explains that the term "PAS" is sometimes used in reference to a "more complex concept" and notes that "PAS" typically refers to a child with

---

[7] We discuss the controversy over parental alienation as a diagnosis in the *Diagnostic and Statistical Manual of Mental Health Disorders* (DSM) later in this chapter.

parental alienation, who manifests some or all of eight characteristic behaviors described by Gardner. Bernet uses the term "contact refusal" to describe the behavior of a child or adolescent who adamantly avoids spending time with one of the parents. He states: "Contact refusal is simply a symptom that could have a number of possible causes, one of which is parental alienation. This terminology is similar to *school refusal*, which is simply a symptom that could have a number of possible causes" (Bernet, von Boch-Galhau, Baker, & Morrison, 2010, p. 79).

Bernet writes:

> Parental alienation and PAS do not describe or pertain to different groups of children. On the contrary, we believe that the children who experience parental alienation are almost exactly the same children who manifest PAS. The latter is a subset of the former. We believe that the great majority of children who experience parental alienation also manifest some or all of the eight characteristic behaviors of PAS. In other words, parental alienation is simply a general term that is not encumbered by the baggage associated with PAS, e.g., the eight behaviors or symptoms that constitute the syndrome. In our use of these terms, parental alienation and PAS are typically descriptors of the child. We are explaining these definitions in detail because we realize that some authors have given other meanings to "parental alienation." For example, some authors use "parental alienation" to describe the behaviors of the alienating parent and "PAS" to describe the condition of the child. Also, some authors use "parental alienation" to describe any estrangement between the child and a parent (including situations in which the parent was abusive) and "PAS" to describe the child's unjustified rejection of a parent (i.e., when the parent was not abusive). (Bernet et al., 2010, pp. 79–80.)

Joan Kelly and others prefer to avoid the term "parental alienation," as it leads to confusion. She stated:

> Are we talking about the parent fostering alienation or are we talking about the parent that has become alienated from the child? So, I prefer the term, *the alienated child,* because we start with what seems to be the major problem—a child resisting or rejecting contact. Then, you find out why is that, what is going on.[8]

The literature and our interviews confirm this confusion. The parent referred to in the label "parental alienation" may be identified as the rejected parent or the alienating parent or both. The use of the term "alienation" addresses this confusion.

---

[8] Interview, April 21, 2010.

2.3 Affinity and Alignment

In many cases, differentiating the various factors or types of parent–child contact problems poses significant challenges.

A child, while maintaining contact with both parents, may have an affinity or be closer emotionally with one parent because of temperament, gender, age, familiarity, greater time spent with that parent, or shared interests. Sometimes, the child experiences anxiety separating from one parent. *Affinity* does not involve a rejection or negative feelings toward a parent but is a preference for spending time with a specific parent in specific situations. Nor is affinity fixed; preferences a child has for one parent or the other typically ebb and flow over time depending on situational factors, the child's mood, and developmental factors, such as the child's age, and the child's gender as well as the parent's gender.

Alignments between the child and the preferred parent may develop before, during, or after the separation because of the other parent's nonexistent, interrupted, or minimal involvement, or inexperience or poor parenting, even if these shortcomings do *not* reach the level of abuse or neglect. Like with affinity, alignment does not involve rejection of a parent but results in a resistance or reluctance to have contact with a parent. What may start as an affinity or alignment may, without early intervention, develop into alienation or justified rejection.

If separated parents have a reasonably good relationship, they may be able to identify and address the issues that arise when affinity or alignment are occurring without professional intervention (and, of course, without using any such terminology). However, when parents do not have a good relationship, they may involve professionals or the courts in a case that, upon assessment, is affinity or alignment and not alienation. One of the challenges of these cases is that it can be very difficult in the early stages of affinities and alignments to predict which of these cases may develop into alienation or justified rejection. In cases of affinity or alignment, the transition from one home to the other may be difficult for the child, especially the younger child, though in these cases the children often settle down soon after they make the transition. However, the parents may misinterpret the behavioral difficulties of the child and incorrectly blame the other parent. For example, the rejected parent may blame the favored parent for alienating the child while the favored parent may blame the other parent for poor or even abusive parenting and advocate on behalf of the child's right to refuse contact.

Although it is often difficult for legal and mental health professionals to predict whether affinities or alignments will develop into alienation or justified rejection, these cases allow for opportunities for early intervention. Often, there is an expectation that the problems will resolve with time without intervention. However, without early and appropriate intervention, these difficulties may snowball, and what started out as a mild strained parent–child relationship or contact problem becomes alienation. If addressed early enough with preventative measures such as education, brief counseling, or direction from the judge, some strained parent–child relationship problems can be ameliorated.

Also, alignments may develop for what are referred to as expected divorce-specific reasons, such as when a child or adolescent becomes angry or upset with a parent who leaves the family, starts a new relationship, or remarries. In this circumstance, a triangulation of family dynamics occurs; the child who is reacting to the parental separation or experiencing loyalty conflicts identifies and sides with the "left parent," who feels hurt, upset, abandoned, or angry. And, consistent with developmentally expected behavior, adolescents may form their own moral judgments about right and wrong.

UK sociologist and researcher Carol Smart stated:

> . . . drawing on cases from our research, some children withdrew
> from the parent they were going to visit because the parent seemed
> to be much more interested in doing their own thing, spending
> time with the new partner, and their new children. And, there is
> always the problem for children of going on a visit, say, with the
> non-residential father and his new partner where there are other
> children in the household that he is living with all the time, and
> then his own, biological child/children comes along every other
> weekend, or whatever it might be, and they have got to fit in;
> and there are jealousies between children, and maybe they have
> to share a bedroom with these children, and so on. We talked
> to children quite a lot about what actually happened in making
> these transitions, and it is quite an emotional, psychological sort
> of transformation they have to go through when they are shifting
> themselves from one household to another and then back again, and
> so on. So I think a greater understanding is needed of what it is like
> being a child, having to move back and forth, and to integrate into
> these different households . . . instead of always focusing on the idea
> that it must be the residential parent that is causing these problems.[9]

In other circumstances, adolescents may want to spend less time with one parent, not because they prefer to be with the other parent, but rather for developmentally appropriate reasons. In this situation, the adolescents may be more interested in staying in the home they are accustomed to and the same neighborhood, and being with their friends and participating in local activities, than spending time with either parent.

Alignments in the absence of abuse or neglect may also develop before the separation when parents invite their children to take their sides in the parental conflict. Australian social worker and family therapist Robyn Fasser (Fasser & Duchen, 2010) notes the importance of examining the current

---

[9] Interview, May 24, 2010.

family dysfunction in the context of the rigid family patterns and boundary problems of several previous generations.[10]

Alignments also occur in response to ongoing or emergent parental conflict, such as that related to financial disputes, remarriage, or a parent's desire to relocate. The literature and our interviews with leading experts clearly establish that not all children exposed to parental conflict or alienating behaviors actually become alienated from one parent. The child's upset or moral indignation or his or her resistance to see a parent was initially an understandable reaction to the separation. This reaction on the part of the child is not viewed by most experts as alienation in the way we have defined it, but rather as an alignment. Like affinities, these alignments, which may well be an expected reaction to parental separation and conflict, are nevertheless red flags. If not addressed early on, an alignment may develop into alienation where the child's rejection of a parent becomes disproportionate to his or her experience with the rejected parent. We return to a discussion of differentiating alienation from justified rejection later in this chapter.

2.4 The Role of the Adversarial System and Professional Advisors

Kelly and Johnson (2001) and others have noted the multiple factors associated with different types of parent–child contact problems, unanimously noting the negative impact of the adversarial system and others such as friends, family, and helping professionals, which cannot only exacerbate parental conflicts but may also precipitate these conflicts (Altobelli, 2011; Bernet, 2010; Drozd & Olesen, 2004; Garber, 2007, Kopetski, 1998a; Martin, interview, April 12, 2010; Stoltz & Ney, 2002). These people have been referred to as "negative advocates" (Eddy, 2010) or "cheerleaders" (Johnston & Roseby, 1997).

During our interviews, almost all the expert informants pointed out that mental health and legal professionals can *facilitate or exacerbate* problems by reinforcing an erroneous belief that the parent–child relationship problem is due to an unjustified rejection or alienation when it is the result of other factors or circumstances, but do not *create* alienation. Only a couple of the experts interviewed believed that overzealous or ill-informed therapists, lawyers, or other advocates could *cause* the problem in the absence of the favored parent's direct or indirect, conscious or unconscious, alienating behavior.

Attempting to address the problem of alienation in the family justice system may, in some cases, exacerbate contact problems. For example, Janet Johnston stated: "Court delays, and doing nothing and messing up in court and taking ages to get results . . . All of these entrench the child's fear and avoidance and makes the situation a lot worse."[11] Philip Epstein, a senior family law

---

[10] Interview, June 2, 2010
[11] Interview, May 10, 2010.

lawyer, in Toronto said: "I think that professionals can contribute to the problem by supporting the preferred parent in views that are not sustainable."[12]

Ideas disseminated in the media and popular culture can also exacerbate parent–child contact problems. Elizabeth McCarty, of the Ontario Children's Lawyer said:

> The media has also popularized the term parental alienation. The legal system can certainly be influenced by the proliferation of discussion around parental alienation in the media. Cases can be framed in a way that presents them as alienation cases when that is not the case. Both the media and the legal system can fall prey to the mischaracterization of a case, which can have a direct impact on your ability to resolve the issues.[13]

In our interviews, judges unanimously agreed that the negative impact of the adversarial system often has as a result of the absence of early identification and delays. Justice Marcus, from Israel, identified "juridogenic" problems (taken from the medical term "iatrogenic") as "...the damage the court process can do without any intention of doing harm, simply because the procedure goes on too long or because the wrong turns have been taken on the road; assumptions have been made without basis and that can happen."[14]

Judge Boshier, the Principal Family Court Judge in New Zealand said:

> Lawyers can exacerbate alienation simply because they are paid to advocate their client's cause and that is, in the common law world, the nature of the adversarial role of the lawyer. The other example is possibly unwitting, a counselor who is counseling a child and not challenging the child, but reinforcing or supporting a child who is articulating their dislike of a mother and father...A counselor who regards their role as nonchallenging and therapeutic is probably adding to the alienation by almost justifying it to the child. Now by that I don't mean to be controversial nor provocative. I'm just simply making the observation that it is not the job of the counselor to challenge the child necessarily, but to be therapeutic and supportive, and I think that may have the consequence of adding to alienation.[15]

Reflecting similar views, Australian Federal Magistrate Tom Altobelli stated:

> First, I see it in the intensely adversarial behavior of some family lawyers, not all family lawyers. I also see it in the context of what

---

[12] Interview August 15, 2010.
[13] Interview, July 14, 2010: a joint interview with Elizabeth McCarty and Dan Goldberg, both lawyers at the Office of the Children's Lawyer, Ministry of the Attorney General of Ontario.
[14] Interview, June 1, 2010.
[15] Interview, May 23, 2010.

I call the partisan expert, as opposed to the single-joint expert. So what happens with that expert is that they buy into the dispute and inadvertently add fuel to the fire, so to speak.[16]

An opposing view is provided by lawyer and women's advocate Joan Meier:

> Again, this is where I come back to the fact that alienation is not a useful concept, it is an obviating, pathologizing concept. Why is it helpful to call it alienation instead of to say the lawyer is fueling the conflict or the mediator is whitewashing the accused, or whatever you want to say is creating problems? Why is it helpful to call that alienation? All I think it does is confuse. But if I had to give a yes/no, I would say no, because I do not think... even if there is a legitimate thing called alienation that we should be concerned about, I do not think the role of lawyers and mediators is part of it.[17]

In speaking about child abuse or domestic violence, Meier goes on to say:

> [Pro-alienation theory] lawyers very much fuel the notion, the misconception in courts that when children have been abused that they have actually just been alienated and there is actually no abuse. The main contributors to that view are custody evaluators, most of whom are not abuse experts, despite some assertions to the contrary. These evaluators typically use the term alienation to rebut abuse claims. I have many, many cases of that sort. And so, they are the main purveyors of the concept in question. In terms of actually causing alienation of children from one parent? No, I do not think that lawyers [for custodial mothers alleged to have alienated children] have anything to do with that and I do not think that mediators have anything to do with that. One might believe that if one believed that litigating abuse furthers alienation because the abuse is false. But I don't believe that, because I do not believe that lawyers and moms who are litigating abuse are doing it when it is false. Maybe once in a thousand or in a hundred cases, but in 99 out of 100 the abuse is true, and the abuse claims are being disbelieved. So no, they are not furthering alienation—they are trying to protect the kids, or their clients' kids. In short, this whole debate, just as with any given case, comes back to the question of whether abuse claims are true or false. And the problem with alienation—as it is commonly used in family court—is that it simply *assumes* one answer to that question.

---

[16] Interview, June 3, 2010.
[17] Interview, April 21, 2010.

2.5 Alienation Within the Context of High-Conflict Separations

The American psychiatrist William Bernet et al. (2010) argues that there is an important difference between PAS and parental alienation:

> PAS typically includes the idea that one of the parents actively influenced the child to fear and avoid the other parent. Although we believe that occurs in many instances, it is not necessary to have an alienating parent for parental alienation to occur. Parental alienation may occur simply in the context of a high-conflict divorce in which the parents fight and the child aligns with one side to get out of the middle of the battle, even with no indoctrination by the favored parent. (p. 79).

As noted above, the literature and our interviews with experts clearly establish that not all children exposed to parental conflict or alienating parental behaviors actually become alienated from one parent. The distinction made by Bernet et al., that parental alienation can occur even in the absence of alienating behaviors by a favored parent and solely on the basis of a child's reaction to parental conflict, is important, and to the extent that it is operative in any particular case, it may help both parents to engage in interventions without blaming each other.

However, several of our interviews with experts revealed doubts about whether alienation can occur in the absence of alienating parent behavior and solely as a result of a child's response to parental conflict. In significant measure, these disagreements reflect differences in how alienation is defined. Most key informants concluded that while there are multiple contributing factors, alienation requires the contribution of the favored parent's behavior, direct or indirect, conscious or unconscious. When unconscious, mental illness or a personality disorder may be a factor. Some of the experts whom we interviewed clarified that alienation can occur as a result of a family member or sibling's alienating behavior and in the absence of the favored parent's alienating behavior; however, this was observed to be much less common, and likely to accompany the favored parent's alienating behavior, not to act alone.

One important question is whether it is even possible for there to be total absence of alienating parental behaviors, conscious or unconscious, when there is parental conflict? As Chief Judge Carey of the Probate and Family Court in Massachusetts stated:

> In essence parents are acting by engaging in the conflict, they are driving a child to finally saying: "I cannot take the conflict anymore, and if I pick one parent perhaps the conflict will go away because they don't have anything to fight about."[18]

---

[18] Interview, June 29, 2010.

In other words, intrinsic in the high parental conflict are the negative views, attitudes, and feelings the parents have for one another, expressed directly or indirectly, and painfully evident to the child. The majority of experts interviewed believe that some involvement of the favored parent is necessary for alienation to occur.

There are clearly cases where a child's anger, or moral indignation or their resistance or refusal to see a parent, should be viewed, at least initially, as the child's own expected reactions to the separation or the parental conflict— what we referred to earlier as divorce-specific reasons. Most experts do not view such a reaction on the part of the child as alienation in the way we have defined it, but rather, as an alignment or to a lesser degree as an affinity as previously discussed. Generally, as an alignment, it is viewed as a milder form of a strained parent–child relationship or contact problem that, if left unattended, might mushroom into alienation.

According to Joan Kelly:

> We have often talked about children who resolve their dilemma of being in the middle, by rejecting one parent and totally aligning with the other. But, I do not think we have much research that really observes that process. It may be a component of what kids do, but we are talking in alienation of an enormously vitriolic response on the part of the child that is rejecting the parent, so opting out of the conflict may not be… opting out of the conflict by aligning and rejecting the other parent, I think isn't going to be a primary reason but may contribute.[19]

In addressing whether alienation can occur solely in response to parental conflict and in the absence of the favored parent's alienating behavior, Richard Warshak stated:

> It may, on some level, help the child; it may give the child a way to cope with conflict between parents by taking sides and disowning a parent. But favored parents, if they're doing their job right, shouldn't accept their child rejecting the other parent, if the other parent is a good parent. The [favored] parent will say "well, it's not me, that's just my child's choice and it's just their way of managing the tension between me and my ex." My response is that you should do everything possible to help your children adjust in healthy ways to the divorce just like you help them adjust to other changes in their life. If they change schools, or if a sibling is born, you don't necessarily support a child's unhealthy way of coping with difficult events in their life.[20]

---

[19] Interview, April 21, 2010.
[20] Interview, April 15, 2010.

2.6 Distinguishing Alienation From Justified Rejection

The need to differentiate alienation from justified rejection (or realistic estrangement[21]), where the child's resistance or refusal to have contact with a parent results from the trauma of witnessing intimate partner violence or from experiencing physical abuse, unreasonably harsh discipline, sexual abuse, or significantly inept or neglectful parenting by the rejected parent was recognized in Gardner's formulations of alienation and subsequently was elaborated by Johnston and her colleagues as well as others (Warshak, 2002). In justified rejection cases, children do not exhibit the eight behavioral manifestations of alienation first introduced by Gardner, while alienated children do (Baker & Darnell, 2006). Unlike alienated children, those who have been abused or neglected often want some contact with the abusive parent and often do not exhibit rejection or resistance to contact,[22] though they often exhibit symptoms of posttraumatic distress disorder (PTSD).[23] Baker notes that children in the child protection system, where there is abuse and neglect and often only one active parent, may not be the same as children from divorce, where two parents are fighting over the child.

In cases where the rejected parent has been abusive or violent with the other parent, or neglectful, abusive, or significantly inept with the child, the more correct "diagnosis" is a justified rejection, explained *primarily* by the rejected parent's behavior. While the preferred parent may be justifiably concerned and protective, the child's reaction to the rejected parent is relatively independent and occurs irrespective of the preferred parent's attitudes and behavior. In alienation, the child's rejection is *primarily*, though not always exclusively, the result of the alienating parent's conduct, conscious or unconscious, subtle or obvious, direct or indirect. That is, in alienation cases, without the influence of the favored parent, the child would not reject the other parent. The favored parent may be malicious and vindictive, feel above the law, and deliberately act to keep the child from the other parent. Alternatively, the favored parent may have a personality disorder or mental illness that may be marked with disordered thinking or paranoia, suggesting that his or her protective behavior is genuinely motivated or unintentional. In this circumstance, the favored parent, due to his or her own earlier experiences, may be predisposed to certain vulnerabilities and unable to sufficiently differentiate a perceived risk from an actual risk to the child. Often, this parent projects his or her own fears and anxieties onto the child. The alienating parent is unable to differentiate sufficiently his or her own needs

---

[21] The term "realistic estrangement" is used by some writers. We prefer avoid this term as it can be confusing because the word "estrangement" has a broader range of meaning and connotations.

[22] Interviews with Amy Baker (April 30, 2010) and Bill Eddy (April 29, 2010).

[23] Interviews with Amy Baker (April 30, 2010), Leslie Drozd (June 23, 2010), and Janet Johnston (May 10, 2010).

and experiences from that of the child's. The literature consistently indicates, as do our interviews with experts,[24] that notwithstanding this parent's vulnerability and genuine belief that the child is at risk, this can still be an alienation case.

Psychologist Peter Jaffe stated:

> I recently was involved in a custody assessment involving abuse allegations that had no basis in fact whatsoever. It had been thoroughly investigated, and it was clear that the allegations of sexual abuse were a total misunderstanding and overreaction stemming from the parent's personal history. The [allegedly abusive] father and his uncle took a polygraph test, which supported their innocence. It is one of those rare cases where there is not even a real question about what happened. No abuse happened. In that case I am trying to work with the mother's therapist to basically say: "Your client has a problem here, and her historical problems are going to impact the two boys' ability to have a good relationship with an excellent father." The boys are also going to miss out on an opportunity to connect with their paternal relatives as well as another sibling (half-sister). Now, there are other cases where there is some basis in fact underlying the allegations being raised, but the system professionals can't quite agree on making findings [or abuse by the rejected parent], or there is a finding, but the professionals involved do not appreciate the impact that it is having. It's almost easier dealing with a case with a parent where there is no basis in fact to find a way to salvage it. I have cases where there is abuse, and someone says: "Forget it, get over it, it's ancient history." But, a parent has been traumatized, and those cases are very difficult to resolve. These matters lead to experts being set up on both sides that prolong litigation and the conflict.[25]

As noted, another complicating factor when attempting to reliably differentiate alienation from justified rejection is determining what, from the child's perspective, is justified or unjustified. While the term "disproportionate" to describe the child's reaction in cases of alienation is accepted by many, some object to referring to a child's rejection as unjustified given that this is how the child feels, and it is invalidating to label his or her feelings "unjustified." Further, given the subjective nature of a child's feelings, it can be extremely difficult to make determinations regarding what is justified or unjustified,

---

[24] Interviews with: Justice Tom Altobelli, June 3, 2010; Peter Jaffe, June 23, 2010; Janet Johnston, May 10, 2010; Justice June Maresca, April 12, 2010; Robin Deutsch, June 14, 2010; Jennifer McIntosh, July 14, 2010; Joan Kelly, April 21, 2010.

[25] Interview, June 23, 2010.

reasonable or unreasonable.[26] As previously noted, it is this difficulty that in part has contributed to Johnston's revised definition of alienation, which focuses on the parent's alienating behaviors and the impact of this on a particular child. Still, it appears that there is less issue taken with the concept of a "justified rejection" than an "unjustified rejection."

Echoing the concern about the subjectivity in determining what is justified or proportionate and what is not, socio-law professor Linda Neilson, said:

> I think there is a huge potential to make errors in terms of what is disproportionate and what isn't because traditionally people have tended to divorce domestic violence from child abuse. And, we now know that domestic violence can have very serious implications for children and long-term implications and those reactions continue long after the domestic violence ends. Then, if we combine that with what we know from medical research on child brain development and the impact of trauma on the child's brain, we know that genuine fear, which is a learned response, can continue a long time after the domestic violence ends, even after it seems, on an objective basis, that the parent has changed in a positive way.[27]

An associated issue is raised by some who note that many custody evaluators are inadequately trained and thus not competent to recognize abuse and domestic violence. Consequently, both the short- and long-term impact of abuse and violence on the child and custodial parent are often minimized, while inaccurate conclusions are reached about warranted protective behavior and alienation.[28]

In some instances of justified rejection, the favored parent's reactions may be disproportionate to the circumstances and even emotionally harmful to the child (Friedlander & Walters, 2010; Johnston, Roseby, & Kuehnle, 2009). The protective response of the favored parent in *both* alienation and justified rejection may seem like alienating behavior. Different opinions, though, exist with respect to what the remedy should be. Domestic violence advocates and others express concern about punitive measures and custody reversal, even in cases of emotional abuse or severe alienation, for several reasons, including the potential risks of separating the child from the favored parent and because the favored parent, while misguided, is trying to protect the child. Others express concern for the child if the favored parent remains unresponsive to intervention geared at helping him or her to recognize the child is not, in fact, at risk and, further, is at risk if he or she is cut off from the rejected

---

[26] Interviews with Jennifer McIntosh (July14, 2010), Janet Johnston (May10, 2010), Loretta Frederick (June 28, 2010), Robert Marvin (April 20, 2010), and Joan Meir (April 21, 2010).
[27] Interview, June 21, 2010.
[28] Interviews with Loretta Frederick, June 28, 2010, Linda Neilson, June 21, 2010, Joan Meir, April 21, 2010.

parent and the extended family. Treatment and judicial remedies will necessarily be different depending on the nature and intensity of the parent–child
contact problem. We will return to this in Chapter 7 on interventions, and
Chapter 9, on legal responses and remedies.

Johnston has emphasized the difficulty in many cases of differentiating
the reasons for the parent–child contact problem (interview, May 10, 2010;
Johnston et al., 2009). She notes there is often no "bright line" between the
rejected parent's abusive behavior (violent, endangering, terrorizing of child,
witness to family violence); marginal or poor parenting (lacks empathy, self-
preoccupied, passive and neglectful); or overly punitive, coercive control in
response to the child. As previously noted, more recently she has proposed
moving from the concept of the "alienated child" to a more general definition with a focus on what the alienating parent is doing. Consistent with the
work of Baker and Darnall (2006), who focus more on parental behavior and
alienating strategies exhibited by the favored parent, Johnston proposes that
the parents' and children's behavior be defined independently and suggests
that with the development of valid measures, it should be possible to reliably identify these behaviors. She suggests using the term, "parental alienating
behavior" (PAB), which refers to false, malicious, or unjustified negative communication and behavior by one parent that has the *potential* to negatively
influence a child's relationship with and wish to spend time with the other
parent. PAB is considered to be emotionally abusive. She uses the phrase "visitation resistance and rejection" to describe the child's behavior toward the
rejected parent without any presumptions as to the cause.

Alienation *and* justified rejection may range from mild to severe. While
clear-cut cases may be less common than mixed cases, some cases may be
clearer than others. Many of the experts whom we interviewed, both legally
trained and mental health professionals, stated that based on their experience,
it is not particularly difficult to differentiate alienation from justified rejection at the extreme ends. The differences are undoubtedly clear at the end
of the continuum. However, as we move away from the ends of the continuum, it becomes more difficult to make what ends up being finer and finer
distinctions.

When attempting to differentiate alienation from justified rejection, it is
important to recognize that lapses in good parenting are common; there are
no perfect parents. Incidents of poor parenting by the rejected parent occur in
many cases of alienation, though not in all cases. What may have started out
as a normal parenting flaw, accepted by the child, may come to be a contributing factor to the child alienation. Without the alienating behaviors by the
favored parent, siblings, or extended family, the child would not have rejected
the parent.

In other cases, rejected parents are good parents, both before and after the
alienation surfaces (Baker & Fine, 2008; Johnston et al., 2009). Here, the child
enjoyed a good relationship with the parent, with any deficits in the parent's
personality or behavior clearly insufficient to cause a rift in the relationship.

It is also possible that the previously accepted parenting behavior changes for the worse after the separation, because the soon-to-be rejected parent is parenting in a different context and without the other parent as a support or buffer. These cases may be viewed as mixed or hybrid, with elements of alienation and justified rejection. However, when poor parenting is present in alienation, it does not rise to the level of neglect, emotional abuse, or physical abuse; if it did rise to this level, the identification should not be alienation but justified rejection. Amy Baker stated: "When there is *a bona fide* abuse or neglect, then alienation is off the table. It doesn't matter how manipulative or undermining the preferred parent may be." It is *primarily*, although not exclusively, the disproportionate reaction *of the child*, in combination with the alienating behavior, intentional or unintentional, that makes it alienation.

The ultimate question is whether or not it is in the child's best interest to attempt to repair the relationship with the rejected parent, irrespective of the cause of the strained relationship, and whether the rejection is justified or unjustified. A good custody evaluation will assist the family justice system in making what is often a difficult differentiation and can weight assignment of the contributing factors. An evaluator's analysis and categorization of parent–child contact problems can, in turn, inform the nature of the intervention.

Classification is not an exact science but, rather, involves both art and science (Gould & Martindale, 2007). Ultimately, in an individual case what is critical is not the subtle distinctions in terminology or classification, but rather, gaining a good understanding of family dynamics and making a plan that will promote the best interests of the child. What is key to the family dynamics in alienation cases is a good assessment of *how* the favored parent responds to instances of poor parenting by the rejected parent: that is, not only what the alienating parent does overtly, covertly, or nonverbally, but also what this parent does *not* do, which also may be indirect behavior. Silence can send a strong message to the child that the favored parent does not support the child's relationship with the other parent. In addition, in alienation cases, the favored parent often puts a spin on the rejected parent's flaws, which are exaggerated and repeated. "Legends" develop, and the child is influenced to believe the rejected parent is unworthy, and in some cases dangerous and abusive.

In alienation cases, the child's relationship with the rejected parent is not supported by the alienating parent; the child is not encouraged to see both the good and not so good in the other parent. Nor is the child required to sort out and resolve the difficulties or conflicts, as the favored parent would very likely expect of the child in other situations, such as when the child complains about a friend, teacher, or coach, giving the child the impression that the child's continued relationships with other people are more important than having a relationship with his or her other parent. For example, when difficulties occur between the favored parent and a relative of that parent, the parent is likely to expect and require the child to sort out those difficulties, and not to avoid them or sever ties with the people with whom the child experienced the conflict.

However, in alienation cases, the favored parent exploits the rejected parent's inevitable foibles and shortcomings and often purports to "leave the decision" about whether to have contact or even making efforts to resolve conflicts, to the child, thereby sending a strong message that the relationship is not that important. Interestingly, it is not uncommon for a favored parent who is noncommittal when it comes to the child seeing the other parent to assert firm expectations when it comes to the child's behavior in other respects, such as homework, being polite with relatives and neighbors, chores, extracurricular activities, or school. Good parenting includes not only listening and validating a child's feelings, but also helping them to see things from another person's perspective; resolving, not avoiding conflicts; having expectations; and modeling compassion, empathy, and forgiveness—practices that are not part of the truly alienating parent's repertoire when it comes to the rejected parent.

Often, the alienated child develops an anxious and phobic-like response. Like other phobias, the continued avoidance of the anxiety-provoking circumstances (parental conflict, loyalty bind), or feared object (the rejected parent), known as "anticipatory anxiety," reinforces the child's avoidance and rejection. The child's resistance or refusal is reinforced by the favored parent's approval and extra attention. Further, a mutually escalating cycle of fear and anxiety develops between the child and favored parent; the more upset the child is, the more protective and concerned the parent is, which in turn escalates the child's reactions, and so on.[29] Learning theory posits that the correction (extinction) of the avoidance is extremely difficult and requires exposure and systematic desensitization to the avoided circumstance or feared object.

Another important consideration when differentiating alienation from justified rejection is the rejected parent's behavior toward the child. When considering behavior of the rejected parent that may seem inappropriate or counterproductive, it is necessary to assess whether that behavior is *reactive* to the child's resistance or rejection, or behavior on the part of the rejected parent that predates the alienation and thus is *causal*. Ultimately, though, the impact on the child, irrespective of cause or intention of either parent, is most important. Even inappropriate, although understandable, reactive parental behavior that can be counterproductive may mushroom to the point that the child's rejection becomes "justified." This view was reflected by many experts in our interviews, who noted the diagnostic significance of determining whether a rejected parent's inappropriate behavior is causal or reactive. Was the behavior part of a preexisting pattern of abuse or inappropriate parenting, or was it an isolated incident or uncharacteristic behavior? These experts note, however, that this distinction has less importance when considering the child's feelings.

---

[29] Separated, high-conflict parents often have no direct contact with each other and rely on second-hand information, including from their child, to form opinions about each other. See Campbell (2005) for further elaboration on the role of ambiguity and attribution theory in the development of anxiety and negative stereotypes that are highly resistant to change.

From the child's perspective, the fact that the parent's behavior was reactive does not change how the child's feels about the parent. Johnston stated:

> I don't think it feels much different for a child whether it's reactive. It is a self-fulfilling prophecy that they hated that parent and felt very afraid of that parent...To a child that has been convinced all along that a parent is abusive, I don't think that it feels any different.[30]

In speaking about the impact of causal compared with reactive behavior by the rejected parent, Elizabeth McCarty, a lawyer at the Ontario Office of the Children's Lawyer, said:

> In the cases that I deal with I want a focus on how behaviors impact on a child. Determining whether a parent's behavior is causal or reactive can make a difference legally and can impact how a case is labeled, but it is the child's reaction to the behavior and their point of view that is most important. The child may be responding to reactive or causal behavior, but in dealing with solutions you need to focus on how the child has interpreted the relationship and how best the dynamics between the child and that parent can be addressed. It is important to keep it child focused.[31]

While the child's feelings about the behavior of a parent may not initially be influenced by whether that parent's inappropriate conduct is reactive or causal, a mental health professional who is working with the child may attempt to help the child understand these distinctions and the implications this may have on the child's feelings of rejection toward that parent.

2.7 Mixed or Hybrid Cases

Empirical studies have found a strong correlation between alienation, alienating parental behaviors, overprotective parenting, and an enmeshed[32] dynamic

---

[30] Interview, May 10, 2010.

[31] Interview, July 14, 2010.

[32] The term "enmeshment" has been widely used in the family therapy literature since it was popularized by Salvador Minuchin. "Enmeshment" refers to an "extreme form of proximity and intensity in family interactions...In a highly enmeshed, overinvolved family, changes within one family member or in the relationship between two family members reverberate throughout the system...On an individual level, interpersonal differentiation in an enmeshed system is poor...in enmeshed families the individual gets lost in the system. The boundaries that define individual autonomy are so weak that functioning in individually differentiated ways is radically handicapped." (Minuchin, Rosman, & Baker, 1978, p. 30).

between the alienated child and the favored parent (Baker & Darnall, 2006; Kelly & Johnston, 2004; Johnston, Walters, & Olesen, 2005b), as well as in case studies and clinical experience (Everett, 2006; Kelly & Johnston, 2001). With more research and experience, some legal and mental health professionals have noted that in their practices pure (clear) cases of alienation and justified rejection are less common than mixed or hybrid cases (Friedlander & Walters, 2010). Friedlander and Walters (2010) have expanded the earlier reformulated model and refer to "hybrid" cases, which they explain have varying degrees of enmeshment and boundary diffusion between the favored parent and the child, and *some* degree of inept parenting by the rejected parent. Reacting with anger, fear, or a need to retaliate, the favored parent may attempt to protect the child from harm by cutting off contact rather than addressing the parenting issues. Cases involving enmeshed and overinvolved parenting, however, are not in our view, mixed or hybrid in the same way that cases involving alienation and justified rejection are, given the preponderance of enmeshment in alienation cases. In other words, the presence of enmeshment with the favored parent does not make the case any less of a purer alienation case. To the contrary, the presence of enmeshment is defining and often a risk factor when observed in the younger child's interaction with his or her favored parent. While this child may not be entirely resisting or refusing contact, he or she may be showing early signs of becoming alienated. The presence of enmeshment dynamics, though, will inform the choice of interventions, which we discuss further in Chapter 7.

In their proposed hybrid model, Friedlander and Walters (2010), describe "realistic estrangement" as including cases where relatively minor emotional insensitivities or reactions by the rejected parent contribute to the parent–child relationship problem. The inclusion of minor insensitivities in realistic estrangement cases, thereby lowering the threshold for what would constitute a justified rejection, is a departure from earlier conceptualizations, where realistic estrangement was limited more typically to situations where the rejected parent perpetrated abuse or violence toward the other parent, or abuse, neglect, or very poor parenting toward the child. Minor insensitivities, though, are common to most parents. Psychologist Robin Deutsch stated:

> ...those rejected parents should be responsive to treatment or to parent guidance with a skilled clinician. If they are not responsive, then you've got something else that I would not consider the behavior a minor insensitivity. The definition of alienation incorporates the concept of a child using exaggerated and unjustified reasons for refusing contact. Minor insensitivities or flaws may be used as a basis for refusing contact. They are not generally included in realistic estrangement as in many families a parent is neither 100% emotionally attuned or may have parenting lacunae.[33]

---

[33] Interview, June 14, 2010.

While it can be difficult to make these distinctions, in our view, cases where minor parenting flaws or emotional insensitivities by the rejected parent have contributed to the child's rejection should not be regarded as cases of justified rejection or realistic estrangement. In such circumstances, the child would not reject the parent in the absence of the parental alienating behaviors.

More importantly, the critical factor when making these distinctions and identifying the most appropriate clinical interventions and legal remedies is the responsiveness to guidance and redirection by the court, lawyers, and mental health professionals by *both* the rejected parent, who may have reacted negatively to being rejected or mistreated by the child, and by the favored parent, who may have been misguided or mistaken in his or her conclusion that the child needed protection from the other parent.

We conceptualize "mixed" or hybrid cases as those involving elements of:

1) alienating behaviors and strategies (a process of alienation) on the part of the favored parent, *and*
2) behaviors and attitudes on the part of the rejected parent, including inflexibility and unresponsiveness to changing behavior, that lend to a justified or proportionate resistance or rejection to contact on the part of the child.

These mixed cases do *not* include other types of parent–child contact problems summarized earlier, such as an affinity due to a normal developmental preference or shared interests, or the child not having established a positive a relationship with the parent.

2.8 Dynamics in Alienation Cases

Recently, some writers have used the framework of gatekeeping to distinguish a child's resistance or refusal to have contact with a parent when the favored parent, typically the father, is "abusive" to the child or has been a perpetrator of domestic violence, from alienation in other circumstances when the favored parent, typically the mother, is not abusive in this way, but rather is "protective"[34] (Drozd & Olesen, 2009, 2010; Johnston et al., 2009).

In some situations, the favored parent genuinely believes that contact with the other parent will be harmful to the child. In some of these cases, the child's rejection is justified and the parent is justifiably protective; efforts to protect the child may look like parental alienating behavior when it is not. These are cases of justified rejection, not alienation.

In other cases, although the favored parent is genuinely concerned that contact with the rejected parent places the child in harm's way, the favored

---

[34] Drozd, interview, June 23, 2010; Jaffe, interview, June 23, 2010; Johnston, interview, May 10, 2010.

parent is misguided, as there is no real risk to the child. These cases are distinguished from the more severe alienation cases where the favored parent feigns his or her concerns and makes unfounded allegations that the rejected parent is sexually, physically, or emotionally abusive to the child. Drozd, Kuehnle, and Olesen (2011) refer to this deliberate behavior as "restrictive/negative gatekeeping." In these cases, the favored parent intentionally and maliciously discourages, interferes, or prevents contact with the other parent. This is severe alienation and amounts to emotional manipulation, intrusive parenting, and emotional abuse of the child by the favored parent.

Although protective parenting may be justified, it may be problematic or emotionally harmful to the child. In these cases, Drozd et al. (2011) in their presentation refer to "counterproductive protective parenting," which they define as: "…efforts of a concerned parent to protect the child from a genuinely abusive parent, when those efforts are clumsy, overly reactive, poorly regulated or otherwise look alienating." They view this behavior as protective gatekeeping as opposed to restrictive gatekeeping on the part of the favored parent. In their attempt to protect the child, the favored parents project their own earlier or current experiences of trauma onto the child; the parents' reactions are disproportionate to the experiences and may involve distortions, even paranoia, resulting in compromised, possibly emotionally harmful or abusive parenting.

Some feminists and domestic violence advocates argue that protective parenting of any sort, justified or unjustified, is not alienation, claiming that the parent (usually the mother) either genuinely believes there is risk to the child, or that there is likely some good reason for the concerns even if these cannot be identified by a custody evaluator or proven in court. For example, Joan Meier (Meier, 2010), an advocate for victims of domestic violence, asserts that significant (i.e., effective) alienation by custodial mothers is rare, but "alienation" by violent and abusive fathers is a significant concern; through a process of control and intimidation, children identify with the aggressor, become aligned with the abusive father, and reject their victimized mother.[35]

Drozd and Olesen (2010) prefer to identify the actions of the abusive and aggressive (also alienating) parent as "sabotaging," a process involving a violent or abusive parent who turns the child against and undermines the victim parent. In such cases, Johnston refers to the child's "pathological bonding with an abusive partner" consistent "with the Stockholm Syndrome and notes it is a form of PTSD to attach to that parent and be very fearful of leaving that parent."[36] The child identifies with the aggressor and may have posttraumatic stress disorder (PTSD). In this circumstance, the alienating behaviors and

---

[35] Interview, April 21, 2010. See Rand (2011) for a critical analysis of the issues in historical context.

[36] Interview, May 10, 2010.

strategies on the part of the favored parent can be viewed as part of an abusive pattern that might include mental illness or substance abuse.[37]

Loretta Frederick stated: "This behavior is yet another 'tactic' of the abusive parent's repertoire, and I do not see this as 'alienation' per se."[38] Similarly, Linda Neilson stated, "I prefer the term manipulation…where the domestic violator parent actually manipulates the children and creates an alignment such that the children align with the abusive parent against the other parent."[39]

Clearly, the dynamics of each family are different, and a thorough assessment is required to ensure that appropriate interventions are provided on the basis of different dynamics and the nature and severity of the alienation, as well as any issues of patterns of abuse and intimate partner violence (Jaffe, Ashbourne, & Mamo, 2010; Jaffe, Johnston, Crooks, & Bala, 2008; Kelly & Johnson, 2008).

2.9 Alienation and False Allegations of Abuse

While Gardner initially reported a much higher prevalence of false allegations of sexual abuse in alienation cases, he later reported that 10% to 20% of the alienation cases he had seen included these malicious allegations, and these cases were identified by him as exhibiting severe PAS (Gardner, 1998b).[40] Gardner also noted that PAS-indoctrinating fathers sometimes accuse the mother's new male partner or stepfather of sexual abuse. More recently, Kopetski, Rand, and Rand (2006) reported that in their study, false allegations of child abuse occurred in more than half of the cases referred for a custody evaluation, with neglect alleged primarily by alienating fathers and sexual abuse alleged primarily by alienating mothers.

In a study based on Canadian child protection data from 2003 (Bala, Mitnick, Trocmé, & Houston, 2007), separated fathers and mothers seem about equally likely to make unfounded allegations of abuse or neglect to child protection agencies, though mothers are more likely to make unfounded allegations of child sexual abuse, and fathers more likely to falsely claim that mothers are neglecting their children. Although the rate of unfounded allegations of child sexual abuse in the context of parental separation is relatively high (65%), the incidence of deliberate lying by the accusing parent seems relatively low (18% of cases in this study). Child protection workers report that most of these unfounded allegations are a product of miscommunication or misunderstanding, which may be exacerbated by hostility surrounding

---

[37] Neilson, interview, June 21, 2010; Jaffe, interview, June 23, 2010.

[38] Interview, June 28, 2010.

[39] Interview, June 21, 2010.

[40] In this second edition, Gardner provides further elaboration on the differential diagnosis of PAS from bona fide abuse and/or neglect.

parental separation and resulting distorted perceptions, rather than deliberate fabrication by the accusing parent.

As discussed later in this book, it is clear that one of the characteristics of more severe alienation cases is the making of false allegations of abuse and neglect, and child protection authorities are not infrequently involved in these cases in conducting repeated investigations. However, children whose parents have separated may also face heightened risk of abuse or neglect, so child protection agencies must take reports made in this context seriously.

2.10 Debates About Parental Alienation as a Diagnosis or Condition

As noted, Gardner was the first to propose that parental alienation is a "syndrome" (PAS) that should be treated as a childhood psychiatric disorder and classified in the *Diagnostic and Statistical Manual of Mental Disorders* (DSM). Subsequently, during the 1980s and 1990s, debate evolved, and numerous publications surrounding the notion of parental alienation as a "syndrome" or "diagnosis" emerged, primarily based on a conceptual or theoretical analysis, or clinical experience, as opposed to empirical research. Those supporting PAS as a diagnostic syndrome included Bone (2003), Brody (2006), Burrill (2006b), Kopetski (2006), Leving (2006), Lorandos (2006a), Rand (1997a, 1997b), Rand, Rand, and Kopetski (2005), and Walsh and Bone (1997).

Others maintained that PAS is not a clinically valid "diagnosis" and that evidence of such a diagnosis or syndrome should not be admissible in court (Bruch, 2001; Drozd & Olesen, 2004; Emery, 2005; Faller, 1997; Johnston & Kelly, 2004; Kelly & Johnston, 2001; Walker, Brantley, & Rigsbee, 2004b; Williams, 2001; Zirogiannis, 2001). These writers noted that PAS was not included in the current edition of the *Diagnostic and Statistical Manual of Mental Disorders, Fourth Edition* (DSM-IV) (American Psychiatric Association, 1994). Gardner's reply (2002b, 2004) explains that submissions were never made for PAS to be included; thus, the Committee responsible for the DSM-IV did not have occasion to reject it. He added that in the 1980s, when he began noticing and writing about PAS, it would have been premature to consider PAS for DSM-IV since there were too few articles in the literature to warrant a submission for inclusion to the DSM committees that started meeting in the early 1990s.[41] Years ago, Gardner predicted that the Committees for DSM-V would be likely to consider a submission for inclusion, given that there were well over 100 articles at that time on PAS, including 18 by Gardner in peer-review journals,

---

[41] He further cites the stringent criteria for inclusion in the diagnostic manual, noting by way of example that although Tourette's was first described as a syndrome in 1885, it was not included as a disorder in the DSM until 1980. Similarly, Asperger's syndrome was first described in 1957; however, it took 37 years for it to be included in DSM.

66 by others, and 51 on the phenomena of pathological alienation (see list available from www.rgardner.com and www.warshak.com). There have been numerous articles written on the topic since then. The DSM committees are now considering PAS as a diagnosis for inclusion in the next edition, scheduled to be released in 2013. The issue of inclusion of PAS in DSM-V is highly controversial and is further discussed below.

Psychologist Deirdre Rand (2011) provides a historical summary of the controversy about PAS as a psychological concept. She identifies two major groups of PAS critics. The first group includes primarily mental health professionals, divorce researchers, and other mental health professionals who work with high-conflict separation/divorce families, including those who are engaged in disputes over child custody or contact (e.g., Wallerstein; Johnston and Kelly group). For this group, the two most contentious issues are Gardner's emphasis on the causal role of the favored parent (as manifest in the child), and the "extreme interventions" that Gardner proposed, including the possibility of confinement of an alienated child in a juvenile custody facility.

In 2004, Janet Johnston, sociologist, and Joan Kelly, psychologist, wrote in *Family Court Review*:

> We reject Gardner's proposal that PAS should be granted the status
> of a diagnostic syndrome or that it be included as a psychiatric
> category in future editions of the DSM. Proponents of PAS continue
> to insist, without adequate empirical evidence, that a brainwashing
> parent is the primary causal agent and ignore or minimize the role
> of all other agents of a child's alienation. In this respect, PAS does
> not meet the American Psychiatric Association's (1994) criteria for
> a syndrome, which is defined as a cluster of symptoms, appearing
> together that characterize a disease that has "commonly recognized,
> or empirically verified pathogenesis, course, familial pattern, or
> treatment selection." (p. 626)

Gardner (2004) responded in the same 2004 issue of the *Family Court Review*, addressing the objections raised by Johnston and Kelly. Gardner and his supporters maintained that the criticisms of his work were unfounded in many respects. He argued that throughout his publications, including not only those on PAS but also those written before, he emphasized that a family systems perspective was needed to understand all childhood disorders, including PAS (Gardner, 2004). He maintained that his writings (1992b, 1998b, 1999), including his first publication on the topic in 1985, routinely differentiated PAS from other forms of justified rejection of a parent (or realistic estrangement) resulting from child abuse, neglect, or abandonment, or as a manifestation of adolescent rebellion. Moreover, he noted that he introduced the concept of PAS precisely because of the need to differentiate it from other types of parent–child and contact problems about which he had written previously. Other models of parental alienation or child alienation, though, include various types and causes of the parent–child contact problem, which he maintained contributed to the diagnostic confusion and controversy. In his reply commentary, Gardner reiterated his original 1985 definition: "[PAS]...results from a *combination* of a programming (brainwashing) parent's indoctrination and the child's own vilification of the target parent" (2001, p. 61).

Rand (2011) argues that the harshest critics of Gardner are the second group, advocates for women (e.g., the American group, National Organization of Women [NOW]), and especially advocates for female victims of domestic violence (e.g., Bruch, 2001; Faller, 1997; Meier, 2009; Walker, Brantley, & Rigsbee, 2004a). One advocate for abused women, Joan Meier,[42] claims that, in effect, alienation, as used in family courts, is a fabricated concept for denying abuse or other criticisms of a noncustodial parent (usually the father). She argues that PAS was "invented by Gardner to refute [child] sexual abuse." These feminist critics object to Gardner's views on child sex abuse and often equate false allegations of sex abuse with his definition of PAS. They argue that in response to allegations of abuse against them, male perpetrators advance counterallegations of PAS or alienation as a "smoke screen" for their own violent and abusive behavior (Meier, 2009; Walker et al., 2004b). Feminist critics charge that this often results in the courts awarding custody to abusive fathers, despite the fact that battered mothers are justifiably protecting, and not alienating, their children from their fathers. These writers appear to be arguing that if PAS or alienation were not accepted in the courts, such counterallegations against victim mothers would not be as frequent and would not carry as much weight. Some advocates of victims of domestic violence assert that there is no evidence to support the claim that mothers are falsely accusing fathers of domestic or child abuse (Bruch, 2001). They caution that Gardner's theory, which has been "conveniently" adopted by many fathers' rights advocates, is yet another manifestation of "mother and victim blaming."[43]

It is accepted now that a child's rejection of a parent is to be expected and is, in fact, a healthy response to both child abuse or direct or indirect exposure to domestic violence; accordingly, this reaction is not alienation (or parental alienation or child alienation). Rejection in this context is characterized as "realistic estrangement" by Gardner, though as previously noted, we prefer to use the term "justified rejection" to characterize these cases. However, some feminist critics deny that a parent (mother) can induce a child to make or go along with false allegations of abuse against the other parent. In other words, it is claimed that children who reject a parent or are reluctant to have contact *must* have a good reason, such as having witnessed domestic violence, bona fide abuse or parental maltreatment. In addition to concerns about the overlap in abuse and domestic violence cases with cases of resistance to contact are concerns about the inability of custody evaluators and other professionals to reliably identify and assess domestic violence and abuse and their impact on

---

[42] Interview, April 21, 2010.
[43] There are also groups headed by mothers advocating greater awareness of PAS. See http://www.thelizlibrary.org/. Retrieved on March 16, 2012.

children and their mothers.[44] As noted above, feminist critics are especially concerned about lack of understanding of various professional groups about domestic violence and abuse.

Rand (2011) argues that the feminist critics "dismiss the idea that children of divorce may align with one parent to do battle against the other, amplify their complaints about the other parent, and become obsessed with denigrations of the rejected parent which are out of all proportion to the child's experience with that parent." (p. 54). Rand notes that for the most part, these critics deny the existence of the PAS phenomenon, by whatever name, whether it be called "parental alignments," "overburdened child," or "pathological alienation."

It is important to recognize that while the two groups of critics as discussed both reject the idea that alienation is a "syndrome," they differ markedly on important aspects related to the existence, definition, and treatment of alienation. For example, the feminist group is generally opposed to the possibility of court-ordered counseling or a change of custody to the rejected parent as a response to alienation or resistance to contact with a parent, while Janet Johnston and most other mental health critics recognize that these remedies are likely to be necessary in the most severe cases.

Reflecting the views of the former group, feminist commentators Walker and Shapiro (2010) maintain that alienation as a diagnosis of any sort should not be included in the DSM due to "the lack of scientific and empirical data underlying the construct" (p. 283) and "the inability to differentiate the symptoms from trauma, specifically child abuse and domestic violence from PAD [Parental Alienation Disorder]" (p. 268). They maintain that the risks of identifying the child as having a mental disorder during a high-conflict or abusive custody battle are likely to be greater than giving the child the opportunity to have a break from a relationship with one parent and a chance to restore contact later when the parental conflict has subsided or the "fears and trauma triggers" subside. They conclude that:

> there are insufficient data to determine that rejection of a parent
> is harmful to the child or that the child and parent will remain
> disconnected over time if the child is permitted to reestablish
> a new safe and secure environment. What is being termed as
> alienation may well be a normal variant of family structure based
> on many variables in that particular family system and that forcing
> reunification may itself be more detrimental to the parent–child
> relationship over a period of time. (p. 284)

Richard Warshak (2001, 2006) specifically cautions against the use of "PAS" in forensic settings (2006). Warshak (2001) and many others[45] argue

---

[44] Interviews with Linda Neilson, June 21, 2010; Loretta Frederick, June 28, 2010; and Joan Meir, April 21, 2010.

[45] Interviews with psychologists Stephen Carter, Janet Johnston, Joan Kelly, Justice June Maresca, Federal Magistrate, Tom Altobelli, and family law lawyer Philip Epstein.

against the use the term "parental alienation *syndrome*" in reports and testimony, instead recommending descriptions of family dynamics and behaviors, and inclusion of illustrative statements made by parents and children.

More recently, while intentionally excluding any reference to *syndrome*, William Bernet, a child and adolescent psychiatrist, and his coauthors submitted a proposal that parental alienation be considered as either Parental Alienation Disorder (PAD) or as a Relational Disorder (see Bernet's Appendix B) (Bernet, 2010).[46] A similar proposal has also been made to *The International Classification of Diseases, 9th Revision, Clinical Modification* (ICD-9-CM), Sixth Edition.[47] The proposal was signed by 70 individuals, primarily, although not exclusively, mental health and family law professionals. Bernet's bibliography includes published articles, books, and dissertations (total of 630 references) from Canada, United States, the United Kingdom, Europe, South Africa, Japan, Malaysia, Mexico, India, Israel, South America, Australia, and Cuba.

Bernet notes that efforts have been made to move away from any emphasis on the blame of one parent. The diagnosis of PAD is based on the *child's* behavior (duration at least 2 months), with specific criteria consistent with Gardner's eight behavioral manifestations.[48] PAD is *not* diagnosed if the rejected parent maltreated the child. Bernet et al. (2010) defines alienation as a:

> mental condition in which a child—usually one whose parents are engaged in high conflict divorce—allies himself or herself strongly with one parent (the preferred parent) and rejects a relationship with the other parent (the alienation parent) without legitimate justification. (p. 76)

Bernet and his coauthors maintain that parental alienation is not a minor problem but a significant and tragic one representing a serious mental condition. The child's refusal to see a parent is maladaptive and "driven by the false belief that the alienated parent is a dangerous and unworthy person." They maintain that PAD is an important and widespread problem and estimate

---

[46] Further information on the status of the committee's work may be obtained from the DSM website (www.dsm5.org).

[47] The ICD-9-CM is maintained jointly by the National Center for Health Statistics (NCHS) and the Centers for Medicare & Medicaid Services (CMS).

[48] These include: 1) a persistent rejection or denigration of a parent that reaches the level of a campaign; and 2) weak, frivolous, and absurd rationalizations for the child's persistent criticism of the rejected parent; and two or more of the following six attitudes and behaviors: 1) lack of ambivalence; 2) independent-thinker phenomenon; 3) reflexive support of one parent against the other; 4) absence of guilt over exploitation of the rejected parent; 5) presence of borrowed scenarios; and 6) spread of animosity to the extended family of the rejected parent. The disturbance causes clinically significant distress or impairment in social, academic (occupational), or other important areas of functioning (Bernet et al., 2010).

that parental alienation occurs in 1% of all children and adolescents in the United States (i.e., about 250,000 children and youth). They maintain that it is important to properly recognize the problem so that it may be researched, prevented, and treated.

The reasons cited for inclusion into DSM are:

1) relational disorders are included in DSM-V, and PAD is an exemplar of this type of mental disorder;
2) despite controversies regarding terminology and etiology, the phenomenon of PAD is almost universally accepted by mental health and legal professionals;
3) existing research indicates that PAD is a valid and reliable construct;
4) more research is needed, and establishing diagnostic criteria will make it possible to study PAD in a more systematic manner;
5) establishing diagnostic criteria will reduce the opportunities for abusive parents and unethical attorneys to misuse the concept of PAD in child custody disputes; and
6) establishing diagnostic criteria will be helpful for many, including clinicians who work with divorced families, divorced parents who are trying to do what is best for their children, and children of divorce, who desperately need appropriate treatment that is based on a correct diagnosis.

As an alternative to PAD, Bernet proposes the diagnosis of Parent–Child Relational Problem. The proposal states:

> Parent–Child Relational Problem (a V-code) is the appropriate diagnosis if the focus of clinical attention is on the relationship between a child and his or her divorced parents, but the symptoms do not meet the criteria for a mental disorder. For example, a rebellious adolescent may not have a specific mental disorder, but may temporarily refuse to have contact with one parent even though both parents have encouraged him to do so and a court has ordered it. On the other hand, parental alienation disorder should be the diagnosis if the child's symptoms are persistent enough and severe enough to meet the criteria for that disorder.[49]

The proposal notes that more people will be able to obtain insurance-funded treatment if PAD is accepted as a diagnosis in DSM-V. Bernet clarified that although this is an important consideration, it is not one of the primary reasons for the inclusion.[50] American psychologist Robin Deutsch[51], who is

---

[49] V codes in the DSM represent additional conditions that may be a focus of clinical attention (American Psychiatric Association, 1994).

[50] Interview, June 2, 2010.

[51] Interview, June 14, 2010.

not in favor of PAD being included in the DSM, notes that there is already pro-vision of a diagnosis, Parent–Child Relational Problem (V61.20) in the DSM, which should be sufficient for insurance coverage when treating parent–child contact problems.

Janet Johnston and Joan Kelly reiterated their earlier objections in a letter to the DSM committee, in which they opposed Bernet's proposal to include PAD as a diagnosis in the DSM. Thirty-five mental health and family law professionals signed their letter in support of their position. The objection to including alienation as a mental disorder of a child (i.e., PAD) is supported by the majority of the experts whom we interviewed,[52] many of whom support the diagnosis of these cases as a Parent–Child Relational Problem.

In their letter to the DSM committee, Johnston and Kelly maintain that inclusion of PAD does not meet the DSM-V criteria for a new diagno-sis category as proposed by Kendler, Kupfer, Narrow, Phillips, and Fawcett (2009).[53] Johnston notes that only two of these five criteria are met. One factor that is met is that there is a broad consensus of expert clinical opin-ions that alienation exists, and the other is that alienation identifies a dis-tinct group that needs intervention. However, Johnston notes that PAD does not satisfy the criterion that the diagnosis should *not* have a sub-stantial overlap with other diagnoses. As discussed, there is a substantial overlap of factors contributing to the problem, such as developmentally expected reactions, reactions specific to the divorce, or alignments that result from the child's efforts to cope with parental conflict, that makes diagnosis extremely difficult. While there are some pure cases of either alienation or justified rejection, many cases are mixed. In her comments made at AFCC plenary in Denver in June 2010, Janet Johnston cautioned that there is "no bright line" between abusive parenting (violent, abusive, endangering, terrorizing of the child, witness to family violence) and mar-ginal or poor parenting by the rejected parent (lacks sufficient empathy, self-preoccupied, passive and neglectful and/or overly punitive in response to the child's rejection and physically forces compliance). She noted that ultimately, alienation and justified rejection may co-occur. She concludes that there is insufficient diagnostic validity with respect to etiology, course (including degree of distress, disability, or impairment of functioning to the child), treatment, or prognosis.

Similarly, Canadian legal scholar Linda Neilson stated:

> The problem I see with including it in the DSM is that it takes our attention away from the complexity of these cases, away from close examination of parenting and the whole dynamic of the family

---

[52] Exceptions include Bernet, Baker, Boch, Ludmer, and Samery.

[53] Interview with Janet Johnston, May 10, 2010; see also her comments at the AFCC Denver Opening Session, Parental Alienation and the DSM-V (Baker, Bernet, Elrod, Jaffe, & Johnston, 2010).

because it is focusing on one thing: the child's rejection of a parent, and I think there are so many other elements and dynamics that go into a best interest of the child determination.[54]

Finally, those like Johnston who object to inclusion of PAD as a diagnosis note that the benefits of inclusion must outweigh any risks, which they do not agree is the case. There is a concern that given the need to make sense out of complexity quickly, the courts and professionals may rely on a diagnosis of PAD for convenience, resulting in a high risk of misdiagnosis. While the intention may be, as Bernet states, to move away from an emphasis on parental fault or blame, dissenters maintain that the diagnosis of PAD will necessarily promote blame and polarization in the adversarial system and thus be counterproductive to resolution and parents working together to assist their children. Johnston states:

> Diagnosis should not cause any harm, but I think parental alienation allegations can be generated, thrive, and are reified in an adversarial legal system. There is something about the very nature of this particular condition that a finding of PA or PAS in court [that appears to] offer a simple, clear-cut answer to who is right and who is wrong for these litigants, who are often ashamed and are intent on proving that they are the good parent and the other is the bad parent, and for the lawyers who are charged with zealously advocating for their clients there is no nuance here. You are either one or the other. And despite this attempt [in Bernet's proposal] to...get the nuance back in and make allowance for these other contributing factors, the way the court operates is often to strip down these cases and see something as clear-cut. In that sense, it is only going to contribute to the blaming, mistrust, and polarization and undermine the capacity for coparenting. In this context I think the diagnosis can be viewed as doing more harm than good. In custody litigation there is proclivity of clients and advocates to prefer simplicity and clarity at the expense of nuance and complexity in these family situations...There is something about this diagnosis that is just attractive; it uniquely thrives in the adversarial litigation arena. And I don't know what other diagnosis does.[55]

Similarly, lawyer and social worker Bill Eddy stated:

> I think the issue is really more of a systems issue. My fear is that it's going to get identified as an individual cause, and so mom or dad are going to be hit over the head with this if it happens and courts will say "now, it's a syndrome" or "now it's a diagnosis," and

---

[54]   Interview, June 21, 2010.
[55]   Interview, May 10, 2010.

therefore, x, y, z and we're going to stop examining anything else. My concern also is that there are cases of true abuse that need to be investigated, and as soon as you say "here is the diagnosis," you're also saying it's not any other diagnosis. And there are cases where it may be another diagnosis, and it's easy to jump to conclusions. Unfortunately, in this day and age, people are becoming more comfortable jumping to conclusions, especially in legal matters, in an all-or-nothing way. I'm concerned it may feed that. I'm concerned courts will be stuck arguing over the diagnosis, rather than focusing on what to do right away to help both parents and the children.[56]

A diagnosis of the problem as a "mental disorder" is believed to be simplistic to the extent that it does not adequately consider the role of the family court systems and both the legal and mental health professionals who often play a part in the exacerbation of the problem. Most of our expert informants emphasized that alienation, by whatever name, is a family and systemic problem, not an individual pathology or mental disorder of the child that can be adequately captured using the medical model or the DSM.[57] Significant concerns were also expressed about labeling a child with a mental disorder. Johnston concludes:

At best, PA is a non-diagnostic syndrome that sheds no light on cause, prognosis or treatment. Including PA in the DSM-5 with its potential misuse in custody litigation at this juncture does not add any information that would enlighten the court, the clinician or the clients, all of whom would be better served a more specific description of the parents' and child's behavior in the context of his family together with a thorough assessment of all factors potentially contributing to the child's negative's beliefs and behaviors vis-à-vis the other parent. More empirical research is warranted. (Handouts from AFCC Annual Conference Denver, 2010, p. 13)

The majority of the mental health professionals whom we interviewed believe that parental alienation does not meet the criteria for a mental (psychiatric) diagnosis (an individual pathology), but indicated that it could be a *family* relational problem (not only a parent–child relational problem) that is exacerbated by the adversarial legal system. The acceptance of this as a diagnosis, however, does not appear to be consistent with how a parent–child relational problem as a diagnosis is proposed by Bernet. He proposes that the

[56] Interview, April 29, 2010.
[57] Interviews with Francine Cry, May 27, 2010; Stephen Carter, June 16, 2010; Robin Deutsch, June 14, 2010; Leslie Drozd, June 23, 2010; Robyn Fasser, 2010; Benjamin Garber, May 21, 2010; Peter Jaffe, June 23, 2010; Joan Kelly, 2010.

parent–child relational problem designation should be a designation for the less severe cases that do not meet the threshold for PAD.

In an Internet survey of 448 (a response rate of 46%) mental health and legal professionals, Bow, Gould, and Flens (2009) report that the respondents were "cautious and conservative/moderate in their view of parental alienation (PA) and very reluctant to support the concept of parental alienation *syndrome* (PAS). Also, they did not view PAS as meeting admissibility standards" (p. 1). Seventy-four percent indicated that PAS did not meet the American expert evidence *Frye* Standard of "general acceptance" in the "scientific community," and 88% stated that in their view it did not meet the alternate (a higher) *Daubert* standard for admissibility in court (a criteria based on the acceptance of a reliable and valid scientific concept.). Bow et al. conclude that the lack of a single definition has contributed to an ongoing debate about the existence, etiology, and characteristics of alienating dynamics.

More recently, in a survey of 1,000 audience members conducted at the AFCC 2010 Annual Conference in Denver, 310 members completed the survey. Nearly all respondents (98%) agreed with the following question: "Do you think that some children are manipulated by one parent to irrationally and unjustifiably reject the other parent?" (Baker, Jaffe, Bernet, & Johnston, 2011). However, only one third of respondents thought parental alienation should be included in the DSM. The majority (85%) said there would be unintended negative consequences if it were included, while about half said there would be negative consequences if it were excluded.

At present, the debate continues, but it seems that PAS will not be included in DSM-V. Vice-Chair of the APA Task Force drafting DSM-V, Dr. Darrel Regier, said (Crary, 2010, October 1): "There is not sufficient scientific evidence to warrant its inclusion in the DSM." He described chances for inclusion of parental alienation as "slim"—given that it has not been selected for field trials that normally would be a prerequisite for official recognition (Crary, 2010).

While prior to 2000 it was common for reported court cases from the United States, Canada, and the U.K. to use "syndrome" terminology, reflecting the usage of experts who appeared as witnesses, it has become much less common. Even if not a DSM diagnosis, courts will continue to permit the inclusion of behavioral descriptions of children and their parents and will very likely continue to use "alienation" and "parental alienation." Further, judges recognize that it is for mental health professionals, not the courts, to decide whether parental alienation is a "syndrome."

2.11 Summary

In this chapter, we reviewed the various types of parent–child contact problems, including alienation and justified rejection. There is not presently a clear consensus about how best to define alienation, which creates difficulties when attempting to assess its occurrence, related factors, and consequences. Although we were unable to find a consensus about the terminology to be used to define alienation, alienation is a complex phenomenon, and the field should move away from simplistic, unidimensional definitions. Instead, understanding the complexity of alienation requires a comprehensive approach to determine how best to assess and measure for the presence of alienation, thereby differentiating it from other parent–child contact problems. It is also important to recognize that clear (or pure) cases of either alienation or justified rejection are likely less common than mixed cases. In the next three chapters, we review the empirical evidence regarding risk factors, indicators, and available measurement tools to assess for alienation and other parent–child contact problems.

3

Risk Factors and Indicators Involved
in Alienation

3.1 Extent and Limitations of Research on Alienation

As new research begins to emerge regarding the factors associated with alienation, it is important to delineate the correlates of alienation. This chapter reviews the current research regarding risk factors and indicators of alienation, and discusses the current state of the literature to provide guidance in this emerging area of research and clinical development.

Although there is a rapidly growing body of literature on alienation, there is a long-standing recognition that not all research designs are equal in terms of the generalizability of findings (external validity), and the ability to control for risk of error and minimize bias in the results. Assessing the quality of the literature relevant to alienation provides the ability to highlight the strengths and limitations of the evidence and to determine areas that need further research (Saini, Johnston, Fidler, & Bala, 2012).

Some research methods provide better evidence than other methods when seeking answers to specific questions. For example, qualitative methods of interviewing participants about a particular phenomenon are preferred for understanding the unique experiences of included participants. However, given the small samples required to gain a rich description of the phenomenon, qualitative studies are not well suited for making inferences to a larger population. Random sampling of a population to survey responses about a phenomenon is a more valid way to make inferences back to the target population based on the sample responses. The most valid observational studies use both random sampling and randomized control comparison groups to isolate any associational relationships found in the target sample that are found to be different than the comparison group. Unlike qualitative studies, observational studies often do not provide the rich context of these relationships, due to the closed-ended questioning required to manage data collection and analysis of large samples.

Questions about the effectiveness of interventions are best answered using random control trials to isolate the salient variables and minimize the risk of confounding factors influencing the results. As a result, controlling for error and bias, randomized control trials (RCTs) are often considered to be the most valid method for finding the true effect of an intervention. These controlled experiments permit the investigation of a hypothesized cause and effect relationship to determine whether the manipulation of a condition (e.g., providing children an intervention) causes the other variable to change (e.g., children's relationship with a parent improves postintervention). However, randomized trials are expensive to undertake, and there are significant practical and legal impediments in undertaking such research for court-controlled interventions.

The degree of confidence in research findings is directly related to the research design used, the sampling strategies, the environment or setting of the studies, and the methods used to control for error and bias. Assessing the evidence allows consumers of research to consider not only the strength of the findings, but also the external validity, generalizability, or transferability of findings across multiple samples.

With an understanding of the levels of evidence in the empirical literature, it is important to consider the current state of the empirical evidence of alienation within the context of separation and divorce. The results of the rapid evidence assessment (REA) of peer-reviewed literature undertaken for this book uncovered many conceptual articles arguing the merits of alienation, but there are few empirical studies that have tested these clinical hypotheses (Saini et al., 2012). Turkat (2002) argues that published clinical observations about alienation are nevertheless important contributions to the field, given that most clinical hypotheses developed by mental health and legal professionals never reach the stage of being empirically tested and most are rarely published. In his view, if clinical observations "receive attention in the literature from others, that is usually a sign that the idea has some degree of merit" (p. 155). However, others have argued that clinical observations regarding alienation do not constitute valid empirical evidence (Johnston & Kelly, 2004; Saini et al., 2012).

Empirical studies conducted to investigate risk factors, indicators, and consequences of alienation are limited to one-shot cross-sectional studies and qualitative studies using small samples of nonrandom participants. However, with the growing body of research and some degree of consistency in the findings, it is possible to draw some tentative conclusions about alienation.

3.2 Current Evidence on the Social and Psychological Factors Associated With Alienation

The majority of studies share common limitations that restrict the generalizability of their findings, including nonrandom samples, data analyzed retrospectively, and use of descriptive statistics rather than mathematically calculated comparisons. The children and parents in these studies, therefore, are not necessarily representative of all children and families from divorced or separated populations, or even those involved in alienation cases. The findings of these studies are further limited by the use of different definitions for "alienation" (e.g., parent alienation syndrome, child alienation, parental alienation, child refusal, etc.), including the inability to reliability differentiate alienation from other types of strained parent–child relationships, including justified rejection. This lack of consensus on the definitions of alienation and the use of varying terminology in the studies further provides confusion in determining the potential of integrating findings across studies. This point was echoed by the psychiatrist William Bernet:

> There needs to be a standard definition so that everybody can communicate and when people do research they are using the same criteria, whatever the criteria might be. There needs to be a standard definition for the diagnosis and standard criteria for making the diagnosis. How can you do research on a large scale without having that? Currently it's like trying to write a dictionary in the Tower of Babel. There are not only different definitions for the phrase, parental alienation—there are 4 or 5 definitions for that term— but there are different names for the situation in which a child adamantly refuses to have contact with one of his parents without justification.[1]

In considering the social and psychological factors associated with alienation, it is important to distinguish between risk factors that make alienation more likely to occur in a specific case, and indicators that suggest that alienation is present. Unfortunately, much of the current literature does not make this distinction because studies have generally not separated samples by those at risk of alienation and those currently involved in alienation. Risk factors consider characteristics that are related to the increase in likelihood that alienation will occur within the context of separation, including factors specific to the parents, the relationship between the parents, factors regarding the parent–child relationships, factors specific to the child, and macro level factors (e.g., the adversarial system).

Indicators are observable symptoms that point toward the presence of alienation in a specific case. In contrast to risk factors that consider the

---

[1] Interview, June 2, 2010, William Bernet.

likelihood of occurrence, indicators are factors that help to distinguish the presence of alienation from cases where alienation is not present. In addition, indicators address the frequency, nature, and severity of alienation by addressing symptomatology, or the combined cluster of symptoms that would suggest the presence of alienation in a given case. This is further complicated because there is substantial overlap in the alienation literature between risk factors and indicators. For example, one cannot say with certainty whether parental mental health problems occur before the separation, thereby making it a risk factor for alienation, or whether the onset of mental health problems after the separation contributes to the presence of alienation, making this factor an indicator.

Despite these limitations, there is a growing literature that has considered the various factors of alienation. To provide clarity of the current evidence, factors are presented by considering the findings according to whether the factor addresses the interparental relationship, factors regarding the favored parent, factors of the rejected parent, and factors that are specific to the child. Although risk factors and indicators are often presented as one dimensional and isolated (child, favored parent, rejected parent, interparental, and the macros system), it is important not to consider these as discrete categories, as no one factor should be considered solely without considering the intersections of the risk factors and indicators present at all levels of the family system.

As Chief Justice Carey of Massachusetts stated:

> I define alienation as a culmination of factors…I view it as a triad, which would include one parent who perhaps is engaging in the alienating behaviors, another parent who may be engaging in alienating behaviors, or just by personality may be contributing to the alienating issues, and it could be child's temperament or just the mere fact that the child is caught in the middle.[2]

This was echoed by psychologist Richard Warshak in determining the cause of parental rejection:

> If there is rejection, I look for various possible contributing factors, including the rejected parent's behavior, the circumstances of the family situation, the favored parent's behavior, and the child's own contributions. Most important, I try to determine whether the child would be better off remaining alienated from the parent, or whether the child really would be better off if the relationship was repaired.[3]

---

[2] Interview June 29, 2010, Chief Justice Paula Carey, Probate and Family Court, Massachusetts.

[3] Interview, April 15, 2010.

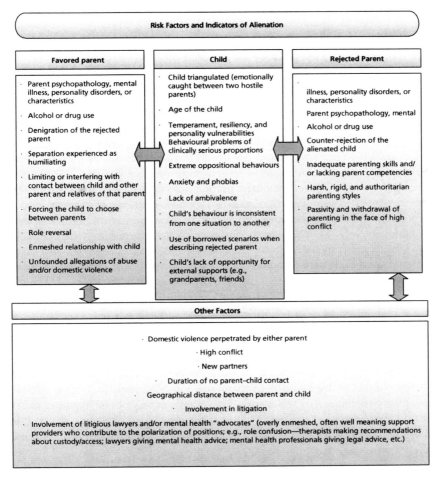

Figure 3.1 Summary of Risk Factors and Indicators of Alienation

In Figure 3.1, a combination of risk factors and indicators of alienation is presented to provide a general overview of this complex issue. Within a multidimensional view of the factors of alienation, no one factor provides sufficient evidence of the presence of alienation. But rather, each case should be assessed for the presence of all potential factors and the interactions among these factors to provide a more complete picture of the complex dynamics of alienation. Each of these individual factors is further explored below, noting that a comprehensive assessment (see Chapter 4) is needed to distinguish between mild, moderate, and severe cases of alienation and the relationship of the presence of alienation with the frequency and intensity of these factors on a case-by-base basis.

3.3 Interparental Factors Following Separation or Divorce

3.3.1 Intimate Partner Violence Perpetrated by Either Parent

Intimate partner violence has been suggested to be a significant factor in distinguishing justified rejection (realistic estrangement) from alienation (Johnston, Walters, & Olesen, 2005b; Lee & Olesen, 2001).

In the Johnston, Walters, and Olesen (2005c) study of 125 children drawn from an archival database of documentary records describing parent–child relationships in separating and divorced families, they found that intimate partner violence had occurred in 44% of high-conflict families, with fathers almost three times more likely to be perpetrators than mothers. Intimate partner violence was not directly related to children's rejection of a parent, and it was not found to be a predictor of rejection of either parent, an indication that in families where there is intimate partner violence, the children are not likely to resist or reject the perpetrator. As discussed previously, there are also cases where a child is alienated from a parent who is the victim of abuse as a result of intimidation or identification with a parent who is the perpetrator of abuse.[4]

3.3.2 Interparental High Conflict

There were no known studies that found an empirical link between high-conflict divorce or separation cases and alienation, although clinical observations have suggested that children's rejection of one parent commonly occurs in the context of high-conflict separation. Vassiliou and Cartwright (2001) assert, for example, that the dissolution of high-conflict marriages and court proceedings can increase conflict among the separating parents and that it is believed that this conflict propels and intensifies the occurrence of parental alienation.

3.3.3 Parents' Involvement in Entrenched Litigation

It has been asserted that involvement of the courts by parents to solve their custody and contact issues contributes to or exacerbates the occurrence of alienation. Based on her experience as a judge in British Columbia, Donna Martinson (2010) suggested that "Not only is harm caused by the alienating behavior and the conflict associated with it, but the court process itself may exacerbate the conflict, placing the children in the middle and affecting their lives on a daily basis in highly destructive ways" (pp. 180–181). Likewise, Kopetski (1998a) suggested that alienation can be exacerbated by legal proceedings that coincide with and strengthen the pathological defenses alienating parents use to avoid experiencing psychological pain of internal

---

[4] Interviews with Loretta Frederick, June 28, 2010; Janet Johnston, May 10, 2010; Linda Neilson, June 21, 2010; and Leslie Drozd, June 23, 2010.

conflict. Kelly and Johnston (2004), providing some support for this position, found that children of divorce referred from family courts compared with a community-based sample of separated families had higher rates of alienation. It should be noted that there could be a "selection bias" for these studies as parents with allegations of alienation are very probably more likely to turn to the courts to help resolve disputes issues. In other words, it seems clear that parents in cases with alienation allegations are more likely to seek resolution by a family court judge (and less likely to settle on their own) than in cases without such allegations, but it is far from clear that the family justice process exacerbates the problems in these cases.

3.3.4 Geographical Distance Between Parents

There is relatively little empirical evidence on the impact of geographic distance between parents on the occurrence of alienation, though some commentators have suggested that alienation may be more likely to occur or worsen if parents reside far apart, making contact less frequent. Clinical commentaries have noted that an application to the court by a custodial parent to relocate with a child after divorce may be a risk factor for alienation. Once the issue of relocation is raised, then the custodial parent may attempt to influence the child to support the move or may raise allegations not raised before to justify the move (Warshak, 2000).

Waldron and Joanis (1996) suggest that when there is large geographic distance between homes, an alienating parent has a good deal of time to work with, which can reduce the likelihood that the child will be able not to succumb to the alienating parent's attempts to involve him or her in the campaign of denigration against the rejected parent. Others have noted that time and distance away from a rejected parent can further perpetuate alienation because the child is unable to experience positive interactions with the rejected parent, which can further polarize the child's beliefs about that parent (Vassiliou & Cartwright, 2001).

3.4 Factors of the Favored Parent

3.4.1 Exposing the Child to Denigration of the Rejected Parent

Kelly and Johnston (2001) describe the child's "denigration of the rejected parent" as a result of the communication of extremely negative views about the rejected parent by the favored parent, which are then freely, angrily, and repeatedly expressed to the child. They note that "the effect of the continued drumbeat of negative evaluation of the parent is to erode the child's confidence in and love for the rejected parent. These evaluations may also be expressed indirectly, covertly, or unconsciously and may include innuendos of sexual or child abuse or implications that the parent is dangerous in other ways"

Table 3.1 Factors of the Favored Parent

Factor	Description	Citations
Exposing child to direct, indirect, conscious, or unconscious denigration of the rejected parent	Bad-mouthing, portraying other parent as dangerous or as having abandoned or rejected the child, removing all signs of the other parent from the home, negative body language when other parent is mentioned, etc.	Kelly & Johnston, 2001; Baker, 2006; Kopetski, 1998a, 1998b; Lowenstein, 1998; Steinberger, 2006a; Vassiliou & Cartwright, 2001; Waldron & Joanis, 1996
Parent psychopathology, mental illness, personality disorders, or characteristics	Favored parent sees self as "virtuous." Rigid thinking; externalizes responsibility onto others; histrionic, suspicious, or paranoid; narcissistic; psychotic; vulnerable to loss and conflict related to attachment and separation; need for control; parent–child role reversal; lack of warm and involved parenting; child abuse	Baker, 2006; Clawar & Rivlin, 1991; Everett, 2006; Hoppe & Kenney, 1994; Kopteski, 1998a, 1998b; Johnston, 1993; Johnston & Campbell, 1988; Johnston et al., 2005a; Lampel, 1996; Rand, 1997a; Racusin & Copans, 1994; Siegel & Langford, 1998; Turkat, 1994, 1999; Warshak, 2001
Separation experienced as humiliating	A parent feels humiliated by the events and/or circumstances of the separation.	Kelly & Johnston, 2001
Alcohol or drug use	A parent uses drugs or alcohol after the separation.	Baker, 2006
Remarriage of favored parent	A parent becomes involved with a new partner after the separation, which leads to remarriage.	Warshak, 2000
Withdrawing of love from, or becoming angry with, the child if child displays affection toward other parent	A parent blames the child for having a continued relationship with the other parent.	Baker, 2006; Steinberger, 2006b; Waldron & Joanis, 1996
Limiting or interfering with contact between child and other parent	Arranging for activities during planned time; letting the child decide to have contact or not; seeking restraining or supervision orders; interfering with access to child-related health, education, or activity information	Baker, 2005b, 2006; Baker & Darnall, 2006; Johnston et al., 2005b; Kelly & Johnston, 2001; Kopetski, 1998a, 1998b; Vassiliou & Cartwright, 2001

Table 3.1 (Cont'd)

Factor	Description	Citations
Limiting contact of child with rejected parent's extended family	A parent blocks or interferes the child's time with the other parent or arranges activities during planned time with extended family of other parent	Baker, 2006
Forcing the child to choose between parents	Emotionally harmful tactics to manipulate, bully or verbally pressure child to be frightened of other parent; ignoring the other parent; isolating child from usual social interactions with rejected parent, friends; corrupting child by lying, manipulation, and aggression	Baker, 2006; Clawar & Rivlin, 1991; Rand, 1997a, 1997b
Abusive behaviors by favored parent	Knowingly or without reasonable basis makes false allegations of physical, sexual, or emotional abuse about the other parent; punishes child for speaking positively about the other parent; delusional statements or repeated gross distortions and exaggerations about the other parent	Baker, 2006
Role reversal	Boundary problems, psychological intrusiveness, parentification, adultification	Garber, 2010; Johnston et al., 2005a; Kelly & Johnston, 2004
Enmeshed relationship with child	Collusion, one-sided alliance, poor boundaries, infantilization	Baker & Darnall, 2006; Ellis, 2007; Everett, 2006; Garber, 2011; Steinberger, 2006a, 2006b; Waldron & Joanis, 1996;

(p. 257). Baker (2006) reported that adult children from her retrospective study talked about being exposed to relentless bad-mouthing of the rejected parent by the favored parent. Constantly bad-mouthing, attacking the rejected parent's character, and sharing with the child a distorted, essentially negative perception of the rejected parent have been found to be present in both empirical evidence and clinical observations (Baker, 2005a, 2006; Kelly & Johnston, 2001; Kopetski, 1998a; Steinberger, 2006a; Vassiliou & Cartwright, 2001; Waldron & Joanis, 1996). Steinberger (2006a) states that a favored parent may attempt to denigrate the other by issuing moral judgments on the rejected parent's values, lifestyle, choice of friends, career, or financial or relational successes or failures in life (p. 12). Clawar and Rivlin (1991) note that one of the critical consequences of denigrating the other parent to the child is that it teaches prejudice and perpetuates rigid ideas of all-or-nothing thinking about the child's relationships with significant others.

3.4.2 Personality Traits or Disorders of the Favored Parent

The favored parent's psychopathology and personality disorders have received by far the most attention in both the empirical evidence and clinical observations as significant factors that contribute to the presence of alienation (Feinberg & Greene, 1997; Friedman, 2004; Hoppe & Kenney, 1994; Johnston, 1993; Siegel & Langford, 1998). Psychological testing indicates that these parents tend to be rigidly defended and moralistic; they tend to perceive themselves to be flawless and virtuous, externalizing responsibility onto others and thereby lacking insight into themselves and the effect they have on others (Bagby, Nicholson, Buis, Radovanovic, & Fidler, 1999; Bathurst, Gottfried, & Gottfried, 1997; Siegel, 1996). Examining alienation using the Minnesota Multiphasic Personality Inventory (MMPI-2)[5], Siegel and Langford (1998) found that alienating parents participating in a custody evaluation were significantly more defensive on two validity indicators (e.g., scales F and K) than both the normative sample of noncustody litigants and a group of custody evaluation participants not identified as alienators. Other clinical observations and test results indicate that favored parents in comparison with rejected parents have more psychological disturbances, including histrionic, paranoid, and narcissistic personality disorders or characteristics, psychosis, and suicidal behavior (Baker, 2006; Clawar & Rivlin, 1991; Gardner, 1992b; Hoppe & Kenney, 1994; Johnston & Campbell, 1988; Johnston, Walters, & Olesen, 2005a; Kopetski, 1998a, 1998b; Lampel, 1996; Racusin & Copans, 1994; Rand, 1997a; Siegel & Langford, 1998; Turkat, 1994, 1999; Warshak, 2001).

Kopetski (1998) examined data obtained from the evaluation of 600 parents in custody disputes through a 20-year period and developed four unique characteristics of the alienating parent: 1) an orientation of paranoia and narcissism, often as the result of an underlying personality disorder; 2) an overreliance on a coping mechanism for psychological defenses; 3) engagement in an unhealthy grieving process regarding one's divorce; and 4) difficulties within the alienating parent's family of origin.

---

[5] MMPI-2 is a 567-item test to identify personality structures and disorders, including perception and preoccupation with their health and health issues, depressive symptoms level, emotionality, control issues, gender stereotypes, trust, anxiety, cognitive impairments, motivation, and sociability. It is one of the most widely used measures by mental health professionals in various fields of practice with adults with mental health problems (Butcher, Dahlstrom, Graham, Tellegen, & Kaemmer, 1989).

Rand (1997a, 1997b) also summarized a number of common personality factors, including: (a) an underlying narcissistic vulnerability, (b) attempts to conceal one's parental deficits by deflecting scrutiny of one's underlying personal problems via externalizing alienation strategies, (c) preexisting vulnerability to loss and conflict with regard to attachment and separation, and (d) a high intrapersonal need for control.

Johnston and her colleagues compared the Rorschach protocol ("ink blot" test) of parents, some of whom were alienating and participating in custody evaluations, with data from two current nonpatient samples (Johnston et al., 2005a). Clinical judgments of parenting behaviors, such as alienating coparenting, parent–child role reversal, lack of warm and involved parenting, and child abuse, were tested to see if these could be validated by the parents' responses on the Rorschach. Preliminary results suggest that the Rorschach test provides indications about a parent's capacity for empathy and ability to cope with stress and conflict, both of which are associated with warm and nurturing parenting (Johnston et al., 2005a). They found that custody litigants were significantly different from the nonpatient samples on numerous dependent variables, most notably their lack of resilience to separation and their experiences of loss.

In Baker's (2006) qualitative study of 38 adults who were alienated from a parent when they were children, 14 of the participants were characterized as having their alienation experiences resulting from a custodial mother's narcissistic personality and conduct during divorce, while 8 of the participants were described as having alienation resulting from narcissistic mother in a nondivorced family.

Everett (2006) states that many alienating parents display clear psychiatric symptoms and/or disorders, and these disorders render the parent vulnerable to stress, conflicts, and changes or threats in their emotional milieu. Everett also suggests that these parents depend on the marriage and/or family structure, or explicitly on their enmeshing role with their children, for support and help to contain their psychiatric symptoms. This is consistent with Garber's discussion of parentification, adultification, and infantilization, three forms of role corruption that commonly occur in the enmeshed favored parent–child dynamic in both alienation and justified rejection (Garber, 2011).

3.4.3 Separation Experienced as Humiliating by the Favored Parent

Kelly and Johnston (2001) note that a favored parent who encourages a child to reject that other parent may have experienced the separate as a deep narcissistic injury and a complete abandonment from the other parent, which results in profound humiliation and rage. Earlier childhood trauma may be triggered. They suggest that this rage of the narcissistically wounded spouse might result in vengeful behaviors, vindictiveness, cognitive distortions, and a complete blurring of boundaries between the parent and child.

3.4.4 Alcohol or Drug Abuse of the Favored Parent

It has been suggested that a factor contributing to the favored parent's alienating behavior is the use of alcohol or drugs. Based on Baker's (2006) qualitative study of 38 adults who had been alienated as children, half the alienating parents were alcoholic. Due to the small sample size, further research is needed before suggesting that this is a common factor of alienation.

3.4.5 Remarriage of Favored Parent

Warshak (2000) suggests that remarriage of the favored parent can trigger alienation, as the new couple attempts to unite around a common enemy and "make room" for the stepparent. The introduction of new partners can also precipitate the conflict between parents, even after a period of calm due to the perceived threat of the new partner's role with the child. As the conflict escalates, so, too, can the "making room" phenomena increase as the new couple reinforce their couple boundaries. More research is needed regarding the involvement of new partners to better understand their potential role and contributions to cases of alienation.

3.4.6 Withdrawing of Love, or Becoming Angry Toward the Child

Based on clinical observations, Waldron and Joanis (1996) note that alienation can become exacerbated by the favored parent rewarding any sign of negative interaction between the child and the rejected parent or by punishing the child, sometimes very directly, for not adhering to the campaign of denigration of the rejected parent.

In her retrospective study of adults who had been alienated as children, Baker (2006) cites adults who reported threats by the favored parent of withdrawing love if the child indicated affection for the rejected parent, thereby instilling fear in the child. Baker (2006) notes that this was one of the main strategies the favored parent used to heighten the child's dependency on the favored parent. In her study, Baker noted that the favored parent withdrew love and affection in at least 20% of sample of adults who had experienced alienation as a child.

Steinberger (2006a) notes that when the child begins to detect the anger of the favored parent after an expression of positive feelings about the other parent, the child seeks to avoid it and begins to understand that rejecting the other parent is the easiest way to do that, and this becomes complicit in the alienation taking place.

3.4.7 Limiting Contact Between Other Parent and Child

Interfering with the child's time with the rejected parent is a recurring factor found in the literature (Baker, 2005b, 2006; Johnston et al., 2005b; Vassiliou & Cartwright, 2001). Baker (2006) found that approximately two thirds of her sample of adults alienated as children reported some form of interference with parenting time and contact, including not following through on planned time (29%), the alienating parent arranging fun activities during planned time to entice the children away from the targeted parent (18%), and letting the child decide whether or not to visit (12%). This latter group is particularly important to consider; although presented by the alienating parent as "the child's right" to choose, the child may not be able to make independent decisions regarding contact with the other parent that are free from the denigration, hatred, or hostility expressed by the alienating parent.

Baker and Darnall (2006) found almost two thirds of their sample of adults alienated as children reported some form of interference with court-ordered or agreed-to parenting time and contact, and one third of the sample reported interference with their mail and phone contacts.

Based on clinical observations, Kopetski (1998a, 1998b) notes that alienation is characterized by a favored parent attempting to attenuate, control, or exclude contact with the rejected parent through behaviors such as the removal of the child from physical proximity to the other parent. Kopetski also reports alienating parents engaging in repeated litigation aimed at enforcing exclusion, indefinite supervision, or attenuation of the relationship.

Kelly and Johnston (2001) report that the favored parent may "seek restraining and supervised visitation orders, finding reasons to cancel visits when orders for contact exist to limit child's contact with alienated parent, out of misguided belief that rejected parent is dangerous" (p. 258). They further state that phone calls, messages, or letters are often not passed on to the child in these cases. In the most extreme alienation cases, they report that alienating parents effectively prohibit any reference to the other parent in their residence.

Baker (2006) found that many of the adults alienated as children reported that the favored parent interfered with access to information regarding the child, including not providing the alienated parent with information from the school, doctors, and social activities (19%).

3.4.8 Limiting Contact of Child With Rejected Parent's Extended Family

A child's continued positive relationship with extended family members post-separation is considered a protective factor against negative adjustment. In cases of alienation, the favored parent may limit the contact the child has with the rejected parent's extended family, which can interfere with the child's relationship with significant family members. Baker (2006), for example, notes that this strategy was identified by at least 20% of the sample of adults who had experienced parental alienation as a child.

3.4.9 Forcing the Child to Choose Between Parents

Alienating parents may use emotionally harmful tactics to manipulate a child into choosing them over the other parent (Rand, 1997a). Some of these tactics can include bullying or verbally pressuring the child into being frightened of the other parent; ignoring the other parent; isolating the child from normal social interactions with the rejected parent, and relatives and friends of that parent; and corrupting the child by lying, manipulation, and aggression toward others (Rand, 1997a). Likewise, Baker (2006) found that the adults who were alienated as children reported that they were made to feel guilty about the relationship with the other parent and were forced to choose or express loyalty.

Clawar and Rivlin (1991), in a published study of 700 separating and divorcing families followed over 12 years, identified eight stages of the alienation process that resulted in severe alienation. This process in and of itself lends credence to the fact that the bond is tenable and not healthy and that alienation can be maintained for long durations (see Table 3.2). Although

Table 3.2 Stages of the Alienation Process (Adapted from Clawar & Rivlin, 1991)

Stage	Description
1	A theme for the rationalization of the rejection of the alienated parent is chosen. This may include reasons of family unity, religion, or ethnicity: e.g., your father/mother never spent time with you, wanted you, respected your (our) spiritual beliefs.
2	A sense of support and connection to the alienating parent is fostered: e.g., s/he doesn't attend to child's emotional needs.
3	Feeling of sympathy for the alienating parenting is fostered: e.g., the other parent left me without money, was unfaithful, betrayed us.
4	The child shows support for the beliefs of the alienating parent such as expressing fear of visiting the other parent or refusing to talk to that parent on the phone.
5	The child's compliance is tested, and s/he is subtly rewarded for negative behavior toward the alienated parent that is considered desirable by the alienating parent: e.g., yelling, running away, hitting.
6	The child's loyalty is tested by the child's behavior and attitude, which demonstrate preference to the alienating parent: e.g., calls to come home during time with the other parent.
7	Ramping up the alienating occurs by looking for behaviors that reinforce the alienation: e.g., new or embellished allegations whereby the child rejects the alienated parent without hesitancy.
8	Maintenance alienation. Subtle ongoing reminders that maintain the alienated state: e.g., praying for the alienating parent.

these stages provide insight into the formation of alienation, the approach does not differentiate the severity of behaviors that could inform a differential approach.

3.4.10 Abusive Behaviors by the Favored Parent

In the Baker (2006) study, half of the adults alienated as children reported that the alienating parents were physically, emotionally, sexually, or verbally abusive toward the children. She notes that 16 of 40 (53%) of participants described their alienation experience as resulting from a relationship with a cold, rejecting, or abusive alienating parent.

3.4.11 Enmeshed Relationship With Child

Steinberger (2006a) suggests that collusion or a one-sided alliance by the child with the favored parent is a signal of the potential for alienation. Similarly, Everett (2006) views these enmeshing behaviors between the child and favored parent as a prealienation condition. The child's dependent and enmeshed relationship with the favored parent is considered a significant factor used to identify cases of alienation, especially when there is the creation of alliance with the child in the parental battle (Ellis, 2007; Waldron & Joanis, 1996). In Baker and Darnall's (2006) cross-sectional study of 97 rejected parents, they found that 29% of these respondents reported some form of enmeshment between the child and the favored parent.

Role reversal can occur in alienating cases when the favored parents use the children for their own emotional support or to meet their own needs, thereby sabotaging their children's relationship with the other parent (Kelly & Johnston, 2004). Likewise, Johnston et al. (2005a) examined the extent of boundary problems, role reversal, or psychological intrusiveness between each parent and child and found that parents involved in alienation had difficulty distinguishing their children's feelings from their own and often treated their children as confidantes to their adult interests and concerns.

3.5 Factors of the Rejected Parent

3.5.1 Counterrejection of the Alienated Child

There is less evidence regarding the factors that may be associated with being an alienated parent. Clinical observations have noted that in response to a child's resistance to contact, a rejected parent may exhibit counterrejecting behavior toward the alienated child. They may also seem withdrawn, especially in the presence of interparental conflict, and appear self-centered and

Table 3.3 Factors of the Rejected Parent

Factor	Description	Citations
Counterrejection of the alienated child	Reactive behavior such as venting, anger, withdrawal, harsh or rigid parenting	Gardner, 1998b; Kelly & Johnston, 2001; Turkat, 1994; Warshak, 2003a
Inadequate parenting skills	Withdrawal, permissiveness or punitive parenting, lack of interest, lack of empathy, attempts to induce guilt, use of force	Fidler & Bala, 2010; Kelly & Johnston, 2004; Tucker, 2006
Harsh and rigid parenting style	A parent uses an authoritarian parenting style as the dominant parenting strategy.	Kelly & Johnston, 2001
Passivity and withdrawal in the face of high conflict	A parent avoids contact with the other parent and refuses to engage with the other parent during exchanges.	Baker, 2006; Fidler & Bala, 2010; Gardner, 2002a; Kelly & Johnston, 2001; Kopetski, 1998a, 1998b; Vassiliou & Cartwright, 2001

immature, and may have critical and demanding traits (Gardner, 1992a; Turkat, 1994; Warshak, 2003a). In some alienation cases, the rejected parent may back off entirely from efforts to see the child, breaking off all contact. Kelly and Johnston (2001) note that when a rejected parent feels that he or she is being treated negatively by an alienated child who is refusing efforts to reconnect, the rejected parent can become highly affronted and offended by the lack of respect and ingratitude afforded him or her. In these situations, the counterrejection may be felt by the child, and exploited by the favored parent, "as confirmation of the rejected parent's lack of interest and love, which often leads to intensified condemnation of the 'bad' parent" (p. 259).

3.5.2 Inadequate Parenting Skills of the Rejected Parent

Tucker (2006) suggests that the rejected parent can have difficult and rigid parenting styles and may also lack empathy toward the child (also Gardner 1992a; Turkat, 1994; Warshak, 2003a). Few rejected parents are prepared to deal constructively with some of the extreme behaviors manifested by alienated children, including belligerence and aggressive behaviors (Fidler & Bala, 2010). Kelly and Johnston (2004) found in the study of 215 children of divorce referred from family courts and the general community that a lack of warmth, involvement, and competence in parenting by the rejected parent (whether mother or father) was strongly predictive of the child's rejection of that parent.

3.5.3 Harsh and Rigid Parenting Style

Kelly and Johnston (2001) note that rejected parents can also exhibit harsh and rigid parenting styles. Although they do not rise to the level of emotional or physical abuse, these rigid parenting styles resonate and conjoin with alienated children's prior experiences, leading alienated children to reject the parents. Likewise, Kelly and Johnston (2001) note that critical and demanding behaviors by the rejected parent can further contribute to the child's alienation in the context of other operative factors.

3.5.4 Passivity and Withdrawal in the Face of High Conflict

Kelly and Johnston (2001) note that some rejected parents, made anxious or immobilized by interpersonal and legal conflict, withdraw from the battle over contact with their children for some considerable period. Likewise, Fidler and Bala (2010) suggest that the rejected parents often react with passivity and withdrawal in an effort to cope with the parental conflict that may predate separation. Often at the advice of friends, family, and legal and mental health professionals, they decided to give the children "space" to have their feelings come around. These reactions, which in fact are consistent with what the children are asking for, may be exploited by the alienating parent, thereby reinforcing the allegations made against the rejected parents, including abandonment, disinterest, and poor parenting (Baker, 2006; Gardner, 2002a; Kelly & Johnston, 2001; Kopetski, 1998a, 1998b; Vassiliou & Cartwright, 2001). Kelly and Johnston (2001) state that alienated children, having been bombarded with messages that the other parent does not love them, see withdrawal as a lack of interest and abandonment. The decision to give the child space, something that initially was positive and child focused, is distorted into being a negative response on the part of the rejected parent. Further, giving the child space is often inconsistent to the extent that the rejected parent vacillates between backing off and coming on stronger to resolve the situation and see the child, a pattern that serves to confirm the allegations made by the favored parent and child (Fidler & Bala, 2010).

3.6 Factors of the Child

Kelly and Johnston (2001) suggested that a child's response of alienation may be influenced by a number of factors: the personality of the favored parent; the favored parent's negativity about the rejected parent that reinforces the child's aligned response; and the child's age, cognitive capacity, temperament, and vulnerability, including having special needs (see also Racusin & Copans, 1994). Additional factors include: a more conflicted divorce and intense litigation; marital history, especially when there are intense emotions around the separation (such as shame or humiliation); multiple professionals or extended

Table 3.4 Factors of the Child

Factor	Description	Citations
Child triangulated (emotionally caught between two hostile parents)	Brought into the middle of the parents' relationship	Baker & Darnall, 2006; Cyr, interview, 2010; Kelly & Johnston, 2001; Steinberger, 2006a; Stoltz & Ney, 2002; Waldron & Joanis, 1996
Age of the child	Onset of pre- or early adolescence (9–15 years)	Everett, 2006; Johnston et al., 2005b; Kelly & Johnston, 2001; Waldron & Joanis, 1996
Temperament, resiliency, and personality vulnerabilities	The child's capacity for dealing with changes and routine adjustments	Drozd, interview, 2010; Kelly & Johnston, 2001; Steinberger, 2006b
Behavioral or emotional problems of clinically serious proportions	Acting out, depression, anxiety, phobias, underachievement	Johnston et al., 2005c; Kopetski, 1998a, 1998b; Lampel, 1996; Lowenstein, 1998, 2006
Extreme oppositional behaviors	Expressions of anger, hostility, rudeness, swearing, physical aggression, destroying properly, lying, spying	Johnston et al., 2005c
Anxiety and phobias	Panic reactions, hypochondriacal symptoms, psychosomatic complaints	Lowenstein, 1998, 2006
Lack of ambivalence	All-or-nothing thinking, idealization of favored parent/ devaluation of rejected parent, cognitive distortions, poor reality testing	Baker, 2006; Johnston et al., 2005c; Kelly & Johnston, 2001; Kopetski, 1998a, 1998b
Child's behavior is incongruent from one situation to another	Inconsistencies, contradictions, thoughts and feelings do not match actual behavior	Lowenstein, 1998, 2005; Steinberger, 2006; Waldron & Joanis, 1996
Use of borrowed scenarios when describing rejected parent	Use of same words, adult-like language and phrases, sounds rehearsed, wooden, brittle	Gardner, 1992a; Kelly & Johnston, 2001; Waldron & Joanis, 1996; Weir, 2011
Child's opportunity for external supports	E.g., therapists, extended family members, trusted adults, increased dependency on favored parent	Kelly & Johnston, 2001

family and friends who align themselves in the conflict; and an older sibling who is refusing contact with a parent, as this can contribute to a younger sibling becoming afraid or resistant.

Kelly and Johnston (2001) note that prior to separation, some parents use their children in the expression of the marital conflict by inviting the children to take sides in intense conflicts, by supporting them in the conflict or being a messenger of the conflict, and by encouraging children to be punitive toward the other parent. In prolonged adversarial divorce proceedings, these hostile dynamics involving children can continue and escalate, placing the child at greater risk for becoming alienated. Waldron and Joanis (1996) note that when children are put in the middle of the adult conflict in cases of divorce, children can become involved in the "spy game" of reporting back to the parents and by becoming the principal communicator between the parents. Dynamics where a parent pressures the child to take sides in the battle between the parents, by discussing issues with the child that should only be discussed with the other parent or professionals, can develop into alienation (Baker & Darnall, 2006; Steinberger, 2006a; Stoltz & Ney, 2002). Psychologist Francine Cyr observes that the child's triangulation is one of the most important factors to consider when assessing for alienation:

> The research shows.... one solution that children develop is to take sides and then they become aligned totally to one parent and they reject the other and no ambivalence toward the other parent. That is one factor that I want to stress, that the splitting and the total lack of ambivalence and total lack of recognition of the good aspects...good and bad aspects of both parents is a distorted view of one's parents and is often associated with high degree of alienation...[6]

3.6.1 Age of the Child

Waldron and Joanis (1996) suggest that the children most vulnerable or at risk to become alienated, due to several converging developmental issues, are in the 8 to 15 year old range. Kelly and Johnston (2001) also note that most children whose alienation is consolidated are older than 7 or 8 years of age because the children need to have sufficient cognitive maturation and capacity to make moral valuations. They suggest that the most common ages of the alienated child are between 9 and 15 years old. Johnston et al. (2005b) suggest that strident rejection of parent tends to develop when children are older, into late latency and early adolescence. While the younger child tends to have a

---

[6] Interview, May 17, 2010, Francine Cyr, Professor of Psychology at the Université de Montréal.

shifting allegiance and form of splitting off, in an effort to cope with the contradictory information, the older child, who now has the cognitive maturity to keep all views in his or her mind simultaneously, denies all positive feelings and attitudes about the rejected parent. This results in a process of the demonization of the rejected parent and an idealization of the alienating parent. Everett (2006) states though that the younger a child is, the easier it is to accomplish the induction process.

3.6.2 Temperament, Personality, and Developmental Vulnerabilities

Kelly and Johnston (2001) note that a child's vulnerability to alienation increases with greater psychological adjustment problems in the child. Anxious, fearful, and passive children lack the resiliency to withstand the intense pressures of the custody battle and the favored parent's alienating behaviors. Children with special needs and developmental challenges have been identified as being more vulnerable to parental influence and alienation (Johnston et al., 2005c; Racusin & Copans, 1994).

Steinberger (2006a) suggests that children with anxious, fearful, or passive character traits, or low self-esteem, lack the resiliency to withstand the intense pressures of the custody battle and the favored parent's alienating behaviors. It might be psychologically easier for them to choose a side to avoid crippling anxiety. In contrast, children who are insightful, clear thinking, and morally developed can often maintain greater balance through the high-conflict divorce.

Children's resiliency is also an important factor to consider because two children experiencing the same alienating behaviors by a parent may react very differently. As Leslie Drozd notes:

> Some children are resilient and some are not. Temperament, disposition, as well as age and stage of development are resiliency factors that can make a difference. On the other side of the coin are the child's vulnerabilities. Some children are more vulnerable than others. Some take in and internalize everything a parent says. Other children write off what their parent says and might think, 'Oh, that's just mom' or 'that's just dad. He (or she) is just kind of angry and really doesn't mean what he (or she) says.' These children do not find the need to pair up with that parent. They do not eat, sleep, walk, think, and feel the same way as that parent and are, thus, able to gain some distance. These children are the resilient ones whereas the more vulnerable ones may take in and believe everything bad that one parent says about the other. Sadly they often see themselves as bad, too.[7]

---

[7] Interview June 23, 2010, Leslie Drozd, psychologist.

3.6.3 Behavioral and Emotional Problems of Clinically Serious Proportions

Based on a study of 20 sets of parents and children in custody litigation, Lampel (1996) found that aligned children were angrier than nonaligned children. Likewise, Johnston et al. (2005c) found that the favored parent often reported that their alienated children had more behavioral and emotional problems of clinically serious proportions, including depression, withdrawal, somatic complaints, and aggression than those children who were able to maintain relationships with both parents. According to parent ratings, children who were alienated were significantly more disturbed within the whole group of children of high-conflict custody. Kopetski (1998a, 1998b) noted that alienated children are more likely to become defiant and rigid, and refuse to attend school. Based on his clinical experience, Lowenstein (1998, 2006) suggests that alienated children are also likely to develop eating disorders and sleep disturbances.

3.6.4 Extreme Oppositional Behaviors

Johnston et al. (2005c) note that severely alienated children may appear emotionally constricted, but they are also likely to behave very inappropriately at times and manifest conduct disorders, at least in the presence of the rejected parent. They note that "expressions of hatred, rage, contempt, and hostility can be acted out in rudeness, swearing and cursing, hanging up the phone, spitting at or striking a parent, sabotaging or destroying property, stealing, lying, and spying on the rejected parent" (p. 42).

3.6.5 Phobias and Anxiety

Lowenstein (1998, 2006) suggests that in severe cases of alienation, the favored parent can create a seriously unhappy situation for the child who will often develop panic reactions when he/she is asked to spend time with the rejected parent. He further notes that children may fear being abandoned or rejected when they have been induced to feel that one of the partners in a relationship is less than desirable. Anxiety factors about the custodial parent may induce a school phobia, which is fear of attending school, due to the fear of leaving the favored parent. Some children suffer from hypochondriacal disorders and tend to develop psychosomatic symptoms and physical illnesses. Such children fear for the future and the safety of the custodial parent.

3.6.6 Lack of Ambivalence

The alienated child's lack of ambivalence about the rejected parent is an indicator of alienation. It can be reflected in all-or-nothing thinking to reduce ambiguity and can contribute to poor reality testing and rigid thinking. Kelly and Johnston (2001) note that the alienated child often idealizes or speaks glowingly of the favored parent as both an adult and parent, while entirely devaluing the rejected parent. (This characteristic of all-or-nothing thinking is frequently observed in the favored parent as well.) These children often refuse to consider any information that might undermine this viewpoint of their "perfect companion and parent" (p. 263). Waldron and Joanis (1996) note that for these children, everything seems to have life-and-death importance.

Based on her qualitative study of adults alienated from a parent as children, Baker suggests that there are comparisons between favored parents and cult leaders. Baker (2006) states that adults in her study reported feeling all good feelings about the favored parent and all bad feelings about rejected parent. She notes that more than one participant made a comment such as: "I remember thinking he [the rejected parent] should go ahead and die. I wish he'd just go get in a car accident. I wish he'd die. I didn't want him to come home." Baker (2006) notes that the utter lack of ambivalence is a hallmark of parental alienation, while children involved in child protection cases usually have ambivalent feelings about genuinely abusive or neglectful parents.

Johnston et al. (2005c) comment on their clinical observations of children with poor reality testing, at least with respect to their views of either "idealized" or "demonized" parents. For these children, their interpersonal perceptions tend to be distorted or inaccurate and their reasoning capacities appear disordered. They state that "compared to most children of divorce, they appear relatively free of painful loyalty conflicts as if they lack the capacity for ambivalence" (p. 41).

Kopetski (1998a) reports that children's poor reality testing can be considered a symptom of alienation, whereas the child mirrors the distorted perceptions of the favored parent, and this becomes fixed and rigid in the child's opinions and ideas.

3.6.7 Child's Behavior Is Incongruent From One Situation to Another

Steinberger (2006a) states that another factor or indicator of alienation is a child who shows affection to the rejected parent when the favored parent is absent but acts differently or defiantly to the rejected parent when in the presence of the favored parent. This disconnect is frequently observed by children's lawyers and mental health professionals working with these families. Waldron and Joanis (1996) note that in these cases, the child will often display a split identity, or vertical splitting, where the child will appear to be rejecting a parent in the presence of the favored parent, but when with the rejected parent, the child will display affection, attachment, interest, fun, and freedom from the oppressive alignment with the alienating parent. Despite their protests to the contrary, Weir (2011) found more than a 50/50 chance that the child appeared to enjoy the experience of contact once it was insisted that a visit take place as part of the assessment process. Lowenstein (1998, 2006) suggests that children in these situations practice deception in order to placate the favored parent, while at the same time seek to form some kind of warm relationship with the rejected parent. This splitting off of one part of the self, referred to a "false self" or "inauthenticity," poses a risk to the child's psychological health. Waldron and Joanis (1996) note that the children's own statements are often contradictory, or they contradict factual history or the perceptions of unbiased individuals.

3.6.8 Use of Borrowed Scenarios When Describing the Rejected Parent

Kelly and Johnston (2001) note that alienated children tend to speak about the rejected parent by using replicas or slight variants of the favored parents' allegations and stories, thus creating legends. Generally, alienated children sound rehearsed, wooden, brittle, and frequently use adult words or phrases. Waldron and Joanis (1996) state that alienated children often parrot themes of the favored parent, even using the same words while borrowing the alienating parent's scenarios to describe the other parent.

3.6.9 Lack of External Support for the Child

Another factor and indicator of alienation is the lack of external support for the child. Kelly and Johnston (2001) note that when children have few external resources—such as therapists, extended family members, or other trusted adults—their vulnerability increases, particularly if they are emotionally isolated with the favored parent.

3.7 Summary of Factors and Indicators

Many factors and indicators of alienation have been proposed in the conceptual literature, though more sound empirical research is needed to clearly identify and differentiate each of these. Better research will provide mental health and legal professionals with valid and reliable criteria to assess both the risk and occurrence of alienation after separation or divorce. Based on the available evidence to date, one factor that is significantly associated with alienation is the favored parents' symptoms of psychopathology and personality disorders. An important indicator of alienation is the child's refusal to visit a parent with whom the child previously had a positive relationship.

Children who experience alienation are likely to suffer a range of short- and long-term negative effects, including behavioral problems. Less is known about the characteristics or circumstances of the rejected parent that may contribute to the risk and perpetuation of the alienation, which is an important area for future research. Future research should include random samples with sufficient sample sizes using comparison groups of nonalienated children to reduce error and bias in the empirical evidence and to strengthen the scientific knowledge in this area.

4

Assessment and Measurement Tools
for Alienation

To advance the scientific knowledge base of alienation and deal more effectively with alienation cases, there must be reliable and valid methods for assessing and measuring the presence of alienation, which could include standardized measures, structured interviews, rating scales, or some other scientifically based protocol that has been tested for its psychometric properties (Turkat, 2002). Standardized tools should be developed for four separate purposes:

1) to screen for potential alienation cases from the general population of separating parents;
2) to identify the presence of alienation in cases where allegations of alienation have been made, and help determine whether problems with resistance to contact may be due to the conduct of the rejected parent or other factors;
3) to assess the risk of continued alienating behaviors once alienation has been substantiated; and
4) to assess for the potential risk of alienation before a child resumes contact with a parent from whom he or she has been separated because of previous alienating behaviors by that parent.

Currently, there is a lack of reliable or valid assessment protocols and measures for alienation. As discussed in this chapter, there are some measures of alienation in current use that have some utility, but none have been demonstrated in research studies to have reliability or validity (Baker, 2006; Turkat, 2002), and little distinction is made in current measures between screening (assessing potential for alienation before it occurs) and assessing for the risk of recurrence of alienation (where there has already been a finding of alienation).

The development of reliable and valid measures involves several years of work to test and refine the measures, and it requires the accumulation of several empirical studies to investigate the empirical relevancy and accuracy. Such measures have to accurately and consistently distinguish the presence or absence of alienation, and discriminate alienation from other phenomena, such as justified rejection, high conflict, violence, and child maltreatment (Turkat, 2002).

The challenge of developing a valid measure to distinguish alienation from other situations of resistance to contact with a parent is compounded by the different theoretical efforts in the field to define, describe, or refor-mulate alienating behaviors (Darnall, 1998; Kelly & Johnston, 2001; Rand, 1997a, 1997b; Waldron & Joanis, 1996; Walsh & Bone, 1997; Warshak, 2001). There remains little consensus on the precise definition and terminology of alienation, and until the scientific community and mental health and legal professionals reach some basic consensus regarding the operationalization of alienation, it is likely that no one assessment tool or measure will satisfy the requirements of both face validity and content validity. Joan Kelly suggested that there is a real need to build consensual measures to assess for alienation, but the development of these measures "would have to be done on the task force consensual basis in order to be accepted by a broad range of people."[1]

4.1 Clinical Judgment

When allegations of alienation are made, the accurate and timely identifica-tion of alienation is essential for early intervention, case management, and planning for effective treatment options. Incorrect assessment and decisions can lead to a number of detrimental outcomes, including leaving children in potentially dangerous or emotionally damaging environments, or subjecting children and parents to overly intrusive interventions. Most of the experts whom we interviewed reported that they were either unaware of measures to classify alienation, or they did not use any of the existing measures in their clinical or legal practice. Many indicated that they relied upon their profes-sional experience, intuition, and individual heuristics to determine the pres-ence of alienation. Toronto lawyer Philip Epstein, for example, stated: "It's like obscenity, you know it when you see it."[2] Psychologist Francine Cyr noted:

> A lot of [professionals] rely on what Gardner had said, but we know that has not been proven or demonstrated or validated. So it's more the clinical intuition and clinical experience of people and their

---

[1] Interview April 21, 2010, Joan Kelly, psychologist.
[2] Interview August 15, 2010.

guts and their goals that make them diagnose or not the presence of alienation. So, the diagnostic of alienation is not as rigorous as it should be and I think there is a need to develop more standardized measures to detect the presence, the degree of this condition.[3]

Richard Warshak pointed out that there are some research tools being used, but that the clinical judgment of custody evaluators remains the most common method for assessing for alienation:

[Custody evaluations] involve clinical interviews, taking a careful history, perhaps psychological testing, observations of parents and children, speaking with other people who have some other information that may assist the assessor—usually they're called collateral contacts. So I think the way to assess alienation is to use multiple methods to gain information about the family.[4]

There were a number of experts interviewed who described their processes for assessing parent–child contact problems within custody evaluations. For example, Robyn Fasser, a clinical psychologist from South Africa, described her approach of being attuned to the language family members used during interviews:

I like to see the parents first because I like to hear the language that the parents use. So that is the first stop. In any custody evaluation, whether it is to investigate alienation or not, I like to see the parents first. I like to see if the children use the same language as the parents and whether, for examples, it is age-appropriate language or not. That would be one of the ways that I identify, whether there are elements of interference or the influence of adult concepts in a child's view of the world. Interestingly you can also hear from children and the language they use in telling their story, when you're in tune with them how they see the world, and with which parent they are psychologically comfortable. Their use of language, the ease and natural spontaneity with which they describe their experiences is an indication of where they feel they are psychologically heard. That is a primary cue for me.[5]

Linda Neilson described the importance of considering parenting behaviors to assess for the root cause of parent–child contact problems:

I think one needs to look at parenting behaviors over time and of both parents in a lot of detail. I see manipulating a child against one parent as an element of that but not as a bigger element than all the other things. I mean you've got to look at the parenting practices of

---

[3] Interview May 27, 2010, Francine Cyr.
[4] Interview April 15, 2010, psychologist.
[5] Interview, June 2, 2010.

both parents, the degree to which they put the child's interest first, the degree to which each parent has been involved with the child, the degree to which each parent is supporting the child, the degree of benefit and positive influence each parent offers to the child.[6]

Billy Eddy pointed out that the clinical assessment of parent–child contact problems should include a focus on whether there has been an escalation of the child's refusal to contact the parent:

> A child says "I don't want to see my parent," and there is a degree of "I would really rather not go this weekend," or "I'm angry at my other parent so I don't want to spend time with them today" to "I don't want to go" repeatedly to "I don't want to go at all" to "I hate the other parent," and it's an absolute. So I see that whole range. Often what I've seen is that it grows through all of that, as the child absorbs the escalating conflict and parents misunderstand and reinforce their resistance. So it starts out with, "I'd rather not" to "I'm really angry and I refuse and I'm not going to even communicate."[7]

Although professional experience is important, clinical judgments about the presence of alienation can be compromised by varying individual and contextual factors and biases, which can make the assessment of alienation too complicated and unreliable to evaluate objectively.

Misclassification and inaccurate identification of alienation can have serious repercussions for children and families, which can lead to either exposure of a child to potential harm and possibly unwarranted separation between a child and a parent erroneously believed to have been alienating the child, or a continuation of exposure to alienating parent behavior that results in a child losing a relationship with the other parent and extended family members.

4.2 Decision Trees and Assessment Protocols

Decision trees and assessment protocols have been developed by researchers applying theories and current evidence of alienation. Several authors have published decision trees and assessment criteria for considering the presence of alienation (Bricklin & Elliot, 2006; Drozd & Olesen, 2004; Ellis, 2007; Fidler, Bala, Birnbaum, & Kavassalis, 2008; Garber, 2007; Stahl, 1999).[8] Within each

---

[6] Interview June 21, 2010, law and social work academic.
[7] Interview April 29, 2010, lawyer and social worker.
[8] See also the following that provide more general and useful custody and access assessment protocols (Ackerman, 2006; Birnbaum, Fidler, & Kavassalis, 2008—see Chapters 2 and 3 and the accompanying appendices; Gould, 2006; Gould & Martindale, 2007; Leonoff & Montague, 1996; Lee, Calloway, Nachilis, & Marvin, 2010; Ludolph & Bow, 2010; Marvin, interview April 20, 2010; Schutz, Dixon, Lindenberger, & Rutter, 1989; Stahl, 1994).

"decision tree," questions are put forward to consider the presence of alienation. For some of these, the suggested presence of alienation is determined by a minimum number of affirmative answers to the questions posed within the instruments.

A major focus of these decisions trees is to assess the presence of alienation by considering whether the child's behavior toward the rejected parent has justification, or whether the child has a false sense and a disproportionate dislike for the rejected parent. These decision trees and assessment protocols consider the behaviors of the favored parent (including his or her contribution to the child's feelings and behaviors toward the other parent), the child, and the rejected parent. Some of the questions used in these decision trees consider whether the favored parent supports the child's relationship with the other parent and whether attempts are made to encourage the child's relationship with the rejected parent.

Table 4.1 lists questions that Fidler et al. (2008) recommend that a custody evaluator consider when dealing with allegations of alienation.[9]

Table 4.2 lists typical behaviors exhibited by the child, the favored parent, and the rejected parent, as proposed by Fidler et al. (2008).[10] Determining the presence of these behaviors is an important assessment function, when intervening in cases of alleged alienation.

Ellis (2007) proposes three key questions to consider when deciding whether allegations of maltreatment are highly exaggerated, false, and consistent with alienating behaviors or are consistent with the actual occurrence of maltreatment:

1) Is there a readily identifiable reason for the strained contact (e.g., violence, maltreatment, poor parenting)?
2) Do the allegations of abuse appear to be false or highly exaggerated?
3) Does the child proclaim a total absence of love, affection, or positive feelings for the rejected parent?

Ellis suggests that answering "no" to the first question and "yes" to the second and third indicate that there is more likely the presence of an alienated child.

---

[9] Adapted from Fidler, B., Bala, N., Birnbaum, R., & Kavassalis, K. (2008). Chapter 7: Child custody assessments, recommendations, and judicial remedies regarding alienated children. In *Challenging Issues in Child Custody Disputes: A Guide for Legal and Mental Health Professionals*. Toronto, Canada: Carswell Thomson.

[10] Adapted from Fidler, B., Bala, N., Birnbaum, R., & Kavassalis, K. (2008). Chapter 7: Child custody assessments, recommendations, and judicial remedies regarding alienated children. In *Challenging Issues in Child Custody Disputes: A Guide for Legal and Mental Health Professionals*. Toronto, Canada: Carswell Thomson.

Table 4.1 Assessing Allegations of Alienation (Fidler et al., 2008)

Questions to consider using all sources of information (e.g., from each parent, the child, parent–child observations, collateral sources, court documentation) when assessing allegations of alienation:

1) Has either parent, through covert pressure and innuendo, or more overt indoctrination, influenced the child's preferences?
2) Is there a role reversal, with the child attempting to provide emotional support or care of the parent whom the child perceives is lonely, unstable, without supports, unhappy, or angry about the separation?
3) Is the child's need for empathy conditional on sharing the distorted perceptions of a humiliated parent?
4) To cope (for self-protection), does the child placate the angry parent by negatively distorting reports of how much s/he enjoyed the time with the other parent?
5) Is the child concerned about losing one parent the way the other parent was seemingly lost?
6) Is the child's reluctance to leave one parent and go to the other a developmentally expected age- or gender-related affinity to the preferred parent, or a preference due to familiarity and shared interests?
7) How consistent are the child's stated views or preferences of resistance or rejection with the child's actual behavior during observations with the rejected parent, or as reported by the rejected parent?
8) Are the child's fears and anxieties understandable reactions to the nonpreferred parent's inept, rigid, and/or insensitive parenting?
9) Are there divorce-specific reasons for the child's rejection of the parent, such as anger and hurt for initiating separation or a premature introduction to a new partner or stepsiblings?
10) Has the favored parent exploited the child's hurt and angry feelings about the separation, thereby cementing the child's alignment against the other parent? If so, how and to what extent?
11) How long has the rejection been occurring?
12) How amenable does the favored parent seem to be to intervention or discussion by the custody evaluator?
13) Is the child's alliance related to the preferred parent's having few, if any, behavioral expectations or offering more material rewards?
14) Is the child's resistance or refusal a justified reaction and trauma-coping mechanism in reaction to being abused by that parent, or having witnessed that parent's violence and abuse with the preferred parent?

Questions to assess the child's experience of parenting and his or her manner of reasoning:

1) What was the child's experience of parenting before and after the separation?
2) To what extent was each parent involved in the child's care?
3) Was one parent more of a disciplinarian?
4) What was the nature of the child's emotional relationship with each parent before and after the separation?
5) Did either parent's behavior toward the child change significantly after the separation?
6) Does the rejected parent have positive relationships with any of the children?
7) Is the child's reaction long-standing or recent?

Table 4.1 (Cont'd)

8) Does the child reject the parent consistently or only occasionally?
9) Does the child express some ambivalence, or are his or her feelings and attitudes fixed and unambivalent?
10) What is the sequence and context surrounding the rejection?
11) Can the child recognize positive qualities in the rejected parent and negative ones in the favored parent?
12) Does the child reject obvious facts: for example, his or her evident enjoyment as captured in a video or photograph?

Questions of inquiry relating to the favored parent include:

1) Is the favored parent concerned about the difficulties that the child is having in the relationship with the other parent, and if so, does the parent's concern translate into more than just listening and validating?
2) Does the parent do more than pay lip service to the child's need for a relationship with the other parent?
3) If so, what does the favored parent suggest happen to resolve the parent–child relationship problem?
4) Does the favored parent propose giving the child indefinite time to change attitudes toward the rejected parent, suggesting that the problem will improve in time without doing anything?
5) Would the parent be as passive if the child were repeatedly upset about other concerns, such as a problem with a teacher, grandparent, other relative, or a same-age friend?
6) Does the favored parent share with the child the notion that the other parent abandoned them both (e.g., did not want to continue to work on the marriage) and in so doing reinforce the child's hate and rejection?
7) Does the favored parent claim that s/he had a similar experience with the rejected parent and know how the child feels, and assert that the child is justified and should not be forced to see the other parent?
8) Does the parent exploit the child's feelings in the service of lending validation to his or her own feelings about the other parent?

Questions relating to how each parent responded or did not respond to incidents where the child witnessed conflict between the parents:

1) In the case of an isolated incident, did the favored parent attempt to protect the child from exposure to the incident?
2) How does the favored parent comfort the child after the incidents?
3) Did the favored parent attempt to protect the child from his or her own emotional reaction, or did that parent emphasize the perceived trauma to the child in order to gain support, and in effect be parented by the child?
4) Did the favored parent help the child not only to identify and express his or her feelings, but also to cope with them by resolving and repairing the relationship with the other parent?
5) Does the rejected parent acknowledge the transgression, apologize, and proceed to learn from his or her mistakes, or does the parent remain defensive, externalize responsibility, and repeat the same mistakes?

Table 4.2 Alienation: Typical Behaviors Exhibited by Child, Favored Parent, and Rejected Parent (Fidler et al., 2008)

Typical Behaviors Exhibited by Alienated Child:
- Opinion of parents is one sided, all good or all bad; idealizes one parent and devalues the other
- Vicious vilification of rejected parent; campaign of hatred
- Trivial, false, and irrational reasons to justify hatred
- Reactions and perceptions unjustified or disproportionate to parent's behaviors
- Talks openly and without prompting about rejected parent's perceived shortcomings
- Extends hatred to extended family and pets of rejected parent (hatred by association)
- No guilt or ambivalence regarding malicious treatment, hatred, etc.
- A stronger, but not necessarily healthy, psychological bond with alienating parent than with rejected parent
- Anger at rejected parent for perceived abandonment; blames that parent for divorce
- Speech about rejected parent is brittle, a litany; obsessed; has an artificial quality; affect does not match words; no conviction; uses adult language; has a rehearsed quality
- Stories are repetitive and lacking in detail and depth
- Mimics what siblings report rather than own experience
- Denial of hope for reconciliation; no acknowledgment of desire for reconciliation
- Expresses worry for preferred parent, desire to care for that parent; or, defensive denial that child is indeed worried about parent

Typical Behaviors Exhibited by Favored (Alienating) Parent:
- Insists that the child has the right to make decisions about contact
- Rarely talks about the other parent; uninterested in child's time with other parent after contact; gives a cold shoulder or silent treatment, or is moody after child's returns unless child expresses dissatisfaction about the contact
- No photos of rejected parent in the home; removes reminders of the other parent
- Refusal to hear positive comments about rejected parent; quick to discount child's good times as trivial and unimportant
- No encouragement of calls by child to other parent between contacts; rationalizes that child does not ask
- Tells child fun things that were missed during the child's time with other parent
- Indulges child with material possessions and privileges
- Sets few limits or is rigid about routines, rules, and expectations
- Refuses to speak directly to parent; refuses to be in same room or close proximity; does not let rejected parent come to door to pick up child
- No concern for missed time with other parent
- Makes statements and then denies what was said
- Body language and nonverbal communication reveal lack of interest, disdain, and disapproval
- Engages in inquisition of child after time spent with the other parent
- Rejected parent is discouraged or refused permission to attend school events and activities
- Telephone messages, gifts, and mail from other parent to child are destroyed, ignored, or passed on to the child with disdain
- Distorts any comments of child that might justify the accusations about abusive parenting or negative behavior
- Doesn't believe that child has any need for relationship with other parent

Table 4.2 (Cont'd)

- When child calls during contact with other parent and is quiet or noncommunicative, parent wrongly assumes pressure from rejected parent, or that child is not comfortable with rejected parent; evidence of bad parenting as favored parent does not appreciate that child is uncomfortable talking to alienating parent in presence of rejected parent
- Portrays other parent as dangerous; may inconsistently act fearful of other parent in front of child
- Exaggerates negative attributes of other parent and omits anything positive
- Delusional false statements repeated to child; distorts history and other parent's participation in the child's life; claims other parent has totally changed since separation
- Projection of own thoughts, feelings, and behaviors onto the other parent
- Does not correct child's rude, defiant, and/or omnipotent behavior directed toward the other parent but would never permit child to do this with others
- Convinced of harm, when there is no evidence
- False or fabricated allegations of sexual, physical, and/or emotional abuse
- Denigrates and exaggerates flaws of rejected parent to child
- Says other parent left "us," divorced "us," and doesn't love "us"
- Over-involves child in adult matters and litigation
- Child required to keep secrets and spy or report back on other parent
- Child required to be messenger
- Overt and covert threats to withdraw love and affection from child unless other parent is rejected
- Extreme lack of courtesy to rejected parent
- Relocation for minor reasons and with little concern for effects on child

Typical Behaviors Exhibited by Rejected (Alienated) Parent:
- Harsh, rigid, and punitive parenting style
- Outrage at child's challenge to his/her authority
- Passivity or withdrawal in face of conflict
- Immature, self-centered in relation to child
- Loses temper; angry, demanding, intimidating character traits, but not to level of abuse
- Counterrejecting behavior
- Lacks empathic connection to child
- Inept and unempathetic pursuit of child, pushes calls and letters, unannounced or embarrassing appearances at school or activities
- Challenges child's beliefs or attitudes and tries to convince him or her otherwise
- Dismissive of child's feelings and negative attitudes
- Attempts to induce guilt
- May use force to reassert parental position
- Vents rage, blames alienating parent for brainwashing child, and takes no responsibility

Note. Reprinted by permission of Carswell, a division of Thomson Reuters Canada Limited.

Table 4.3 outlines Ellis' (2007) proposed questions for determining whether alienation is occurring by establishing that at least 10 of the following 15 child behavior indicators are present (p. 18).

American psychologist Benjamin Garber (2007) proposed a hierarchical "decision tree" for deciding whether alienation is present or not. The presence

Table 4.3 Ellis' (2007) Criteria for Determining Presence of Alienation

1) The child maintains a delusion of being persecuted by a parent who is viewed by the child in exceptionally negative terms.
2) The child uses the mechanism of seeing one parent as all good and the other as all bad (splitting) to reduce ambiguity.
3) The child's behavior toward the targeted parent is incongruent from one situation to another.
4) The child denies any positive feelings for the targeted parent.
5) The attribution of negative qualities to the targeted parent may take on a quality of distortion or bizarreness that borders on loss of touch with reality.
6) As evidence of the targeted parent's bad behavior, the child includes recollections of events that occurred out of the child's presence so that the child could not have witnessed them, or before the child would have been old enough to remember them, or that are highly implausible.
7) When it is pointed out to the child that the story is not internally logical, the child alters the story or the explanations in an attempt to make them consistent.
8) The child's hatred and sense of persecution by the targeted parent have the quality of a litany.
9) The child, when faced with contact with the targeted parent, displays a reaction of extreme anxiety, including panic attacks, stomach aches, vomiting, hysterical crying, falling to the floor, clinging, hyperventilating, clutching transitional objects, and wailing.
10) The child has a dependent and enmeshed relationship with the alienating parent.
11) The child is highly compliant, cooperative, and adaptable with all adults other than the targeted parent.
12) The child views the alienating parent as a victim—as having been persecuted by the targeted parent and having suffered greatly as a result of that parent's actions.
13) The child maintains a complete lack of concern about or compassion for the targeted parent but instead holds an attitude of exploitation toward the targeted parent.
14) The child minimizes the significance of the targeted parent in the child's life.
15) The child insists on calling the targeted parent by his first name or refers to his or her stepfather as "Dad." Children may insist they should be the ones to decide whether they see the targeted parent.
16) The child's belief system is particularly rigid, fixed, and resistant to traditional methods of intervention.

of alienation is rated by moving from more developmentally expectable and environmentally manageable factors, such as affinity and alignments, through to those more systemically entrenched and pathological behaviors typical in more severe alienation cases (see Table 4.4).

Drozd and Olesen (2004) also proposed a decision tree with questions to help determine whether a parent is engaging in alienating behaviors (p. 77) (see Table 4.5).

4.3 Measurement Scales

In an effort to address the limitations of "clinical judgments" regarding the presence of alienation, there have been some recent attempts to develop

Table 4.4 Garber's Hierarchical Decision Tree for Alienation (Garber, 2007)

1) Is the child only saying what s/he believes the listener wants to hear?
2) Does the child resist separation from the sending/alienating parent in general?
3) Does the child resist contact with the receiving/rejected parent in general?
4) Is the receiving parent notably more or less strict or demanding than the sending parent?
5) Is the receiving parent sensitive and responsive to the child's needs?
6) Is the sending parent supportive of the receiving parent?
7) Can the sending parent be enlisted to help facilitate the child's security with the receiving parent?
8) Can the receiving parent be engaged to provide the child with corrective experiences?
9) Are measures to limit the sending/alienating parent's contact with the child necessary, practical, and appropriate?
10) Are measures to limit the receiving/targeted parent's contact with the child necessary, practical, and appropriate?

standardized measures to assess the presence of alienation. Janet Johnston (2004) developed the Alienating Parenting and Supportive (Co) Parenting Scales (see Table 4.6), which is an extensive coding manual based on process interviews, preparation of custody evaluation reports, and clinical summaries to rate alienation. Initially, the scales were used by researchers to rate archival data on high-conflict litigating families. The interrater agreement of the scales was assessed by a 15- to 20-year longitudinal follow-up of a representative sample of 22 children from an initial study of 90 families.

Johnston (2010) more recently modified the scales to also allow them to be used directly by family members (e.g., to rate one another).

Adult children were administered the scales by asking them to retrospectively rate their parents at the time they were in grade school. The results

Table 4.5 Drozd and Olesen's (2004) Decision Tree to Assess Alienating Parental Behaviors

1) Does the parent believe the things s/he is saying about the other?
2) Is s/he genuinely frightened and protective, even if mistakenly so?
3) Is there a financial or any other kind of gain that would help explain the reason for the behavior if genuine fear does not seem to be present?
4) Is there a personal or family history of rejection that is being repeated in this new family?
5) Is the parent developmentally stuck in black-or-white thinking for reasons that may or may not be related to a past or present history of abuse, and does that parent see most things as win–lose or all-or-nothing?
6) Is there documented psychopathology that would explain any existing problems with flexible and clear thinking?
7) Is the parent prone to form relationships that are merged, and does the parent see the child as an extension of him/herself?

Note. Reprinted with permission from "Is It Abuse, Alienation, and/or Estrangement?," by L. M. Drozd and N. W. Olesen, 2004, *Journal of Child Custody,* 1 (3) p. 77. Copyright by Taylor & Francis Ltd, http://www.tandf.co.uk/journals.

Table 4.6 Subscales and Items of Johnston's (2011) Alienating Parenting and Supportive (Co) Parenting Scales

Alienating Parenting and Supportive (Co) Parenting Scales

Subscale	Items
The Allegations and Substantiation scale	Allegations of child neglect
	Child physical abuse
	Child sexual abuse
	Alcohol abuse
	Drug abuse
	Domestic violence
	Child stealing
	Other criminal activity
	Whether these allegations were cited as reason for litigation or referral
	Whether these allegations were substantiated against the mother or father
Child's Attitude and Behavior Toward Parents	Child rejection of parent
	Child enjoyment of parent
	Child visitation resistance with parent
	Child aligned with parent
	Child worry/sadness about parent
	Separation anxiety from parent
Alienating Parenting Behavior	Alienating parenting
	Supportive coparenting
	Distrustful coparenting
General Parenting Behaviors (II) scale	Warm/involved parent
	Negative-angry Parent
	Role reversal with parent
Ex-Spousal Relationship scale	Anger/blaming of ex-spouse
	Tension/fear of ex-spouse
	Obsession with ex-spouse

showed that correlations of these child ratings with the ratings made 15–20 years ago by clinicians were moderate, providing some evidence of concurrent validity. Johnston notes that several studies have supported the scales' predictive validity (Johnston, 2003; Johnston & Goldman, 2010; Johnston, Olesen, & Walters, 2005a, 2005b, 2005c; Johnston, Roseby, & Kuehnle, 2009).

Another instrument that measures the extent of alienation is the Relationship Distancing Questionnaire (RDQ), developed by Moné and Biringen (2006). The RDQ is a 30-item tool used to measure the extent to which adult children recall their parents' behaviors as alienating and the extent of their own memories about being alienated by one or both parents. The scoring of the tool assumes that alienation can occur by both parents, so the rating of each parent's alienating behaviors is scored separately (Mother section and Father section).

The RDQ contains several factors on each of the Mother and Father sections, and preliminary results show acceptable internal consistency for both sections of the tool (Moné & Biringen, 2006). The RDQ also shows good test-retest, suggesting consistency of reporting from one time to another. The RDQ has also been tested with other measures with similar theoretical constructs of parent–child contact problems, which showed RDQ to have convergent validity with these similar constructs (Moné & Biringen, 2005). No other study has used RDQ, so its reliability and validity testing is still in its infancy. Further testing is needed to replicate the reliability and validity reported in Moné and Biringen's (2005) study, and further testing is needed to explore whether the RDQ can discriminate alienation from other parent–child contact problems.

Amy Baker recently developed the Baker Parental Alienation Syndrome Questionnaire (BPASQ), a 28-item paper-and-pencil instrument administered to children.[11] Items in the tool focus on the children's perceptions of each parent and whether the children take sides when their parents disagree. Preliminary testing of the measure has been completed with two sets of children, identified as either alienated or estranged (10 alienated and 8 estranged). Baker identified the two groups by reviewing extensive custody evaluation reports and court transcripts and applying the eight behavioral manifestations of parental alienation syndrome (PAS) identified by Richard Gardner (1992a). She then assessed whether these two groups could independently be reclassified based on their responses to a series of questions on the BPASQ.

Preliminary results showed that all (8 of 8) of the court-referred alienated children were correctly coded as alienated, while 9 of the 10 court-referred estranged children were correctly coded as estranged. In all, 94% were properly coded and 6% were not. This tool is the first attempt at classifying cases as either alienation or estrangement. Since both groups of children were previously classified (without using the tool) during their involvements with the courts, the results show good concurrent validity with these prior classifications, but it remains unclear whether the tool would report similar results when classifying children from a broader sample of children. No other study has used the BPASQ, so its reliability and validity testing is still in its infancy.

4.3.1 Use of Existing Scales

Existing scales, such as the MMPI(2), the Rorschach, Perception-of-Relationships Test (PORT), and the Bricklin Perceptual Scales (BPS), have been used to test the psychological profiles of parents and children where alienation has been suspected (Gordon, Stoffey, & Bottinelli, 2008; Johnston

---

[11] E-mail correspondence with Amy Baker on August 28, 2010.

& Goldman, 2010; Johnston, Roseby, & Kuehnle, 2009; Lampel, 1996; Siegel & Langford, 1998). Gordon et al. (2008), for example, investigated psychological profiles of alienating parents (mothers and fathers) using the MMPI(2) compared with nonalienating parents (mothers and fathers who were in custody litigation, but without PAS) while the control parents had normal range scores. Siegel and Langford (1998), also using the MMPI(2), found that alienating mothers were more likely to deny and project compared with normative samples.

Bricklin and Elliot (2006) suggest the use of the Perception-of-Relationships Test and the Bricklin Perceptual Scales to assess alienation, based on the assumption that strongly stated verbal opinions of a child about a parent's value in creating emotional comfort can be compared with what is reflected in the validated test scores to determine inconsistencies found in cases of alienation. However, the general use of the Bricklin measures has been criticized, and they should be used cautiously if at all (Birnbaum, Fidler, & Kavassalis, 2008; Wood, Nezworski, Lilenfeld, & Garb, 2009; Zervopoulous, 2008).

4.4 Differentiating Levels of and Responses to Strained Parent–Child Relationships

With the continued debate about appropriate responses to children resisting contact with one parent, there is a clear consensus that there is an urgent need to identify strained parent–child relationships early in the separation process so that appropriate prevention and intervention strategies can be applied. Parent–child contact problems, including alienation, generally become more difficult to address with the passage of time, as children and parents are more likely to become entrenched in their positions, which may be further exacerbated by the litigation process.

Delays or use of ineffective interventions are likely to entrench the alienation, making it more difficult to remedy. When attempted solutions are not matched to the unique factors of the case, alienation can be exacerbated by ineffective attempts to address the problems in the family. Differentiating alienation from other types of strained parent–child contact problems requires a careful assessment of the factors that contribute to the presence of alienation and an understanding of the level of severity of factors that are more likely to lead to families being entrenched in their positions.

The identification of differential levels of and responses to strained parent–child relationships builds on existing approaches to distinguish the nature, severity, and frequency of strained parent–child relationships within the context of alienation (Clawar & Rivlin, 1991; Gardner, 1992a). Differentiating the severity of strained relationships is the first step in determining the most appropriate prevention or intervention strategy for families. Prevention or intervention will depend on the nature and reasons for the strained parent–child contact, the degree and frequency of parents not supporting the child's relationship with the other parent, the conduct of the parents, the duration and intensity of these negative behaviors, the impact of parental behaviors on the children, the child's level of receptivity and responsiveness to these negative behaviors, and the intentionality to prevent a relationship with the other parent.

Based on Gardner's (1992a, 1996) eight criteria for the presence of alienation as manifest in the child, he proposed a framework for assessing the severity of alienation (see Table 4.7) as mild, moderate, and severe.

Mild alienation includes some but not all of the eight symptoms. Bad-mouthing and denigrating of the resisted parent are mild and intermittent. Any difficulties with the child's transition from the custodial to noncustodial parent are short-lived, and the child is able to resume comfort once out of the realm of the alienating parent. Further, symptoms of alienation are not transferred to the extended family members.

In moderate cases, all eight symptoms are likely to be present and more severely than in mild alienation, while not as pervasive as in severe cases. Alienating behaviors are stronger and more varied than in the mild cases. Gardner emphasized that moderate cases often include more difficulties during transitions with the child protesting that s/he does not want to have contact the rejected parent but ultimately goes. In these cases, the child eventually settles once with the rejected parent but remains guarded in his or her interactions with that parent. Symptoms resurface or escalate prior to the transition

Table 4.7 Gardner's Differential Diagnosis of the Three Types of Parental Alienation (1996)

	Mild	Moderate	Severe
Primary symptomatic manifestation	Mild	Moderate	Severe
The campaign of denigration	Minimal	Moderate	Formidable
Weak, frivolous, or absurd rationalizations for the deprecation	Minimal	Moderate	Multiple absurd rationalizations
Lack of ambivalence	Normal ambivalence	No ambivalence	No ambivalence
The independent-thinker phenomenon	Usually absent	Present	Present
Reflexive support of the favored parent in the parental conflict	Minimal	Present	Present
Absence of guilt	Normal guilt	Minimal to no guilt	No guilt
Borrowed scenarios	Minimal	Present	Present
Spread of the animosity to the extended family of the hated parent	Minimal	Present	Formidable, often fanatic

back to the preferred parent. Symptoms are also transferred to extended family members.

In severe cases, which Gardner believed were a minority of between 5% and 10% of all cases, the child exhibits all eight symptoms to a significant degree and may have temper tantrums or panic or phobic reactions. The child and alienating parent may share paranoid fantasies. The contact is likely impossible with the child threatening harm to him- or herself or the rejected parent, destruction of property, or incessant rejecting behaviors. Usually, if the child does spend time with the rejected parent, these behaviors do not subside during the course of the contact, and the child remains distant, fully guarded, and hypervigilant to the perceived threat of the rejected parent (see Table 4.7).

As discussed, although some of Gardner's views remain controversial, his differentiation of mild, moderate, and severe cases is an important contribution to adopting a differential response for parent–child contact problems.

Building on the need to develop a differential approach for the assessment of and interventions with various levels and types of parent–child strained relationships, we are proposing a differential response (see Figure 4.1) based on the factors associated with alienation (covered in Chapter 3) and the levels of severity of each of these factors (mild, moderate, and severe) that should be considered in the assessment and differential response to prevention and intervention strategies.

Factors that we propose be included in the assessment of severity of alienation are:

1) the parents' conduct;
2) protection versus the probability of harm;
3) rigidity of child's perceptions toward his/her parents;
4) the frequency of parent–child contact;
5) the duration of strained relationships;
6) the history of rigidity;
7) the responsiveness of each parent to education and therapy as suggested; and
8) the level of compliance with court orders.

Each of these factors needs to be assessed to determine whether the case is mild, moderate, or severe as the frequency, intensity, and duration of these factors will provide insight into the overall severity of the parent–child strained relationships and provide guidance to the manifestation of the contact problems.

4.4.1 Mild Cases

For mild cases, while there are instances of problematic behaviors, these have not developed into rigid patterns. Children may temporarily or occasionally resist contact with a parent due to affinity, alignments, and situational issues.

Favored parents may show signs of minimal interference or bad-mouthing. In these cases, the favored parent often values the child's relationship with the other parent but occasionally may display misguided protective behavior. The children demonstrate that they value the relationship with both parents but occasionally may display unjustified discomfort. Mild cases may have interruptions of parent–child of contact due to late or missed contacts, but these are considered infrequent, and attempts are made by the favored parent to compensate for interruptions of the parenting schedule. The presence of strained parent–child contact is often situational. Further, the parents usually interact with flexibility regarding changes to the parenting schedule. When education or therapy is offered to these parents, they are expected to be receptive to treatment to improve the parent–child relationships, and to comply with court orders and agreements.

4.4.2 Moderate Cases

For moderate alienation cases, favored parents may engage more frequently in episodic interference of the child's relationship with the other parent and bad-mouthing of the other parent in frustration and anger. As the anger and mistrust increases, a parent's overprotection of the child can undermine the child's relationship with the other parent. Children's reactions to these episodic interferences are mixed, confused, or inconsistent, which can lead to contact with the other parent, which is sporadic, infrequent, or delayed. In moderate cases, there begins to emerge a pattern of missed opportunities for parent–child contact due to the more frequent interruptions of parent–child contact. Because the favored parents' thinking is more rigid at this level, there is less opportunity to make up these missed opportunities given that the parents are often unwilling to make adjustments to the parenting schedule to accommodate changing schedules. When therapy is offered to these favored parents, they may appear to be complying, but their attendance is likely to be sporadic and/or with minimal success. In moderate cases, there may also be more instances of not adhering to court-ordered parenting plans.

4.4.3 Severe Cases

In severe cases, psychologically abusive conduct by the alienating parent is often related to mental health or personality disorder issues of that parent. There is interference in contact with the other parent, and severe and frequent denigration ("bad-mouthing") of the other parent. In these cases, favored parents may intentionally attempt to block the child's relationship with the other parent but usually identify it as protection, despite repeated investigations or evidence that demonstrates that the risk of future harm is improbable. Alternatively, in severe cases the alienating parent may identify the conduct as a result of desire to promote the rights or wishes of the child. Children in severe cases may be observed as rigid and having extreme reactions to the

Figure 4.1 Differential Response to Strained Parent–Child Relationships

Assessment: Level of Severity	Mild	Moderate	Severe
1. Parental conduct	1. Minimal interference/ badmouthing	1. Episodic interference / bad-mouthing	1. Psychologically abusive alienating behaviors related to mental health issues (e.g., paranoia)
2. Protection vs. the probability of harm	2. Parent values child's relationship with other parent but occasionally displays misguided protective behavior.	2. Parent's overprotection (unwittingly or intentionally) undermines the child's relationship with the other parent.	2. Identifies actions as protecting (rights of) child, despite repeated investigations or evidence that demonstrates that the risk of future harm is improbable, or makes malicious allegations knowing they are unfounded
3. Rigidity of child's perceptions/ behavior toward his/her parents	3. Child values relationship with both parents but displays discomfort (not extended to extended family).	3. Child displays more resistance than at mild level, although reactions are mixed, confused, or inconsistent (e.g., before or during transitions, while with resisted parent).	3. Rigid/extreme child reaction to RP (e.g., threats to run away, of harm to self or other, acting out, or aggressive behavior)
4. Frequency of parent–child contact	4. Minor interruptions of parent-child contact (e.g., late, missed visits, short-lived transition difficulties in presence of FP).	4. Contact is sporadic, infrequent, and/or delayed.	4. No or very infrequent contact between child and RP
5. Duration of strained relationships	5. Situational and infrequent relationship strain (e.g., due to affinity, alignment, expected and time-limited upset over parents' separation)	5. Pattern of missed opportunities for parent–child contact; child takes longer to settle in after transition than at mild level and may become unsettled closer to return time to FP	5. Chronic parent–child disruptions
6. History of parents' rigidity	6. Generally flexible but can be rigid	6. Generally rigid but some instances of flexibility	6. Inflexible position taking
7. Responsiveness to education/ treatment as suggested	7. Responsive to education/ treatment to improve parent-child relationships	7. Attends treatment but sporadic and/or with minimal success	7. Refusal of treatment / previous attempts for treatment unsuccessful
8. Compliance with court orders, parenting plans, treatment agreements	8. Compliant with parenting plan, treatment agreement and court orders	8. Inconsistent compliance with parenting plan, treatment agreement and court orders	8. Noncompliance with parenting plan, treatment agreement or court orders

Legal Interventions: From court support, monitoring to intervening	Detailed parenting plan, including specified parenting time with RP, and primary residence care with FP Early case conference Court management and monitoring Referral to parenting education or counselling with experienced therapist Warning of sanctions for noncompliance of parenting plan and orders	Highly detailed parenting plan (specified court ordered parenting time for child with RP) Court monitoring Continuity with one judge Warning of sanctions or custody reversal Sanctions for noncompliance (contempt of court, opportunity to purge contempt) Consideration for joint custody to ensure involvement of the RP in child-related decision making Consideration for extended periods of contact over holidays with RP (e.g., summer school break) Consideration for equal parenting time Court appointment of a therapist experienced in alienation	Strong sanctions for noncompliance implemented Possibility of transfer of custody to RP with one or more of the following: • interim interruption of contact with (at least 3 months) with FP or until behavior change demonstrated • monitored or supervised contact with FP • use of transitional site to prepare for transfer of custody to RP • eventual return to FP if there is an absence of parental alienating behaviors demonstrated
Client Interventions: Map interventions to client needs	Preventive parent education Psychoeducational groups for children Family therapy (members seen in various combinations) Therapist reporting back to court when there is noncompliance with parenting plan, orders, or treatment agreement	Court-ordered family therapy (members seen in various combinations) to repair relationships and implement court-ordered parenting time with RP Additional therapy for child, rejected or FP Intensive residential family intervention (may be with one family or group therapy), with both parents and children, combining therapy and psychoeducation (e.g., family camp program, weekend workshop) Therapist reporting back to court for noncompliance with parenting plan, orders or treatment agreement Parenting coordinator (case manager / monitor interventions)	Custody reversal (as above) accompanied by reintegration intervention with child and RP, followed by intervention/therapy to reunify FP Parent education and individual therapy for FP with a view to reunification with child Therapist reporting back to court when there is noncompliance with parenting plan, orders, or treatment agreement Parenting coordinator (case manager / monitor of interventions)

Note: FP = favored parent; RP = rejected parent.

rejected parent, despite a history of positive interactions. As a result of these patterns, it is common for there to be no or little contact between the child and the rejected parent.

Often, parents and children maintain a rigid position about any parent–child contact. At this point, the alienating parent may suggest to the child to see the other parent, knowing that the child will refuse, which is then used as further demonstration of the child's refusal to have contact with the other parent. In these cases, the alienating parent will argue that the child's views and preferences should be heeded (which takes focus off of the parent's behaviors). When therapy is offered to these parents or their children, it is likely met with refusal and a lack of cooperation. Often in severe cases, there have been previous attempts for treatment that have been unsuccessful. It is important to carefully consider any previous efforts that were unsuccessful so that similar approaches are not repeated, thereby reinforcing the alienation and the child's negative reaction to the failed efforts. Ineffective interventions are not only a waste of resources but can also result in escalating polarization (Schepard, 2001). In severe cases of alienation, there are usually examples of parents disregarding treatment contracts and court orders.

4.4.4 The Differential Model of Alienation

Early assessment by a court-appointed mental health professional with specialized knowledge in alienation, abuse, and intimate partner violence is highly desirable. Therefore, we propose a differential model for considering the nature, severity, and frequency of strained parent–child contact problems after separation. In Chapter 7, we connect specific mental health and legal interventions for children and families based on the overall severity of the strained parent–child contact.

4.4.5 Summary

As empirical research about risk factors and indicators of alienation is limited, measurement is clearly an issue that needs further development and research. Although progress has been made in this area, there is still no assessment tool that has been validated by rigorous empirical research that can be used to readily establish the presence of alienation and differentiate it from other types of parent–child contact problems. Decision trees can be clinically useful in assessing the presence of alienation and other parent–child contact problems, but these are subject to biases and the chance of error in making accurate decisions. Promising measures to assess the presence of alienation include the Alienating Parenting and Supportive (Co) Parenting scales (Johnston, 2004, 2011), the Baker Parental Alienation Syndrome Questionnaire (e-mail correspondence with Amy Baker on August 28, 2010) and the Relationship Distancing Questionnaire (Moné & Biringen, 2006). However, further testing and refinement are needed for these measures using multiple samples and various sample settings. In addition, more research is needed to determine whether these measures can accurately distinguish levels of severity, frequency, and duration of alienation across multiple populations.

Further attention is also needed to reach consensus on the salient issues that can accurately distinguish alienation from other related phenomena. While better assessment and measurement tools are needed, every family is different and will require a careful and comprehensive assessment of the child's needs within the particular family context, using information from many sources (e.g., from parents, collateral sources, psychometrics, observations, court documentation, etc.), to determine the nature of parent–child contact problems and suggest what is in a particular child's best interests. As discussed in Chapter 6, failure to accurately detect the presence of alienation and intervene accordingly can have serious consequences for children and can alter their pathways into adulthood.

5

Prognosis and Long-Term Consequences of Untreated Alienation on Young Adults and Their Families

5.1 The Impact of Alienation on Children and Adults Who Were Alienated as Children

Understanding the short- and long-term effects of alienation on children is crucial when considering if, when, and how there should be intervention. Although there is little, if any, well-controlled and empirically based evidence about the effects of alienation, clinical observations, cases reviews, and qualitative studies have demonstrated with few exceptions that alienated children are at risk for short-term emotional distress and long-term adjustment difficulties (e.g., Burrill, 2006a; Cartwright, 1993; Clawar & Rivlin, 1991; Dunne & Hedrick, 1994; Gardner, 1998b; Garrity & Baris, 1994; Johnston, 2003; Johnston, Roseby, & Kuehnle, 2009; Kelly & Johnston, 2001; Kopetski, 1998a, 1998b; Lampel, 1996; Lee & Olesen, 2001; Lowenstein, 2006; Lund, 1995; Racusin & Copans, 1994; Rand, 1997a, 1997b; Rand, Rand, & Kopetski, 2005; Stahl, 1999; Stoltz & Ney, 2002; Turkat, 1994, 1999; Waldron & Joanis, 1996; Wallerstein & Blakeslee, 1989; Walsh & Bone, 1997; Ward & Harvey, 1993; Warshak, 2001).

In their mixed-gendered study of 74 children from litigating families, Johnston, Walters, and Olesen (2005c) reported that children aged 5 to 12 tended to exhibit early signs of alienation (e.g., children exhibiting separation anxieties related to emotional enmeshment toward the favored parent and parent–child role reversal) while older latency-age children (aged 10 to 13) tended to exhibit a more consolidated alienated stance (e.g., children experiencing strong and persistent negative views toward the rejected parent with a general lack of pleasure and affection toward that parent). Compared with nonalienated children from custody-litigating families, alienated children had more difficulties with information processing, coping, self- and other representation, and affective functioning. Alienating custodial parents reported that alienated children had more emotional and behavioral problems than both their nonalienated counterparts and the normative samples. The alienated children were more vulnerable, exhibiting emotional and behavioral problems and social incompetence, but an inflated self-confidence.

In the 20-year follow-up of children in high-conflict divorces, some of whom were alienated, Johnston and her colleagues (Johnston & Goldman, 2010; Johnston et al., 2009) reported that 60% of youth from 18 to 21 years of age had impaired emotional functioning, and 84% had difficulty forming secure intimate relationships. Emotional dysfunction was found more frequently in those who had severed contact with a parent than in those who had not.

Amy Baker (2007a) conducted a qualitative retrospective study of 38 adults recruited from the Internet who reported being alienated as children.[1] Many continued to suffer with low self-esteem into adulthood. As children, they internalized the negative attributes of the rejected parent that were communicated both directly and indirectly by the favored parent or aligned others. One explanation for their low self-esteem is because they believed, as children, that the alienating parent must have also hated the aspects of their personalities that were similar to the rejected parent. As children, they reasoned that since they were genetically similar to the rejected parent, they too must have been "bad." In addition, respondents indicated that they had ultimately accepted their alienating parent's campaign of assertions that the rejected parent did not love them and had abandoned them. Self-hatred and self-blame were common among the 38 respondents, often resulting from feeling guilty for rejecting the parent and from having abandoned their younger siblings who continued contact when the alienated child did not.

Baker noted that the results of her retrospective and qualitative study must be treated cautiously, as the study did not include a comparison group of adult children of divorce without the experience of parental alienation. Further, her study population was relatively small, recruited by advertisements and self-selected, which may have resulted in a self-selection bias of those most severely alienated and unhappy that this had occurred. Consequently, one cannot conclude that the outcomes are due to an alienation process per se; the outcomes may have been a result of the divorce itself, parental pathology, or other precursors. Nevertheless, Baker concluded that the voices and felt experiences of these adult children provide a good foundation for future, better-designed research.

---

[1] The results of Baker's research project are summarized in this 2007a book as well as several articles (2005a, 2005b, 2005c, 2006).

5.2 Spontaneous Reconciliation

Researchers have followed cases and observed various types and degrees of spontaneous reconciliations (Baker, 2006; Darnall & Steinberg, 2008a, 2008b; Johnston & Goldman, 2010; Rand & Rand, 2006). Maturation, independence, emancipation, and life cycle trigger events have been identified by these writers and clinicians as precipitants for reconciliation of parent–child relationships, sometimes years after the conclusion of court proceedings. Such life events include graduation, getting married, having a child, a rift in the relationship with the custodial/favored parent, attending therapy, intervention of a significant other or family member, and death or serious illness of a family member.

The adults studied by Amy Baker (2007a) reported that reconciliation occurred from 6 to 47 years after the initial rejection of a parent. Participants in this study ranged from 19 and 67 years of age ($M = 40.5$, $SD = 11.5$).

Johnston and Goldman (2010) were able to locate and study about one third (37) of their original sample of custody-disputing families (90), 15 to 20 years after clinical and legal interventions. This original sample included various types and degrees of parent–child contact problems, including those where the child's rejection was justified and where it was due to alienation. Extreme cases of child abuse or neglect or intimate partner violence were not included in the sample. Johnston interviewed both parents and the grown children and examined each child's treatment record. All of the sample had received court-ordered counseling as children and specified parenting time with the rejected parent.

All of the grown children, now adults, reported painfully remembering their parents' overt and covert alienating behaviors when they were children. Despite this, between the ages of 18 and 21 years, nearly all initiated some contact with their rejected parents. The sustainability of these relationships, however, was mixed. Most (80%) reported eventually having frequent and close contact with both parents. While recognizing their parents' limitations and as a result having low expectations for them, about one third of the sample as adults expressed positive attitudes toward both parents, while two thirds had negative views or continued to have little or no contact with the rejected parent, mostly in cases where that parent struggled with significant problems, such as substance abuse, significantly compromised parenting, or violent behavior. In this latter group, where there were continued strongly negative views of a rejected parent, it appears that most of the cases involved justified rejection rather than alienation.

Many of the sample, who later initiated contact with the rejected parent as adults, perceived that the longer-term voluntary therapy was helpful for reestablishing a relationship with a rejected parent. However, repeated referral for court-ordered reunification therapy during childhood and adolescence was recalled negatively by some respondents. Johnston and Goldman (2010) note that an unjustified rejection that emerges for the first time in early adolescence is a common coping strategy in high-conflict divorced families and serves an important developmental function. Based on their preliminary findings, they suggest that in such circumstances, when the rejection commences only in adolescence compared with when it starts earlier, the alienation is unlikely to last beyond a couple of years. They propose that a "strategy of supportive voluntary counseling and/or backing off and allowing the youth to mature and time to heal the breach" (p. 113), instead of forcing adolescents to participate in counseling. They conclude that teenagers who feel that their autonomy has been respected, and in turn feel empowered, are better able to distance themselves from the alienating parental conduct and family conflicts and, consequently, are more likely to subsequently initiate contact with the rejected parent.

As noted, in this study of children who were alienated for long periods of time and who later initiated contact with the rejected parent, many had been previously required by the court as children to attend reunification counseling that they did not want or that they perceived at the time as unhelpful. In examining retrospectively the cases in this study where the sample later initiated contact with the rejected parent as adults, they reported these reunifications as voluntary and not occurring as result of counseling or therapy. However, it is impossible to know on the basis of these self-report data the extent to which maturity, the court-ordered counseling, or some other factor or combination of factors was responsible for their decision to initiate contact with their rejected parent. It is possible that the counseling that they received reluctantly as children was a contributing factor in their later desire to initiate contact with their rejected parent regardless of how they viewed the counseling as children.

Findings reported by Baker (2007a) and Clawar and Rivlin (1991), indicating that many of the adults who rejected a parent postseparation secretly wished as children and adolescents that someone would have recognized that they did not mean what they said when they were rejecting their parent, is an important consideration when identifying an appropriate intervention.

Darnall and Steinberg (2008a, 2008b) studied 27 adolescents and young adults who were aged 4 to 17 at the time of the alienation; the subjects experienced varying degrees of spontaneous reunification without "any significant intervention from the court or mental health professional" (2008b, p. 254). The length of time the child had no contact with the rejected parent ranged from three months to nine years. It was possible to identify various common situations as noted above that precipitated reconciliation.

Of the 27 who had some degree of reconciliation, one third (9) sustained positive relationships, leaving two thirds (18) who ended up breaking off the relationship again. All of their reports of spontaneous reunification, irrespective of the specific category of crisis, had one or more of the following in common:

1) the favored parent had eventually come to support the reunification in some way, either for his or her own economic self-interest or by following the child's lead;

2) the court became involved, in effect threatening a crisis for the alienating parents, such as a third-party caring for the child;

3) the alienated child was influenced by siblings who had continued to have contact with the rejected parent; *or*

4) the child had found a way to appease the favored parent by claiming it was the court that made the reunification happen or by showing that the favored parent would benefit (e.g., having the rejected parent help to pay for college).

Consequently, although most of these adolescents and young adults reported their efforts to reconcile as "spontaneous," like in the Johnston and Goldman follow-up, it remains unclear the extent to which the earlier court orders for contact and treatment contributed to this eventual outcome.

5.3 When to Suspend Efforts or Letting Go

Rejected parents may increase the likelihood of a sustained reconciliation, if it eventually occurs, by keeping photos, life- or scrapbooks, memory boxes, letters or poems, or returned gifts or cards, and creating Web sites or keeping current contact information. Such items will provide the child with concrete evidence that the rejected parent never stopped loving him or her or wanting to have contact. Additional guidance to parents about if and how to let go is available (e.g., Darnall, 2010; Warshak, 2010b).

In some severe alienation cases, legal or mental health professionals may advise rejected parents to suspend their efforts to enforce parent contact, believing this is the least detrimental alternative at the time for the child involved. For some of these professionals, use of the contempt power of the court is viewed as likely to be ineffective, and a reversal of custody and residing with the rejected parent are expected to be more harmful than beneficial.

There is an assumption that once the rejected parent gives up and is out of the child's life, the child's exposure to parental conflict and bad-mouthing will abate. Reports from our interviews with key informants, however, indicate that one cannot assume the child will necessarily be protected from parental conflict even when the rejected parent chooses to suspend litigation or contact with the child has been terminated or (e.g., interviews with: T. Altobelli, June 3, 2010; A. Baker, April, 30, 2010; G. Czutrin, April 19, 2010; R. Deutsch, June 14, 2010; W. Eddy, April 29, 2010). While the rejected parent may have given up his or her claim for parenting time, litigation may continue over spousal or child support or property, or perhaps over the rejected parent's right to information about the child to which the child may be privy.

There are different views by professionals on whether children and particularly adolescents should be pressured to reestablish a relationship with the rejected parent. Further, in some cases a rejected parent will decide, without professional advice, not to continue with seeking to legally enforce a relationship with an alienated child. This may be a result of lack of financial or emotional resources of the rejected parent to obtain the necessary legal or mental health services needed, or because of a concern about the effects of a prolonged struggle on the children. Unfortunately for children, in some cases it may be that the better-adjusted parent is the one who decides to withdraw from the conflict, leaving the children solely in the care of a less capable parent.

The existing data on spontaneous reconciliation and the sustainability of the contact and relationship are preliminary and mixed. There is a real need for empirical, longitudinal data on the long-term consequences of alienation. What is clear is that these cases are often extremely complex, and the intervention or lack of it must be determined on a case-by-case basis. However, if a relationship is discontinued during childhood, there may be the hope, but not the certainty, that it may later be reestablished. Even if it is reestablished in late adolescence or adulthood, the loss of a relationship, often for many years, during childhood creates permanent losses for the parent and child.

6

Prevention

One of the primary goals of working with children and parents where alienation or other parent–child contact problems are occurring is to help improve strained parent–child relationships. As we have discussed in Chapter 4, early identification of the nature, frequency, and severity of parent–child contact problems is critical so that families receive the appropriate services to properly address strained relationships post separation and divorce. In this chapter, we focus on prevention to avert parent–child contact problems from becoming more severe.

A number of experts whom we interviewed emphasized the importance of addressing strained parent–child contact problems before these relationships develop into more severe contact problems. As Justice Philip Marcus[1] from Israel explains, the identification of alienation patterns and how best to stop the contact problems from happening is the best way to respond to alienation problems because once the contact problem has set in, it becomes far more difficult to resolve. Likewise, psychologist Richard Warshak[2] stated:

> I guess the most exciting aspect is the potential to prevent problems
> from developing or prevent problems from becoming more severe
> than they already are. It's almost always easier to overcome a
> problem in the early stages of the problem before it becomes too
> entrenched, and certainly when it comes to alienation.

---

[1] Interview, June 1, 2010.
[2] Interview, April 15, 2010.

Psychologist Peter Jaffe[3] suggests that the most important process for these cases is early identification, triaging based on the severity of the case and then providing prevention to less severe cases so that these families receive education and support early in the process and before family members become entrenched in their positions. As he notes, "early on, the parents like you and you are seen as neutral. It is preferable to use that relationship to intervene clinically or get people to the right clinicians, and suspend any [custody evaluation] report that gets people more polarized." Janet Johnston[4] notes that prevention is also important for younger children before alienation may be crystallized. She notes: "early intervention, prevention is extremely important and it makes a huge difference when you see these kids at around 8, 9, 10 [years of age] beginning to develop the attitude of resistance and to move in and do preventive work. That is much more effective than trying to start intervention with a child or adolescent that is really stuck—at 12, 13, 14 [years of age] and really doesn't want to see the other parent and has been refusing for some time."

Parent–child contact problems are complex and require different approaches to address the variability of these strained relationships. Differences in the severity of parental alienating behaviors, factors that contribute to different types of contact problems, and the duration of these issues all contribute to the need to differentiate prevention and intervention approaches so that they are tailored to the needs of families. As we have discussed, parent–child contact problems and alienation can change over time, in some cases swiftly, from mild to severe if strategies are not put in place to help families improve strained relationships early in the process of separation.

There are a number of prevention approaches, strategies, and programs that have been developed to address different levels of severity of parent–child contact problems. These are generally separated into three different categories of prevention, each with their unique focus and target groups:

1) primary prevention focuses on the entire population who may be at risk of parent–child contact problems after separation;
2) secondary prevention targets children and parents who have been identified at greater risk of becoming involved in alienation; and
3) tertiary prevention targets children and families involved in more severe levels of parental alienating behaviors.

6.1 Universal or Primary Prevention

This form of prevention targets the entire population of separated parents and children and includes public announcements, awareness campaigns,

---

[3] Interview, June 24, 2010.
[4] Interview, May 10, 2010.

or presentations in the community or given to children at school about the risks of strained parent contact after separation. The ultimate goal of universal prevention strategies is to help establish protective factors before a problem develops (Ripple, 2004). For example, by offering education to all parents after they separate about the potential of contact problems, it is assumed that these parents will generally be better equipped with the knowledge and skills needed to protect their children from the potential of contact problems with both parents. These strategies are directed toward enhancing protective factors within the identified risk domains of alienation, including school, community, family, and individual and for building community knowledge and capacity for organizational change. Rather than seek out families most at risk of parent–child problems, these programs are provided to all families, regardless of the risk of developing future contact problems. Primary prevention strategies are attractive because the cost of delivering the service per individual is low. Because the strategies are geared toward the general population of separating families, there is minimal risk of stigmatizing effects for children and families (Williams & Van Dorn, 1999) who may be struggling with strained relationships.

6.2 Public Awareness

There are several initiatives that have been developed to bring public awareness to the impact and effects of alienation (see Table 6.1). The designation of April 25 of each year as Parental Alienation Awareness Day is an international initiative developed by advocates to bring awareness and information about alienation to the general public, as well as parents, the courts, teachers, the police, and so on. The aim of this day is to make the general public more aware of the problems associated with alienation and to encourage parents who might engage in alienating behaviors to seek mental health support or parenting education (www.paawarenessday.com). It is challenging to do research to evaluate whether or not public awareness campaigns are producing the desired impact. However, it seems likely that these campaigns will have the least effect on the most serious cases, as these parents are most likely to be resistant to recognizing and addressing their behaviors.

6.2.1 Parent Education Programs

Another, more focused primary prevention strategy has been to mandate or suggest that all parents involved in litigation participate in a parent education program before they can proceed with the litigation process. Parent education sessions have been developed to offer parents the knowledge and skills to navigate the court system and to consider alternative dispute strategies, with the aim of encouraging an expeditious resolution of disputes and reducing interparental conflict associated with entrenched litigation. Parent education

Table 6.1 Examples of Public Awareness Initiatives

Event	Country
Semana Brasileira de Conscientização da Alienação Parental	Brazil
"Bubbles of LOVE"	Australia
Fun in Park, theme "Bringing Families Together" in support of International Parental Alienation Awareness Day	Bermuda
Bubbles of Love Day	Canada
Love Is for Everyone! Bubbles of Love	Canada
Red Deer PA Awareness Day & Bubbles of Love BBQ!	Canada
Toronto Bubbles of Love Day	Canada
Light up the Sky	United Kingdom
Public Information Desk for PAAD	Germany
Easter Bubbles of Love	Poland
Dia Internacional para a Consciencialização sobre a Alienação Parental	Portugal
Bubbles of LOVE in Sweden	Sweden
Mothers for Justice Peaceful Protest for Parental Alienation Awareness	United States
Bubbles of Love Day Illinois	United States
Gathering of Family and Friends of Targeted Parents	United States
West Virginia Annual Parental Alienation Awareness Day Candlelight Vigil	United States
Philadelphia Bubble and Candlelight Visual for Parental Alienation Awareness Day	United States
Trophy Club Texas Bubbles of Love	United States

programs vary in duration (from 2 hours at one session to 12 hours spread over 6 weeks), content (information about the courts, alternative dispute resolution options, impact of separation and conflict on children), and format (presentation, video, vignettes, educational materials, role playing, and development of communication skills)[5]. Recruitment also varies, as programs can be court mandated or voluntary.

While a detailed discussion of parenting education programs is beyond the scope of this book, recent reviews (Fackrell, Hawkins, & Kay, 2011; Kierstead, 2011; Sigal, Sandler, Wolchik, & Braver, 2011) suggest that parents are generally satisfied with the content of the knowledge provided (Brandon, 2006; Criddle, Allgood, & Piercy, 2003; Faircloth & Cummings, 2008; Shifflett & Cummings; 1999; Yankeelov, Bledsoe, Brown, & Cambron, 2003). However, mandatory parent education programs have resulted in mixed results in demonstrating behavioral changes in the way parents relate between themselves

---

[5] See Pollet (2009) for a survey of programs in the United States for children of divorcing or separating parents.

and their children (Bacon & McKenzie, 2004; Goodman, Bonds, Sandler, & Braver, 2004; Grych, 2005; Whitworth, Capshew, & Abell, 2002). There are several methodological limitations of the current research that limit the generalizability of these findings, including a lack of comparison groups, the use of nonstandardized parent self-report data, and a lack of fidelity checks for the consistent delivery of these approaches.

Further, these programs are aimed at all separating parents involved in litigation, and less is known about the impact of these programs specific for high-conflict families. However, the available research suggests that parenting education programs have the least effect on parents involved in the high-conflict separations that are likely to develop into alienation (Bacon & McKenzie, 2004; Fackrell et al., 2011; Neff & Cooper, 2004; Sigal et al., 2011).

6.3 Selected or Secondary Prevention

Secondary prevention approaches are purposively aimed at populations that have been identified as having more risk of alienation than the average population of separating parents. The early identification of problematic parent–child contact issues is critical in determining which families are best suited for these approaches so that strategies are targeted and tailored for the types of factors that interfere with positive parent–child relationships after separation and divorce. Similar to universal prevention strategies, selected prevention efforts seek to reduce these risk factors by actively developing protective factors (Ripple, 2004) but are delivered with the specific aim of identifying and ameliorating strained parent–child relationships.

Secondary educational and clinical prevention approaches to address parent contact problems are typically implemented by mental health professionals[6] at various stages of the separation process, in addressing mild and moderate contact problems. The development of these programs is still in its infancy, and there are few empirical evaluations to assess the potential effectiveness of these to improve parent–child relationships postseparation. The current evidence is mainly guided by clinical anecdotes, case studies, within-group evaluations, and a few qualitative studies involving small samples.

The specific clinical or psychoeducational intervention chosen will depend on both the nature (e.g., alienation, justified rejection, elements of both—a mixed case) *and* the level (mild or moderate) of parent–child contact problems, as well as on the services available and on the willingness of family members to participate. Secondary prevention approaches involving education or therapy tend to be suitable for mild and some moderate cases, which may include the relatively clear alienation or justified rejection cases, or the mixed cases, which have elements of both justified rejection and alienation.

---

[6] We also refer to these professionals as therapists and counselors throughout this book.

Included in these less severe cases may be those where the child, while resisting contact due to an affinity, age, gender, or divorce-related alignment, continues to have some contact with the nonfavored parent.

There are a growing number of psychoeducational group programs available for children and both residential and nonresidential parents of separation and divorce experiencing strained parent–child relationship problems. These may be court connected, community, or school based. Based on the risk and protective factors associated with parent–child contact problems and postdivorce adjustment problems, three critical factors have been identified as the key points of prevention: 1) managing parental conflict; 2) parenting effectiveness combining warmth, discipline, and limit setting; and 3) positive parent–child relationships (Pedro-Carroll, 2010). Contributing to these is the parents' own well-being and psychological functioning.

6.3.1 Secondary Prevention Programs for Parents

Prevention and skill developing parent education programs are considered essential for families when children are at risk as they are in "high-conflict" families. With a focus on the negative impact of conflict on children, secondary prevention programs aim to provide parents with parenting effectiveness training rather than information only. To specifically target high-conflict families, many of these programs go beyond providing information and focus on activating skill-building components, which include modeling role play and feedback to help parents build their skills for effective parenting and to reduce interparental conflict. These secondary programs are usually not court mandated, but rather, parents are recruited by building on their motivation to strengthen the quality of their parenting and to not undermine the other parent.

Skill-based programs geared at changing behavior, which are likely to require more than the typical 2 to 6 hours of primary prevention parent education, are likely to be more effective than programs limited to basic information about the court process (Wolchik, Sandler, Winslow, & Smith-Daniels, 2005), but there remains insufficient evidence to determine the impact of these secondary programs.

Kids' Turn is a six-session divorcing parent education program offered to all family members, with each parent in different rooms and the children in separate groups based on their ages (e.g., 4–6 years, 7–9 years, and 10–14 years). Although most aspects of the Kids' Turn program have not been rigorously evaluated for efficacy, the authors report that based on a pre- and post-preexperimental design (e.g., no comparison group) of 61 participants, they found that after completion of the program, parents reported a reduction in parental conflict (intensity and frequency), parental alienating behaviors, parent anxiety and depression, and children's internalizing problems (anxiety and depression) (Cookston & Fung, 2011). Improvements in child and adolescent adjustment problems at follow-up to varying degrees have been reported in programs for residential parents, such as Parenting Through Change (PCT) (Forgatch & DeGarmo, 1999; Stolberg & Mahler, 1994) and New Beginnings Project (Wolchik et al., 1993, 2002; Wolchik, Sandler, Weiss, & Winslow, 2007).

Even fewer secondary prevention programs have been developed for nonresidential parents. However, one such program is the Dads for Life (DFL) program (Braver, Griffin, & Cookston, 2005), developed to help noncustodial fathers enjoy positive relationships with their children.

Few programs specifically target mild and moderate parental alienating behaviors and parent–child contact problems. This is clearly a gap in services to parents, given the importance of targeting alienating behaviors early in the process to ensure that parents receive the necessary support and to improve strained parent–child relationships at risk of severe alienation.

6.3.2 Programs for Children and Adolescents

With children, typically, education-based programs assist them to develop skills to cope with stress of the parental separation, identify and discuss their feelings, and develop strategies to cope with an array of feelings, including those related to parental conflict and loyalty binds.

One of the most widely researched and empirically validated programs for children is the Children of Divorce Intervention Program (CODIP) (Pedro-Carroll, 1985; Pedro-Carroll & Cowen, 1985). This is a school-based group support program designed to assist children with their adjustment and coping skills. Based on reports of their parents, teachers, and group leaders, children of various ages and cultural backgrounds who participated have demonstrated improvements in physical symptoms, in their social and emotional adjustment, including reductions in anxiety, improved self-esteem, and general improvement in their perceptions about the divorce (Pedro-Carroll, 1997, 2005; Pedro-Carroll & Alpert-Gillis, 1997; Pedro-Carroll, Alpert-Gillis, & Cowen, 1992; Pedro-Carroll, Sutton, & Wyman, 1999). These results have been replicated by others using the CODIP for children from kindergarten through Grade 6, with effects still present 2 years postintervention (Velez, Wolchik, & Sandler, 2011).

Other psychoeducational prevention programs for children have reported improvements in perceived competence and internal locus of control, and decreased depression (Garvin, Leber, & Kalter, 1991; Stolberg & Mahler, 1994). Using the Children's Support Group (CSG) program, Velez et al. (2011) report positive effects on overall adjustment, social skills, and self-esteem with children and younger adolescents, with these results sustained at the 1-year follow-up.

Velez et al. (2011) provide a brief summary of the evidence-based programs for children and adolescents that have empirically demonstrated effectiveness. They conclude that prevention programs for children in divorced families intended to teach coping skills and adaptive emotional expression can be effective in reducing postdivorce adjustment problems and delinquency, while enhancing social, academic, and emotional well-being, especially for youth who have more problems when they enter the program. They note that teaching parents about the impact of parental conflict, effective parenting and discipline, and methods to enhance the quality of the parent–child relationship will benefit children's postdivorce adjustment.

With prevention in mind, Andre and Baker (2009) developed a book and workbook for children called *I Don't Want to Choose: How Middle School Children Can Avoid Choosing One Parent Over the Other*. These are part of a 17-week activity-based school curriculum for groups of 10 to 20 middle school children whose parents are separated or divorced.[7] The purpose of the program is to teach children critical thinking skills, including how they can resist the pressure to choose between their parents. Currently, the program is being implemented in several schools in the United States with a plan to increase the number of schools and to assess outcomes.

Welcome Back, Pluto: Understanding, Preventing, and Overcoming Parental Alienation is a preventative educational DVD prepared by Drs. Richard Warshak and Mark Otis for children, teenagers, parents, and practitioners working with separated and divorced families.[8] Primarily, it has been an educational prevention tool to help repair a damaged relationship and prevent further deterioration. The developers also use the educational DVD to help repair a damaged relationship, and it can be used by therapists conducting reintegration therapy. The DVD "teaches children and parents how to preserve a good relationship in situations that threaten to undermine love and respect. The DVD identifies warning signs of trouble, why children become alienated, how parents can avoid common errors, how rejected parents feel, practical tips for parents, and tips to help kids avoid taking sides" [on jacket of DVD]. Richard Warshak stated:

> My hope is that the materials that my colleagues and I are
> developing will help families who are at risk for having children
> reject parents, and that it will help children and the parents avoid
> the problem. My hope is that this will be seen by families just at the
> moment when parents first separate, that attorneys will have their
> clients watching this program, that parents will sit down with their
> children to have them watch it, that if they go to court and the court
> senses that this is a family that might be on track for developing a
> problem with a child rejecting a parent that the court will advise
> the parents to get a hold of this program and have children see it,

---

[7] Further information is available at www.amyjbaker.com.
[8] This DVD is accompanied by a user's guide, costs $20 (U.S.), and is available from www.warshak.com.

and that therapists working with the family will be able to use these materials to educate the children and the parents on how to better handle the situation.[9]

6.4 Indicated or Tertiary Prevention

Tertiary prevention strategies are directed at high-risk populations such as families where there is severe alienation. "Tertiary prevention is sometimes compared to treatment because of the higher level of problems among the target group, and because more intensive services are needed" (Ripple, 2004, p. 28). This prevention effort would serve to prevent any further progression into the alienation cycle. Severe justified rejection cases, where it has been determined that it is in the child's best interest *to attempt* to repair the child's relationship with the abusive or neglectful parent, require a different approach. In some of these cases, individual therapy or rehabilitation for the offending parent and individual therapy for the child for posttraumatic stress disorder, with ongoing assessment to determine if and when parent–child reintegration is indicated, may be appropriate. Chapter 7 is devoted to interventions for the less severe levels of parent–child contact problems, and Chapter 9 addresses legal and clinical remedies for more severe alienation.

6.5 Summary

Primary prevention programs may be helpful before parents find themselves having relationship difficulties or are in the early stages of separation. These programs and approaches can help to build awareness of the difficulties associated with parent–child contact problems and can assist them in developing effective plans for protecting their children from the negative consequences of strained parent–child relationships. Educational programs for separating parents that are intended to explain the various methods of nonadversarial dispute resolution and the negative effects of parental conflict and litigation are valuable. While such programs may not prevent the most severe cases of alienation from occurring, they have positive value for many parents and children.

For secondary prevention programs to be effective, there is a clear need for early identification and screening of high-conflict cases, including recognition and responses to strained parent–child contact problems, irrespective of cause. Effective early identification of strained parent-contact problems will be assisted by the development of validated screening instruments. Early assessment by a court-appointed mental health professional with specialized

---

[9] Interview, April 15, 2010.

knowledge in alienation, abuse, and intimate partner violence is highly desirable. Parent–child contact problems, including alienation, generally become more difficult to address with the passage of time, as children and parents are more likely to become entrenched in their positions, further exacerbated by the litigation over parenting and financial matters.

Even though many of the experts interviewed spoke about the importance of early identification and prevention (before matters escalate to more severe alienation), there are very few examples of primary approaches to educate people about alienation (other than the public awareness campaigns by advocacy groups) and even less attention toward secondary approaches specific to families at risk for alienation, as most focus on high conflict more generally. The majority of approaches specific to alienation have been developed to respond to parent–child contact problems rather than proactively address strained parent–child relationships before it becomes a serious problem.

7

Interventions, Educational and Therapeutic

Various mental health interventions, approaches, and strategies are discussed in the literature for responding to cases when alienation or other parent–child contact problems are present (e.g., Baker & Andre, 2008; Baker & Fine, 2008; Campbell, 2005; Carter, Haave, & Vandersteen, 2009a, 2009b; Cartwright, 2006; Darnall, 2010; Everett, 2006; Fasser & Duchen, 2010; Fidler, 2011; Fidler, Bala, Birnbaum, & Kavassalis, 2008; Fidler, Chodos, Nelson, & Vanbetlehem, 2009; Freeman, Abel, Cowper-Smith, & Stein, 2004; Friedlander & Walters, 2010; Greenberg, Fick, Perlman, & Barrows, 2010; Johnston, Walters, & Friedlander, 2001; Lowenstein, 1998; Ludolph & Bow, 2010; Marcus & Lehmann, 2010; R. Marvin, interview, April 20, 2010; Mone, 2010; Otis & Warshak, 2009; Sullivan & Kelly, 2001; Vanbetlehem, Chodos, Geraldo, & Mingorance, 2010; Waldron & Joanis, 1996; Walters, Friedlander, & Harper, 2010; Warshak, 2010a, 2010b; Weitzman, 2004). Although there is variability among these intervention models, they all involve both psychoeducation and counseling or therapy, and are implemented at various stages of the separation process.[1]

Most approaches have been developed within the past 10 years. There are a few empirical evaluations to assess the potential effectiveness of these interventions. The current evidence, though, is mainly guided by clinical anecdotes, case studies, a few qualitative studies involving small samples, and within-group evaluations.

Deciding the most appropriate intervention for children and families will depend on the nature of the parent–child contact problem (alienation,

---

[1] The terms "therapy" and "counseling" and the corresponding terms "therapist" and "counselor" are used interchangeably.

justified rejection, elements of both—a mixed case, other dynamics such as enmeshment, age-appropriate reactions, degree of intentionality on the part of the favored parent to exclude the other parent) *and* the level or extent of the parent–child contact problem (mild, moderate, or severe; responsiveness to intervention and court orders on the part of the favored parent).

Generally, therapeutic and educational interventions tend to be suitable for *mild and some moderate cases,* which may include the relatively pure alienation, or justified rejection cases, or the mixed cases that have elements of both justified rejection and alienation. Included in these mixed or less severe cases may be those where the child, while resisting contact due to an affinity, age, gender, or divorce-related reaction or alignment, continues to have some degree of contact with the nonfavored parent. In the more severe cases, education or therapy alone, in the absence of a temporary interruption in contact with the favored parent, and possibly an accompanying change in custody, is unlikely to reverse the alienation. While improvements may be observed during therapy, these are unlikely to be sustained once the child returns to the orbit of the favored parent, and perhaps other influences, like the extended family. Further, therapy in the more severe cases, which may include some moderate cases, may be associated with the alienation becoming more entrenched.

Cases of severe justified rejection, where it *has* been determined that it is in the child's best interest *to attempt* to repair the child's relationship with an abusive or neglectful parent, are likely to require a different approach, including individual programs and therapy for the rejected parent. These cases of severe justified rejection may quite possibly also require individual therapy to treat the child, who may or may not have posttraumatic stress disorder. Ongoing assessment is necessary to determine if and when family counseling and parent–child reintegration are indicated.

7.1 The Role of the Court in Educational and Therapeutic Interventions

The role of the court is often critical to the effectiveness of educational or therapeutic interventions that are intended to respond to alienation. The need for ongoing court involvement to provide structure and support for these remedies is strongly recommended by both legal and mental health professionals as noted in the literature and during our interviews. Clinical psychologist, educator, and researcher Leslie Drozd stated:

> In any kind of system, including the family law system, there
> is going to be a pull to come up with a simple solution. But the
> reason that so many of these cases are going back through the
> court system and are revolving doors is because these family

systems are recalcitrant and won't change unless there is incredible accountability.... there has to be external motivation before there is going to be any kind of internal motivating.[2]

The mental health professional, who may take on a dual function of educator and therapist, can assist with the implementation of any court-ordered parenting time. However, a therapist should not be in a position of determining the amount of the parenting time, as this would interfere with the counselor's neutrality and likely compromise any progress. Unlike traditional therapy, in cases of alienation, court-directed counseling only has limited confidentiality (Johnston, 2005b; Sullivan & Kelly, 2001). Parents need to be accountable, and the court needs to monitor the family and enforce orders as required and in the best interests of the child. The therapist may report to the court, an arbitrator, or a parenting coordinator on the progress of the therapy and may, where appropriate, provide a status report including whether the therapy is progressing or not or clinical impressions and observations about the case. When there is more than one professional involved, open communication between them is necessary to maintain consistent child-focused goals and avoid alignments and all-or-nothing thinking (splitting), which may occur with less experienced professionals, but also more seasoned therapists working with high-conflict cases. We discuss the structural components of the mental health interventions, including the role of the court; problems associated with the therapist assuming multiple roles and the limits of confidentiality; legal responsibilities and remedies; and the need for accountability, court orders, and counseling contracts in Chapter 9.

In this chapter, we begin with a summary of the common features related to most therapeutic approaches or programs, followed by a discussion of seven specific interventions intended to respond to parent–child contact problems. Some of these have reported preliminary outcome research, which we summarize. We conclude with a discussion about the costs and accessibility of these interventions.

7.2 Principles and Guidelines

Referrals for mental health interventions may come from the court, lawyers, parents, other therapists, family physicians/pediatricians, schools, or custody evaluators. While counseling and parent education can have an important role in helping to remedy strained parent–child relationships and restore contact, the mental health professional must understand the ethical considerations and the dynamics of these cases and be prepared to address the varied causes of resistance or rejection. Further, mental health professionals

---

[2] Interview, June 23, 2010.

must be prepared to work with the court, which in most cases assumes an important role in the overall intervention.

A comprehensive child custody evaluation will assist the therapist dealing with strained parent–child relationships or contact problems. With or without the benefit of a prior comprehensive custody evaluation, a therapist needs to conduct a careful clinical assessment to identify the multiple causes of the strained relationships and family dynamics in order to develop and then implement the most appropriate treatment plan. This clinical assessment will inform the development of a child-focused treatment plan that protects children from the damaging effects of the family circumstances and various contributing factors to the parent–child contact problem. A fundamental principle is that every family is different, so there is no "one size fits all" treatment plan for cases where a child is alienated or resisting contact with a parent for other reasons.

7.3 Goals of Counseling

Articulating the counseling goals in a court order and therapy contract is imperative.[3] In alienation cases, this type of intervention is often referred to as reunification, reintegration, or reconciliation counseling or therapeutic access. However, it is important to recognize that while the goals may include the child's reunification with the rejected parent, the primary focus needs to be the whole child and his or her overall adjustment, including social, emotional, physical, and academic adjustment. The family functioning including effective parenting and family communication is also an important goal of any intervention. The child's relationship with one parent rarely is entirely independent from the child's relationship with the other parent. Consequently, a related goal toward improving the child's relationship with the rejected parent is to do the same with his or her relationship with the favored parent, which is likely to be compromised in some way, even if this is not immediately evident. Children generally benefit from the involvement of both parents in their lives, in the absence of serious abuse or neglect issues. Further, when the reasons for rejection are unjustified by an objective standard or do not accord with reality, it is not emotionally healthy for a child to learn to cope by avoiding problems or severing ties with a parent.

As we have noted previously, children living in these circumstances often, although not always, experience adjustment problems, not only those relating to a rejected parent, but also to the favored parent or with their peers. Some children, however, continue to do well in school and socially. This positive adjustment in some contexts does not necessarily mean the child is not also

---

[3] See Appendix A for a sample Family Treatment and Intervention Agreement. Chapter 9 includes a checklist of items recommended for inclusion in the court order for treatment (see Table 9.1).

struggling emotionally or behaviorally in other contexts. Behavior checklists and school report cards provide gross, or sometimes even inaccurate, measures of a child's overall adjustment or development. Overachievement in school or in an athletic or extracurricular context may be an effective coping mechanism in response to stress or anxiety (Conger, Stocker, & McGuire, 2009). The peer relations may be limited, or the socialization of these seemingly "well-adjusted children" may be restricted to the favored parent's perspectives. In situations involving genuine alienation, on the surface children may appear to be doing well, but on a deeper level these are inevitably emotionally troubled children, and it may only be a matter of time before adjustment difficulties surface.

It is likely that the favored parent will find the notion of treatment more palatable and, in turn, will be more likely to support the child's attendance at counseling, if the goals include improving the child's overall adjustment. Johnston (2005b) and others advise that additional goals of treatment should be identified, in addition to repairing the child's relationship with the rejected parent and implementing court-ordered parenting time. These goals may include:

a) protecting and removing the child from parental conflict;
b) fostering the child's healthy relationship with *both* parents;
c) restoring the parents' adequate functioning and appropriate roles;
d) correcting the various cognitive distortions, polarization, and splitting present in parents and child;
e) augmenting the child's coping skills and improving appropriate expressions of the child's affect;
f) replacing inaccuracies and distortions with more realistic perceptions that reflect the child's actual experience with both parents; and
g) improving the child's peer relationships.

Addressing the child's poor self-esteem and loss of identity, teaching right from wrong, and preventing relapse are additional goals identified in the literature (Baker, 2006; Waldron & Joanis, 1996; Walters & Friedlander, 2010; Warshak 2010b).

In other words, treatment involves assisting children to differentiate themselves from others, become autonomous, and, in effect, reach their own conclusions about both parents and their relationships with relatives. Teaching children critical thinking skills has been identified as an essential component of all educational and therapeutic interventions. Sometimes, with explanation and education, an older child may come to understand how and even why the alienation occurred and how they came to believe what they did (Rand & Warshak, 2008; Warshak, 2006).

7.4 Treatment Modalities, Approaches, and Strategies

Therapeutic and educational interventions in cases of parent–child contact problems tend to be eclectic and involve varying degrees of different therapies, such as structural (Minuchin, 1974) and strategic family therapy (Haley & Hoffman, 1994), brief solution-focused therapy (Berg, 1994; de Shazer, 1988), and narrative therapy (White & Epston, 1990). In addition, typically, elements of a cognitive-behavioral approach are used. Cognitive behavior therapy (CBT) involves a systematic examination of how thinking impacts on feelings and actions. By changing the way that parents and children think, their feelings and responses can be changed, and ultimately their functioning improved (Dobson & Dozois, 2001). CBT may be used with children, adolescents, and adults (Kendall, 2005) and has been shown to improve many different problems, such as anxiety, depression, panic attacks, phobias, posttraumatic stress disorder, and mood and eating disorders (Butler, Chapman, Forman, & Beck, 2006). CBT is often used as a general term that may involve specific techniques such as cognitive restructuring, in vivo exposure therapy, imaginal exposure therapy, and systematic desensitization, which have been shown to have probable effectiveness in the treatment of anxiety disorders (e.g., panic disorder, social anxiety, school phobia, etc.) (Silverman, Pina, & Viswesvaran, 2008), and are likely to be useful with some parent–child contact problems.

A family systems approach is needed for therapy in alienation cases.[4] This involves the participation of the entire family in various combinations, sometimes including other relatives such as stepparents, stepsiblings, and grandparents (Cartwright, 2006; Everett, 2006; Friedlander & Walters, 2010; Gardner, 1998a, 1998b, 2001b; Johnston, 2005b; Johnston et al., 2001; Lee & Olesen, 2001; Lowenstein, 1998; Sullivan & Kelly, 2001; Walters & Friedlander, 2010). Within this approach, the therapist works with the entire family in various combinations; family members are seen individually, the child with each parent, the parents together, siblings in various combinations, and the entire family as the therapist deems appropriate.

The intervention plan in parent–child contact cases usually proceeds gradually in a stepwise process that typically takes at least 6 months and can take as long 2 years to successfully complete. Sessions may be once a week or more frequent, especially in the early stage of the counseling. Although every situation is different, typically the process begins with several sessions with each parent alone and sometimes together. While continuing with the rejected parent individually, the child is seen with the favored parent to introduce the process, and then the child is seen individually for a number of sessions. The child and favored parent are seen together as needed. Depending on the nature and intensity of the child's reaction and alienation, individual sessions may help the child prepare for eventual sessions with a rejected parent. Next, a child's contact with a rejected parent may be limited, indirect contact by way of letters or photographs and gradually include more direct contact by way of telephone or observations from behind a one-way mirror. In some cases, this

---

[4] This requires training and experience in systemic therapies, high conflict, separation/divorce, alienation, child custody–disputing families, and personality disorders.

gradual approach is not necessary, and once the individual contacts have been made, the child and rejected parent can be seen together quite quickly. Next, if therapy is progressing, sessions with the child and rejected parent continue, followed by gradually increasing contacts outside the therapy that are then followed up on in subsequent therapy sessions. In some cases, the child may be having supervised contact outside of the sessions along with the weekly therapy. Individual work continues with the rejected parent and the favored parent as the reintegration of the child with the rejected parent is occurring. In some cases, work can be done with the parents jointly to address their communication and coparenting. Every family is different; the composition of who attends, the sequence, and the timing of sessions may vary considerably.

The role of the court is to encourage and monitor this gradual progression. For example, the court order may require that the child attend three individual sessions, followed by three months of therapeutic access (sessions with the rejected parent and with the favored parent's participation as directed by the therapist). The therapist's office can be used as a transitional site where the therapist meets with family members (including the favored parent), both before and after parent–child contact that occurs outside the therapist's office. The ultimate goal is for the detailed, court-ordered parenting time to occur without the need for the therapist's involvement. Sessions before and after parent–child contacts, for example, on the Monday morning after a weekend contact, can monitor and assess the family's progress and provide expedient intervention, dealing with problems as they arise.

If risk of abuse has been ruled out, it is important that the therapist's involvement with contacts to foster reconciliation of a child with a rejected parent *not* be referred to as "supervised visitation." These contacts should not take place at a supervised visitation center, as this is likely to reinforce the irrational fears of the child or favored parent (Johnston, 2005a). During the interviews for this book, several judges noted that in some cases supervised contact may initially be indicated in an effort to maintain the child's contact with the parent, while allowing time to investigate the allegations. However, continuing with the supervised parenting time can exacerbate the parent–child contact problem, if it goes on too long and there is no objective basis upon which to continue the supervision.

Several practitioners have drawn from *parent–child interactive therapy* (PCIT)[5] (Herschell & McNeil, 2005; Timmer, Urquiza, Zebell, & McGrath, 2005) in the development of programs for alienated children. PCIT is a program for parents who have been physically abusive with their children. Research has found that these abusive parents do not say more negative than positive comments to their children, but they make few positive comments.

---

[5] PCIT is provided by many mental health treatment agencies in 27 states in the United States, Hong Kong, and Australia. Numerous studies have demonstrated positive outcomes in reducing child behavior problems. More information may be obtained from www.pcit.tv.

Using in vivo coaching,[6] the program teaches parents better communication skills, including making more positive comments to their children.

When conducting child custody evaluations with high-conflict families with children up to 7 years old, where allegations of alienation may be present, psychologist Robert Marvin and his colleagues use separation-reunion procedures[7] and adaptations of other attachment procedures[8] with both parents and the child to assess attachment in parent–child relationships. In some cases, after the evaluation, the parents view the recording with the evaluators, who provide feedback and education about the difficulties the child experiences with the separations and transitions. Marvin notes the potential benefit to the parents' increased understanding when they can observe and be educated about the child's behavior during transitions and interacting with the other parent. He explains:

> What the child is saying is not really, 'I don't want to go to daddy's
> house or I don't want to go to mommy's house'; they are saying
> 'I hate this separation.' For older children, I think it is partly,
> 'I hate this separation and it is partly, 'I hate being caught in the
> middle here.' Using the recording with parent education hopefully
> helps to deescalate some of this conflict and some of the mistaken
> impressions about how the child feels about being with the other
> parent.[9]

In their text on conducting the methodology for conducting child custody assessments, Birnbaum, Fidler, and Kavassalis (2008), write:

> It is important to note that attachment is but one element of the
> parent–child relationship, and stands separate from other important
> components, such as providing for instrumental needs, discipline
> and teaching. In addition, the parent's own attachment has been
> shown to be highly predictive of child adjustment, behavior and
> attachment (Hesse, 1999; van IJzendoorn, 1995). In other words,

---

[6] This involves the therapist coaching the parent in real time during his or her interactions with the child.

[7] See for example, the Strange Situation (SS), originally developed by Mary Ainsworth (Ainsworth, Blehar, Waters, & Wall, 1978; Marvin, Cooper, Hoffman, & Powell, 2000).

[8] See for example, the Adult Attachment Interview (AAI), a semistructured interview process developed by George, Kaplan, & Main (1985) to assess attachment. The parents provide reports of their own childhood experiences of separation, rejection, loss, and past and current attachment experiences. Research has identified four types of adult attachments—a) secure and the insecure; b) dismissing; c) preoccupied; and d) unresolved (Main & Goldwyn, 1998)—and the Working Model of the Child Interview (WMCI) (Zeanah & Benoit, 1994).

[9] Interview, April 20, 2010.

inquiries into how the parent perceives his or her childhood and early relationships, and not only parent–child observations, are central to understanding the quality of the parent–child relationship (Schmidt, Cuttress, Lang, Lewandowski & Rawana, 2007). Note that both the AAI and the SS are research tools, and as such should not be used for clinical work without considerable training. Notwithstanding this caveat, incorporating questions from these tools into the child custody assessment protocols is likely to provide an abundance of relevant information related to child development and parent–child relationships that can then be considered with all of the other information obtained during the assessment (p. 115).

7.5 Summary of Specific Interventions, Protocols, or Approaches

7.5.1 Cognitive-Behavior Desensitization Using the One-Way Mirror

Weitzman (2004) describes a protocol used with anxiety disorders, which uses observation through a one-way mirror as a tool to reintroduce children to an alienated or estranged parent, thereby allowing the child to initially view the parent without being seen. "The one-way mirror provides a physical and psychological barrier from direct contact with a parent whom the child fears and allows the clinician to more easily control the pace of the reunification process." (p. 27). Viewing the estranged parent from behind the one-way mirror can reduce the child's anxiety, permitting the reunification process to proceed gradually. The parent and child can talk to one another through the speaker system. Using the mirror and audio equipment can also be fun for many children, thereby assisting with the process of reunification. The child can simply observe the parent with the therapist, and when ready the child can ask the parent questions. After informed consent and confidentiality are addressed, the protocol involves the following stages:

1) Therapist has initial meeting with parents;
2) therapist meeting with the child;
3) orienting the child to the viewing room;
4) commencing the use of the one-way mirror with child observing estranged parent;
5) interviewing the estranged parent in the child's presence; and
6) repeating interviews with estranged family members, if required initially from behind the mirror.

Once the parent–child relationship is reestablished, the family can move to having contacts together in public places or to more traditional family therapy.

7.5.2 Model for Reconnection (Toronto)

This model was developed at Families in Transition (FIT, Family Service Association [FSA], Toronto) and is one of several services offered by this nonprofit social agency for separated and divorced families (Freeman, 2008; Freeman, Abel, Cowper-Smith, and Stein, 2004).[10] Support from the United Way enables FSA to offer subsidies for all FIT programs.

This model identifies three types of requests for reconnection, each involving a different approach to the intervention:

1) establishing a connection where the child has no prior relationship with a parent (e.g., parents cohabited but separated before birth of child), in which case the approach provides an introduction and opportunity to establish a relationship;
2) reconnection where there has been an interruption in parent–child contact ranging from 3 months to many years, and the child has some memory of the estranged parent; and
3) when the child cannot remember the absent parent, the reintroduction model includes six stages:

    i. the reconnection assessment process (includes safety and risk assessment) and the development of a child-centered timeline;
    ii. preparatory work with the child and both parents;
    iii. planning the first face-to-face meeting;
    iv. facilitating early child–parent meetings;
    v. revising the parenting plan; and
    vi. supporting the child–absent parent relationship.

The model places importance on maintaining a child-centered focus and timeline that is determined primarily by the child's readiness. Careful attention through early and ongoing assessment is paid to safety and risk factors that may involve implementing an appropriate safety plan. Professional consultation and teamwork are identified as key features of the model.

In an interview with Rhonda Freeman, executive director of Families in Transition, she reported that there is currently no quantitative outcome data regarding the program because they are still building the model and making modifications as needed.[11] She noted that some of the key lessons learned so far include:

1) working with both parents is critical;
2) working with the residential parent is especially important for the success of the intervention;

---

[10] FIT also provides individual counseling and psychoeducational groups for both parents and children
[11] Interview, May 25, 2010.

3) the involvement of the court is sometimes helpful to encourage the residential parent to support the child's relationship with the other parent;
4) it is important for the therapist to delay seeing the child until both parents are engaged with the intervention; and
5) there are no quick fixes to this work.

She further stated that success is not necessarily defined by face-to-face contact between the child and the rejected parent being achieved and that it is expected to take time before this contact occurs.

7.5.3 Family Restructuring Therapy (Edmonton)

This future-oriented and action-focused intervention is practiced by a team of psychologists in Edmonton and has been presented at workshops and a preconference institute at the AFCC annual conference (Carter, Haave, & Vandersteen, 2006b, 2009a, 2009b; Carter, Vandersteen, Haave, Trussler, & Bateman, 2008).[12] It is described as an "active, directive process that assists families in conflict to modify maladaptive interactions."

In addition to voluntary interventions, the Alberta Court of Queen's Bench (superior trial court) may invoke its Family Law Practice Note 7 (Trussler, 2008) and may order the team, as independent parenting experts, to provide the intervention. The court may direct that neither parent make an application to the court during the intervention process. The therapy is not confidential, and the team may communicate directly or indirectly with the court. The parties do not receive a copy of any letters or reports to the court unless ordered by the court.

The therapy involves at least three professionals working with the family: one for each parent and one for the child or children. There may be a case manager or parenting coordinator as well. The parents may at some point be seen together, if appropriate and useful, but this does not happen in every case. The scope of the therapeutic mandate is identified, and a retainer agreement and consent forms are completed. Individual meetings occur with each parent initially, followed by the development of a case plan. The therapy involves different team members meeting with different family members in various combinations, addressing the issues, including the gradual reestablishment of the child's relationship with the rejected parent. The team meets regularly to share information. This model includes both therapy and assisting the parents to develop a parenting plan through a directive meditative process. There is no public funding, and parents are responsible for paying the fees in full by way of a retainer to the team.

Outcome research on the Edmonton program has not been conducted. Anecdotally, Carter and his colleagues have reported that "the intervention

---

[12] Stephen Carter has also presented this approach at other legal and National Judicial Institute trainings. See also Carter (2011).

is highly effective in teaching parents to co-parent, in re-uniting parents with 'alienated' children, and in developing concrete, practical parenting plans" (Carter et al., 2006a, p. 574) and judges seem satisfied with the outcomes (Trussler, 2008). Based on clinical impressions, Carter estimates that they have achieved positive outcomes with approximately one third of the cases, partial success with another third, and lack of any progress with one third (interview, June 16, 2010; Carter et al., 2006a).

7.5.4 The Multi-Modal Family Intervention (MMFI) (Bay Area of California)[13]

MMFI was initially developed by Johnston et al. (2001) and later refined on the basis of a study of clinical experience of 55 cases by Friedlander and Walters (2010). The children ranged from 2.5 to 18 years of age. Younger children were identified as being at risk for alienation, while a more definite reluctance or refusal for contact with a parent was generally the reason for intervention for children at 5 or 6 years of age and older.

In this program, either both parents consent and execute a treatment contract, or the court provides an order for the therapy. The MMFI requires the active involvement of both parents and the children. Concurrent work is done with the child and each parent individually as well in dyads or triads. A thorough assessment is conducted to understand the multiple factors that have contributed to the child's reluctance or refusal to spend time with a parent. A range of specific techniques are used including individual psychotherapy, family therapy, case management, and education and coaching (Walters & Friedlander, 2010). All of these are aimed at increasing the

---

[13] Similar approaches have been developed by others. For example, Family Solutions in Toronto, of which Dr. Fidler is a founding member, is a team of experienced senior psychologists, social workers, and a psychiatrist committed to providing professional services to families in conflict. Members of the team have written and presented widely at conferences and other educational trainings for judges, lawyers, and mental health professionals (e.g., Fidler, 2011; Fidler et al., 2008, 2009; Fidler & Vanbetlehem, 2011; Vanbetlehem et al., 2010). See www.familysolutionstoronto.ca for further information.

Another example in Sonoma County, California, is offered by Transitioning Families (Bailey, n.d., www.transitioningfamilies.com). This team of psychologists and other professionals provides family and individual counseling, various reunification programs and family workshops, coparenting counseling, and supervised visitation services. Their programs are experiential and are based on a strong psychodynamic background. They include the use of the outdoors, animal- and equine-assisted therapy, growth, and learning culinary experiences. The families they serve have suffered the abduction of a child, parental alienation, trauma, and intensely conflicted child/parent relationship problems.

understanding of parents and children, and modifying feelings, beliefs, and behaviors. The broader treatment goals include understanding and addressing the impact of the separation and divorce on the child, teaching the child coping strategies; changing the child's distorted, "good/bad" views and polarized feelings toward both parents into more realistic ones; and restoring appropriate coparental and parent–child roles in the family. Treatment contracts are used, and case management is provided by a judge, a parenting coordinator, or the child's lawyer, either independently or as an integral part of the MMFI.

Friedlander and Walters (2010) report that 85% of their treated families were "hybrid cases," including "some with significant components of [realistic]estrangement and/or enmeshment" (p. 109). A noteworthy minority of 15% were found to be "uncomplicated" or "pure" cases of alienation. Based on feedback from the families and clinical judgment of the service provider, the researchers concluded that "a significant majority of outcomes were positive as evidenced by resumption of a relationship consistent with the capacities of the parent and child and adjusted time-share reflecting that change" (p. 109). In addition, and irrespective of the amount of time the child spent with the rejected parent, they concluded that the intervention helped to prevent significant alienation from developing in a significant number of cases. Negative outcomes, including therapy ending or a decrease in parenting time or no time with the rejected parent, occurred in only a few cases. They caution that cases of justified rejection or severe alienation may not be appropriate for the MMFI as these cases may require more extreme measures. For example, in cases of severe alienation a change in custody to the rejected parent or removal of the children from the family and placement in a residential treatment program, foster care, or boarding school may be required (Friedlander & Walters, 2010). We discuss the possible use of transitional residential programs for severe cases in Chapter 9.

In their addendum to Friedlander and Walters (2010), discussed previously, Johnston and Goldman (2010) report on their 15- to 20-year follow-up of the outcomes of the confidential family counseling[14] approached from two sources. The first source was 37 young adults between the ages of 20 and 30 years, from 22 families. All had received 20 to 30 hours of the MMFI at the time of the custody dispute when they were between the ages of 4 and 14 years (also see Johnston, Roseby, & Kuehnle, 2009). The second source included treatment records of 42 children from 39 litigating families who were resisting a parent during their counseling for an average of nearly 10 years. These children were between 2 and 17 years old when first seen and between 9 and 29 years when last seen in therapy. Referrals were made specifically to address two groups: where the child resisted or refused contact with a parent and where

---

[14] Reporting to the court by the counselor was limited to whether or not the family attended the counseling and was cooperative, and the status of the treatment in terms of stage of completion.

the referral was for other more general reasons relating to the parental conflict. These two referral groups were not studied separately. Data included the young adults' retrospective reports from clinical interviews and ratings of the clinical files, both conducted by the first author, who was also the children's therapist years prior.[15] In addition, the young adults completed standardized measures of their emotional functioning, relationships, and the quality of the relationships and feelings toward their parents over their childhood and adolescent years. Currently, these researchers are obtaining further data on the short- and long-term outcomes of MMFI.

Johnston and Goldman (2010) note that while the goals of their interventions include parent–child reintegration, the objectives go beyond that and include better overall child adjustment, the correction of distorted and polarized thinking, and improved parenting and coparenting functioning. Noting the descriptive nature of the studies and small samples, they provide preliminary and speculative hypotheses with respect to outcomes and the adult children's attitudes and feelings about their experiences in counseling and the judicial system. The range of resistance and rejection and outcomes varied depending on many factors, including the family dynamics and parental behaviors, the causes of the resistance or rejection, the age of onset, and the chronicity of the family dysfunction. In summary, they observed that retrospectively the young adults had strong negative views and feelings when they were forced by the court to participate repeatedly with different therapists for reunification therapy, while those who had a single supportive long-term therapist found the experience beneficial.

In addition, 19% of the young adults from families having earlier, chronic family dysfunction and realistic concerns on the part of the young child continued to express strong negative feelings toward one parent and to refuse all contact during their young adult years. Based on these preliminary data, the researchers concluded that highly successful outcomes are achievable with a minority of families and are more likely when the resistance manifests during adolescence as a coping mechanism in response to parental conflict compared with when the difficulties with contact began in earlier childhood. Johnston and Goldman (2010) hypothesize that in families where rejected parents have persistent parenting limitations within a chronically conflicted family, positive outcomes may occur when children are helped to achieve a strategic or emotionally safe distance from the more difficult or demanding parent, where contact is brief, less frequent, and limited to structured and mutually enjoyable activities. Most poor outcomes are likely to involve a rejected parent with serious parenting deficiencies. They further propose that when an evaluation indicates that the alienating parent is mentally ill or seriously character disordered and is avoiding, refusing, or sabotaging therapy or court orders, a change in custody to the better functioning, rejected parent or a third party

---

[15] This is a common methodology used in conducting qualitative research (see, for example, Friedlander & Walters, 2010, and Warshak, 2010b).

is warranted. Johnston and Goldman conclude that the findings of their follow-up studies support the need for early intervention and preventive measures, before litigation escalates and child's resistance become entrenched.

7.5.5 Baker and Fine (2008)

In an article written primarily for rejected parents, "Beyond the High Road: Responding to 17 Parental Alienation Strategies Without Compromising Your Morals or Harming Your Child," Baker and Fine (2008) set out 17 alienating behaviors/strategies identified in their research and paired each of these with specific advice for what to say or do with the alienating parent or child.[16] Examples of parental alienating behaviors or strategies include bad-mouthing, limiting contact, withdrawing love, creating the impression that the rejected parent is dangerous, asking the child to spy on or keep secrets from the rejected parent, or referring to the rejected parent by his or her first name. Strategies to respond to these include becoming educated about parental alienation, obtaining a "reality check," extending a hand to the alienating parent, obtaining mental health and legal advice, picking your battles, to not take it personally, having empathy for your child, being the best parent you can be, and not taking the bait. Baker and Fine suggest using the article in combination with counseling with the rejected parent. This could be done in individual sessions with the rejected parent in the context of the larger family therapy or when it is not possible to engage the child or favored parent. In those cases where the favored parent or children are participating in therapy, the strategies contained in the article may assist rejected parents who oftentimes are unaware of some of their own behaviors that may be exacerbating the problem. Rejected parents are encouraged to take the "high road"—not confront the favored parent in front of the children and not say anything that could be construed as critical about that parent to the child.

7.5.6 New Ways for Families (California)

A court-based early intervention program called New Ways for Families has been developed by Bill Eddy, a lawyer and social worker at the High Conflict Institute (2009, 2010) in Southern California. This is a short-term and highly structured cognitive-behavioral counseling program designed to address high-conflict court cases including those involving allegations of alienation or abuse as early as possible.[17] New Ways also relies on research and principles drawn from parent–child interaction therapy (PCIT) (Herscell & McNeill, 2005; Timmer et al., 2005), child-inclusive mediation (McIntosh & Long, 2006; McIntosh, Wells,

---

[16] This is an excellent article not only for the rejected parent, but also for mental health professionals and lawyers to assist them in their work with parents.

[17] For further information and materials, visit www.highconflictinstitute.com or contact newways@highconflictinstitute.com.

Smyth, & Long, 2008), dialectical behavior therapy (DBT) (Dimeff & Koerner, 2007; Linehan, 1993) and cognitive behavioral therapy (CBT).

The program is currently being piloted in family courts in Calgary and Medicine Hat in Canada (each with 3-year funding of $500,000 by Alberta's Safe Communities Initiative), and in San Diego and Salt Lake City in the United States (with fees paid solely by parents). It includes a research component in all four cities. As of July 2011, approximately 30 families had completed the program in San Diego, where it began in 2009. Eddy has given training presentations in 10 of the United States and three Canadian provinces (British Columbia, Alberta, and Ontario). There are plans to implement court-affiliated New Ways programs in several other cities in the United States, and consideration is being given to have these programs at other sites in Canada.

Eddy[18] explains that many parents who begin the court process are not ready to resolve their disputes in a child-focused manner. Consequently, New Ways is intended to be implemented before the court makes final decisions. New Ways can be ordered by the judge at court hearing (preferably the first one) or consented to by the parties. The order or consent does not assign blame to either parent. Interim orders for parenting arrangements, including supervised parent–child contact, may be made by the judge in the interim while the family is participating in the program. Each parent participates in an identical counseling structure with the same counselor; parents select a counselor from a roster of trained professionals. If the parents cannot agree on a counselor, the judge, who also has had a training session, selects the parent–child counselor from the roster. The parents pay privately for the counseling based on a sliding scale, although the scale does not go to zero. Costs for the counseling may be reallocated by the court at a later time.

New Ways is based on the working assumption that high-conflict families have three common problems: "all-or-none" thinking, unmanaged emotions, and extreme behaviors. The goal is to assist parents early on with communication and conflict resolution skill development that hopefully will enable them to make better use of services to develop their postseparation parenting plans and arrangements. The counseling includes five specific goals to:

1) reduce the likelihood of the families becoming high-conflict families;
2) help parents teach their children resilience;
3) strengthen both parents' ability to make parenting decisions;
4) assist professionals and the courts in assessing each parent's potential; and
5) give parents a chance to change in court cases of abuse or alienation (Eddy, 2009, p. 6).

The program involves four steps. Step 1 is called "Getting Started" and involves the referral and intake. Step 2 is comprised of 6 weeks of individual

---

[18] Interview, August 15, 2010.

and *confidential* parent counseling[19]. Step 3 includes a further 6 weeks of *non-*confidential, parent–child counseling. Each parent has his or her own counselor whom he or she has selected from the roster of trained professionals. Using a parent workbook, the individual parent counseling sessions focus on learning and strengthening three key skills: flexible thinking, managed emotions, and moderate behavior. During the parent–child counseling, each parent meets with the child three times and teaches the child the same three skills that the parent learned during the individual parent sessions, also relying on a workbook to guide them through the process. The same counselor is used for the mother/child sessions and for the father/child sessions. The parent–child counselor is permitted to report to the court on the nature and extent of the progress in therapy. Neither the individual parent counseling nor the parent–child counseling requires the parents to have contact with each other at any stage of the process, thereby addressing any concerns relating to abuse and safety. Step 4 involves family or court decision making. The expectation is that after the counseling, some families will be able to resolve their parenting arrangements on their own or through some form of alternative dispute resolution. If not, the parents may return to court, and the parent–child counselor will provide a report to the court on the parent–child sessions.

7.5.7 Overcoming Barriers Family Camp (New England)

Overcoming Barriers Family Camp (OBFC) is an innovative 5-day family camp designed to treat separating and divorced families where a child is resisting contact or totally rejecting a parent. The program includes an evaluation and training component. The camp has been operating in Vermont and combines psychoeducation and therapeutic interventions in a safe, "fun" environment. Both parents must participate with the children and often stepparents participate as well (Sullivan, Ward, & Deutsch, 2010). An important tenet of this program is working with the entire family and not separating, even temporarily, the child from either parent. A court order is required for participation. The camp may be suitable for families with varying degrees of parent–child contact problems resulting from multiple factors, including hybrid cases. However, it is likely that the intervention is not suitable for the severest and most entrenched of alienation cases.

The first OBFC was held in 2008, and it has run for 3 consecutive years.[20] The OBFC is held at an existing family summer camp where experienced camp

---

[19] In this step involving the parent counseling, reporting to the court is limited to whether or not the parents attended. No further disclosure is made by the therapist.

[20] In 2012, a nonprofit organization, Overcoming Barriers, which provides psychoeducational programming for high-conflict families, was established in California. Two of these programs are available in Massachusetts; one is a 12-session (once per week) psychoeducational group, and the other is a

counselors and directors offer an array of recreational activities (yoga, hikes to the creek, outdoor and indoor games, etc.), arts and crafts, and typical family camp offerings (campfire, sing-alongs, music, a talent show, etc.). Family members also spend part of each day involved in psychoeducation and intensive therapy provided by experienced therapists.

The camp experience allows family members to informally interact with each other in a relatively informal setting, as well as to meet with others experiencing similar situations and observe their interactions.

To date, several experienced clinical psychologists have provided the following interventions:

a) a daily 3-hour psychoeducational group for parents (separate groups for the favored and rejected parents) and children;
b) coparenting therapy for both parents together to address parental conflicts and parenting plan disputes; and
c) interventions designed to reconnect rejected parents and their child(ren) during the camp activities in the afternoons and evenings. These interventions include observing the child, engaging in an activity with the child, and family meetings with one or both parents and the child.

Children bunk with a counselor in cabins with other children their age and are separated at night and during parts of the day from their parents. The 5-day camp experience provides many opportunities to develop the children's age-appropriate autonomy and to begin to repair and realign relationships, both with the rejected and favored parent. While the children are encouraged, they are not forced to engage in activities with a rejected parent. However, these reluctant children have an opportunity to see that parent from a distance throughout the day and evening activities and programs. They observe other children engaging with their own parents as well as with that child's parents. They hear other children talking about those experiences, both with their parents and with other children's parents. Experiences and incidents arise throughout the day and evening, providing many opportunities to process feelings, ideas, and behaviors, and in effect, build bridges toward repaired relationships all in nature with leisure, music, and fun activities interspersed.

In the last 2 years of the program, an aftercare component has been included. Each family leaves the camp with a customized aftercare plan to help support the implementation or further development of any parenting plans discussed between parents during their time at OBFC. The clinical team makes recommendations for specific professionals in the parents' home communities

---

weekend group program for two families. In addition, there is a 5-day High Conflict Divorce Camp, for six families at a time, near San Francisco, CA. This family camp ran for the first time in July, 2012, and is modeled after the camp that ran in Vermont and is discussed here. See www.overcomingbarriers.org for more information.

who would be suitable for providing additional support. Parents sign releases of information to allow clinical insights gleaned during the program to be shared with other professionals working with the family in aftercare, and the courts if necessary.

As of 2010, a total of 16 families completed the camp intervention; 5 in each of the first 2 years and 6 in the third year, 2010. The evaluation, conducted by trainees, observers, or the psychologists who subsequently reported to the court, is limited to exit interviews and a 6-month follow-up for the first 5 families.

Sullivan et al. (2010) report preliminary positive parent satisfaction at the exit interview. For the 2008 participants, when asked in exit interviews to rate their experience from 1 to 5, 5 out of 11 adults rated it a 5 (very good), and 6 out of 11 rated it a 4 (good). In other words, all of the adult participants considered the camp a good or very good experience. The 2009 adult participants' assessment of the camp during the exit interview was more positive than that of the first year: 9 of 10 rated it a 5 (very good) and 1 rated it a 4 (good). Verbal feedback from parents has also been encouraging. Many 2008 participants asked for a longer camp, while comments from the 2009 group included compliments on the sense of safety provided by the camp environment. Feedback from the children in 2008 focused on what their parents should do to better parent and coparent. One child said the parents should come on their own without the children, and after the parents learn some things, then the children can come! One child said, "Give your parent a chance." The children said they benefit from the group experience with other children and knowing that they were not alone.

Follow-up contact with participants of the 2008 program indicated mixed results. Some families experienced improvements, such as the development of a joint parenting time and coparenting plan, and children beginning to have contact with a previously rejected parent on alternate weekends. Others, though, showed less improvement, including the continued rejection of parents by children and continued litigation. One month follow-up after the 2009 session, aimed at determining whether the family had connected with the recommended professional services, indicated that three of the five families sought the assistance of a parenting coordinator. However, the 6-month follow-up indicated the need for more vigilant follow-up of the proposed aftercare plans given to the parents when they left the camp. Three of the five families, some of whom had made observable positive gains at camp and at the 1-month follow-up, were again embroiled in litigation. In one family, the father died due to illness without having the opportunity to make contact with his children.

The cost of the camp in the first 2 years was $7,500 for a family of four, plus travel expenses to get to the camp. In 2010, the cost increased to $8,000. In addition to this cost, which includes all food, lodging, and camp activities, each child and each parent receives at least 15 hours of group therapy, which amounts to a total of 45 hours of therapy for a family of three, more if more than one child attends the camp. Additional therapy is provided throughout the day, including coparenting, individual, parent–child, and family sessions. The service providers note that the cost charged to families does not, in fact, cover the actual costs, and to date the camp intervention has been subsidized by the Common Ground Center, which is the nonprofit organization where the camp occurred, as well as by donations to cover counselors' salaries and overhead costs to run the camp. To date, the clinical team has been working pro bono. Further and significant costs that are not remunerated in any way include extensive professional hours required for managing the intake process and determining which families are suitable and not suitable for the camp intervention.

While this program may be an option that may assist some families, OBFC faces significant challenges. Based on the preliminary results, it is likely that this intervention may not be appropriate for the severest of cases and is likely to have more success with the milder or moderate parent–child contact problem cases. These may include those where the problem is primarily due to alienation, justified rejection, or a combination of both. While important bridges may be built and connections made during the program, what happens after the family leaves the camp and resumes their usual patterns is critical. Establishing available and appropriate aftercare for numerous families is imperative and may pose unique challenges, including further litigation. Limitations include the camp occurring only once a year and requiring a complex and time-consuming referral process that requires consideration of out-of-jurisdiction referrals and court orders. Additional challenges include the program becoming financially viable and making it available in more local jurisdictions.

To address fiscal and availability challenges and with the primary objective of prevention, the program's founding psychologists, Ward, Deutsch, and Sullivan, and camp director Carole Blane developed an intensive weekend group workshop called, "Forging Families' Futures." This weekend workshop is for the entire family, including new partners and stepsiblings, where a child (between 9 and 18 years of age) is resisting or refusing contact with one parent. The workshop includes two families and provides a program and structure similar to that of the camp that is adapted to 3 days. In addition to group activities during the day and evening, there are three psychoeducational groups that meet daily during the mornings: one for the children who are about the same age, one for the favored parents, and one for the rejected parents. Children sleep with their peers and a team member. To date, three weekends have been provided with more in the planning stages. Outcome data are not available (Ward, Deutsch, & Sullivan, 2010).

7.5.8 Family Bridges: A Workshop for Troubled and Alienated Parent–Child Relationships

In severe cases, where a child refuses or strongly resists contact with a parent, a program such as "Family Bridges: A Workshop for Troubled and Alienated

Parent–Child Relationships" (Family Bridges) may assist the family to transition after the court has ordered a change in custody to the rejected parent (Rand & Warshak, 2008; Warshak, 2010a).[21] This experiential and educational program is one option to consider *after* a court determines that an interim or permanent change in custody to the rejected parent is in the child's best interest. Family Bridges (FB) is intended to address alienation of a child, and is not suitable for:

> children whose rejection is reasonable and warranted by the history of the child's relationship with the rejected parent, such as those harmed by a parent's substance abuse or violent behavior; families in which the court finds that a child's relationship with a rejected parent is severely damaged but that overall it is in the child's best interests to remain with the favored parent; children whose alienation is not likely to become severe; and families in which children who reject a parent spend most of their time away from that parent, or who will be with the rejected parent only for a short period of time before returning to the home of the favored parent. (e.g., school vacation periods) (Otis & Warshak, 2010, pp. 2–3).

Family Bridges was first developed in the early 1990s by American psychologist Dr. Randy Rand for child abduction cases, and then later modified for cases of severe alienation by Drs. Richard Warshak and Deirdre Rand. The program provides a 4-consecutive-day workshop for one family at a time, facilitated by two professionals who work with the child(ren) and the rejected parent.[22] A program can also later be made available for the favored parent, should he or she agree to participate in a subsequent workshop or aftercare treatment, though this has not happened often.

Like other interventions that have been discussed, the goals of Family Bridges go beyond improving the child's relationship with the rejected parent. They include:

a) facilitating, repairing, and strengthening the child's ability to maintain healthy relationships with the parents, preferably with both of the parents;
b) improving the child's critical thinking skills;
c) helping the child and parents remove the child from parental conflicts;
d) protecting the child from becoming alienated in the future;
e) helping the child to maintain balanced and realistic views and perceptions of both parents and of himself/herself;

---

[21] Previously, this intervention was known as "The Family Workshop for Alienated Children."

[22] A comprehensive description of Family Bridges and summary of preliminary outcome data are available in Warshak (2010b).

f) helping the child develop a compassionate view of each parent's actions rather than an excessively harsh or critical one;

g) strengthening the family communication and conflict resolution skills; and

h) improving parenting skills and ability to nurture of the rejected parent while also setting and enforcing appropriate limits.

The structure and content of Family Bridges are based on research in cognitive, social, and developmental psychology, sociology, and social neuroscience, including the efficacy of multimedia instruction, techniques for teaching critical thinking, factors affecting misperception, negative stereotype formation, suggestibility, the influence of authority figures and groups on an individual's attitudes and behavior, and the impact on children of exposure to parental conflict.

In some cases, there will be an order for the rejected parent and child to participate in the workshop. In other cases, the court will permit the previously rejected parent who now has custody to make final decisions with respect to educational or health decisions, including attendance at the workshop. Parents ordered to attend against their will are not accepted into the program. Lawyers or clients interested in making a referral have direct contact with one of the potential workshop leaders to determine if the referral is appropriate, and if so, consultation is provided regarding the various steps that need to be taken prior to the workshop commencing. If a referral is made and the previously rejected parent and children attend, after an orientation and risk assessment to determine suitability, the workshop proceeds through four phases:

Phase One: Basic Concepts and Information,
Phase Two: Divorce-Related Concepts and Integration of Learning,
Phase Three: Application of Learning, and
Phase Four: Acquisition and Practice of Communication and Conflict Resolution Skills.

Family Bridges concludes with the development of an aftercare plan for the family, which involves efforts to sustain the child and previously rejected parent's renewed relationship in their home community and to resume the child's relationship with the favored parent.

Most rejected parents and children who have participated in Family Bridges have previously participated in some form of therapy that was not successful. Warshak (2010a) notes that when the child and parents are made aware of the court's expectations for the child to reintegrate with the rejected parent, notwithstanding the child's resistance or refusal, the child is emotionally freed up to participate meaningfully in the program. Further, experience from these workshops indicates that children usually feel relief at having the decision to choose one parent over the other taken away from them. While children are required by their parents to start the program, after some participation they may choose to opt out, which Warshak reports has not occurred during any of the workshops he has conducted.

Warshak (2010b) reports preliminary outcome data on 23 children (8–16 years old) from 11 families with whom he conducted the workshop. All of these families had attended other counseling previously without positive outcomes. Seven of the 11 families attended the workshop with an accompanying order for change in custody to the rejected parent. Some had orders for the workshop. All were severely alienated at the outset. Twenty-two of the 23 children restored a positive relationship with the previously rejected parent by the end of the 4-day workshop.

Seventeen of these 22 (77%) maintained this positive relationship a year or more later. Those who did not maintain the positive relationship had contact with the favored parent soon after the workshop was completed. In Warshak's view, an insufficient period of no contact and the lack of participation in the aftercare program were important factors in these negative outcomes.

Family Bridges is typically combined with a family vacation after the conclusion of the workshop. For example, many have attended the workshop in California and then gone to Disneyland. There are also ample opportunities for leisure time and activities during the 4-day workshop at the end of the day or evenings in proximity of the workshop, which is often a hotel suite.

To date, the workshop has usually occurred outside the family's jurisdiction, frequently although not necessarily, in either Texas or California, where the principal workshop leaders reside.[23] Questions and sometimes harsh criticisms have been advanced in the literature and in our interviews with some judges and mental health professionals with respect to FB occurring outside of the family's jurisdiction. The noted concerns relate to the additional costs as well as the comfort of the child and parents.

There have also been concerns expressed in the media about children being "dragged" to this out-of-jurisdiction program in "handcuffs."[24] There are actually no cases in which force has been used to bring a child to the program (let alone handcuffs used). Children have complied with the court order changing custody and accompanied the rejected parent to the vacation setting where the program is held, some albeit initially reluctantly. In a few cases, the transition to the workshop has had to be assisted by transport agents who are experienced, privately retained childcare workers, with the rejected parent traveling separately.

---

[23] More recently, a number of professionals in the United States and Ontario are in the process of being trained or have been trained to provide Family Bridges and are offering the program in other locations. Requirements for licensing are a factor. For example, it is not permissible for an out-of-province psychologist to practice in Ontario. Other jurisdictions may have different rules. An out-of-jurisdiction psychologist may provide training to a licensed psychologist, who effectively assumes responsibility for the case.

[24] "Coercion adds to trauma," Editorial in *Globe & Mail*, February 9, 2010.

Clearly, if a court is planning to award custody of a severely alienated child to the rejected parent, there must be careful consideration of how the child is to be informed and the logistics of the custody transfer, an issue we discuss more fully in Chapter 9. However, if handled properly, there should not be any need for use of force.

There are several reasons why it is preferable to have the FB program away from the child's home (though it need not be in Texas or California). While Family Bridges may be conducted in or near the rejected parent's home, and while this may be preferable to the extent that the child feels comfortable in that home, a different or unfamiliar environment may be more constructive for many children. The child may not, in fact, feel comfortable in the rejected parent's home because he or she has come to associate it with negative experiences and feelings. Further, if the child is in a familiar locale, there may be heightened risk of a violation of a court-imposed restriction on communication between the favored parent and children, which can jeopardize the program. Indeed, if the workshop is conducted locally, some of the travel expenses will be saved. However, the expense of a hotel suite may still be necessary when it is ill advised to conduct the workshop with the child staying in the rejected parent's home.

Other concerns have been noted by some judges and mental health professionals about removing children from their familiar environment to attend Family Bridges or Overcoming Barriers because they equate these programs with "residential" interventions (similar to youth custody or placement in a mental health facility). A residential program, however, is typically one that the child attends without either parent and is much longer than the 4 or 5 days of either FB or the camp program.[25] Family Bridges usually involves the child attending with his or her siblings and the rejected parent with whom the child previously had a good, reasonably good, or excellent relationship.

As mentioned, attendance at FB requires a court order for custody reversal to the rejected parent, who then has the legal authority to make health care decisions for the child. In addition, an order for a temporary interruption in the contact with the favored parent, usually at least for 3 months, is necessary to allow for the reintegration with the rejected parent to take effect and solidify. In these severe cases, where in many instances counseling has failed, the temporary interruption in contact with the favored parent is believed to be necessary for the reintegration of the child with the rejected parent. The goal is for the child to ultimately have a good relationship with both parents. For this to happen, the intervention must proceed sequentially: first, the child's relationship with the rejected parent must be reestablished, and then the child can be gradually reintegrated with the favored parent. FB also offers a program for the favored parent; however, it has provided this infrequently to date given the unwillingness of the favored parents to participate. FB facilitates an aftercare

---

[25] The 5-day camp program, Overcoming Barriers, requires the attendance of the entire family and thus is also not a "residential" program.

program for the children and the previously rejected parent in the local juris-diction once the workshop has been completed. The favored parent is invited to participate as well.

Family Bridges costs about $20,000 for the professional services, which includes 64 hours of professional time (e.g., two professionals for four, 8-hour days[26]). This is comparable to 2 hours of weekly therapy extended over 7 or 8 months.[27] Additional costs are required for travel expenses (transportation, lodging, meals) for the family to attend the workshop out of their home juris-diction (or to allow for the workshop leaders to travel to the family's location to deliver the program). Further costs include any associated legal and court fees to get to the point where the workshop can proceed (i.e., an interim order for a custody reversal) and costs of any follow-up contacts or consultation with workshop leaders. Postworkshop aftercare treatment adds further to the ongoing costs for these families. This is clearly an expensive intervention that is beyond the means of many parents.

In her commentary on Family Bridges, Joan Kelly (2010) states:

> The most striking feature of the Family Bridges workshop was the empirical research foundation underlying the specific content of the 4-day educational program. The lessons and materials were drawn from universally accepted research in social, cognitive, and child developmental psychology, sociology, and social neuroscience. Although this body of research was not specifically developed nor tested with populations of high-conflict parents and children, materials more commonly used in college classrooms were adapted for the developmental and cognitive abilities of children and their circumstances in high-conflict families. The content of Family Bridges is intended to directly address underlying mechanisms and processes that are most likely to contribute to the child's alienation from, and rejection of, a parent. (p. 83)

---

[26] In reality, in addition to time taken during the referral stage and the period from the point of the order for the custody reversal to arrival at the workshop, the workshop leaders work many more hours each day to debrief on the day and prepare for the next day. Further, they are essentially "on call" to assist if necessary during the family's leisure time. The same can be said for any professionals providing intervention in these situations that sometime require crisis intervention or on-call services, such as those at Overcoming Barriers or therapists providing reintegration counseling; many hours of planning, thinking, and direct service are provided without remuneration and after typical work hours.

[27] Compare these costs with those of Overcoming Barriers previously discussed, and with as many as 3 years of weekly therapy, usually more than 1 hour a week, which is often required for the more traditional reintegration family therapy approaches where the child continues to reside with the custodial parent.

Kelly goes on to list these mechanisms, including distortions in memory, perception and thinking, suggestibility and negative stereotype formation, the influence of authority figures, the development of critical thinking, communication, and conflict resolution skills.

Kelly (2010) provides insightful comments about possibilities for future research, the limited availability of the program due to the specific and associated financial costs, and the need for careful training to ensure consistent and quality delivery of the workshop. The training takes considerable time given the need for practitioners to experience several workshops before they can deliver the program on their own. Increasing the number of professionals who are adequately trained to deliver the workshop will hopefully make this option available to families more widely in the United States and other countries at a lower cost to the extent that travel expenses will be avoided. Another important consideration noted by Kelly is the challenge inherent in later engaging the favored parent's participation in a parallel or subsequent workshop (i.e., favored parent with professional in absence of child and rejected parent). According to Kelly, the current lack of such programs "undermines the lasting effectiveness of the program in some cases, particularly when contact is resumed within weeks of the intervention" (p. 85).

7.6 Aftercare, Training, Accessibility, and Costs of Interventions

More intensive interventions, such as a camp program or weekend workshop, provide an opportunity for the family to engage in a more profound experience to initiate some change. In some cases, appropriate follow-up or aftercare is necessary to consolidate and further develop the obtained gains or to work on additional goals. Such efforts may be especially important in situations where the child continues to have contact with both parents, including the alienating parent, who may struggle to correct their parental alienating behaviors. Speaking of these types of interventions, Leslie Drozd states:

> …an inoculation can happen where there is some intense work
> done as the family members immerse themselves in a concentrated
> effort to heal. Families can sometimes forge through impasses and
> work through things better in weeklong or weekend programs
> as opposed to the often times slow and laborious work done in
> an outpatient setting. The key to success in intense programs is
> the follow-up after the intense work, because no matter what has
> gone on in the week or the weekend, once everyone returns home,
> there will be a tendency for there to be a change-back reaction.
> Unless there is some sort of support or accountability and unless
> professionals work with a given family upon their return, the

significant and concentrated work that they did will be lost, and the family will fall back into old and dysfunctional patterns.[28]

Intervening successfully is labor intensive and challenging even for the seasoned practitioner. Psychologist Jennifer McIntosh stated, "…these cases make me draw a very long breath, and I really have to examine in myself whether I am in a time and a place, whether I have the personal fortitude to take a particular case on, because there is nothing easy or straightforward in the diagnosis or treatment of these matters…"[29] Often, the work involves crisis intervention "after hours" as the therapist provides the much needed support to family in between sessions not only to implement the parenting time schedule smoothly but also to be available in a timely manner before and after these contacts. In addition to office sessions, therapy can be done in the community or in the parents' home.

Delivery of intervention for alienated or estranged children requires specialized knowledge and substantial experience working with high-conflict families engaged in child custody disputes. In addition to knowledge, skill, and experience, therapists will rely on their creativity and at times need to "think out of the box" to develop well-timed and effective interventions. Therapists need to remain introspective and be prepared to examine their own biases. They need to remain aware of the tremendous "pull" of these families and the ease with which one can align with one parent or the other, or succumb to confirmatory bias.[30]

Experienced professionals will benefit from regular peer consultation and continuing education. Those with less experience and training should obtain regular and substantive supervision. To begin with, the therapist should have the knowledge and training required to conduct custody evaluations. Additional knowledge and training related to various therapy approaches, strategies, and modalities is required. Given the need for substantial experience and specialized knowledge, the hourly rate is likely to be substantial; private services can range from $150 to $300 (U.S.) per hour, depending on the specific professional and location of practice. Services tend to cost more in larger urban centers compared with smaller centers.

7.7 Concluding Comments

As discussed in this chapter, there is insufficient outcome data on all interventions developed for parent–child contact problems, including affinities,

---

[28] Interview, June 23, 2010.
[29] Interview, July 14, 2010.
[30] The tendency for professionals to favor information that confirms their preconceptions and discounts information that does not support their perceptions.

alignments, justified rejection, or alienation. In addition to the small samples, methodological limitations typically include the evaluation being conducted by the clinician who delivered the intervention. Some assert that interventions for the more severe cases, like Family Bridges, are more intrusive and thus ought to be held to a higher research standard than other interventions, such as the MMFI therapeutic program by Johnston and her colleagues (Jaffe, interview; June 23, 2010; Jaffe, Ashbourne, & Mamo, 2010). This raises an important question. Is a program like the OCBC camp or FB more intrusive than court-monitored weekly counseling that occurs for a year or two? Since FB usually operates within the context of a custody reversal and a suspension of contact with the favored parent for a period of time, the workshop and the custody reversal (including the separation from the favored parent) necessarily co-occur. It is difficult, then, to know the respective impact of the each of these. Further, different interventions are suited for different types and severities of parent–child contact problems. Johnston and her colleagues and others have consistently noted that MMFI and similar therapies are not indicated for the most severe cases, where indeed a custody reversal and intervention to assist with that transition may need to be the last resort. More and better research on all interventions is required.

It is important to recognize that all of the available interventions—be they brief (e.g., OBFC for groups or Family Bridges for a single family) or longer term family (reintegration) therapy of the general or more specific type, such as MMFI—are very expensive and out of reach for most families. Often, therapy is intensive and requires at least 9 to 12 months to complete, often as many as 2 years. In many instances, numerous hours are spent during the referral stage and for planning and consultation throughout the intervention that are not billed for. These cases often require more than one therapist, and some families will require a case manager or parenting coordinator, adding further to the costs. The significant difference between interventions such as OBFC or Family Bridges and therapy or counseling is that the costs for the camp or workshop are paid primarily all at once, while the costs of therapy can be expended over time, making it easier for many families. Any court or legal fees to obtain the necessary court orders and ongoing case management and monitoring, which can be substantial, are applicable to most interventions to one extent or another. The OBFC camp and FB often require aftercare therapy or counseling, adding further to the already significant costs. Thus, irrespective of the particular intervention, access to services is a serious problem as most families will not be able to afford services. As discussed previously, preventive measures are necessary and preferable to intervening once the problems have developed and become entrenched.

Appendix A: Family Treatment and Intervention Agreement

Between: _____ and _____
          (Father)   (Mother)

Objectives

1. The parents agree that the objective of this counseling is not to determine IF it is in the child(ren)'s best interest to have contact with one of the parents. Rather, the parents agree that it IS in the child(ren)'s best interests to have meaningful relationships with both parents, and this Agreement is intended to help the child(ren) have a meaningful relationship with both parents.
2. To meet the goals listed below, the parents have agreed to engage the services of [insert therapist's name] (also referred to as "the therapist" in this Agreement) and will contact him or her no later than _____ to schedule appointments.
3. The goals of the treatment/intervention are:

   a) to foster healthy child adjustment;
   b) to facilitate the implementation of the previously agreed-to or court-ordered parenting time schedule, dated _____;
   c) to restore adequate parent functioning, parenting, and roles;
   d) to restore and/or facilitate contact between _____ and _____, age_____, (DOB)_____;
   e) to work with each parent and his or her child(ren) toward the goal of identifying and separating each child's needs and views from each parent's needs and views;
   f) to assist the parents to fully understand the needs of each child and the negative repercussions for the child(ren) of a severed and/or compromised relationship with a parent in their young lives and as adults;
   g) to work with each family member to help form more appropriate parent–parent and parent–child roles and boundaries;
   h) to correct the child's distortions and replace them with realistic perceptions to reflect the child's actual experience with both parents;
   i) to assist the child to differentiate self from others and exercise age-appropriate autonomy;
   j) to help each parent to distinguish valid concerns from overly negative, critical, and generalized views relating to the other parent;
   k) to assist parents to resolve relevant parent–child conflicts;

l) to improve our parenting skills and family communication skills;

m) other (specify)_____.

4. While the parents may have different views about the causes and reasons for the child(ren)'s refusal or reluctance to see _____, they agree not only to the objectives defined above, but also that they each need to be a part of the solution to meet those objectives.

Role and Authority of the Therapist

5. The parents have agreed to the involvement of the entire family, in various combinations, as directed by [insert therapist's name]. The process will include meetings between the therapist and each of the parents and the child(ren) individually and jointly. The process may include interviews and/or meetings with other family members as deemed necessary by [insert therapist's name].

6. [insert therapist's name] will not be making decisions regarding the child(ren)'s time with each parent (access) and/or legal decision making (custody). Rather, he/she will be assisting to implement the previously agreed-to and/or court-ordered parenting plan. Notwithstanding, we agree that [insert therapist's name] may [insert here scope of authority, if any, e.g., to determine the nature of transitions, e.g., rules of parental communication or engagement, location, and pacing of the parent–child contact consistent with the court-ordered parenting plan, etc.]. [insert therapist's name] may make recommendations to the parents, lawyers, and the court to the extent that he/she has obtained sufficient information.

7. [insert therapist's name] may choose to contact other professionals involved with the family to both give and receive information to better meet the aforementioned objectives and goals of the therapy. Toward this end, the parents will sign all releases of information required by [insert therapist's name] to implement the process. The parents shall provide all records, documentation, and information requested by [insert therapist's name] as soon as possible upon request.

8. From time to time, the interests of the child(ren) will be best served by the engagement of additional professionals. For example, [insert therapist's name] may make recommendations and referrals for an additional therapist, for the parents, child(ren), or extended family who are involved in the process. *Optional: In the event the parents disagree with each other or [insert therapist's name], [insert therapist's name] shall assume authority for the determination of the need for and the selection of any additional professionals. The therapist will also maintain authority for the termination of other therapists who may be involved.*

Responsibility of the Parents

9. Both parents will overtly support the therapy and [insert therapist's name] to the child(ren). This includes respecting the child(ren)'s right *not* to discuss with the parents their sessions with the therapist. To this end the parents will not ask the child(ren) for information about their therapy sessions or parenting time with the other parent.

10. The parents will refrain from scheduling new after-school activities, lessons, or events during the scheduled therapy. Reasonable efforts will be made in scheduling appointments to avoid the child(ren) missing school or their currently scheduled after-school activities. However, this may not always be possible, in which case the child(ren) may be required to miss some school or after-school activities.

11. Given the risks of information being taken out of context or being incomplete, the parents agree that they will not restate, summarize, or paraphrase in court documents any feedback provided by [insert therapist's name] to them or their children. If necessary, they can request a report, and [insert therapist's name] will be responsible for communicating any feedback or information about the therapy process to the court.

Duration of Services

12. The therapy shall continue for at least _____. [*Insert term in months or number of sessions.*]

OR

13. In the event that either party wishes to terminate therapy, he or she will provide 15 days notice to the therapist and the other parent in writing. The parents will attempt, with the assistance of counsel, to agree on an alternate to replace [insert therapist's name]. If the parents are unable to agree within 30 days, an alternate will be appointed by [insert "the court" or the specific name of the Arbitrator or Parenting Coordinator for determination in a summary fashion].

14. Neither parent may unilaterally withdraw from this Agreement prior to the completion of the term identified in #12. With their joint consent in writing, both parents may terminate this Agreement. [insert therapist's name] may resign any time [he/she] determines the resignation to be in the best interests of the child(ren) and will make a referral to another therapist after giving 4 weeks notice.

Confidentiality

15. While [insert therapist's name] is bound to maintain confidentiality and not disclose information to anyone not involved in the process, the parents understand that the process may involve sharing of information between those involved in this process, as well as with various professionals and the court. [insert therapist's name] may use his/her discretion to exchange information as necessary between parents, between the parents and the child(ren), and between the children. [insert therapist's name] shall be free to disclose all information, documentation, and correspondence generated by the process with the lawyer for each parent and with the court. [insert therapist's name] may at his/her discretion exchange information with other relevant professionals currently or previously involved and may speak with the lawyers ex-parte. This signed agreement serves as the parents' informed consent for [insert therapist's name] to obtain information from the court, counsel, and both parents AND for [insert therapist's name] to provide information received from all sources to the court, counsel, and the other parent.

16. The parents understand that [insert therapist's name] is required to report to the appropriate child welfare authority (i.e., Metropolitan Child(ren)'s Aid Society, Catholic Child(ren)'s Aid Society, or Jewish Child & Family Service) if he/she has a reasonable suspicion that a child(ren) is/are being abused and/or neglected. In addition, he/she is obliged to notify the proper authorities if he/she has a "reasonable suspicion" that a client may harm himself or herself or the other parent.

Fees

17. Unless otherwise agreed or by court order, Father and Mother shall share all costs equally at a rate of $____.00 per hour. Fees are applied to all time expended in any/all professional activities, including administrative matters. This includes time spent in reviewing documents and correspondence; writing memos to the file; writing reports; voice mail; writing and reviewing received e-mail; meetings; and contacts/telephone calls with the parents, their counsel, and other professionals involved. Also included are any unpaid fees charged retroactively from the time that services are initially requested and the file is opened. This also includes disbursements paid to collateral sources for verbal and/or written reports and agency/hospital reports should these be required by the source.

18. Fees related to report preparation shall be paid for by the parent requesting the report, subject to reallocation by the court. Fees related to preparation for or attendance at court (e.g., trial, settlement conference, discoveries) are billed at $____.00 per hour.

19. Fees for attendance at court, testifying in court, or discoveries are billed by a minimum half-day rate of $_____.00. Any court-related fees (i.e., preparation time, attendance, and travel) shall be provided in advance by retainer by the parent requesting [insert therapist's name]'s attendance at court. A separate contract for these services (detailing cancellation policy, etc.) may apply and be provided at the time of any request.

20. Record keeping requirements make it necessary to log each e-mail, telephone call, and/or message and make a record of even the briefest telephone call. For this reason contacts in excess of 5 minutes are charged at the prorated hourly rate stipulated in the service agreement

21. Father and Mother will each provide a retainer of 10 hours of services, that is, $_____.00. At all times each parent shall maintain a retainer of at least $_____.00 (2 hours) in the account of [insert therapist's name], who shall advise in advance when a further retainer is required. A statement of account will be provided to the parents from time to time. If the above terms are not satisfied, [insert therapist's name] will postpone all services until the retainer terms are met. Nonpayment of fees shall be grounds for the resignation of [insert therapist's name].

22. Appointments cancelled without at least 48 hours advance notice may be charged at full fee independent of the reason for the cancellation. Monday and Tuesday appointments must be cancelled by 5:00 p.m. on the previous Friday. The parents will each be responsible for bills arising from his/her own cancellation with insufficient notice and/or failure to attend a scheduled appointment.

To Evidence their Agreement, Father and Mother have Signed this Agreement before a Witness. Certificates of Independent Legal Advice are Attached.

DATE:

Witness   Father

DATE:

Witness   Mother

8

Hearing the Voices of Children in Alienation Cases

It is important for parents, professionals, and judges to consider children's perspectives and preferences about the arrangements for their care, but the stated wishes of a child are not determinative of the child's best interests or of the decisions to be made by parents or courts, even when expressed by an older child or adolescent.[1] The opportunity to be heard is not equivalent to a right to make decisions. Further, the involvement of children should always be arranged in a way that is sensitive to their capacities and vulnerabilities.

8.1 Children's Stated Wishes: Clinical Perspectives

Mental health professionals, lawyers, and judges have conflicting opinions about how, and even whether, to involve children in family litigation over parenting arrangements. Some argue that asking children their opinions about residence or parenting time may place them "in the middle" of their parents' dispute and may increase the harmful effects of the separation and litigation process on children, especially if alienation is an issue (Altobelli, 2011; Emery, 2003; Warshak, 2003b), while others argue that children want to be active participants in the decisions that affect their lives and should be part of the decision-making process postseparation (Birnbaum & Bala, 2010b; Brown, 1995;

---

[1] In all jurisdictions, case law, or more commonly legislation, provides that the wishes of the child are *a* factor in determining the child's best interests; for example, in Australia, the *Family Law Act* s. 60CC(3)(a).

Carl & Karl, 2011; Paetsch, Bertrand, Walker, MacRae, & Bala, 2009; Parkes, 2009; Timms, 2003).

Generally, research suggests that *appropriate* participation by children in decision making can reduce the negative effects on them of parental separation and family breakdown (Cashmore, 2003; Kelly, 2002; Neale, 2002; Smart, 2002). Most children want to be kept informed and want their views heard by the decision makers who are making arrangements for their care and activities, including their parents, but they do not want the responsibility for making decisions.

Children's articulated wishes need to be assessed for the impact of loyalty conflicts and undue influence, and then interpreted and weighed by taking into account many factors, including their age, competence, maturity, coping skills, family dynamics, and the nature of the parent–child relationship. In cases involving domestic violence, a child may identify with or be intimidated by an abusive parent to reject the other parent (Johnston, Walters, & Olesen, 2005b; Warshak, 2003b).

Notwithstanding the value of giving children a voice, consideration needs to be given to the possibility that in individual high-conflict or abuse cases, the risks of soliciting preferences, even if these could be reliably obtained, may outweigh the benefits (Warshak, 2003b). In high-conflict cases where a child is resisting contact with a parent, *even if* the risk of harm from emotional or physical abuse or neglect is ruled out, it is unlikely to be in the best interests of a child to be given the final authority to determine what constitutes reasonable contact, as this responsibility may unduly burden the child (Gardner, 1998b; Johnston & Kelly, 2004; Warshak, 2003b).[2] Such responsibility may frighten or overwhelm children, especially younger ones, inducing feelings of guilt. Furthermore, this responsibility may reinforce their unrealistic sense of power and encourage disrespectful behavior, phobic reactions, or distortions of reality. In many alienation cases, clearly removing children from the role of "decision maker" allows them to save face, in effect giving them the needed excuse, to rebuild their relationship with the rejected parent (Gardner, 2001a; Johnston, Walters, & Friedlander, 2001; Warshak, 2003b). Australian child psychologist Jennifer McIntosh, reflecting the views of a number of experts,

---

[2] In *I.S. v D.S.*, [2010] B.C.J. 413 (S.C.), Arnold Bailey J. commented (at para. 129):

> I declined to hear the preferences of the children in this case because
> I was of the view that the pressure such an interview would place upon
> them would be, at a minimum, detrimental to their well-being, and that
> any information the Court received would be of virtually no value. This
> was so because of the very negative comments about the [mother]...that
> the [alienating father]...had repeatedly expressed to the children in the
> past; his telling them they could choose which parent to live with at the
> age of 12 years; and the [father's]...prolonged "over-sharing" of adult
> information about these court proceedings that cast the [mother]...in
> a decidedly negative light.

noted the importance of listening to children, but not burdening them with the responsibility of decision making:

> From the age of about 6 or 7, and even earlier, I pay very careful attention to the children's opinions as an expression of what it is like to be them, now, in this circumstance, and at this stage of their childhoods. Their opinions should inform decision making by the court and should inform parents' understanding of their child's subjective experience and developmental needs, but the children are not the decision makers. With alienation cases, I think therapeutically it is very important never to give the child the impression that they have made the decision for contact to stop...it is a terrible burden for them to carry for the rest of their lives...the justice system has got be very clear that it has made the decision...because this gives the child a better position to come back from. [3]

8.2 Children's Right of Participation

Increasingly, children are regarded as having the *right* to participate in legal processes that resolve disputes about their care (Cashmore & Parkinson, 2009; Eekelaar, 1992). Further, there is a growing body of research that recognizes the value for both decision makers and children in having the children involved in family dispute resolution processes. There is, however, considerable controversy about how to involve children in these processes, and in particular about whether and how they should communicate directly with the judges who will make the decisions that profoundly affect their future.

Almost all countries in the world have ratified the *United Nations Convention on the Rights of the Child*,[4] an international treaty that clearly recognizes the right of children to participate in the family justice system, with Article 12 providing that:

1) States Parties shall assure to the child who is capable of forming his or her own views the right to express those views freely in all matters affecting the child, the views of the child being given due weight in accordance with the age and maturity of the child.
2) For this purpose, the child shall in particular be provided the opportunity to be heard in any judicial...proceedings affecting the

---

[3] Interview, July 14, 2010.
[4] The United States is one of only two countries in the world that has not yet ratified this international treaty, the other being Somalia. The failure of the United States to ratify gives the *Convention* much less legal weight in that country, though it is cited as a persuasive (but not binding) source of law by judges and scholars in the United States.

child, either directly, or through a representative or an appropriate body, in a manner consistent with the procedural rules of national law.

While the *Convention* does not have the same legal force as legislation or the constitution of a country, it is cited by the courts in many jurisdictions as having persuasive value or an aid in interpreting and applying the law.[5] The importance of the *Convention* for establishing the child's right to be "heard," including in an alienation case, was, for example, recognized by Martinson J. in the 2010 Yukon decision in *B.J.G.* v. *D.L.G.*, where she wrote:

> ...in my respectful view all children in Canada have legal rights to be heard in all matters affecting them, including custody cases. Decisions should not be made without ensuring that those legal rights have been considered. These legal rights are based on the *United Nations Convention on the Rights of the Child* and Canadian domestic law.
>
> The *Convention*... says that children who are capable of forming their own views have the legal right to express those views in all matters affecting them, including judicial proceedings. In addition, it provides that they have the legal right to have those views given due weight in accordance with their age and maturity. There is no ambiguity in the language used. The *Convention* is very clear; *all* children have these legal rights to be heard, without discrimination. It does not make an exception for cases involving high-conflict, including those dealing with domestic violence, *parental alienation*, or both. It does not give decision makers the discretion to disregard the legal rights contained in it because of the particular circumstances of the case or the view the decision maker may hold about children's participation.
>
> A key premise of the legal rights to be heard found in the *Convention* is that hearing from children is in their best interests. Many children want to be heard and they understand the difference between having a say and making the decision. Hearing from them can lead to better decisions that have a greater chance of success. Not hearing from them can have short and long term adverse consequences for them. While concerns are raised by some, they

---

[5] The legal weight given to international treaties by national courts is a complex topic, with variation in different countries, and in many countries is also influenced by the nature of the proceedings and the treaty. Suffice it to say that the *Convention on the Rights of the Child* is cited by courts and scholars throughout the world, including the United States, which has not ratified the *Convention*, for guidance in dealing with child-related issues. However, given the vagueness of its provisions and the limited effect of this treaty on the law of any country, there is significant judicial discretion in deciding how much weight to give the *Convention*.

can be dealt with within the flexible legal framework found in the *Convention*.[6]

It has also been argued that children in alienation cases, especially older children and adolescents, should be encouraged to participate in the legal process in some way, as they may be more likely to comply with an order that is contrary to their stated wishes if they have the feeling that they have at least been "heard." There is a related argument that they may be more fully legally bound to comply if they have been made parties to the action, or at least afforded the opportunity to state their case to the judge.[7]

8.3 Children's Stated Wishes: Weight in the Courts

In general, those who are making recommendations, parenting plans, or decisions about the care of children, including judges, assessors, and parents, give considerable weight to the perspectives and preferences of children, especially as they get older. However, in cases where there are concerns about alienating parental behavior and influence, children's stated wishes may not be true reflections of their genuine and deeper feelings or their actual behavior when in the presence of the resisted or rejected parent, let alone determinative of their needs and interests. In cases where alienation is a concern, the courts are clearly not bound by the stated preferences of a child, regardless of how consistently and fervently these wishes may be stated.

Judges have long held that children's stated wishes are only one consideration in determining their best interests. In one of the first reported cases to use the concept of "alienation," the 1991 Quebec case of *P.S.-M. v. A.J.-L.C.*,[8] the Quebec Superior Court dealt with a case of four children caught up in a heated custody dispute between their parents. Although both parents worked during the marriage, the mother was the primary caretaker of the children. Following separation, the children went to live with their father and after a while refused all further contact with their mother. When the mother attempted to exercise her right to parenting time, the children called the police. A court-ordered psychological assessment established that the children were alienated from their mother. Several interim court orders attempted to reestablish contact between the children and their mother, all of which were sabotaged by the

---

[6] *B.J.G.* v. *D.L.G.*, 2010 YKSC 44, at para 2–4. Emphasis added. For an Australian case discussing the effect of the *Convention* on a child's right to be heard in a dispute between parents, see *Dylan & Dylan* [2007] FamCA 842.

[7] See Robert Boyden & Soby Lenz, Parent Alienation: The need for a clear and unequivocal response (July 2010, National Family Law Program, Victoria B.C.). In *S.G.B. v S.J.L*, [2010] O.J. No. 3619, (Ont.C.A.) per Epstein J.A. (In Chambers), the failure of the trial judge to hear from a sixteen-year-old boy in an alienation case was accepted as a reason for staying the decision.

[8] Unreported, [1991], SCM 500–12-184613895 (Que. Sup.Ct.).

father, and the children were finally put into foster care by child protection authorities. When foster care was no longer available, the children returned home to their father. Once back at his home, the children refused to engage in counseling with various mental health professionals, including the court-appointed psychologist who had been trying to reestablish contact with the mother. At the conclusion of the trial, the two older children were permitted to remain with their father, as it was evident they would run away if they were made to live with their mother. The two youngest, however, were placed in the custody of their mother. Contact for the younger two children with the father and the two older children in his care was suspended for a period of 6 months to allow the younger children to stabilize in their mother's home. In determining the weight to be given to the desires of the children, Justice Gomery stated:

> In determining questions of custody, the court must be guided by
> the best interests of the child. The desires and preferences of each
> child are factors to be taken into consideration, particularly in cases
> where the child's wishes are freely expressed and are not influenced
> by pressure or manipulation. In this case, the wishes of the children,
> especially the younger children, may be safely ignored because they
> are a result of distortions of the truth that their father has told them,
> and the psychological pressure to which they have been subjected...
>   Children do not always know what is best for them. The law
> leaves it up to the court to decide this question, when their parents
> are unable to agree, and the law does not state anywhere that the
> court must be guided by what the children have to say, although it
> does require that they should be given an opportunity to be heard.
> At their request, as it was expressed through their own lawyer, the
> court has listened to them. What they have said, and the way they
> have said it, has served to strengthen the court's opinion that it
> would not be in their best interests to continue to let them have
> their own way.[9]

A 2009 New York appellate decision, *Burola v. Meek*,[10] took a similar approach to the wishes of a child in a case involving same-sex partners with a child born to one woman and adopted by the other. The partners separated when the girl was 9 years old, and entered into a comprehensive agreement, which was incorporated into a consent order that provided for joint legal custody with a primary residence with the biological mother but significant time in the care of the adoptive parent. By the time that the child was 11 years old, the adoptive mother was experiencing serious problems seeing the child. The child said she did not want overnight contact with her adoptive mother. The adoptive mother brought the matter to Family Court, seeking increased time with her daughter.

---

[9] Ibid. at p. 19.
[10] 64 AD 3d 962, 882 N.Y.S. 2d 560 (3d Dept., 2009).

The Family Court judge, after hearing evidence from the parties and other witnesses, including the child's therapist, concluded that the biological mother had "deliberately engaged in a course of conduct that was designed to alienate the child" from the adoptive mother. For example, the biological mother engaged in conduct that increased the child's anxiety about contact, and encouraged the child to abandon use of the adoptive mother's surname, even though it was her legal name. The biological mother failed to keep the other parent informed of the child's ongoing activities and removed photographs from the child's room that had pictures of the three of them together. The Family Court judge determined that the child "would only enjoy a wholesome relationship with both of her parents—something that was clearly in her best interests—if her time" with the adoptive mother were significantly increased. The trial judge ordered an arrangement of alternating weeks of custody for each parent. In rejecting the appeal of the biological mother for an order for sole custody, Kavanagh J. commented:

> [the] Family Court did take into account the fact that the child did not want to continue overnight visitation with respondent. After twice meeting with the child, Family Court was well aware of the child's wishes and clearly took them into account in reaching its decision. However, as noted by the court, *a child's wishes are but one factor and are not determinative regarding decisions relating to custody and visitation.* This is especially true where the evidence received at the hearing supports the court's finding that the child has been manipulated by one of the parties and the child's views regarding her relationship with the other party are the product of that manipulation.[11]

In a 2007 Ontario case of *Figliano v. Figliano*, where the court found that the children had been alienated, Mesbur J. emphasized that children and their parents need to be aware of the limited role of a child's expressed preferences:

> At trial, there was a great deal of discussion about the children expressing a wish to live with their father. I want to make clear at the outset that the children do not have to choose which parent to live with. That is not their job. It is their parents' responsibility to make that decision, in their best interests. When their parents cannot agree, then the responsibility falls to the court. *My role is to take on that task, and to make the decision of what is best for the children. Their wishes are only one factor to consider. What children say they want is not necessarily what is best for them. What children say they want does not necessarily reflect their real wishes.* It is important

---

[11] *Burola v. Meek*, 64 AD 3d 962, 882 N.Y.S. 2d 560 (3d Dept., 2009). Emphasis added.

that both of the parents, the children, and both extended families understand this.[12]

While courts are not obliged to follow the wishes of children, especially in alienation cases, when children are older adolescents there may come a point at which attempting to enforce contact between a child and alienated parent becomes effectively impossible. The degree of respect to be accorded the wishes of the child will depend not only on chronological age, but also on the child's emotional and cognitive maturity, as well as the determination of the individual child to make a decision. As Toronto lawyer Philip Epstein notes: "Once a child has reached 14, 15 or 16 years of age, it's probably too late to intervene and the damage from intervention will be worse than the damage caused by the alienation."[13] Older adolescents may start to run away and endanger themselves if they feel that the court is trying to restrict their freedom.[14] With some adolescents, defiance of the court may be a part of their "adolescent rebellion" stage. While such dangerous resistance is almost always usually fueled by the alienating parent, this may be effectively impossible to prove, and in an era of instant and constant communication, it may be

---

[12] [2007] O.J. 530 (S.C.J.); 2007 CarswellOnt 773 (Ont. S.C.J.), at para. 3. Emphasis added.

[13] Interview, August 15, 2010.

[14] The dilemma that the wishes of an alienated but determined child can pose for the justice system was illustrated by the British Columbia case of *C.(A.J.) v. C.(R.)*, [2003] B.C.J. 1150, where an access father was engaged in highly manipulative conduct and phone calls with his 11-year-old daughter, which expert evidence established was "alienating" the child from the custodial mother. On occasion, the father refused to return the daughter after visits, saying that this is what the girl wanted, and as a result he was criminally charged with abduction. The daughter was placed in a foster home, but at that time was very loyal to the father; she wrote to the mother: "If Dad goes to jail, I will hate you forever." The girl began to run away, threatening to live on the streets of Vancouver and prostitute herself if she could not live with her father. The father brought a variation application, and Bennett J. decided that, despite the conduct of the father, it would be preferable for the child to be permitted to live with him, as the child was getting too old for a custody order contrary to her wishes, and that she would endanger herself if she could not live with her father. The court observed: "The issue is what is in the best interests of [the child], not punishing or rewarding [the father] for his conduct." The court ordered that at the end of the school year the child would move from the foster home to live with her father. The court ordered the child was to receive counseling and that the mother would continue to have contact with the daughter. As it turned out, the girl later came to realize how manipulative her father was and later decided that she did not want to have a relationship with him; she was placed in her mother's custody but continued to primarily reside with the foster parents, and contact with the father was eventually limited to correspondence. [*A.C.J. v. R.C.*, [2006] B.C.J. No. 1995 (B.C.S.C.).]

practically impossible to prevent an alienating parent from communicating with and influencing an older child.

The limits of judicial control of older adolescents are illustrated by the 2010 Ontario case of *S.G.B. v S.J.L.*,[15] a case involving alienation of a boy (J.B.) with Klinefelter's syndrome who was 16 years of age by the time of completion of the proceedings. J.B. had a significant learning disability and the "emotional maturity of a child twelve or thirteen" years of age. There was extensive evidence from experts about the alienation of the boy by the father against the mother during the 4 years that he had custody of the boy. The trial judge, Mesbur J., in a lengthy decision, ordered that the mother have custody, with the father having no contact for a 3-month period, during which it was expected that the mother would take the boy to the Family Bridges program. The judge placed significant weight on the boy's special needs, and his immaturity due to his condition.

During the trial, counsel for the father asked the judge to meet the 16-year-old boy (J.B.) and his 19-year-old brother (L.B.). Justice Mesbur declined, writing:[16]

> First, father's counsel was unable to articulate the purpose of my meeting the children. Meeting them would not have provided the court with any admissible evidence. Second, counsel had no clear suggestion of whether the meeting would be confidential, as far as all parties and counsel were concerned, whether counsel would be present, or whether a court reporter would be present. Third, and perhaps more importantly, the children (or at least JB) are not deciding the issues here; the court has that sole responsibility.
>
> I do recognize that children's wishes and preferences are relevant to determining their best interests, particularly in the case of older children such as JB. That said, the court does not have to hear from children directly to find out what their wishes and preferences are. JB has clearly expressed his wishes. He wishes to remain with his father. He does not wish to see his mother or have a relationship with her, at least that is what he told [the court-appointed assessor] Dr. Goldstein. He sees no reason to attempt to repair his relationship with her.
>
> Not only that, JB was quite clear with Dr. Goldstein that if his mother "won" at this trial, he would soon be sixteen, there would be an appeal, and then nothing would happen. JB seems quite aware of a 30-day appeal period. JB is also quite aware that sixteen year old children may have more choices than younger children. All this suggests to me that JB has been far too involved in this litigation up to now, and has far too much information about the legal process than is appropriate for his age and stage of

---

[15] *[2010] O.J. No. 2856*, 2010 ONSC 3717.

[16] *[2010] O.J. No. 2856*, 2010 ONSC 3717, at para. 131–134.

development. Although his brother LB is now an adult, I could not see that speaking either to him or JB would add anything either to my fact finding or legal analysis. As a result, I saw no benefit in meeting with the boys in the course of the trial. To the contrary, I saw only negative effects in doing so, which is why I did not.

Before the order could be enforced, the 16-year-old boy fled and "went into hiding." His father claimed that he did not know where the boy was. Within a few days of the order being made, the police located, apprehended, and detained the boy, who by that time had retained his own lawyer. That lawyer obtained a stay of the original order from the Ontario Court of Appeal, with the judge noting that the case raised some serious issues, including:[17]

> What are the consequences, if any, of the trial judge's decision not to allow J.B. to testify, meet with her or be represented by counsel, particularly when there is evidence... that J.B. objects to the trial judge's having ascertained his views through the evidence of [the assessor] Dr. Goldstein?... Does the court have jurisdiction to order a 16-year old child to submit to medical treatment [by attending the Family Bridges program]? Is it in the best interests of the child to grant an order the effect of which... may well cause him to be a fugitive from the police?

A 16-year-old child in Ontario (and most other jurisdictions) has the right to leave home and cease to attend school, so the appellate decision to stay the enforcement of the order is understandable. As a matter of law in Ontario, even parents with a custody order are not able to prevent their 16-year-old children from moving out of their homes, which presumably includes the right of a child to move into the home of a parent without custody rights. As a practical matter, legally enforcing a custody or contact order regarding determined, older adolescents who can "vote with their feet" may become impossible.

Judges do, however, continue to make orders concerning older adolescents in alienation cases, as illustrated by the 2009 New York case of *Smith v Smith & Pogson.*[18] The mother left the family home when her children were 8 and 12 years of age, to move in with a new partner. Under an informal arrangement with the father, the mother continued to see the children almost daily, but only at the former marital home as the father refused to allow the children to go to her new residence or on vacation with her, even years after the

---

[17] *S.G.B. v S.J.L,* [2010] O.J. No. 3619 (Ont.C.A.) 578. per Epstein J.A. (In Chambers). Interim stay was upheld 2010 ONCA 578. This case, however, was settled before the appeal was heard on terms which provided that the boy, who had been alienated from his mother for 6 years, participate in the 4-day Family Bridges workshop with his mother. As a result, the boy restored his relationship with his mother; see http://warshak.com/blog/2010/12/02/answering-critics-part-1-2/ (accessed Feb. 29, 2012).
[18] 61 A.D. 3d 1275, 878 N.Y.S.2d 814 (3d Dept. 2009).

separation. Four years later the mother perceived that her relationship with the older child, by then a 16-year-old girl, was deteriorating while the 12-year-old boy told his mother that he wanted to spend more time with her. The mother commenced a Family Court application, and was granted sole custody of both children, with a fixed parenting time schedule for the father. The father was unemployed, despite being well educated, and there was evidence that he was not addressing the children's increasingly apparent behavioral problems. The Family Court judge had met with both the children and was aware of the girl's wishes but determined that it was in the best interests of both children to reside with their mother and have only limited contact with their father. The father and the Law Guardian for the children appealed the Family Court order, but the appeal was dismissed. In affirming the Family Court decision, Stein J. observed that the "children's wishes are but one factor to consider," commenting on the significance of the father's attitude and conduct:

> The father . . . sees no need to enroll the daughter in counseling
> to address undisputed self-destructive and risky conduct on her
> part. Significantly, the evidence demonstrates that the father
> continues to harbor anger and resentment towards the mother, to
> which he exposes the children. Despite his protestation regarding
> the mother's adulterous relationship with another man, he has
> steadfastly resisted attempts to resolve issues surrounding a
> dissolution of the marriage, including custody of the children. In
> addition, he has done nothing to address the daughter's animosity
> towards her mother and, indeed, appears to condone it.[19]

The court in *Smith* was clearly concerned about the welfare of the daughter and prepared to make an order for her custody, even though she was 16 years old. Although not explicitly mentioned by the court, the fact that this older adolescent had a younger brother with a positive attitude toward the mother may have been a factor in the court's approach, hoping that his presence might ease the transition of the older girl to her mother's custody. It can be very difficult for a court, a parent, or anyone, to force a determined older adolescent to do anything, but with the right structure, support, and direction, these children may realize that a custody order is in their own best interests and will comply with it.

8.4 Methods for Courts Hearing the Views and Wishes of Children

While lawyers for parents who are involved in child custody cases recognize the importance of the court hearing evidence about the perspectives and views of the children, it is generally considered inappropriate for lawyers for

---

[19] *Smith v Smith & Pogson*, 61 A.D. 3d 1275, 878 N.Y.S.2d 814 (3d Dept., 2009).

the parents to interview the children or attempt to directly involve them in the litigation by calling them as witnesses to testify in court, where they could be subjected to cross-examination.

There are several different ways through which courts can receive evidence of the perceptions and wishes of children:

- hearsay evidence about the child's views and preferences as the basis for the testimony of a parent or other adult;
- a letter, written statement, or recording of the child;
- a report or testimony from a mental health professional who has interviewed the child in the context of preparing a court-ordered assessment;
- a report or testimony from a mental health professional, lawyer, or community volunteer about an interview the child (sometimes called a Views or Voice of the Child Report);
- a lawyer appointed for the child; and
- a judicial meeting with the child.

There are advantages and disadvantages to each of these methods for bringing the child's views before the court (Bala, Talwar, & Harris, 2005). Not all of these options are available in all jurisdictions, and there may be resource or legal constraints on use of some of these options in some jurisdictions. A decision about which method, or combination of methods, is to be used in a particular case depends on such factors as:

- the age and maturity of the child;
- the consistency and strength of the child's wishes;
- the attitudes of the judge, lawyers, and parents;
- the legal provisions in the jurisdiction;
- the professional resources available, whether provided by the government or paid for by parents; and
- the preferences of the child about the method of participation. (This last factor is often ignored but arguably should be important.)

There are a number of factors to balance when deciding what approach to follow in ensuring that the child's voice is heard, including:

- providing the court with as much accurate information as possible,
- minimizing trauma to the child,
- ensuring a fair process for the parents,
- ensuring a fair process for the child, and
- resolving the dispute as cost effectively as possible for the parties and the state.

Some of the variation between jurisdictions in terms of the methods used to bring the "voice of the child" before the court is a function of the legislation, resources, and institutional structures available.

8.4.1 Children's Statements as the Basis for Parents' Testimony

A widely recognized part of the common law of evidence—the hearsay rule—at least in theory, prevents a witness from testifying about what a person told that witness. While the hearsay rule is important, especially in criminal cases, it is widely ignored in family cases, and in any event one of the traditional exceptions to the hearsay rule allows a witness to testify about the out-of-court statements of another a person to reveal the "state of mind" of that person. This exception to the hearsay rule has long been used to permit adult witnesses in a family case to testify about a child's wishes.[20] There are, however, special considerations if parents want to testify about what the child told them. One important judicial concern is the desire to discourage parents from questioning their children about ongoing litigation.[21] Further, there are significant concerns about the reliability of this type of evidence, not just about the honesty or accuracy of the parent's testimony, but also about the effect that the parent *may* have had on the child's candor. Some judges will refuse to admit this type of evidence in family law cases, while most others will give it very little weight.

8.4.2 Letters, Recordings, and Other Statements of Children

It is not uncommon in alienation cases for children to write letters or e-mail to a judge, or for a parent to want to submit a letter, audio recording or a video recording of a "statement" made by the child, purporting to set out the child's preferences. There are understandable judicial concerns about the manipulation of children in these cases. Since there is no reliable information about the context in which such a statement was made, and judges want to discourage parents from involving their children in litigation in this way, judges generally refuse to receive such statements, or, if they are admitted, they are given little or no weight.[22]

In a few jurisdictions, such as Scotland,[23] social workers may assist older children in preparing written or video recorded statements that can be submitted to the court. This process has the advantage of providing assurance that the views expressed are not the result of direct parental influence or pressure, and that the preparation of the statement is not emotionally disturbing to the child.

In a few jurisdictions, a child may be permitted to file an affidavit (sworn statement) setting out his or her preferences for a custody decision. In most

---

[20] See, e.g., *Strobridge v. Strobridge* (1994), 4 R.F.L. (4th) 169 (Ont. C.A.); and *C.K. v. C.S.*, [1996] N.S.J. 609 (Fam Ct.).

[21] See, e.g., *M. (D.G.) v. M. (K.M.)*, [2000] A.J. 1001 (Q.B.); *Keeping v. Keeping*, [2004] N.J. 293 (U.F.C.), per Cook J.

[22] There are very different rules for the admission of video recordings of interviews of children made by investigators in abuse cases.

[23] See Sheriff Court Form F-9, www.scotcourts.gov.uk.

jurisdictions, however, children are strongly discouraged, or prohibited, from making sworn statements or being called as witnesses in family cases. In Ohio, for example, parents are not permitted to file affidavits from their children in family cases,[24] and in Australia, such a statement may only be filed with the permission of the court.[25] Judges will invariably strongly discourage parents from calling their children as witnesses in custody cases and, if the issue is pressed by a parent, will often expressly prohibit this. As discussed below, the issue of the child being called as a witness in court, in the presence of the parents, is very different from the issue of the possibility of the judge meeting the child, typically in the judge's office (or chambers), without the parents or their lawyers present.

8.4.3 Reports from Custody Evaluators[26]

As discussed extensively elsewhere in this book,[27] reports prepared by court-appointed mental health professionals[28] are generally the most thorough and reliable way for determining a child's perceptions and preferences, and bringing evidence of the child's views before the court. The custody evaluator is a social worker, psychologist, or psychiatrist, with professional training and experience in interviewing children. Although the nature and extent of the evaluator's work on a case will vary widely, a distinguishing feature is that the evaluator will rely on multiple interviews, observations, and collateral sources; it is not just a report on an interview with the child. The evaluator will look for confirming and disconfirming information within and across sources of information. The report will set out the evaluator's findings, including a summary of the child's views and preferences, if any, and will often conclude with an include analysis of the case and recommendations.

---

[24] The Ohio *Revised Code* 3109.04 (B)(3) provides that no person shall obtain "from a child a written or recorded statement or affidavit setting forth the child's wishes and concerns" concerning parenting arrangements, though, as discussed below, judicial interviews with children in these cases are common.

[25] Australia *Family Law Act* s. 100B(1). In Texas, until 2009 it was possible for any child 12 or older to file an "affidavit of preferences," but this law was repealed as too many children were being pressured by parents to make such statements.

[26] There is a range of names given to the professionals preparing these reports, including assessors, evaluators, clinical investigators, family consultants. In England and Wales there is a publicly funded agency, the *Children and Family Court Advisory and Support Service (CAFCASS)*, which appoints social workers to prepare reports. In some jurisdictions, these reports are prepared by persons known as a guardian *ad litem* (GAL), though in other jurisdictions the term guardian *ad litem* is used to refer to a lawyer representing the child.

[27] See especially Chapters 4 and 10.

[28] In some American states, reports may be prepared by a volunteer guardians *ad litem* (GAL); these reports are understandably much less reliable and sophisticated.

The evaluator will meet the child, typically more than once, to determine whether the child's views are stable, and will contact other individuals, like teachers, coaches, or therapists, to help understand the child's perspective. The evaluator will invariably interview the parents about their understandings of their children's views and will observe each parent interacting with the child. The report will set out the child's views and wishes and offer an opinion from a trained professional about whether the child has been pressured, manipulated, or improperly influenced to express those views. In addition to considering the independence of the child's views and preferences, an evaluator will attend to the consistency of the child's report from one interview to the next and the consistency or any disconnect between the child's stated feelings and views and their actual behavior when in the presence of the rejected parent. Clinicians report that it is not uncommon for evaluators to observe a disconnect between the child's stated views and preferences, including dislike, hatred, fear, or anger and their actual behavior when they are with the resisted or rejected parent. Some empirical support has been found for this in a study of 58 children involved in custody evaluations, who expressed a strong opposition to having contact with a parent. Weir (2011) reported that many of these children were observed to have positive experiences with the rejected parent despite not having had contact for a significant period of time. In many of these cases, there were unfounded allegations of abuse.

A recently published study of custody and access cases in Canada indicated that the most frequently used method for bringing the views of the child before a trial court is through a court-appointed mental health professional who has interviewed the child (Semple, 2010). The extent of the use of such reports in any jurisdiction will depend, at least in part, on institutional factors and resources. In a number of jurisdictions, including England, Australia, New Zealand, Manitoba, and Ontario, there is government funding for the preparation of reports, and their use is fairly common, especially in cases where alienation is an issue. In other jurisdictions, parents must pay the cost of an evaluation, which limits their use. Even in jurisdictions where there is government funding or a custody evaluation service, like Ontario, it may be limited to some cases; in other cases parents must pay for an evaluation or resolve their case without it.

8.4.4 Voice of the Child Reports

In some jurisdictions, such as British Columbia and Saskatchewan, rather than have a full evaluation done, the court may direct that a social worker or lawyer (or in some American states, a volunteer) interview the child and prepare a relatively brief report for the court. These reports may have such names as a "Voice of the Child" or "Views of the Child" report and are not full evaluation but rather a report solely of the child's stated views, preferences, and perspectives.

These reports, of course, provide much less information than a full evaluation, and if there are issues of alienation, they will not be properly addressed and are unlikely to even be mentioned. However, these reports are much cheaper to prepare, take much less time, and allow the child's statements to be brought before the court without having the child meet the judge, and with some assurance that, at least at the time of the interview, the report provides a reasonably reliable statement of what the child said.

8.4.5 Lawyers for Children

There is very significant variation between jurisdictions in the extent to which lawyers are appointed to represent children, and if they are appointed in the role that they play. While in every jurisdiction where lawyers are appointed for children the child's lawyer must ensure that the court is informed of the child's preferences, in some jurisdictions lawyers are expected to take "instructions" (or direction) from children and advocate based solely on those instructions. In other jurisdictions lawyers may advocate a position based on their own assessment of the child's best interests. This difference in approach is especially significant for alienation cases.

In some jurisdictions there is little or no child representation in cases involving disputes between parents. In jurisdictions where there is a significant amount of such representation, such as Australia, New Zealand, England, and some Canadian provinces, like Ontario and Quebec, and some American states, such as New York, public funding is available to pay these lawyers. Where public funding is available, lawyers representing children are almost always relatively poorly paid; further, the agencies responsible for providing representation have limited budgets, and in most jurisdictions lawyers are only provided in a fraction of child-related cases. New Zealand has one the most extensive programs of child representation; although the government in that country generally pays for a lawyer for the children, the court may order the parents to contribute to the cost of their child's representation.

The role of lawyers appointed to represent children varies both with the nature of the case and the jurisdiction. When children are young, or unwilling to express their preferences (a fairly common occurrence in high-conflict cases not involving alienation), the lawyers for children have to decide on their own what position to advocate, or whether to advocate any position. Commonly, even where a child has views, a lawyer appointed for a child will try to negotiate a settlement, as it will rarely be in the child's interests to have a trial, and children who express views generally have a strong preference for an early resolution without a trial.

Alienation cases present very significant challenges for lawyers for children, and it is in these cases that jurisdictional variation in the professional rules governing the role of lawyers is most significant. In some jurisdictions lawyers appointed to represent children are obliged to be "traditional advocates," basing their position on the instructions of their child "clients," even if the lawyer believes that the child is alienated and not expressing a truly independent view.

Lawyers for children in Quebec are expected to adopt the role of advocate, basing their position exclusively on the stated wishes of the child, even if the child has been alienated from a parent. In 2002, the Quebec Court of Appeal in *F.(M.) v. L.(J.)*[29] ruled that in the province, lawyers who represent children should adopt an advocate role, provided that the child gives clear instructions. In that case, a 10-year-old boy told his lawyer and a psychologist that he did not wish to see his father, but the psychologist who interviewed the boy believed that he was being manipulated by his mother. The trial judge directed that counsel for the child should develop and advocate a position based on counsel's assessment of the child's best interests. The Court of Appeal ordered the appointment of a new lawyer to advocate based on the child's expressed wishes.

In a 2006 Quebec case, the lawyer for a 13-year-old girl appealed the trial decision granting her father specified parenting time for her and her older brother, despite their stated wishes that they only wanted to see their father when they chose to do so.[30] The trial judge had concluded from psychological reports that the children were in danger of parental alienation by the mother. Based on this finding of the trial judge, the Court of Appeal[31] held that the trial judge was justified in ordering contact despite the children's expressed wishes, as it would be in the children's best interests. This illustrates that even in Quebec, where lawyers for children advocate based on their wishes, the courts may decide that it is not in children's best interests to follow their wishes.

While lawyers for children in Quebec, and a few other jurisdictions, are obliged to adopt the "traditional advocate" role, in most jurisdictions lawyers for children have more flexibility. For example, in Ontario, lawyers appointed to represent children from the Office of the Children's Lawyer (OCL) are governed by the Policy Statement on the Role of Child's Counsel, which provides:

Position on Behalf of the Child

In taking a position on behalf of the child, child's counsel will ascertain the views and preferences of the child, if any, and will consider:

a) the independence, strength, and consistency of the child's views and preferences,

---

[29] (2002) D.L.R. (4th) 350, [2002] J.Q. No.480 (C.A.). See also *L. (S.P.) c. L. (L)*. 2006 QCCA 1053, 152 A.C.W.S. (3d) 244, [2006] J.Q. 8690.

[30] *M.E. c. S.G.*, 2006 QCCS 2936, [2006] J.Q. no 5082.

[31] *G.(M.) c. E.(M.) et G.(S.)*, 2006 QCCA 1637, 164 A.C.W.S. (3d) 1003, [2006] J.Q. 13581.

b) the circumstances surrounding the child's views and preferences, and
c) all other relevant evidence about the child's interests.

In … *custody/access* proceedings, child's counsel will not interfere
with a settlement reached by the parties.[32]

Although this Policy avoids explicitly using "best interests" terminology,
OCL counsel is a "protector" of the children's interests, not an advocate for the
child's wishes,[33] and in terms of the commonly used classification scheme for
lawyering roles, should be viewed as a "best interests guardian" (rather than
a "traditional advocate" taking instructions from a client). Although the OCL
may advocate based on the child's wishes, this is only done if counsel considers
this consistent with the child's interests.

---

[32] Ontario Office of the Children's Lawyer, Ministry of Attorney General; first
drafted April 3, 1995, last revised April 1, 2006. Emphasis added.
[33] *In C.R. v. Children's Aid Society of Hamilton, [2004] O.J. 1251, 4 R.F.L. (6th)
98, (Ont. Sup. Ct.) at paras. 26–31, where Czutrin J. explained the role of OCL
counsel:*

> Pursuant to subsection 89(3.1) of the *Courts of Justice Act*, the Office
> of the Children's Lawyer may act as the legal representative of a child.
> The role of counsel appointed under this provision is to provide full,
> complete, and independent representation of the child protecting
> his or her interests. This is true whether or not the child is capable of
> instructing counsel. The role of the Children's Lawyer includes ensuring
> that all evidence relevant to the issue of the child's best interests is before
> the court…
> *To the extent that counsel acting on behalf of a non-instructing
> client represents that child's best interests, and not his or her views and
> preferences, the Children's Lawyer arguably becomes 'not the advocate of
> the children, but a protector of the children'.* In such a role—that is, acting
> without clear instructions—protecting the children's interests "can clearly
> involve presenting the lawyer's perception of what would best protect the
> child's interests." It may become difficult to distinguish counsel's personal
> views, even if motivated by the child's best interests, from counsel's role as
> advocate. If the child is not instructing counsel, who is?
> It is for the children's counsel, ultimately, to present whatever evidence
> that she has or to review the evidence and make submissions to protect
> the children's best interests. These should not be personal views, but
> based on a position that the Children's Lawyer takes, based on the
> evidence and the law, to advance a position to protect the children. It is
> not for counsel to stand up and give personal views or to give evidence
> from the counsel table.
> Ultimately, it is for the court to decide the issues in this case. Counsel
> is not the legal guardian in this case or amicus curiae, but the legal
> representative.

In the Ontario case of *Boukema v. Boukema*,[34] the court was cautioned by the child's counsel about placing emphasis on the child's stated wishes to the exclusion of all other considerations. The parties had entered into Minutes of Settlement that were ultimately incorporated into a judgment of the court. The agreement provided for joint custody of the parties' 11-year-old daughter; the child was to have "primary residence" with her father in Toronto. Almost immediately after signing the agreement, the mother, who had relocated to New Jersey to be with her new spouse, disclosed that she would not abide by its terms; after a 6-week holiday with the mother, the child expressed a wish to go and live with her in New Jersey. The mother claimed that the child's desire to live with her mother was a material change in circumstances justifying new custody and parenting time arrangements. She applied for a variation of the order. A social worker from the Office of the Children's Lawyer concluded that the child's views were not arrived at independently, and for this reason the Children's Lawyer declined to advocate based on the child's views, though he ensured that there was evidence before the court about the child's views as well as about the factors that may had influenced these views. The court found there had been no material change in circumstances to justify changing the child's primary residence from her father, as had been previously agreed to by the parents, and the mother's application was dismissed. The judge further determined that joint custody was no longer feasible and awarded sole custody to the father. In coming to this conclusion, the court considered the child's wishes, but, as the girl had been greatly influenced by the mother, the court attached less weight to her wishes than it might otherwise have done.

A recent paper coauthored by the Ontario Children's Lawyer, Lucy McSweeney (McSweeny & Leach, 2011), both justified the position that she and her lawyers take in alienation cases, while recognizing its challenging nature:

> From our perspective, advocating uncritically the influenced and manipulated views of children is unhelpful and irresponsible. The child's expressed views are typically known to everyone involved, so this approach adds little to the exercise. Furthermore, in many cases, giving effect to a child's wishes to terminate the relationship with the rejected parent may significantly damage a child's long-term psychological well-being…
>
> Unfortunately, this approach often takes a toll on counsel's ongoing relationship with the child. It is not easy to have a frank discussion with an older child about the information that you are going to be sharing with the court: specifically, that while the lawyer will always let the court know of the child's views and preferences, he or she has an obligation to ensure that the court has all of the relevant information, some of which may not be supportive of

---

[34] 31 R.F.L. (4th) 329, 33 O.T.C. 190, [1997] O.J. 2903 (Gen.Div.).

the child's desired outcome. There is nothing more frustrating for children in these circumstances than hearing that their expressed views are considered to be the product of influence, as many firmly believe that they are independently expressed. Similarly, many feel deeply aggrieved that decisions are being made without any consideration of their views and preferences. All of this can lead a child to quickly become disenchanted with her counsel, usually around the same time that her favoured parent begins to raise concerns about the conduct of child's counsel. It can be very difficult to maintain the child's trust and confidence (two critical elements of the solicitor-client relationship) through this process. (p. 16)

As acknowledged in this passage, alienated children may become dissatisfied with a lawyer who is not advocating a position based on their wishes. In a few recent Ontario high-conflict alienation cases, children have rejected representation by OCL lawyers who are not prepared to advocate based on their "instructions" and have retained "their own" lawyers.[35] In cases where this has occurred, alienating parents are very likely encouraging their children to take this position, though some adolescents are savvy about doing their own research on the Internet, and all purport to be acting "on their own."

A 2011 Ontario alienation decision clearly suggests that children, at a certain stage of their development, have the right to retain and instruct their own counsel. In *Durham Children's Aid Society v. A.S.*, a child protection agency was involved in a very high-conflict custody dispute in which the father claimed that the mother had alienated their two children from him. A lawyer in private practice appeared at one of the procedural hearings in the case, stating that he represented the children (whose ages were not specified). The lawyer for the father claimed that the lawyer for the children was, in fact, retained by the mother, and brought an application to remove this lawyer, seeking to have representation for the children provided by the Office of the Children's Lawyer, and hoping that this Office would take a "best interests" approach and support the claim of alienation. The judge dismissed this application, observing:

here the children . . . have become acquainted with, have had considerable positive interactions with, and established a relationship of "trust" with Mr. Jeffery Wilson, counsel and a member in good standing with the Law Society . . .

Throughout the course of the proceeding to date the children have apparently, as Mr. Wilson urges, established [him as their]

---

[35] See, e.g., *Zacconi v Mahdavi*, [2010] O.J. 2513 (Ont S.C.) where a 14-year-old boy contacted the OCL to get his lawyer "changed" to one who would accept his instructions (a request that was not acceded to); and *S.G.B. v S.J.L.*, [2010] O.J. No. 2619 (Ont.C.A.), per Epstein J.A. (In Chambers).

counsel of choice and, to this point, have been compliant in all aspects required of them [as participants in the proceedings].[36]

While upholding the right of the children to choose their own lawyer, and respecting the professional judgment of that lawyer whom the children had the capacity to "retain and instruct," the judge declined to order that the parents or government pay this lawyer, noting that a government-funded office was available to provide representation for the children. The practical effect of this decision is likely to be very limited, since without an order for payment for legal services, children are only likely to have "independent counsel" if a wealthy parent or relative pays for this, and the fact that one parent (or a relative of that parent) alone is paying for that lawyer may raise ethical issues for that lawyer as to whether he or she is truly being "independently retained."

8.4.6 Judicial Meetings or Interviewing of Children: Contrasting Approaches

One of the controversial questions in the area of custody and parent contact cases is whether judges should meet with children who are the subject of a dispute between parents, and if so, what the purpose of this meeting is and how it should be conducted. There have been concerns raised by some about the potential for such meetings to be emotionally traumatic for children, while on the legal side concerns are raised that such meetings are inconsistent with the traditional notions of an adversarial process in which parties introduce and control the flow of evidence placed before the judge.

While in many jurisdictions judges have been reluctant to meet with children, the argument is now being made that children who want to meet the final decision maker have the "right" to do so, and that both children and the judge may benefit from an appropriately conducted meeting. Further, while there is no doubt that children can be traumatized by being "caught in the middle" of a dispute between parents, there is no evidence that children are traumatized by meeting with a judge and, if they wish to do so, expressing their views to the judge.

There is great variation both between, and sometimes within, jurisdictions, in regard to the practice of judges meeting with children. Practices may be evolving in response to both research and to some rethinking of the judicial role in family proceedings. There are, however, challenging issues related to this practice, and there is a need for special consideration in cases where alienation is a concern.

Judicial meetings with children who are the subject of disputes between parents have long been an accepted practice in some, but not all not, American states. In New York, for example, these are known as "*Lincoln* hearings" and

---

[36] [2011] O.J. 1027, 2011 ONSC 1001, at para. 118–119.

were endorsed by the state Court of Appeals in 1969,[37] as permissible, and in some circumstances even required in child custody cases. The judge meets the child outside the presence of the parents and their attorneys, and may directly question the child to ascertain the child's views and preferences. The practice of judicial interviewing of children is also common in Ohio, and judges in that state may meet with children as young as 3 years of age, at least to get a sense of the child's personality (Birnbaum & Bala, 2010b).

In the province of Quebec, the *Civil Code* creates a presumption that children will be directly "heard" by the court:[38]

> Art. 34. The court shall, in every application brought before it affecting the interest of a child, give the child an opportunity to be heard if his age and power of discernment permit it.

As a result of this provision, children as young as 8 years old who wish to communicate directly with the judge appear in court in family law cases in Quebec, though the normal court process is modified for children (Schirm & Vallant, 2004). In recent years, judicial interviewing of children has become more common in Quebec, in part as a result of the 2002 Quebec Court of Appeal decision in *F.(M.) v. L.(J.)*,[39] which held that lawyers who represent children should adopt an advocate role, provided that the child gives clear instructions. It is not uncommon for children in family cases to actually come into the courtroom. Questions that counsel for the parents wish to pose are screened by the court and are asked by counsel for the child or the judge. It is also common for the parents to be asked to leave the courtroom while the child testifies, though their lawyers will usually be present. In some cases, the parents are not even given access to the transcript of the child's testimony, unless an appeal is undertaken and the appeal court determines that this is appropriate (Schirm & Vallant, 2004; Trahan, 2008).

While judicial meetings with children are now common in some jurisdictions, like New York and Quebec, in other jurisdictions the practice has been much less common. For example, legislation like that in Ontario[40] gives judges wide latitude to decide whether to interview children or not. However, this legislation has rarely been used,[41] even though appellate decisions in Canada accept that judicial interviews of children may be conducted without the consent of the parties involved.[42] There are a number of cases in which Ontario

---

[37] *Matter of Lincoln*, 24 NY2d 270 (1969).

[38] L.Q. 1991, c. 64.

[39] (2002) D.L.R. (4th) 350, [2002] J.Q. No.480 (C.A.). See also *L. (S.P.) c. L. (L)*. 2006 QCCA 1053, 152 A.C.W.S. (3d) 244, [2006] J.Q. no 8690.

[40] *Children's Law Reform Act*, R.S.O. 1990, c. C-12, s. 64.

[41] See *Hamilton v. Hamilton* (1989), 20 R.F.L. (3d) 152 (Sk. C.A.); *LaChapelle v. LaChapelle*, 2000 CarswellOnt 4108 (Ont. C.A.) at para. 7.

[42] See *Hamilton v. Hamilton* (1989), 20 R.F.L. (3d) 152 (Sk. C.A.) and *Jandrisch v. Jandrisch*, 1980 CarswellMan 30 (Man. C.A.).

judges have explained their reluctance to interview children (Birnbaum & Bala, 2010b). For example, in the 2004 case of *Stefureak v. Chambers,* Quinn J. reviewed the various methods of bringing a child's views and preferences before the court and, after analyzing the problems associated with judges interviewing children, stated that this should be "only as a last resort."[43] Justice Quinn suggested that it was normally preferable that a mental health professional interview the child and testify about the child's preferences.

In a number of reported cases, judges have refused to interview a child because they feel inadequately qualified to conduct the interview. In *Stefureak v. Chambers,* the parties were disputing the custody arrangement previously arrived at for their 7-year-old child.[44] In making their arguments, both parties were also trying to adduce hearsay evidence of the child's preferences, based on comments supposedly made to them by the child.[45] In refusing to interview the child to resolve the disagreement about the child's views, Quinn J. explicitly stated that "a chambers interview is not feasible...as I have no training or known skill in interviewing children."[46]

Judges appear to be especially concerned about their ability to interview children in cases involving alienation,[47] attachment disorders,[48] or high-conflict disputes;[49] the concern expressed is that such action, by an untrained person, could traumatize the child. In the Ontario case of *S.E.C. v. G.C.,* where the father was claiming alienation of the child by the mother and the mother was alleging serious claims of domestic abuse against the father, the judge decided not to interview the child or permit her to testify in court, observing: "It would be ironic in the extreme on a custody and access issue, where the only factor is what is in the best interests of the child, if the litigation process were used so as to cause harm to the child for the ostensible purpose of ascertaining her wishes or even shedding light on her best interests."[50] Judges have declined to interview children on the basis that they felt that they would accomplish little by doing so and that greater information would be gleaned through the admission of the children's out-of-court statements, or via a children's lawyer or child custody assessment.

8.4.6.1 Growing Judicial Interest in Meeting With Children

Until recently, judges in many jurisdictions have rarely, if ever, met with children in custody and parent contact cases, though the practice of judicial

---

[43] *Stefureak v. Chambers,* 2004 CarswellOnt 4244, 6 R.F.L. (6th) 212 (Ont. S.C.J.).
[44] *Stefureak v. Chambers,* 2004 CarswellOnt 4244 (Ont. S.C.J.).
[45] *Stefureak v. Chambers,* 2004 CarswellOnt 4244 (Ont. S.C.J.) at paras. 2–4.
[46] *Stefureak v. Chambers,* 2004 CarswellOnt 4244 (Ont. S.C.J.) at para. 70.
[47] See *Polsfut v. Polsfut,* 2008 SKQB 63; and *Gibb v. Gibb,* 2008 BCSC 966.
[48] *A.A. v. S.N.A.,* 2009 BCSC 387.
[49] *Ward v. Swan,* [2009] O.J. 1834 (Ont. S.C.J.). See also *Jandrisch v. Jandrisch* (1980), 16. R.F.L. (2d) 239 (Mb. C.A.).
[50] *S.E.C. v. G.P.,* [2003] O.J. 2744 (Ont. S.C.J.) at para. 32.

interviewing has been common in other jurisdictions. Judges in states like Ohio have found that meeting children both helps them to better understand children and make decisions about them, and that children appreciate the opportunity to meet with the judge and learn more about a process that will deeply influence their lives (Birnbaum & Bala, 2010b). One purpose of such a meeting is to allow the children to "put a human face" on the judge and ask any questions that they may have. Such meetings can be helpful both at the pretrial stage, when a judge may be trying to effect a settlement or required to resolve some issues on an interim basis, or at the trial stage. Judicial interviews must be undertaken with due regard for the vulnerability of children, and children should never be forced to meet a judge.

Recently, in many jurisdictions where judicial interviewing has been very rare, there has been growing interest among lawyers, judges, mental health professionals, and advocates for children in giving children the opportunity to meet with judges. In New Zealand, for example, there was a major change in judicial attitudes and practices toward interviewing children between 2006 and 2009, as judges in that country studied the judicial experience in jurisdictions where the practice was common (Caldwell, 2011).

This greater judicial willingness to consider meeting with children was reflected in the 2010 Yukon decision in *B.J.G.* v. *D.L.G.*, where Martinson J. observed:[51]

> While there are many different ways in which children can participate in the process, there are cases in which judicial interviews are necessary and appropriate. Judicial interviews can take place both at the more informal judicial dispute resolution stage, such as at a family case conference or a settlement conference, and during more formal court hearings and trials.
>
> Three broad purposes of a judicial interview have been identified: obtaining the wishes of children; making sure children have a say in decisions affecting their lives; and providing the judge with information about the child... A judicial interview can be useful for all or any one of these purposes. For example, though a judge may have information about a child's wishes through an assessment by an expert, the judicial interview may provide the judge with more general information about the child.
>
> Giving children the opportunity to speak directly to the judge who will be making a decision that could profoundly affect their lives provides meaningful participation, consistent with the values and principles found in the *Convention*. Judges who have to make decisions that have such a significant impact on a child's life should have the benefit of spending the time necessary to get to know that child...

---

[51] *B.J.G.* v. *D.L.G.*, 2010 YKSC 44, at para 54–59.

There will also be cases in which the only way the Judge will be able to hear the child's views is by the use of a judicial interview because of the lack of financial and other resources. Other methods, such as mediation services that involve the participation of children, reports from professionals, and separate legal representation for children, are simply not available.

8.4.6.2 Special Issues With Judicial Interviews in Alienation Cases

While judicial interviews with children can be valuable for both the judge and child, it is also very important to be aware of the purposes and limitations of these meetings. These meetings should not be "forensic" interviews, in that judges should not be questioning children to try to resolve any factual matters that may be in dispute between the parents. It would be unfair to parties to attempt to resolve factual disputes without the parties being present and able to hear and challenge the evidence, and there is no fair way to test the reliability of a child's statement presented in a private meeting with the judge.[52]

Judges who are conducting a trial will generally want to decide at the beginning of the trial whether it will be appropriate to meet with the children, and will make this decision based on information provided by the parents and their lawyers, and the lawyer for the children, if there is one. An important factor in deciding to meet with the children will be whether they want this. The judge will usually only want to meet with children toward the end of the hearing, so that the judge can better prepare for the meeting and contextualize any impressions and information.

In cases where there has been alienating parental behavior, the judge may place no weight on the stated wishes of the children, but the meeting may still be valuable. Even without training in interviewing children, judges who have heard evidence about alienation may be able to see its effect on the children, as illustrated by the 1999 New York case of *J.F. v. L.F*, where the judge heard expert evidence from three forensic evaluators about the alienation from their father of two children, aged 11 and 13 at the time of the trial, and then had the opportunity to meet with the children. The judge described the interview in the following terms:

> [The children] are both highly intelligent and articulate and, in many ways, engaging and charming... They also show a resilience and ability to adapt to situations. Yet, particularly when discussing their father and his family, they present themselves at times in a surreal way with a pseudo-maturity [that] is unnatural and, even, strange. They seem like "little adults." ... The loving way in which the children perceive their mother, and the way in which they

---

[52] *Ward v. Swan*, [2009] O.J. No. 1834 (Ont. S.C.J.).

uncritically describe her as being perfect, stands in stark contrast to their descriptions of their father. Their opinions about their father are unrealistic, misshapen and cruel. They speak about and to him in a way which seems, at times, to be malicious in its quality... Both children used identical language in dismissing the happy times they spent with their father as evidenced in the videotape and picture album as "Kodak moments." They deny anything positive in their relationship with their father to an unnatural extreme.[53]

The Family Court judge in this case decided to immediately transfer custody of the two children from the mother to the father and suspended her contact with them until a therapist recommended that it should be resumed.

In some alienation cases, judges are aware of the child's views (whether from evidence presented at the trial and or through an interview) and decide that it is important to meet with the child after a decision has been made in order to explain the decision and their reasons for not following the child's wishes. In alienation cases, these meetings should be approached with caution, as a child might be angry or sad if the decision is contrary to the child's wishes. While even in severe alienation cases, a child's attitude may "turn" within a matter of hours or days of a custody change, his or her initial reaction to hearing the news from the judge about a custody change may be very angry. It is important for a judge to consider how news of a decision to vary custody will be conveyed to the child, and in some cases it will be preferable for a judge to have the lawyer for the child or neutral mental health professional tell a child about a decision that is likely to upset a child, including providing the child with an explanation of why the decision is in the child's best interests. While judges can and should make it clear to parents the consequences of the failure to obey court orders, a judicial meeting with an alienated child to explain the consequences for the child of disrespecting an order (e.g., running away) may not be helpful if the child feels threatened by the judge. There are, however, cases in which a judge's meeting to explain the decision can be helpful to the child and parents, by giving the child an age-appropriate understanding of the reasons for the decision and an opportunity to ask questions or make comments.[54] Further, some children lacking in internal self-control may benefit from seeing the judge exercising his or her external, quasi-parental control and as a result feel less inclined to act out.

8.4.6.3 Variation in the Practice of Judicial Interviewing

Although in some jurisdictions, like Ohio (Birnbaum & Bala, 2010b), there is appellate jurisprudence or legislation that governs some aspects of judicial

---

[53] *J.F. v. L.F.*, 181 Misc.2d 722, 694 N.Y.S.2d 592 (1999).
[54] See, e.g., *Zacconi v Mahdavi*, [2010] O.J. 2513 (Sup. Ct.); *I.S. v D.S.*, [2010] B.C.J. 413 (Sup. Ct.); and *Haberman v Haberman*, 2011 SKQB 415.

interviewing of children, in most jurisdictions it is a recent and evolving practice. In the absence of clear direction, there is significant variation in how judges conduct these interviews, even in jurisdictions where the practice is now common (Caldwell, 2011), and individual judges will vary their practice from one case to another, depending on the child's age and the circumstances of the case.

Most commonly, judges who interview children will do so without the parents or their lawyers being present, but some judges allow lawyers for the parents to be present (typically expecting them to remain silent and out of the child's line of sight). Most judges meet children in their offices (often called their "chambers"), but some judges will meet children in a courtroom, or on the more informal side, may even meet them in a park or in a child-friendly restaurant. Most judges ensure that there is some type of record of the interview, commonly an audio recording, but in some cases there may just be the notes of a judge. Most judges do not want to be alone with children who are the subject of litigation, and will have a clerk or the child's lawyer present, and some may want a mental health professional present if one has been involved with the case. Some judges, however, meet alone with children.

Perhaps the most significant variation is in the degree of confidentiality that is afforded to these interviews. All judges who engage in this practice know that they must provide some type of explanation of what they have done in the event that there is an appeal. Some judges are of view that parents should get a full transcript of the interview, so that they can introduce evidence or argument to challenge or contextualize what the children say; these judges have a "due process" orientation and should also ensure that the children know that their parents will be fully informed of what they say. Other judges, however, believe that it is sufficient to provide the parents with a summary of what was said, and give the children some assurance that they will have a degree of privacy or protection; these judges may ask the children if there are things that they are especially concerned about their parents being told. A minority of judges will only provide the parents with a terse summary of what the child said as part of their judgment. Judges who decide not to provide parents with a transcript may nevertheless be obliged by the rules of their jurisdiction to have a recording of the interview with the child that can be provided to an appellate court in the event that an appeal is undertaken.

8.5 Concluding Comments: Principles, Policies, and Research

Soliciting the views and involvement of children in postseparation decision making is a challenging and evolving subject. While it is increasingly accepted that children have the *right* to participate, there are questions about *what* the best way to obtain their views and preferences is. There are no easy answers to these questions, and there is only limited empirical research to provide guidance. While lawyers for children can have an important role, representation for children is not appropriate in all contested cases and is not available in many jurisdictions. Not all children want to be or should be interviewed by a judge, but many children want to be included to both give and receive information. Most children do not want to make the final decision and may be reluctant to express preferences about living arrangements; children should never be pressed to "choose" one parent over the other. If a child is adamant about being heard by the judge or giving "instructions" to a lawyer, this may well be a signal that the child has been alienated, though in some cases this could be a reflection of the child's own experiences with a parent or stepfamily situation. However, if children are permitted to participate in the proceedings, they may be more likely to comply with the order made for their care, even if it is contrary to their express wishes, as they may have the feeling that they have at least been "heard."

Clearly, there needs to be a range of options for involving children in decision making about their care. Training and education about interviewing of children are important for all professionals involved in family law disputes, including judges and lawyers. There must also be policies to ensure that there are appropriate resources to allow professionals to meet with children in a comfortable and supportive environment.

Professionals (and parents) should make it clear to the children that "they have a voice, not a choice." High-conflict separations and alienation cases are emotionally traumatic for children, and they often feel "caught in the middle." However, it is the parents who are placing the child in a position of loyalty conflict that causes the emotional trauma. It is living with the loyalty conflict that is hard for the child. A properly conducted interview with professional, whether a custody evaluator, a judge, or a lawyer, is unlikely to further traumatize the child, and there is some research to suggest that children who feel that they have "been heard" in the course of parental separations may have better outcomes.

9

Legal Responses to Alienation and Parent Contact Problems

9.1 Child's "Rights," Parental Duties, and the Best Interests of the Child

Much of the discourse about postseparation parent–child contact through most of the 20th century focused on the "right" of each parent to have a relationship with a child following separation, and in particular on the right of a noncustodial father to have contact with his children, who in this period almost invariably lived with their mother. By late in the 20th century, however, judges and commentators began to say that children have the "right" to have a relationship with both parents after separation. This "children's rights" approach was, for example, articulated by Lord Justice Balcombe in the 1994 English case of *Re J. (A Minor: Contact)*:

> The principles which a court applies in cases such as this are well established. Contact with the parent with whom the child is not resident is the *right of the child* and very cogent reasons are required for terminating such contact.[1]

While there are situations in which it is useful, and indeed important, to use the rhetoric of children's rights, there are also situations in which the use of children's rights discourse can be highly problematic. In particular, where alienation may be present, it is very easy for an alienating parent and an alienated child to shift the rhetoric and say that if the child has the right to *have*

---

[1] [1994] 1 FLR 729, at 735, emphasis added.

a relationship with a nonresidential parent, the child also has the right to *not have* contact with that parent. This rhetoric may then be used in an attempt to inappropriately empower the child, and allow the child to decide to reject a parent. Accordingly, many judges have adopted a different rhetorical approach, preferring to talk about the "duty" of each parent to support their children's relationship with the other parent. Thus, in the 2005 New York appellate decision in *Usack v. Usack*,[2] the court wrote that each parent has a "duty to rise above his anger...to affirmatively encourage the children to have a relationship with" the other parent.

The most appropriate and widely accepted rhetorical approach to relationships between parents and children, however, is to focus not on the rights or duties, but rather on the best interests of the child. Courts and statutes generally presume that it is in a child's best interests to have a relationship with both parents, but this presumption is rebuttable, if for example, there are significant concerns about abuse or violence. The best interests approach was, for example, articulated by the Ohio Supreme Court in 1997 in *Davis v. Flickinger*:

> the best interest of a child encompasses not only the home environment, but also the involvement of both parents. In today's society that fully admits the need for parenting by both parents, each parent should have full involvement in a child's life, where possible and desired by the parent. When one parent begins to cut out another parent, especially one that has been fully involved in that child's life, the best interest of the child is materially affected.[3]

The advantage of a best interests approach is that it focuses on the child, not the parents, and the focus is on the interests and needs of the child, not the child's wishes or rights. While children will often benefit from a relationship with both parents, this will not always be in a child's best interests.

In this chapter we will largely address the issue of contact problems through the lens of the best interests of the child, an approach that is now dominant in the developed world.

There are strongly divergent views among commentators and professionals about the extent to which the best interests of the child are promoted by having the family justice system involved in responding to cases where a child is reluctant or unwilling to have contact with a parent or there are allegations of alienation. Some argue that it is invariably contrary to the best interests of a reluctant child for a court to force that child to spend time with a parent, and futile for a court to make an order for a child or parent to have counseling to help improve their relationship (Bruch, 2001; Walker, Brantley, & Rigsbee, 2004a). Others emphasize concerns about potential harm to children from coercive legal responses and advocate a very cautious approach to judicial

---

[2] 17 AD 3d 736 (3d Dept., 2005).
[3] 77 Ohio St.3d 415 (1997).

involvement in alienation cases (Jaffe, Ashbourne, & Mamo, 2010; Johnston & Goldman, 2010).

Most experienced legal and mental health professionals support early, appropriate, and effective legal responses for high-conflict cases in general, and for alienation in particular. Responding to parent–child contact issues at an early stage may prevent them from becoming severe and entrenched (Fidler, Bala, Birnbaum, & Kavassalis, 2008; Friedlander & Walters, 2010; Jaffe, Ashbourne, Mamo, & Martinson, 2010). While these cases involving parent–child contact problems are complex and challenging, and require a range of responses, many commentators accept that it is in the best interests of children for the legal system to take a lead in identifying and understanding cases where children are resisting contact with a parent. This will often result in a judicial effort to promote the child's relationship with the rejected parent, but there are also clearly cases where it is contrary to the child's interests for a relationship to be maintained, due to issues of domestic violence, child neglect or abuse, or significantly compromised parenting.

This chapter begins with a discussion of the critical role of custody evaluators and mental health experts in these cases. An initial challenge for the courts is to determine the reason for a child resisting contact with a parent: is this is a case of alienation, justified rejection (realistic estrangement), or a "mixed case" with each parent bearing significant responsibility for the situation? The court must then determine what response will be in the best interests of the children involved, sometimes making decisions on an interim basis before there is full knowledge of the cause for the child's resistance to parental contact, and there is uncertainty about how the parents and children will respond to different clinical or judicial interventions. Mental health professionals, especially independent court-appointed evaluators, can have a critical role at this stage.

The chapter then turns to a discussion of the legal responses to a postseparation rejection of a parent by a child that the court concludes is not justified—that is, to cases of alienation. In many less severe cases, the principal role of the judge at a pretrial stage will be educative, exhorting parents to appreciate the importance of their children having a relationship with both parents, and warning a parent who is engaging in alienating conduct and resistant to compliance with court orders about the judicial sanctions available, including the possibility of loss of custody.

In most jurisdictions it is accepted that courts have the jurisdiction to order children or parents to undertake counseling or participate in psychoeducational programs. In some cases, a parent who is being denied contact will seek to have the other parent found in contempt of court, which might result in a fine, an order to provide services in the community, or even imprisonment of an alienating parent, though courts are reluctant to take such a punitive approach to family problems. Courts may also sanction recalcitrant parents by ordering them to pay the legal fees of the other parent, and in a few jurisdictions there may be a suspension of support obligations if a court finds that there has been a deliberate effort by a parent who is receiving support to undermine a payer's relationship with the children. In some cases, the police may directly enforce an access order, though police enforcement is clearly very intrusive and not a long-term solution. In some cases, a court will order a change from sole to joint custody, to give the rejected parent a greater degree of control, and to allow for a strengthening of the relationship between the child and the rejected parent; this may also serve a warning to the favored parent that a full loss of custody may occur if that parent continues to undermine the relationship between the child and the rejected parent.

In some moderate cases and in most severe cases of alienation, a clear warning that in the event of noncompliance with the provisions of the parenting time order, a change of custody is likely to occur, may suffice to ensure compliance with contact orders (Bala & Bailey, 2004; Gardner, 1998a; Johnston & Kelly, 2004; Lee & Olesen, 2001; Sullivan & Kelly, 2001). In other cases, however, a change in custody is required to ensure the ongoing relationship between the child and the rejected parent and to protect the child from the emotional harm being perpetrated by the alienating parent.

The most intrusive response to alienation is an order for placement of the child in the custody of the rejected parent, in some cases with contact between the child and the favored parent also suspended, at least temporarily. While an order for a reversal of custody with a suspension of contact with the alienating parent as a response to alienation—sometimes called a "parentectomy"—is controversial, courts seem increasingly prepared to make these orders in the most severe cases. As will be discussed in this chapter, there are also cases in which the court, or the rejected parent, recognizes that attempting to force a child to have a relationship with a rejected parent will be contrary to the child's best interests, and legal efforts to enforce contact should cease, perhaps with mechanisms in place to try to preserve some minimal contact in the hope that this will allow for a meaningful relationship to be reestablished at some point in the future.

The chapter concludes with a discussion of suggestions for how the family justice system should be structured to allow the most effective responses to children's resistance to parent contact, including a discussion of case management and the need for early identification, and appropriate and effective intervention. Such structures are not only desirable for alienation cases but are also generally the most effective and efficient ways to respond to all high-conflict family cases.

Although there are generally broad similarities in different jurisdictions in the legal responses to cases where a child is refusing to see a parent, there are also some important differences, as responses are affected by legislation, as well as by local resources and court culture. In this chapter, important differences in approach between jurisdictions will be discussed; unless differences are noted, readers can assume that there is significant similarity between jurisdictions, and the reference to cases or statutes in a particular jurisdiction is for illustrative purposes only.

9.2 The Role of Mental Health Experts in Resolving Alienation Cases

The initial, critical issue that a court must face in deciding how to respond to a claim of alienation or resistance to contact with a parent is a determination of the cause of the child's reluctance to have contact with a parent. In every family court system, there is some provision in legislation or the rules of court for a judge to direct the appointment of a neutral mental health professional to conduct an evaluation, assessment, investigation, or home study of the parties and submit a report to the court regarding custody or access issues.[4] These professionals may be social workers, psychologists, or psychiatrists. In England, New Zealand, Australia, and some jurisdictions in North America, the government will often pay for the preparation of such a report, but in many places the parents will be required to pay for any such report, and if they are unable to do so, no evaluation will be done.

Orders for preparation of a report are most often made with the consent of both parties but may also be made by the court on its own motion, or in the face of opposition from one parent. Judges generally recognize the value of an independent, court-appointed expert in cases where parents are litigating about their children, especially where alienation issues arise.[5] While the nature of the investigation undertaken varies considerably by jurisdiction and will depend on the qualifications and training of the expert and the resources available, there will almost always be a number of meetings with the children involved and observation of interactions of the children with each parent, as well as contact with individuals like new partners, grandparents, and teachers. Depending on the qualifications of the expert, there may also be psychological testing. Despite the value of such reports, in some cases concerns about delay, expense, or a lack of availability of a qualified expert may militate against appointment of any expert by the court, and as will be discussed, there are also cases where the opinion of a court-appointed expert is disregarded by the court. There are also cases in which it is clear from the material filed that a claim of alienation is unfounded, and that the lack of contact is justified by abuse or other inappropriate parental conduct; an evaluation in such cases may be viewed as unnecessary, intrusive for the children, and an unjustified expense.[6]

A study of reported Canadian case law on parental alienation from 1989 to 2009, by far the largest study in the literature of court cases on alienation, gives a picture of how these cases present and are dealt with in one country (Bala, Hunt, & McCarney, 2010), including an examination of the

---

[4] See, e.g., *Children's Law Reform Act*, R.S.O. 1990, c.12, s. 30; and *Courts of Justice Act*, R.S.O. 1990, c. C.43, s. 112.

[5] See *Stewart v. Stewart*, [2006] O.J. 5135 (O.S.C.J.).

[6] See, e.g., *In The Matter of E (Children)*, [2010] EWCA Civ 1159.

role of mental health professionals.[7] In this Canadian study, a report about alienation was provided from an independent expert in 187 of the 232 (81%) of the cases. In another 5 cases (2%), the court ordered an assessment for use at a later stage in the proceedings. In 70 of the 232 cases (30%), more than one court-appointed or independent expert was involved, and in 20 of these 70 cases (29%), there was significant disagreement in the opinions of the court-appointed experts. In some of the cases, either the independent expert(s) did not provide an opinion about the question of whether or not alienation occurred, or it was not possible to ascertain the opinion of the expert(s) from the judgment. Of the cases where the independent expert(s) expressed an opinion about alienation, the judge took a different position than the expert(s) in less than 10%. In a number of the cases where the opinion of a court-appointed expert was followed, the court chose between the conflicting views of two (or more) court-appointed experts. Of the 8 cases where the opinions of the court-appointed experts were rejected, some were cases where the judge felt that circumstances had changed since the report was prepared, while in a few cases the judge simply disagreed with the conclusions of the experts.[8]

While most commonly when mental health professionals are witnesses in high-conflict cases involving allegations of alienation they are appointed by the court, in 46 of the 232 cases (20%), one or more privately retained mental health professionals were also called to testify. In 38 of these cases, there was one privately retained expert, while 8 cases involved two or more privately retained experts. In 35 of the 46 cases involving privately retained experts, the experts testified to either critique or support the opinion of the court-appointed expert. The court preferred the opinion of the privately retained expert in only 3 of the 35 cases where there was a difference in opinion between the court-appointed and privately retained expert about whether or not there was alienation.

In the cases in the Canadian study where the court concluded that alienation was present without an expert testifying, there was evidence from child protection workers or police about unfounded allegations of sexual abuse by the alienating parent, or there was proof of abduction by the alienating parent. If there is no evidence from mental health professional, testimony from neutral government employee like a child protection worker or police officer is likely to be important if alienation is to be established, though in a very small

---

[7] The statistical data for 1989–2008 on the Canadian study discussed here were reported in Bala et al. (2010), which provides a detailed description of the methodology for the study. That paper was updated to include 2009 data by one of the authors of this book (Bala).

[8] For examples of cases where the court disagreed with the expert, see *Hooper v. Hooper*, [2003] B.C.J. 1201(B.C.S.C.); *Jefferson v. Jefferson*, 2000 N.B.J.11 (Q.B., Fam. Div.); *Klassen v. Napper*, 2002 M.J. 19 (Q.B.).

number of cases the court was satisfied that alienation occurred even without such evidence.

A similar but less detailed study of reported cases in Australia that raised alienation issues found that the recommendations of a court-appointed expert were followed in 84% of the cases and not followed in 11%, with the remainder unclassified (Bala, 2012).

Although there is clearly some variation between jurisdictions, there is significant reliance on the opinions of court-appointed experts in all countries. On the other hand, in no jurisdiction is the opinion of a court-appointed expert determinative of whether alienation has occurred, nor will a recommendation of the expert necessarily be followed. A party who disagrees with the views of a court-appointed expert always has the right to challenge the expert by cross-examination or by calling other evidence, and it is the judge, not a mental health professional, who makes the final decisions.

An example of the common situation of a court preferring the opinion of court-appointed experts to the view of an expert retained by one party is the 2010 New Brunswick case of *L.B.L. v. S.B.*,[9] where the main issue was the custody of four adolescents. A court-appointed social worker with expertise in child development interviewed all four of the children and concluded that they genuinely preferred to live with the father. This social worker did not believe that the father had "alienated" the children but, to the contrary, testified that they had become "estranged" from their mother by her conduct. The mother called an expert in domestic violence, who also professed to have expertise in alienation and who claimed that the children had been "alienated" from their mother. The court preferred the testimony of court-appointed expert, noting that she made much more reference to the social science literature while the mother's expert did not seem "unbiased, but to the contrary seemed to be an 'advocate.'"

It is understandable that judges generally place significant reliance on independent, court-appointed experts, who are expected to have the education and training to understand the dynamics of these complex cases. Further, unlike a privately retained expert, the court-appointed expert has access to all of the parties, the children, and collateral sources. Of course, in some jurisdictions the parents are required to pay for an expert, and they may not be able to afford one. There are many locales where it is difficult to find a qualified mental health professional to conduct an evaluation, especially for cases as complex as those involving alienation claims, and in some cases it is apparent that the court-appointed expert does not, in fact, understand the complexities of an alienation case.[10]

An interesting example of the court rejecting the recommendations of a court-appointed expert was the 2011 Chicago case of *Wade v. Wade*,[11] where

---

[9] *L.B.L. v. S.B.*, 2010 CarswellNB 474 (Q.B.).

[10] See, e.g., *Elwan v. Al-Tahar*, [2009] O.J. 1775 (Sup. Ct.)

[11] *Wade v. Wade*, Cook County Domestic Relations Court, Case No 07 D11714, March 11, 2011, Judge Renee Goldfarb.

the Domestic Relations Court awarded sole custody of two boys, aged 8 and 3 years, to their father. The court-appointed psychologist suggested that the mother's "alienating conduct and attitudes" were "moderate to severe" but recommended that she was to continue to have sole custody. In rejecting the expert's recommendation, the judge focused on the fact that the expert had made a number of important factual errors in assessing the case and had relied on a number of statements by the mother about her conduct that were proven in court to be lies. Judge Renee Goldfarb found that the mother's alienating conduct was more severe than the psychologist believed, and that she was less willing to support the boy's relationship with their father than the expert expected. The judge concluded:

> This court finds that [the mother] has embarked on an unstoppable and relentless pattern of conduct for over two years to alienate the children from their father, and lacks either the ability or the willingness to facilitate, let alone encourage, a close and continuing relationship between them.

Although the father was awarded sole custody, the mother was to have "regular parenting time" every second weekend plus vacations. It may not be coincidental that in this case the alienated parent who challenged the recommendation of the expert was a prominent, wealthy basketball player with enormous resources that he was able to devote to the trial, which was one of the longest in Chicago family court history, lasting 38 days. His lawyers were able to adduce very detailed evidence to establish that the court-appointed psychologist was gullible to the mother's distortions and lies, and accordingly her recommendations should be disregarded.

9.3 Enforcement Issues and Judicial Remedies

9.3.1 The Challenge of Enforcement and the Role of the Family Justice System

Noncompliance with court orders and separation agreements is common in high-conflict cases, especially those with alienation issues. This in part reflects the fact that alienating parents often persuade themselves that noncompliance is promoting the interests or protecting the rights of their children. It also reflects the high incidence of personality disorders, and the corresponding distortion in perception, in this high-conflict population (Grych & Fincham, 1999; Jenuwine & Cohler, 1999). In these cases, failure to enforce an order against alienating parents only reinforces their narcissism, false sense of power, and disregard for authority (Gardner, 2001a; Johnston, 2005a; Rand, Rand, & Kopetski, 2005). However, judges are aware that enforcement of parenting orders can be very difficult: the law is a blunt instrument and not well designed for the promotion of good parenting.

As Justice Mossip acknowledged in the Ontario case of *Reeves v. Reeves,*[12]

> The most difficult issue with respect to parental alienation and changes in custody with regard to older children is that such orders are very difficult to enforce. There is no point in me taking the difficult path that I have unless I do everything possible to ensure the order is complied with. This order is in the best interests of [the children].... I must ensure that the father and his mother obey this court order.[13]

While in some cases involvement of the justice system is essential if the child is to have a relationship with a rejected parent, resorting to the justice system is costly in both financial and human terms. The justice system is formal and inherently adversarial; each parent is expected to adduce his or her own evidence and challenge the evidence of the other party. As Ontario Justice June Maresca observes, "the fundamental underpinnings of our system are adversarial," which may "contribute" to heightened tensions.[14] In some cases, lawyers may be unscrupulous or ill informed about the deleterious effects of their actions on parental and child conduct. Toronto lawyer Brian Ludmer argues that "the actions and inactions of lawyers acting for aligned parents can be a significant contributor to respect for court orders and respect for the parental role of rejected parents."[15]

Resorting to the adversarial system, and especially the trial process, will tend to push the parents apart, while the optimal outcome for children will involve parental cooperation and compromise. As noted by Massachusetts Judge Carey,[16]

> legal systems can sometimes perpetuate [alienation]...because the more court appearances you have, the higher conflict with the greater opportunity for arguing, and that is a mechanism that a rejected parent in frustration will sometimes use...repeatedly bringing a case to court, but that drives a stake between that parent and the kids. For every court appearance, the emotional level of the parents goes up, and the emotional level of children goes up because they invariably know what is going on or when there is a court hearing, so while the justice system does not create alienation...it can foster it.

Because of the recognition of the potentially harmful effects of resorting to the justice system, judges and other professionals generally encourage

---

[12] [2001], O.J. No. 308 (S.C.J.).
[13] Ibid. at para. 37.
[14] Interview, April 12, 2010.
[15] Interview, May 10, 2010.
[16] Interview, June 29, 2010.

separated parents to resolve their disagreements without a trial, and if possible outside of the justice system. However, it is also recognized that in some cases resorting to the adversarial system is necessary to protect the interests of the children or an abused spouse, and there must always be caution not to pressure a reasonable or abused parent to settle a case with an unreasonable, disturbed, or abusive parent.[17]

Experienced family judges increasingly recognize the importance of early, effective legal responses to alienation and access problems, a view especially clearly expressed by Chief Justice Peter Boshier of the New Zealand Family Court:[18]

> I think that judges have got to be robust. It is not only the discipline of psychology that we have to be conscious of. We also have the integrity of the family court system...the failure of family court systems to act promptly and meaningfully can exacerbate problems and be contrary to the long-term interests of children.

9.3.2 The Role of the Rejected Parent in Seeking a Legal Remedy

Depending on the circumstances, a parent who is having difficulty in exercising his or her parenting time or enjoying a relationship with a child has a range of legal options, but it is important to appreciate that it is up to that parent to decide what remedies, if any, to seek. Unlike with child support, which in most jurisdictions is enforced by a government agency without charge to the recipient, in the absence of voluntary compliance, parents must apply to the courts to have parenting time or contact orders enforced. Applying to the court often requires significant financial resources and emotional energy, and many rejected parents simply give up trying to maintain a relationship with their children.

If the problem is that the alienating custodial parent is not honoring an existing order, then the rejected parent may need to establish that there has been contempt of court—a willful violation of the court order—and the alienating parent should be sanctioned. The rejected parent may also seek variation of the existing parenting order, perhaps to seek a change in custody or residence. Both types of proceedings may be joined together. In practice, there are often a number of court appearances before a matter is concluded, and the judge is likely to try to persuade the parties to resolve their dispute, often

---

[17] Almost all of the interviewees for this book explicitly referred to both the strengths and limitations of the justice system for responding to alienation, and of the need to use alternatives, where appropriate. The recognition of the potential harms of resorting to the justice system was very clearly expressed by all of the judges interviewed.

[18] Interview, May 24, 2010.

urging the alienating custodial parent to respect the rights of the other parent and promote their child's best interests by supporting the relationship with that parent.

Legal responses and penalties for contempt of court (noncompliance with court orders) include:

- requiring the defiant parent and children to undertake counseling;
- compensatory parenting time ("makeup time");
- requiring the defiant parent to pay the legal costs of the rejected parent;
- requiring the defiant parent to pay any financial expenses incurred but wasted (e.g., airfare); and
- finding a parent in contempt of court and imposing a fine, a community service order, or even a jail sentence.

Finally, a court may vary custody in cases of noncompliance, giving the rejected parent joint or even sole custody, though this must not be done to be punitive with the alienating parent, but only if it will promote the child's best interests.

There is a fairly broad consensus that judicial enforcement of court orders is vitally important in alienation cases, though there is considerable debate over the nature and extent of appropriate sanctions (Bala & Bailey, 2004; Clawar & Rivlin, 1991; Gardner, 2001a; Lund, 1995; Stahl, 1999; Sullivan, 2004; Sullivan & Kelly, 2001; Turkat, 1994; Warshak, 2006). Some maintain that the penalties courts have customarily imposed for violation of access orders are too lenient, while others argue that some penalties, such as incarceration or having to pay fines, are excessive and ultimately not in a child's best interest. Furthermore, punitive judicial actions may be counterproductive to the extent that the punished alienating parent is then portrayed to the child as a "martyr," which in turn only serves to reinforce the child's negative reaction and alienation. Some commentators even argue that while judges should "encourage" custodial parents to support their children's relationships with nonabusive, noncustodial parents, coercive judicial action to enforce contact between a child and parent is not appropriate.[19]

9.3.3 The Importance of Detailed Parenting Plan Orders

Separation agreements, minutes of settlement, and court orders that establish a parenting plan for high-conflict families often lack sufficient detail and precision to effectively structure their troubled coparenting relationship. When parents can cooperate, a lack of specificity provides the flexibility to deal with inevitably changing circumstances, but in a high-conflict case,

---

[19] See sharp criticisms presented by Bruch (2001), Faller (1997), and Walker et al. (2004a), who, in addition to objecting to court-ordered treatment and the appointment of parenting coordinators and case managers, denounce orders enforcing parenting time.

ambiguities and insufficient detail in court orders or separation agreements only serve to exacerbate parental conflict. In alienation cases, any opportunity for the favored, often custodial, parent to control the parenting time schedule may be exploited. Incomplete or ambiguous parenting plans provide one such opportunity, as do provisions permitting flexibility in the parenting time schedule; such flexibility is not appropriate for high-conflict and alienation cases. Although legal and mental health professionals are increasingly aware of the need for detailing parenting plans, the need for highly structured and specified terms for high-conflict families cannot be overstated (Fidler, 2007).[20] For a court judgment to be effective in cases of alienation, the order must be detailed, explicit, and comprehensive; these are sometimes referred to as "multidirectional" orders, with directions not only for both parents, but also for third parties such as schools and health care providers (Bala, Fidler, Goldberg, & Houston, 2007; Sullivan & Kelly, 2001; Turkat, 1994).

In high-conflict cases involving parental alienating behavior, the greater the degree of specificity and structure in the order, the higher the likelihood of success in carrying out the terms as envisioned by the judge, and if necessary, to address enforcement. In these cases, the order should be detailed, explicit, unambiguous, and comprehensive.

9.4 Therapeutic Interventions and the Court Process

If children are resistant to contact with a parent, there are often emotional, psychological, or relationship issues that may be addressed through some form of counseling or therapy. In some cases, either or both parents would benefit from therapeutic intervention, while in other cases the child needs counseling; in some cases it may be beneficial for there to be counseling for a parent and child, or for both parents to meet together with a counselor. While judges, lawyers, mental health professionals, and parents themselves often recognize the potential value of therapeutic interventions, there is significant

---

[20] For a more thorough discussion of parenting plans for high-conflict families, see Birnbaum, Fidler, & Kavassalis, 2008). These plans need to address many issues, including: principles of good parenting, rules of engagement, and direction to keep children out of parental conflict; detailed parenting time schedules for both regular and holiday periods; precise start and stop times for parenting times; the location of transitions; who transports the children, and in which direction; parental behavior during transitions; who cares for the children when they become ill in the morning before school and during school; rules about parental communication and information exchange; rules about traveling out of jurisdiction; provisions for how day-to-day (e.g., extracurricular activities, information exchanges, disposition of clothing and belongings, etc.) and major (health/medical, education, religion) child-related decisions are made; parent–child telephone and e-mail contact; procedures for making temporary changes to the schedule, and so on.

controversy about the extent to which judges should order, or even encourage, parents and children to attend counseling or therapy in cases where alienation is a concern.

In this section we explore the differences in judicial attitudes to the question of whether, as a matter of law, a court has jurisdiction to make an order for a parent or child to have counseling, and then consider whether such orders can effect change. In the following section, we turn to some of the practical questions that arise in making orders or agreements that provide for counseling.

9.4.1 Jurisdictional Controversy: Orders or Recommendations?

An initial legal question is whether a court has the jurisdiction to make an order that a child or parents attend counseling as a condition of exercising parenting rights. In most countries, the courts are of the view that judges have the jurisdiction to make orders for parents to have counseling as a condition of exercising custody or contact rights. Further, as discussed below, if a custodial parent is found guilty of contempt for violation of an order for contact, most courts accept that an order to attend counseling may be part of a sentence for contempt.[21] Although more controversial, some courts also accept that a judge can direct that a parent with custody must ensure that a child has counseling, or undertake reintegration or reunification therapy to improve the child's relationship with a rejected parent. Some judges, such as those in Quebec, take the position that they do not have the legal jurisdiction (or power) to make an order requiring counseling for a child or parent, but they are prepared to make "recommendations." In practice, there may not be much difference between these legal approaches, since the real consequences for failure to engage in counseling may be the same, whether the court has made an "order" or a recommendation: as discussed more fully below, if counseling and other therapeutic interventions fail, the court may be faced with the "stark dilemma" of either a variation in custody arrangements or an abandonment of legal efforts to try to force the child to have a relationship with the parent.

9.4.2 Decisions Ordering Parents to Attend Counseling

The 2007 Ontario Court of Justice in *Kozachok v. Mangaw* is an example of a case where the judge in a high-conflict separation situation made an order for *both* parents to "co-operate in engaging the services of a counselor skilled in

---

[21] For an example of counseling being ordered as part of a sentence for contempt, see *Starzycka v. Wronski*, 2005 ONCJ 329, 27 R.F.L. (6th) 159 at para. 17, a case characterized by Wolder J. as "one of the most persistent acts of contempt that this court has ever experienced," where custody was ultimately switched from the alienating mother to the father.

providing child and family counseling in high-conflict separations, and once found, they are to participate in such counseling." Justice Jones observed:[22]

> High-conflict situations do not automatically turn into low conflict situations merely with the passage of time. To expect these parents, without intervention, to learn to co-operate in the interests of their children, is simply unrealistic and potentially harmful to the children's well-being. If I were to accede to the request of the father and force the mother to deliver the children to him for lengthy, unsupervised periods of time, I would expect the conflict to escalate because neither parent would have adjusted his or her behavior or attitude towards the other.
>
> The parties are quite entrenched in their current positions around access. The conflict between the parties, if it continues, is not in the best interests of these children. The parties must accept the fact that neither party is blameless and that the ongoing conflict is fuelled by both...
>
> Third party intervention through counseling is the best option to improve this situation. The parties need to understand the position of the other and how their conduct is negatively affecting the well-being of their children.

9.4.3 Orders for Counseling for a Child and Parent

In many alienation cases in which counseling or therapeutic intervention is ordered for the child(ren), the judge will make the order with the explicit goal of reestablishing the child(ren)'s relationship with the rejected parent, while leaving the child(ren) in the custody of the alienating parent. In these cases the judge is *ordering* that the *alienating parent* ensure that the child attends counseling as a "condition" or "incident" of custody.

In some alienation cases, one or both parents may be ordered to undertake counseling with the objective of improving their communications skills and understanding of the effects of their behaviors on their children. For example, in the 2008 Ontario case of *McAlister v. Jenkins*, Harper J. ordered that the mother was to have no contact with her two daughters, aged 12 and 8, until she was able to interact with the father and his new wife "as parents [are expected to] do" to meet the interests of their children.[23] Further, as a condition of resuming contact with the daughters, the mother was required to attend a program designed to educate parents on how to avoid placing children in the middle of disputes.[24]

---

[22] *Kozachok v. Mangaw*, 2007 CarswellOnt 1069 (Ont. C.J.), at para. 22–24.
[23] *McAlister v. Jenkins*, 2008 CarswellOnt 4266 at para. 188.
[24] *McAlister v. Jenkins*, 2008 CarswellOnt 4266 at para. 188.

The 2008 Ontario decision of Turnbull J. in *L. (J.K.) v. S. (N.C.)*[25] provides a detailed discussion of whether a court can order counseling for a child. In this case, the judge found that the 13-year-old boy had been alienated by the custodial father to reject the mother. The judge ordered that custody be transferred to the rejected mother, and the alienating father's contact with the child be suspended. There was extensive evidence in the decision about the value to the boy of participation in the psychoeducational Family Bridges workshop of Drs. Rand and Warshak. Justice Turnbull recognized that the child faced the very real challenges in adjusting to the sudden change in custody. While the court did not directly order the boy to undertake any treatment and left discretion to his mother to decide what treatment or program the boy would receive, Turnbull J. did require the mother to report on the boy's participation in any such program to court, and thus to the father. Justice Turnbull concluded:[26]

> Our courts have regularly ordered children to participate in counseling. In this case, the order of the court is simply granting custody of LS to his mother with no access for a period of approximately four months by his father. It is not ordering LS to undertake any treatment or to participate in any program. It is leaving such discretion to his mother who, if the workshop program of Dr. Warshak and Dr. Rand is decided upon, is to report such participation to the court…I interpret the law to require the consent of an informed person who has attained the age of 16 to be obtained before a course of treatment is instituted. I do not think it is applicable to a child who the court has ordered to be placed in the custody of a parent, who is able to act in the best interests of the child. To accede to the submission that no treatment or counseling for LS and his mother can be undertaken without LS's consent would effectively mean that there is no remedy in law for an alienated child in these circumstances. It would mean there is nothing the alienated parent could do to remedy the situation and the wrongdoer would be rewarded for his conduct. I do not accept that is the law…
>
> It is inconceivable to me that that…legislation could be interpreted to protect conduct, which a trial court determines is not in the best interests of LS.

In the 2009 Ontario case of *Sickinger v. Sickinger*,[27] Greer J. concluded that the mother of children ages 9, 12, and 16 years, had been alienating them from their father and had been undermining their relationship with him.

---

[25] *L.(J.K) v. S.(N.C.)*(2008), 54 R.F.L. (6th) 74 (Ont. Sup. Ct.).

[26] *L.(J.K) v. S.(N.C.)*(2008), 54 R.F.L. (6th) 74 (Ont. Sup. Ct.), at para. 192–195.

[27] *Sickinger v. Sickinger*, [2009] O.J. No. 2306, 69 R.F.L. (6th) 299 (Ont. Sup. Ct,), per Greer J, aff'd [2009] O.J. 5178, 75 R.F.L. (6th) 1 (Ont. C.A.).

One issue in this case was that the mother had sent one of the children to a therapist selected by her. The father was concerned that this therapist was undermining his relationship with the girl.[28] The judge concluded that it was "imperative" that the girl receive counseling to help her "deal with her anxiety and emotional problems, arising out of her parents' marriage breakdown" and observed that the "therapist must be a person both parents have confidence in." She ordered the mother to cease sending the child to the therapist whom she had selected, and to send the child to a therapist whom the parents could agree upon. Failing their agreement about a therapist, the judge said that she would select a new therapist. The Ontario Court of Appeal dismissed the mother's appeal, implicitly accepting the judge's authority to make such an order, as well as recognizing her wisdom in expecting both parents to agree on the selection of a therapist.

9.4.4 Courts That Will Only "Recommend" Therapeutic Intervention

In some jurisdictions, like Quebec, judges are generally of the view that they do not have the legal authority to make an order for counseling for either parents or children in a family law case. However, these judges are prepared to "recommend" counseling for parents or children in appropriate alienation cases, and to note in their decisions if a parent has agreed (often after discussion with the judge) that counseling will be undertaken.[29]

Until 2008, judges in England could not make orders directing therapeutic involvement or counseling, but the law was changed in that year specifically to allow the courts to deal more effectively with alienation cases and make such orders.[30] In the 2004 English Court of Appeal decision of *Re S (uncooperative mother)*, Lord Justice Thorpe made clear that even where courts cannot order counseling, the failure of an alienating parent to follow recommendations for such therapeutic involvement may result in a change in custody. He explained the value of a therapeutic approach to alienation problems, as well as warning the alienating custodial mother of the potential consequences of not adequately addressing the concerns about the lack of contact by the children with their father.

> Manifestly there are between these adults unresolved areas of conflict which, unless resolved, will continue down the years to

---

[28] As discussed in Chapters 2 and 7 of this book, one of the themes of the authors' interviews with leading experts is that inappropriate therapeutic intervention can exacerbate the alienation of a child, as the therapist may support the child's decision to reject a parent.

[29] See, e.g., *Droit de la famille 083035*, 2008 QCCS 5680; and *Droit de la famille 10936*, 2010 QCCS 1745.

[30] The change in 2008 was the coming into force of Section 11 of the *Children Act 1989* (as inserted by the *Children and Adoption Act 2006*).

resound to the prejudice and harm of these two children. A process of family therapy is infinitely more likely to lead to resolution than continuing litigation between them...So whilst the court has no power to order the [mother] to re-engage in a process of family therapy...if it emerges...that...proposals, reasonable as to time and location have been advanced for the revival of the family therapy and she has continued to refuse, then she must understand that the court may draw adverse inferences against her.[31]

As Thorpe L.J. explains, the consequences for a parental failure to follow through with such a recommendation or undertaking will not be a finding of contempt of court, but it may well affect how a court will deal with custody or contact problems in the future. Thus, there are only limited practical differences between the "recommendation" and the "order" approaches, since a failure to respect a court order to undertake counseling is unlikely to result in a sanction for contempt of court. Perhaps the real difference is psychological, as some parents may feel greater compulsion to follow a judge's "order" than a judicial "recommendation," even if the consequences of noncompliance are similar.

9.4.5 The Limits of Court-Ordered Therapeutic Intervention

Beyond the question of whether courts have the jurisdiction to order counseling, important concerns have been raised about the effectiveness of court-ordered therapy. There is no guarantee that therapy will be effective; mere attendance at counseling is not the outcome that is desired, and individuals who are undertaking counseling only because it is required by a judge may be highly resistant to change. Further, many community agencies that provide counseling without charge or at subsidized rates have long waiting lists for service, and the high cost of fee-for-service interventions are financially inaccessible to many parents.

In cases of less severe alienation, a judicial "push" toward therapy may have positive effects. Counseling is most likely to be effective when a judge persuades parents of its value and of the importance of the child(ren) having a positive relationship with both parents. However, counseling may be ineffective if the parties are highly resistant to counseling and are only attending to avoid a finding of contempt of court.

In the 2009 Ontario case of *Snider v. Laszlo*, Boswell J. accepted that the mother had been alienating the two boys, aged 12 and 14, from their father, but refused the father's request for an order for "reunification therapy," commenting:[32]

> While the court has the inherent jurisdiction to order reconciliation counseling, *such orders are made sparingly...* There should be

---

[31] [2004] EWCA Civ 597, [2004] 2 FLR 710, at paras. 21 & 22.
[32] [2009] O.J. 5032 (Ont. Sup. Ct), at paras. 79–81. Emphasis added.

compelling evidence that the counseling will be beneficial to the participants.

The likely benefit must certainly be questioned where, as here, the counseling is resisted by three of the four proposed participants [the alienating mother and the two boys]. That said, resistance cannot and should not be the sole determining factor when the welfare of the children is in issue. It is not difficult to envision circumstances where the court may be justified in imposing counseling, even though there is opposition to it. But I come back to the fact that there is an assessment just underway. I believe it will be greatly beneficial to have the views and findings of the assessor before imposing any particular form of counseling on the parties and the children.

In more severe alienation cases, counseling alone, while the child continues to reside with the alienating parent, is unlikely to be effective in restoring a relationship between children and a rejected parent, as it will be undermined by the alienating custodial parent. In severe cases, only a change in residence and an interim interruption in contact with the favored parent are likely to allow for the rejected parent to reestablish a relationship with the children. If in a severe case the court awards custody to the alienated parent, that parent will often be well advised to engage therapeutic or counseling services to help the children adapt to a difficult transition and reframe their perception of the rejected parent.

Depending on the jurisdiction, a judge who reverses custody may have the authority to order the new custodial parent to provide services for the child. However, it is generally preferable to allow that parent the discretion to determine what services to seek. While a judge may be well advised to "remain seized" of an alienation case (continue to have responsibility for) after a reversal of custody and to require a review hearing, the custodial parent should generally have the flexibility to decide what services to seek for the child, and to make changes in the therapeutic regime without seeking prior court approval.

9.4.6 Conclusion: Jurisdiction to Be "Cautiously" Exercised

While there is some variation in approach both within and between countries, most judges accept that they have the *jurisdiction* (or legal authority) to order parents to undertake counseling themselves or provide counseling for their children.

Some argue that therapeutic change is necessarily dependent on voluntary participation, and that court-ordered therapy is an oxymoron, as orders are poor motivators to change attitudes and feelings (Bruch, 2001; Darnall & Steinberg, 2008a; Wallerstein, Lewis, & Blakeslee, 2000). This argument has some intuitive appeal, and ultimately no one can be forced to engage meaningfully in therapy. However, the clinical experience of most of the experts interviewed for this book and the literature suggest that in many alienation cases, the education, coaching, encouragement, or threats of a judge can be prime motivators for change, including engagement in therapy.

Many commentators argue that the involvement of the courts is often critical, not only for the effective implementation of a parenting plan (parenting time and decision making), but also for the effective implementation of any treatment or intervention plan in alienation cases (Bala, Fidler, et al., 2007; Baris et al., 2000; Cartwright, 2006; Everett, 2006; Gardner, 1998b, 2001a; Johnston, Walters, & Friedlander, 2001; Lee & Olesen, 2001; Lowenstein, 2005; Lund, 1995; Rand & Warshak, 2008; Sullivan, 2004; Sullivan & Kelly, 2001; Walsh & Bone, 1997; Warshak, 2006). Australian psychologist and therapist Jennifer McIntosh observed:[33]

> Often, I can only do this type of work in the context of a court order, so that I keep the favored parent engaged when the going gets tough, and when we get to the point of trying some reunification visits, that parent is not just at liberty to cut them out.

Therapeutic interventions that focus on helping alienating parents understand the effects of their behavior on their children may facilitate changes in parental behaviors. Changes in parental behavior may then precipitate a shift in attitudes and emotions, even if parents do not gain insight into the psychological roots of their behavior.

However, the judicial jurisdiction to order (or even to recommend) therapeutic intervention should be exercised "cautiously." It should only be done when appropriate resources are available, and when it seems likely that the parent who is the subject of such an order will engage in the process. This parental "willingness" may be a result of judicial persuasion, or even a response to a judicial threat to terminate (or radically alter) that parent's relationship with the child. If the parent seems truly resistant after judicial "persuasion," either there must be a court-ordered change in the relationship with the child, or the judicial effort to effect change should be abandoned.

9.5 The Content of Agreements and Orders for Therapeutic Involvement

9.5.1 The Value of Agreements and Orders

Mental health practitioners recognize that clinical intervention in alienation cases must be based on a detailed written document establishing the framework, objectives, and terms on which services are to be provided. That document could be a contract for provision of therapeutic services, though

---

[33] Interview, July 14, 2010.

in alienation cases it is prudent to have a court order setting out the basic expectations for counseling (Fidler et al., 2008; Friedlander & Walters, 2010; Johnston et al., 2001; Sullivan & Kelly, 2001; Weitzman, 2004). Even if both parents are initially willing to undertake a voluntary response to a child's resistance to contact with a parent, a consent order for therapy may be desirable because it is difficult to know in advance which cases may become severe and require the threat of legal enforcement, and which cases will be less intense with a high degree of voluntary engagement. Without a court order, clients can revoke their consent for treatment for any reason at any time, including the not uncommon circumstances of feeling challenged by, suspicious of, or dissatisfied with the therapist who is redirecting alienating parental behaviors. If treatment is pursuant to a court order, issues related to payment of the counselor or therapist should also be properly addressed in the order.

If the alienation becomes more severe as time and therapy progress, which is not uncommon, it is important for the therapist to be able to provide a summary report back to the court so that the judge can consider the new information when making further orders. The responsiveness by both parents to therapy and changing their own behavior is a critical consideration for a court in dealing with enforcement and variation issues. When reporting to the court, the therapist will necessarily use discretion, limiting where possible details of personal history, and focusing on the parent's receptivity, engagement, and his or her ability and willingness to change behaviors and relationships.

In some jurisdictions, such as Australia, there are significant constraints on the amount of information that government-funded therapists can provide to the courts, beyond the fact of attendance or nonattendance. While concerns about confidentiality of therapy are generally very important, in alienation cases, legal restrictions on information sharing with the courts can undermine the ultimate effectiveness of these interventions, as their effectiveness may depend on an alienating parent having the expectation that the judge will be informed about parents' willingness to truly engage in therapy, as opposed to whether they are merely attend.

9.5.2 Timing: Diverting a Request for an Evaluation Into a Request for Counseling

Given the need for early intervention and the inevitability of delays in securing a court-ordered evaluation report (not to mention the financial cost), a mental health professional approached by lawyers about the possibility of doing an evaluation for the court may choose to explore treatment alternatives with the lawyers during the referral stage. This is an important consideration, as it is not uncommon for treatment to be recommended in any event. As previously noted, alienation is likely to worsen not only the longer it remains unaddressed, but also because the custody evaluation process itself can often result in the child and favored parent becoming entrenched in their positions, in effect upping the ante.

If parents, in the early stages of mild or moderate parent–child contact problems, can agree that it is indeed in their child's best interest to have contact with the rejected parent, irrespective of the cause, a treatment intervention based on an agreement may be indicated rather than a court-ordered evaluation for use in litigation. If both parents agree with this approach and court proceedings have commenced, their agreement should be clearly delineated in an on-consent court order.

In such cases, the mental health professional who has been engaged will need to undertake a clinical assessment to develop a treatment plan, necessarily taking into account the causes of the strained relationships. If serious allegations of abuse emerge during this process, the therapist may need to make a recommendation for a comprehensive court-ordered evaluation (to be carried out by another professional). A further safeguard is that a therapist would be required to report to the child protection authorities any reasonable suspicions of abuse or neglect.

The possibility of diverting a case from custody evaluation and litigation to a voluntary therapeutic response can be appropriate for some less severe alienation cases; judges, lawyers, and mental health professionals need to be aware of this possibility. However, this should only be done if there is genuine agreement by the favored parent that a relationship between the child and the rejected parent is desirable. If the favored parent continues to dispute whether it is indeed in the child's best interests to have contact with the rejected parent, a comprehensive custody evaluation and judicial resolution will be necessary.

9.5.3 Court Orders for Counseling: Elements of the Order

Table 9.1 lists the suggested components of the order governing counseling in alienation cases (Fidler et al., 2008). As will be further discussed in this section, the list recognizes that there may be more than one mental health professional involved in providing counseling, though the number of professionals involved will depend on the nature of the case as well as the resources of the parties.

9.5.3.1 Distinction Between Role of Therapist and Decision Maker

Once it has been determined by the court or agreed by the parents that it is in the child's best interests to attempt to repair the child's relationship with the rejected parent, there may be a provision in the order or agreement for reunification therapy. As previously discussed, while one objective of such therapy is for the therapist to work toward reintegrating the child with the rejected parent, the goals go beyond that and include addressing the child's overall adjustment.

While the therapist's role includes conducting a clinical assessment of the family's dynamics and needs, to develop an appropriate and child-focused

Table 9.1 Court Order for Intervention and Counseling

1) Provide structured and specified parenting plan.
2) Identify objectives of therapy/intervention.
3) Identify minimum duration for therapy/intervention, or clarify the terms for the parents' withdrawal from services and the procedures for selecting new therapists.
4) Identify the names of professionals who will provide therapy/intervention; failing that, a process for selecting professionals in the event the parents cannot agree.[1]
5) Identify the specific role of each professional, including scope of decision-making powers, if any.
6) Name any specific seminars or educational programs parents are to attend.
7) Name family members who are to participate in the therapy/intervention.
8) State that the professionals are entitled to communicate with each other as deemed necessary by the therapists, and that the parents will execute any necessary authorizations to allow for the exchange of information.
9) State that the parents will cooperate with the process as directed by the therapist.
10) Clarify the limits of confidentiality, including reporting requirements to court.
11) Identify enforcement clauses (e.g., sanctions, consequences for noncompliance, options to prevent change of custody, etc.).
12) Specify any grievance procedures.
13) Clarify details of payment for services, including the therapy, and any report or court attendance.

---

[1] This may include a term that there will not be any unauthorized involvement of new therapists.

treatment plan, the therapist is not conducting a forensic assessment in the sense of addressing *if* it is in the child's best interest to have contact with the rejected parent. That determination has already been made by the court or agreed to by the parties. However, in some situations, circumstances may develop to the point that the therapist determines the therapy should cease or that a report to a child protection agency is required.

In undertaking reunification therapy, the therapist attempts to implement a court-ordered or agreed-to parenting time schedule, preferably one that is detailed and unambiguous. If this therapeutic approach is being undertaken voluntarily, it may be helpful to specify that the favored parent is to retain legal custody (decisional authority to make major child-related decisions), provided that the other parent has contact as specified in the order or agreement. This may decrease the favored parent's resistance and insecurities to the extent that he or she participates meaningfully in the treatment intervention, and may also actively encourage the child to do so, as well as outwardly support the child's relationship with the other parent (Rand, 1997a; Warshak, 2001). Further, it may encourage compliance with the treatment plan if the judge gives an implicit, and sometimes explicit, message to favored parents that they can only be assured of retaining custody if they to comply with court orders, engage in therapy, and alter behavior.

The therapist cannot act as the person who will determine the parenting time schedule. The role of the family therapist must remain distinct from that of a mental health professional who might be retained as a decision maker, such as a parenting coordinator or mediator/arbitrator. Assuming the roles of both therapist and decision maker poses ethical issues and clinical obstacles and may raise legal concerns as well (Darnall, 2010; Greenberg, Gould, Schnider, Gould-Saltman, & Martindale, 2003; Kirkland & Kirkland, 2006; Sullivan, 2004).[34] More specifically, if the child and favored parent believe the therapist/facilitator has the authority to determine whether or not parenting time occurs, there is little likelihood of progress to achieve the stated objectives. It is far preferable for a therapist/facilitator to be able to acknowledge awareness of the fact that the child may not want to see the parent, while also noting that the therapist has no control over parenting time schedule/orders. The therapist/facilitator can then advise the child that the objective of the therapeutic intervention is to try to implement the parenting time schedule that was either agreed to by both parents or ordered by the court. Within that broader objective, the child is invited to participate by expressing concerns and feelings, and providing ideas about how to make that time manageable and more enjoyable.

As noted, any order for parenting time assumes that the specific contact is in the child's best interests, and thus this is not open for further determination by the reunification family therapist. Several options exist for the court in establishing a parenting time schedule in cases where reunification therapy is being undertaken. For example, an order might include a specific gradually increasing parenting time schedule, contact may be limited to the therapy sessions only until further order of the court, or contact may be supervised by a family member or at a visitation center and limited to a certain amount of time each week. Frequently, the court-ordered parenting time is not occurring when the therapy begins. In these cases, the order may continue to specify the parenting time that is expected, with the understanding that the objective is for the therapist to gradually implement that ordered plan during the counseling. The therapist may have some authority to determine the pacing of the implementation depending on how the therapy is proceeding, but not to determine whether it is to occur. In these situations it is common for the order to set a date for reestablishing the parenting relationship as specified or for review by the court.

9.5.3.2 Ensuring That the Family Therapy Proceeds

It is not uncommon for difficulties to arise either getting the reunification therapy started or during the therapy; these delays in many cases result in an exacerbation of alienating behaviors. Consequently, the order should indicate

---

[34] See Association of Family and Conciliation Courts (AFCC), *Guidelines for Court-Involved Therapy* (2010), and the AFCC Task Force on Parenting Coordination (2003), and Parenting coordination: Implementation issues, *Family Court Review* (2003), *41*, 533–564. Also see Fidler and Epstein (2008) and *Guidelines for Parenting Coordination* developed by the AFCC Task Force on Parenting Coordination, May, 2005, which can be found at: http://www.afccnet. org.

a date by which the parents must contact the therapist, a court return date to follow up on the treatment progress (or permission to return on short notice), and a provision that neither parent may unilaterally withdraw from the therapy prior to the previously agreed to minimum duration of the therapy or the assigned review date. If treatment is proceeding without incident, this court date can be postponed by the therapist informing counsel and the court. However, when difficulties are encountered, having a specified return date will ensure the court's direction without inevitable delays.

9.5.3.3 Specifying Who Should Attend

As noted, the entire family needs to be involved in the intervention, and seen in various combinations as determined by the therapist. Frequently, the favored parent is hesitant or even unwilling to attend therapy, believing it is the rejected parent who has problems and thus needs therapy before anything else is to occur. The favored parent may also claim an inability to force a child to attend. The order or therapy contract should specifically name the persons required to participate in the therapy or intervention. Blaming one parent is counterproductive to the intervention goals, especially with high-conflict personalities. Regardless of who has "caused" the problem, or the relative contributions of each parent, both parents are important to the solution. These situations are often complex, and sometimes more than one therapist is involved. For example, the child may have his or her own therapist, and one or both parents may also have an individual therapist.

Notwithstanding the need for an approach that involves the entire family, survey results reported by Bow, Gould, and Flens (2006) indicate that the most common recommendation of forensic custody evaluators in alienation cases is for individual therapy for the child and the parents. In cases where there is alienation, judges quite frequently make orders (or recommendations) for the child alone to receive therapy. Individual therapy for the child by either the same or a different therapist working as a member of a team, without the inclusion of other family members, however, is not likely to be an effective intervention for rejection of a parent, as the attitudes of the parents, especially favored parents, often influences their children.[35]

As noted, often, family resources will limit the extent to which an optimal level of services can be provided.

9.5.3.4 Confidentiality and Open Communication Between Involved Professionals

Legal and mental health practitioners generally agree that if a court orders counseling, there should be a mechanism to ensure that the counseling occurs,

---

[35] Frequently, therapists not familiar with high-conflict and custody-litigating families may be of the mistaken view that only individual therapy for the child (or one or both of the parents) is indicated.

which requires the possibility of reporting back to the court. American psychologist Robin Deutsch explained:

> The court has to continue to monitor these cases before and
> after the interventions. There has to be a timeline of scheduled
> reviews. The court needs to know [about what's occurring during
> the therapy]; it's all about informed consent that is set up at the
> beginning.[36]

There are different perspectives, though, on the extent of the information that should be shared with the court. A totally confidential process has the benefit of avoiding the negative impacts of public shame and humiliation, and may encourage more candor by the participants. However, the risk of confidentiality lies in shielding the personality disorders and negative characteristics of parents who tend to show disregard for authority, including court orders or the directions of a therapist (Bernstein, 2007; Greenberg et al., 2003; Johnston & Campbell, 1993; Johnston & Roseby, 1997; Johnston et al., 2001; Lebow & Rekart, 2007; Sullivan 2004; Sullivan & Kelly, 2001). Orders are meant to be followed, and parents need to be held accountable. Further, and elaborated more fully later, in the more severe cases, therapy, especially confidential therapy, is unlikely to be effective. Commenting on the value of the lack of confidentiality on the parents and the success of the therapy, Deutsch observed:

> I don't think its shaming. It is what it is. If people think it is
> shaming, then what does it say about their motivation for their
> behavior? If there is informed consent, and they know it will only
> be disclosed if the process doesn't work or the court subpoenas
> the notes, I think it helps participation. There are other models
> where the therapy ends up being disclosed to the courts, such as
> maltreatment, substance abuse, and anger management and [the
> disclosure] is a very important part.

Completion of therapy in alienation cases usually takes at least 9 months and can take 2 or more years. However, if there is sporadic participation or there has been no change or indications of such in the behavior of the child (i.e., some resumption in contact with the rejected parent) and the favored parent within 3 to 6 months, there will be real concerns about whether therapy will ever be effective in addressing the contact problems.

If at the end of the therapy the parent–child contact problem has not been resolved, the absence of provision for reporting means that valuable information cannot be used by the court, or other professionals who may be involved in the case. Further, in cases where therapeutic intervention is not working, the alienation often becomes worse and more pronounced over the

---

[36] Interview, June 14, 2010.

course of treatment, and reporting can be important to allow for an appropriate legal response.

Circumstances vary, the degree of confidentiality expected should vary with the case, and there should always be special consideration for the confidences that a child shares with a therapist. In our view, however, when difficulties are encountered with the therapy proceeding or with the resolution of the alienation, the benefits to the child of the therapist reporting back to the court exceed any benefits associated with total confidentiality. Depending on the nature of the proceedings, the reporting may be to the court, counsel, an arbitrator, or the parenting coordinator.

In addition, there needs to be some ability for the various involved professionals to exchange information; this provision should be explicitly included in the court order and treatment contract. It is not uncommon for alignments, polarization, and fragmentation to occur among and between the various professionals in the same way that these occur within the family. It is not uncommon for the aligned parent to attempt to prohibit the therapist's access to other previous or current professionals involved. However, the order and treatment contract need to include the provision for full communication between the various professionals (Sullivan & Kelly, 2001).

The order or treatment contract also needs to clarify that there is no confidentiality among family members and therapist in the family therapy. While the therapist will necessarily exercise discretion, if therapy is to be effective in alienation cases, there needs to be some sharing of information provided to the therapist by individual family members with other family members.

9.5.3.5 Appointment of a Parenting Coordinator or Case Manager

Often a number of professionals, including other therapists, physicians, educators, the police, child protection workers, and lawyers for the parents and child, are involved with these families. In many cases, a comprehensive custody and access evaluation has been completed and included recommendations for the clinical interventions. It can be valuable to have a professional who acts as a case manager to coordinate the provision of services and, within the scope of authority vested by the court or agreement of the parties, makes decisions about the day-to-day care of the children that the parents are unable to make together.

In a growing number of jurisdictions, courts are making use of a "parenting coordinator" (or "special master") to deal with cases where the court has found that alienation has occurred. The parenting coordinator may be a mental health professional or lawyer, who assists the parents to implement their parenting plan with minimal conflict and, where they are unable to agree, will have the authority to resolve day-to-day child-related issues that AQ1 are not resolved by the court order or agreement.[37] The scope of decision-making authority of the parenting coordinator may include, for example, the appointment of additional members to the treatment team when parents cannot agree, or a determination of the pacing of the court-ordered parenting time, leaving the therapist entirely out of this role.

In the Washington D.C. case of *Jordan v. Jordan*, the Domestic Relations Court concluded that the custodial mother had been alienating the couple's two daughters, aged 5 and 12 years, from their father, and thwarting his time with the girls. The court responded by awarding joint legal custody to both parents and equal parenting time, and by appointing a parenting coordinator pursuant to the jurisdiction's *Domestic Relations Rules*. The cost of the parenting coordinator was to be borne equally by the parents, and there was an expectation that the older daughter might continue to see an individual therapist to help with the "reunification" process. The Court of Appeal affirmed this decision and explained:

> Dr. Zuckerman [the court-appointed custody evaluator] found both parents to be fit and recommended joint legal and physical custody of the children. Dr. Zuckerman stressed that the children need "to have positive connections with both parents and to be protected from conflict in the post-divorce period." He further emphasized that it is "strongly in E.J.'s [the 12 year old daughter's] best interests to redevelop a good relationship with her father." To facilitate the joint-custody arrangement, Dr. Zuckerman recommended the appointment of a "parenting coordinator." He noted that the parties would need to make significant changes in their attitudes to promote the children's interests, and that the "most important developments" would center around Ms. Jordan, in helping her to normalize E.J.'s relationship with Mr. Jordan. Dr. Zuckerman

---

[37] Roles involving decision making or arbitrating commonly fall under the title of parenting coordinator or mediator/arbitrator (Association of Family and Conciliation Courts, 2005; Baris et al., 2000; Boyan & Termini, 2004; Coates, 2003; Coates, Deutsch, Starnes, Sullivan, & Sydlik, 2004; Garrity & Baris, 1994) and are subject to the jurisdiction's legislation or family law rules relevant to family arbitration. Coates et al. (2004) define parenting coordination as an intervention for high-conflict families in which the coordinator helps the parents implement their parenting plan, most typically one that has already been determined by agreement of the parties or the court. Parenting coordinators are usually retained for a term that lasts between 18 and 24 months. While some jurisdictions have legislation that allows a court to order parenting coordination with the arbitration component, more commonly, any arbitration requires the consent of the parties. A complete discussion of parenting coordination is beyond the scope of this book. For further information, see Kirkland (2008) and Shear (2008).

contemplated that the parenting coordinator would work with the parties "[to create] a plan that would promote the relationships between Mr. Jordan and [his] daughters"; and that the parenting coordinator "should be endowed with authority to speed up or slow down the progress."[38]

In jurisdictions where legislation or the rules of court allow for the appointment of a parenting coordinator, the court must establish the basic legal framework for custody and parenting time, as judges are not permitted to delegate their judicial powers. The use of parenting coordinators is an important innovation; while parents have to pay for the services of this professional, if there are a number of therapists or there are a significant number of court appearances likely, the appointment of a parenting coordinator can ultimately both save the parents money and help the children.

A growing number of jurisdictions have laws to allow for the appointment of a parenting coordinator without the agreement of the parties; in some cases the courts will make such an appointment over the objection of one parent, usually the favored parent, to attempt to address alienation issues.[39] If there is no legislation to allow for the appointment of a parenting coordinator, the parents may make an agreement for such an appointment, with this professional having an agreed-upon authority to act as a mediator, and failing that mediation, as an arbitrator, recognizing that the processes used are to be informal and expeditious (e.g., use of e-mail) and the range of authority limited. However, where legislation or rules of court do not allow for such an appointment, without the agreement of the parties, judges do not have the authority to give a therapist the authority to make any decisions directing when parents will spend time with the children, as this would amount to an improper delegation of authority by a court.[40]

When numerous professionals are involved, careful case management by a parenting coordinator (or case manager) can facilitate collaboration and full communication between the various professionals (Sullivan & Kelly, 2001). The parenting coordinator attempts to ensure team consistency and continuity to avoid the splitting or pitting of one professional against the other, as polarization of professionals is frequently seen in high-conflict families, particularly in alienation cases. As case manager, the parenting coordinator, subject to the ultimate authority of the court, directs and manages the team of professionals, defines *consistent* treatment goals, and facilitates the ongoing exchange of information among the team members, while being mindful not to undermine relationships between therapists and clients.

---

[38] See, e.g., *Jordan v. Jordan*, 14 A.3d 1136 (DC 2011).
[39] See, e.g., *Jordan v. Jordan*, 14 A.3d 1136 (DC 2011).
[40] See *M.(C.A.) v. M.(D.)*, 2003 CarswellOnt 3606 (Ont. C.A.); and *Hunter v. Hunter*, 2008 CarswellBC 656 (B.C. S.C.).

While reporting to the court and an exchange of information among the team of professionals is important, if therapists do not use discretion in disclosing information, work with children can be compromised. When a parenting coordinator is involved, this allows therapists, collateral sources, and children to feel free to communicate with the coordinator, who, in turn, reports to the court. The parenting coordinator may in some instances be able to protect the participants by using different sources of information to formulate any opinions provided to the court or in explaining decisions to the parents (Johnston, 2001; Sullivan, 2004; Sullivan & Kelly, 2001).

In alienation cases it is quite common for favored parents to make repeated allegations of abuse by the other parent, and take the child to different therapists and health care providers to attempt to obtain a report confirming the abuse. To the extent that multiple examinations and investigations are intrusive and pose a risk to the child, it may be necessary for an order to prohibit a parent from taking the child for another investigation or to another therapist without leave from the court, the parenting coordinator, or the consent of the other parent.

9.6 Adjusting Parent Contact and Interim Orders

In cases where there are alienation concerns and a child appears to be rejecting a parent without good reason, a court may respond with a short-term or interim order to change the parenting arrangements. The court may order "compensatory time," with the parent denied contact to make up for lost time with the child. Another option, short of a permanent reversal of custody, is for the court to order a prolonged period of contact with the rejected parent, such as during the summer or an extended vacation, perhaps coupled with restricted or suspended contact with the alienating parent.

Such responses may allow for the restoration of the child's previously good relationship with the rejected parent and prevent the further deterioration of that relationship, and are less disruptive than reversing custody permanently. Further, ordering a temporary change to the parenting time schedule sends a message that the court will respond to alienating conduct while also affording the child and rejected parent the uninterrupted time to repair their relationship.

An example of a court making a short-term change in parenting arrangements is the 2005 Ontario case of *Starzycka v. Wronski*.[41] After extensive court appearances in the year following separation, custody had been granted to the mother of the children; the father was granted alternate weekend and midweek contact with both children, even though only the younger boy was the biological child of the father. Some 8 years after separation, when the younger boy was 9 years of age, the father claimed he was being denied time with his son

---

[41] [2005] O.J. No. 5569 (O.C.J.).

with increasing frequency, and finally that he was unable to exercise any contact with his son. An order was made appointing the Office of the Children's Lawyer to investigate and report to the court. The mother refused to cooperate with the Children's Lawyer's, although she had been previously ordered to do so, and she continued to disobey court orders regarding parenting time, despite several findings against her for contempt. After citing the mother for contempt, the court ordered that the father was to have interim custody of the boy to facilitate an investigation by the Office of the Children's Lawyer. In transferring "interim custody" of the son to the father and denying contact with the mother for that interim period, the court concluded that "[t]he applicant [mother] has refused to follow any orders of this court for the past year and has been found to be in contempt of this court. She has refused numerous opportunities to purge her contempt by cooperating with the Children's Lawyer and by following the directions of this court."[42] The judge granted her custody of the oldest child, for whom the father had not persisted in his claims for contact, perhaps because he was not a biological parent. Justice Wolder was clear that had it not been for the older child who was to remain in her custody, he would have considered incarcerating the mother.

In the 2007 Ontario case of *Pettenuzzo-Deschene v. Deschene*, a court-appointed evaluator concluded that the mother had engaged in a "deliberate campaign of parental alienation," resulting in a 7-year-old girl refusing to spend time with her father, and making it difficult for the father to see his four-year-old son.[43] On an interim motion, Whalen J. decided to transfer physical care from the mother to the father for a 5-week period over the late summer, with the mother to have only supervised access during that period. The intent of the interim order was to allow the children to "re-establish or expand their relationship with their father," with the judge expressing the view that the children might be returned to the primary care of the mother as a result of a trial or settlement, but hopefully with more significant involvement of the father in their lives. There is no report of a trial decision in the case, so it seems likely that this "interim order" had an effect on the mother's attitude and behavior, though they ended up primarily residing with her.

9.7 Contempt of Court: Punitive Sanctions and Behavioral Conditions

One of the most frequently used remedies against a person who is in violation of a court order is a proceeding for contempt of court, which may result in fine, imprisonment, or other judicially imposed sanction. While the contempt process, or more commonly the threat of a contempt proceeding, is enough

---

[42] Ibid at para. 29.
[43] *Pettenuzzo-Deschene v. Deschene*, [2007] O.J. No. 3062, 40 R.F.L. (6th) 381 (Ont. Sup. Ct.).

to secure voluntary compliance with court orders in most types of civil cases, there are real limitations to its use by parents who are being denied contact in violation of the terms of a family court order.

A finding of contempt of court only can only be made if there has been a clear and "willful" violation of a court order. A contempt proceeding is a civil process, initiated not by the state, but by the party whose rights are being violated; however, it may result in an order for the payment of a fine or even imprisonment. Because of the severe sanctions that can be imposed, courts require a high standard of proof before making a finding of contempt of court. In many jurisdictions, a finding of contempt is said to require "proof beyond a reasonable doubt" of the violation of a court order; this is the standard of proof normally required in a criminal proceeding. In some American states, the standard is "clear and convincing" evidence of a violation of a court order, higher than the ordinary civil standard, but not quite as high as the criminal standard of proof.

The heightened standard of proof makes it difficult, though by no means impossible, for a rejected parent to establish contempt of court. Even if contempt is proven, family court judges often exercise restraint in sentencing. There are a number of reasons for this judicial caution. Courts recognize that "the law of contempt...is a blunt instrument that is not particularly well suited to the complex emotional dynamics of access disputes."[44] In other words, a sanction for contempt may not help to secure compliance with the order, especially in the long term. When alienating parents are sent to jail, they will inevitably tell, or it will be evident to the children, that they are sacrificing their liberty as a result of their efforts to protect what they perceive to be the rights or interests of their children not to see the rejected parent; this "martyr-like" response is unlikely to help the child reestablish a relationship with the rejected parent.

More importantly, there is often a concern about the effect of a contempt sanction on the welfare of the child(ren) involved. As one Alberta judge stated in an access enforcement proceeding, "Children are better off if their parents are not in jail or paying fines."[45]

The limitations and challenges of the contempt process are illustrated by the 2010 English Court of Appeal decision in *CPL v. CH-W.*[46] There had been protracted litigation concerning two children, a boy aged 11 at the time of the final proceeding, who resided with his father, and a girl, aged 9 at that time, who resided with her mother. A court order provided that the father "shall allow the mother to have contact" [the English concept equivalent to parenting time, access, or visitation] with the boy on specified weekends. On a number of occasions, the mother came to the father's house to get the boy, and the father indicated that the boy was unwilling to go along with the mother. On

---

[44] *Paton v. Shymkiw* (1996), 114 Man. R.(2d) 303, at 308 (Q.B. Fam. Div.).

[45] Veit J, in *Salloum v. Salloum* (1994), 154 A. R. 65 (Q.B.), para. 10.

[46] *CPL v. CH-W, ML-W, EL-W (by their Guardian ad litem,)* [2010] EWCA Civ 1253.

one occasion, the boy himself came to the door and stated that he did not want to go with her. The trial judge, who had been dealing with the case for some time, found the father in contempt, as he felt that the father had influenced the boy and not done enough to require the boy to go along with the mother. The Court of Appeal reversed the decision. Lord Justice Munby noted that contempt needs to be proven "beyond a reasonable doubt," and the terms of this particular order only required the father to "allow" the boy to have contact with his mother. More generally he noted the importance of the contempt power:

> Committal is—has to be—an essential weapon in the court's armory
> in cases such as this. Nothing in this judgment should be seen as a
> charter for avoiding enforcement of contact orders in whatever is
> the most appropriate way, including, where appropriate, by means
> of committal.[47]

However, the appellate judge accepted that while the boy may well have originally been influenced by his father, by the time of the proceedings in question, the boy was clearly unwilling to see his father, noting: "The boy now has a weapon that no child should possess: by agreeing to see his mother he can save his father from jail; by refusing he can have his father punished." The judge concluded that the welfare of the boy would not be served by committing the father to prison for contempt of court, and observed:

> A common trope...is that committal in this kind of case is or ought
> to be a last resort.

> I agree, but it is important not to misunderstand what is meant by
> this handy aphorism. Committal should not be used unless it is
> a proportionate response to the problem nor if some less drastic
> remedy will provide an adequate solution. But this does not mean
> that one has to wait unduly before having resort to committal, let
> alone waiting so long that the moment has passed and the situation
> has become irretrievable. That point, in the nature of things, is
> often easier to identify with the priceless benefit of hindsight—I
> do not underestimate the difficulties of deciding the right strategy
> in this kind of case. But I cannot help feeling that, on occasions,
> the understandable reluctance to resort to such a drastic remedy
> as committal means that when recourse to it is first proposed it is
> too late for committal, whereas a willingness to grasp the nettle
> by making a committal order at an earlier stage might have ended
> up making all the difference...I have already made. The threat,
> or if need be the actual implementation, of a very short period of

---

[47] *CPL v. CH-W, ML-W, EL-W (by their Guardian ad litem)* [2010] EWCA Civ
1253, at para. 96.

imprisonment—just a day or two—may at an earlier stage of the proceedings achieve more than the threat of a longer sentence at a much later stage in the process. I do not suggest this as a panacea— this is an area in which there is no panacea—but it is something which, I suggest, is worth keeping in mind.[48]

This English decision emphasizes the need to bring a proceeding for contempt of court before the attitude of the children involved becomes so entrenched that it serves no real purpose.

If there is a finding of contempt, the court has the power to impose penalties on the parent who violated the order, primarily intended to encourage future compliance but also as a punishment for the contempt, and may also impose behavioral conditions on the person in contempt to try to ensure that the order will be followed in the future. The court can impose monetary penalties in cases of contempt of custody and contact orders. While fines or community service orders are possible in these cases, they are not often imposed, as they will often harm the children by draining resources from their primary caregiver.

In *Cooper v. Cooper*,[49] Justice Snowie of the Ontario Superior Court of Justice ordered the mother, who was found in contempt of an access order, to pay a fine of $10,000 to the government. In this case, the father had not had contact with the children since the date of separation. Fifteen orders had been made over several years to address the father's contact. Despite significant efforts by the case management judge and mental health professionals involved, the mother had successfully manipulated the situation to sabotage all contact between children and father. In finding the mother to be in contempt, Justice Snowie stated:

> I am satisfied beyond a reasonable doubt that Mrs. Cooper's actions and lack thereof constituted the offence of civil contempt. It is also clear that the actions of the respondent were contrary to the best interests of all three children. These children, as all children do, needed a mother and a father. It is the right of all children to have a relationship with their mother and their father. There is no evidence before this court that would indicate that Mr. Cooper was anything but a good father, a loving father, and a father who throughout the last seven years wanted to be involved in any capacity in his children's lives. He has admirably and heroically been before this court on at least 15 occasions trying, unsuccessfully, to obtain access with his children. He still continues valiantly to attempt to have a relationship with his children.[50]

---

[48] *CPL v. CH-W, ML-W, EL-W (by their Guardian ad litem)* [2010] EWCA Civ 1253, at para. 108.

[49] *Cooper v. Cooper*, [2004] O.J. 5096, 2004 CarswellOnt 5255 (S.C.J.).

[50] Ibid. at para. 57.

In *Cooper,* as is common in contempt proceedings in alienation cases, the alienating mother offered as a defense that she was prepared to comply with the order, but it was the children who were refusing contact. Some judges have responded to this argument by articulating a positive obligation for the custodial parent to encourage the children to attend the scheduled parenting time. In *Cooper,* the custodial mother was found in contempt for having "willfully and deliberately sabotaged"[51] telephone contact between the children and their father. Although she made the children "available" by having them at home when the father called at the appointed time, she would neither answer the telephone nor, in her words, "put the telephone to the children's ears."[52] The court rejected her argument that "it was up to the children to decide whether or not they would answer the phone" and found her in contempt for "shirking her responsibility and obligation directly, and...indirectly conveying to the children her disapproval of telephone access."[53]

As discussed previously, there is some controversy over the jurisdiction and effectiveness of orders for counseling, especially for alienating parents and alienated children, as a condition of a custody order. However, judges clearly have the power to impose behavioral conditions on a person found in contempt of court with a view to attempting to ensure future compliance with the order, and it seems to be generally accepted that courts have the power to order a parent who has been found in contempt of court to undertake counseling as part of the sentence for contempt.

In *Cooper,* in addition to finding the mother in contempt and imposing a fine of $10,000, Snowie J. ordered that the mother was to immediately arrange for and be supportive of counseling for one the children. The purpose of this counseling was the reintegration of the father into the child's life. Justice Snowie ordered the mother to take the child to counseling twice a month without exception for the next 6 months. Additionally, if the mother breached any part of the order requiring her to take the child to counseling, directly or indirectly, the court stated that it would consider this to be a further act of contempt of court and the mother would be required to pay a fine of $15,000. The judge also threatened to impose imprisonment penalties if the breaches of the access order continued. Justice Snowie granted further relief to the rejected father by specifying penalties with respect to possible "future" breaches of her order. While the legal authority for the court to make such prospective punishments may be questioned, as it is not possible to impose a sentence for contempt on a prospective basis, the judge wanted to send the mother a clear message.

The 2005 Manitoba case of *C.A.G* is another example of a decision that accepted the jurisdiction to require a parent found guilty of contempt of court to have counseling. A motion for contempt was brought by the mother against

---

[51] Ibid. at para. 42, Snowie J.
[52] Ibid.
[53] Ibid. at para. 42–43.

the custodial father because of his refusal to allow their two children (aged 15 and 10) to see her. The court found that the "father intentionally acted in such a fashion as to manipulate the children and destroy the relationship between them and their mother...prevent[ing] the mother from exercising access"[54] and held him in contempt. In an attempt to improve the relationship with the mother, the court ordered the father to have the children "attend at and receive therapeutic counseling with the express intention of attempting to assist them to understand the level of hostility they have learned to feel relating to their mother and with the additional goal of attempting to reunify them with their mother."[55] This objective coincided with the legal framework supporting "maximum" parent–child contact, as well as the judicial responsibility to ensure that access orders are respected. In *C.A.G.*, Douglas J. also ordered the custodial father to complete a parenting education course structured "to educate parents about the damage done to children by continuing levels of conflict and animosity between parents."[56]

The courts have generally taken a broad view of their powers to shape flexible responses to findings of contempt in family cases, with a view to attempting to ensure future compliance with the order, with the objective sought by the party bringing the matter to court as well as in the child's best interests. In some jurisdictions, after a finding of contempt (especially a first finding), the judge may delay sentencing to give the parent who has failed to comply with the order an opportunity to "purge" their contempt by complying with the original order until the time of formal sentencing. If the parent complies during that period, the court may decide not to sanction the parent, or reduce the penalty that would otherwise be imposed.[57] This can be an effective method of encouraging immediate compliance.

In addition to imposing fines, courts have also made orders requiring that the aggrieved party be reimbursed for expenses, such as the purchase of an airline ticket, when these expenses were incurred due to parenting time not taking place as ordered. In the British Columbia case of *Poitras v. Bucsis*,[58] the principal issue for the court was whether the evidence supported a finding of contempt against a custodial father for not complying with an order requiring him to facilitate the child's contact with the mother. The father lived in Saskatchewan, and the order required that he send the child to British Columbia for Christmas access. The judge found that civil contempt had been proven, and in addition to ordering additional parenting time for the mother during the next school holiday, the court ordered the father to pay her $1,500 for her legal costs. Additionally, the father was ordered to pay the travel costs of air travel for the extra contact.

---

54 C.A.G. v. S.C., 2005 MBQB 224, 20 R.F.L. (6th) 270 at para. 23.
55 C.A.G. v. S.C., 2005 MBQB 224, 20 R.F.L. (6th) 270.
56 C.A.G. v. S.C., 2005 MBQB 224 at para. 28.
57 See *C.A.G. v. S.C.*, [2005] M.J. 372 (Q.B.).
58 *Poitras v. Bucsis*, 2003 CarswellBC 443, [2003] B.C.J. 460 (B.C.S.C.)

Although there is great judicial reluctance to impose a jail sentence for violation of an access order, in some extreme cases concerns about the need to maintain the integrity of the administration of justice result in this sanction. In *McMillan v. McMillan*,[59] the court noted that the father had to bring four separate contempt motions to enforce an access order and reestablish contact with his children. Quinn J. remarked:

> ... there is a period of time immediately following the separation of spouses when emotions run high and otherwise sensible people are prone to act like vengeful lunatics. A court order deliberately breached during that delicate time frame may attract the compassion of the court. However, a court order which is willfully, deliberately and repeatedly breached many years after such compassions can reasonably be expected to extend, is an entirely different matter. [60]

In light of the repeated defiance of the access order, Quinn J. held that this was an appropriate case to impress upon the custodial mother, and upon other parents involved in a judicial process that "court orders are to be obeyed."[61] In weighing the appropriate sentence, he concluded that the most important factor was "the need to preserve the integrity of the administration of justice; and that, as I see it, can only be achieved through a sentence of incarceration,"[62] which in the circumstances called for a sentencing of 5 days in jail.

An even more dramatic example of a severe judicial response to violation of a court order concerning parent contact is the New York case of *Aurelia v. Aurelia*. The parties shared joint legal custody of their three children; the father had primary physical custody, but he was obliged to facilitate phone calls with the mother and bring the children to the local police station every second weekend so that the mother could have them for the weekend scheduled contact. He consistently failed to comply with the order, the mother was eventually awarded sole custody, and contact with the alienating father was terminated. The Family Court also sentenced him to 6 months imprisonment, a decision affirmed by the Supreme Court, which commented:

> Significantly, respondent [father] testified that he does not think that it is in the children's best interests to have *any* contact with petitioner [mother], that he is against any relationship between petitioner and the children at this time and that he even objects to being required to provide petitioner with written notice of the children's health and educational needs. As long ago as [four years earlier the Family Court found that the father's] ... disparaging

---

[59] *McMillan v. McMillan* [1999] O.J. 285, 44 O.R. (3d) 139 (Ct. J. (Gen. Div.)).
[60] Ibid. at para. 25.
[61] Ibid. at para. 24.
[62] Ibid. at para. 29.

remarks about petitioner in the presence of the children were "particularly vulgar" and that he used the children "to vent his frustrations" about petitioner. We also note that, in response to questions from the children's Law Guardian, respondent testified that, when the children refuse to do something he directs them to do, he disciplines them, but that he does not direct the children to do anything that he feels is not in their best interests.

On this record, we find a complete absence of evidence of any efforts by respondent to facilitate compliance with the court-ordered visitation...there is ample support for Family Court's conclusion that respondent "willfully refused to comply with the parenting order and has actively encouraged the destruction of the relationship between his children and their mother" and that respondent "violated all relevant court orders, permanent and temporary, about the parenting relationship between the petitioner and her children."[63]

Such long sentences for contempt of court by alienating parents are very rare. Significantly in *Aurelia*, the relatively long period of imprisonment would not affect the care of the children and actually helped ensure that there could be no violation of the order since the alienating father was to have no contact with the children.

In most jurisdictions, a party who is found in contempt can be ordered to pay the "costs" or attorney's fees of the party whose rights have been violated.[64] While these awards may not cover all of the legal fees and in some cases may be effectively impossible to enforce, they are intended to both send a message to the party in contempt as well as compensate the party whose legal rights have been violated.

As this discussion reveals, while contempt can be useful in securing compliance with court orders in some situations, it is "blunt instrument" for seeking to improve parent–child relationships. In some jurisdictions, like Australia, there is such reluctance by family court judges to impose a sanction for noncompliance with violation of orders related to residence or contact that alienated parents rarely bother to even commence this type of proceeding.

9.8 Police Enforcement

In some jurisdictions, including most Canadian provinces, legislation specifies that a judge may include a provision in a parenting order directing the police to apprehend and deliver the child(ren) to the person entitled to access.[65] In

---

[63] *56 AD 3d 963, 869 NYS 2d 227 (3rd Dept. 2008).*
[64] See, e.g., *Moudry v. Moudry*, [2005] O.J. 2655 (S.C.).
[65] See, e.g., *Children's Law Reform Act*, R.S.O., 1990 ch. C 12 s. 36.

some other jurisdictions, even without explicit legislative provision, judges may include such "police enforcement clauses" in parenting orders on the basis of their inherent judicial powers. However, an order for police involvement "...is an order of last resort...to be made sparingly and in the most exceptional circumstances."[66]

A Canadian study (Bala et al., 2010) found that police enforcement clauses were included in about 10% of cases involving alienation claims. These orders were almost all made in cases where alienation was found to assist a rejected parent, but also in a few cases where the court concluded that alienation had not occurred but that there were nevertheless concerns about access enforcement. Invariably, judges hope that the fact that a police enforcement order is made will result in compliance with the access order.[67] However, if the police are actually called to enforce an access order on more than one occasion, serious consideration should be given to other solutions.

In all jurisdictions, even without an explicit "police enforcement clause," the police have some obligation to assist in the enforcement of any court order, including a custody or contact order. In practice, however, whether this is a "police enforcement clause" or not, the police are reluctant to become involved in "family matters." If there is an apparent violation of an explicit order granting parenting time, the police may well go to the home of the custodial parent at the request of the parent seeking to enforce the access order to discuss the matter and encourage compliance with the order, but they will be very reluctant to physically remove children from their homes to have contact with a noncustodial parent. As well as being very unpleasant for police officers, such police involvement may be viewed as intimidating by children and perhaps result in further stated fear and rejection of a parent (Sullivan & Kelly, 2001).

While police enforcement orders are appropriate in some cases, especially on an interim basis, it is invariably contrary to the interests of children to have police coming to take uncooperative children to see a parent on a regular basis. This is reflected in the Australian case of *Sawyer & Reid*, where the mother sought a continuing "recovery order that enables the police to intervene" whenever the 10-year-old boy ran away from the mother and returned to his alienating father. In refusing the order, Judge Altobelli observed that such a continuing order "is completely unacceptable and to make such an order would pour petrol on the raging fire that is already burning."[68]

---

[66] *Allen v. Grenier*, [1997] O.J. 1198, 145 D.L.R. (4th) 286 (Gen. Div.).

[67] See *R.L.H. v. G.L.B.*, 2002 ABQB 302 at para. 47: "While I understand counsel's position on not wanting to involve a seven-and-a-half-year-old child with police authorities over the question of access, I believe that the police enforcement clause is the only way that this [father] will live up to the obligations he has under this Court Order to produce the child." The judge hoped that the threat of police enforcement would help ensure compliance by the custodial parent, without the actual need for such enforcement.

[68] [2009] FMCAfam 228, at para. 52.

9.9 Supervision of Contact

Some form of contact supervision for a period of time may be an option in some high-conflict separation cases and can serve a number of different purposes. For example, supervision may be ordered in the early stage of proceedings if allegations of alienation are met with counterclaims of justified rejection due to abuse. Supervision can maintain consistent parent–child contact while these issues are resolved in the court. At an interim stage, before the court has sufficient information to determine the validity of the abuse allegations, the court may decide that it is best for the child to continue to have contact with an alleged abuser but require supervision to ensure that the child is not subjected to the *possibility* of abuse. In some cases, supervision may be provided by a family member of the alleged abuser, such as a grandparent, but if there are significant safety issues, it is preferable to involve a supervised visitation program. Supervised visitation programs have been established in many cities, either as part of the services of an existing agency or at a center specifically intended for this purpose. However, cost factors can limit their accessibility in some jurisdictions for some families, and such programs are not available everywhere.

The personnel at supervised visitation programs are not trained as therapists or to attempt to repair the parent–child relationship. Instead, the purpose of supervised visitation is to observe the parent–child interactions while ensuring the process is neutral and the child remains safe. Depending on the policies of the visitation center, a fact-based observational report may be provided by staff to the court and thus assist the court in making future decisions about the case, but such reports do not provide clinical opinions about the parent–child relationship.

Birnbaum and Chipeur (2010) note that while supervised visitation clearly reduces the risk of abuse of children, there is a lack of evidence about the effects of such contact. They caution that even supervised visitation with an abusive parent is not without emotional risk, as there may be verbal or nonverbal subtle threats or psychological harm.

In some cases, by the trial stage, the child(ren) may be severely alienated and may not have been in contact with the rejected parent for an extended period. Faced with these circumstances, the judge needs to decide whether it is in the best interests of the child(ren) to try to "force" reunification. This requires weighing potential benefits and risks, including any possible trauma that may result if the child(ren) fears the rejected parent, even if that fear is not reasonable. One option in these cases is for the court to order a period of supervised visitation to attempt for gradual reestablishment of a relationship.[69] Such an arrangement

---

[69] See, e.g., *B.R. v. E.K.*, [2007] O.J. 278 (S.C.J) at para. 9, where Wein J. ordered a 5-month period of supervised access because the 10-year-old girl had a "genuine reluctance" to visit with the father and had not seen him for several years after an inconclusive investigation of alleged sexual abuse.

may work to address any fears expressed by the child(ren) and the favored parent. However, as previously noted, the personnel at visitation centers are not trained to conduct counseling. In cases of more significant alienation, it is clearly preferable to have some form of concurrent reintegration therapy with supervised contact, involving a trained therapist to facilitate, monitor, and, where justified, supervise visits and support the reestablishment of a relationship.

Supervised contact with a rejected parent is only appropriate when there are reasonable fears concerning a child(ren)'s safety or, if the fears are unfounded, for a short transition period. Because of the unnatural circumstances in which supervised contact usually occurs, unnecessary supervision may impede the process of reunification. For example, where safety concerns are being unreasonably raised by an alienating custodial parent, supervising visits may suggest to a child that these misperceptions are legitimate, thus increasing the child's fear and resistance to contact. For example, in the Ontario case of *Okatan v. Yagiz*,[70] the trial judge refused to extend an earlier order directing supervised access between a father and his 7-year-old daughter. Though the father was found to have "shown some incredible lapses in judgment in speaking to his daughter,"[71] the judge concluded that absent a risk of danger to the child, supervised access was unwarranted, commenting:

> Supervised access is...reserved for exceptional cases. There is no
> reason to continue it in this case, particularly since [the daughter]
> views supervised access as "proof" that her father is a bad
> man...Having visits at the access centre has simply reinforced what
> [the daughter] no doubt has heard from her mother.[72]

There are also cases where the access parent engages in alienating conduct: for example, by consistently denigrating the custodial parent. In such cases, supervision may be ordered to prevent the alienating parent from engaging in such conduct during the contact.[73] Even if this conduct is not affecting the child(ren)'s attitudes toward the custodial parent, it can be distressing to the child(ren).

Similarly, there are cases where the court orders a reversal of custody, and requires that contact by the alienating former custodial parent is to be supervised, at least for some period of time, to prevent alienating remarks or conduct. In such cases, it may be appropriate to have contact by an alienating parent supervised[74] by an agency or trained professional, as there will likely

---

[70] *Okatan v. Yagiz*, [2004] O.J. 2797 (S.C.J.).

[71] Ibid. at para. 61.

[72] Ibid. at para. 59, 62.

[73] See, e.g., *A.J.C. v. R.C.*, [2003] B.C.J. 1150 (S.C.).

[74] See, e.g., *Sportack v. Sportack* [2007] O.J. No. 313 (S.C.J.) (where supervised access was ordered for a father who was insensitive to the needs of his children and frequently made unfounded allegations of abuse against the custodial mother).

be concerns that a relative or family member would be unable to control this type of insidious but often subtle behavior. Attending therapy may also serve to provide the supervision required to the extent that the child only sees the former custodial parent during the counseling, at least initially, and until any further consent agreements or orders are made.

9.10 Award of Legal Fees

One way for a judge to encourage parents to behave in a child-focused fashion, or at least to comply with explicit court orders, is to require a parent acting unreasonably or using the courts improperly to pay for the legal fees and other litigation expenses of the innocent parent. Such orders are intended to both encourage compliance and compensate a parent for some, or occasionally all, of the litigation costs involved in enforcing a court order. Orders for costs are not uncommon in Canada, especially in high-conflict family cases, provided that the judge concludes that one party is clearly responsible for the situation, and that the child will not suffer economically from a custodial parent having to pay such an award.[75] In the 1988 to 2009 period, legal costs were awarded in 46 out of the 232 (20%) reported cases addressing alienation issues (Bala et al., 2010). The mother had to pay the costs in 22 of these cases, while the father had to pay the costs in 26. The number of cases in which costs were ultimately awarded is undoubtedly higher, as in many reported decisions the court invited future submissions about costs or indicated that the issue of costs would be dealt with at a later stage of the proceedings.

Courts will not only award legal fees to alienated parents who have had to take legal action to enforce orders that give them a relationship with their children, but they may also award legal fees to a custodial parent who has been subject to unfounded claims of parental alienation. This occurred in the California case of *In re Marriage of Torres* where the father claimed that the mother had alienated the children from him and that he should be given custody. The trial court rejected his claim, ordered that the mother should continue to have custody, and awarded the mother $3,250 in attorney's fees, more than half the amount that she spent to defend against his claim. This decision was affirmed by the appellate court, which wrote:

> Viewing the record, we conclude the...trial court awarded [the mother]...attorney fees and costs based on sanctions against [the father]...In her responsive papers...[the mother] asked that the court...award her attorney fees "for this bad faith, ill-conceived and without basis" [application to vary custody]...The trial court found there were no facts to support [father's]...claim

---

[75] See, e.g., *Cooper v. Cooper,* [2004] O.J. 5096 (S.C.J.) and *Chadha v. Chadha,* [2006] O.J. 3744 (C.J.).

and expressly found...[father's] request for change of custody
on the grounds of parental alienation to be "far-fetched." At the
hearing, the court stated such a claim was "a very serious charge
when there really isn't any evidence of it." The...[mother] had to
hire an attorney, and the attorney had to deal with the far-fetched
parental alienation complaints, requiring [the mother]...to incur
a "significant amount" of attorney fees...the long history of the
litigation [reveals]...approximately one dozen experts who were
involved with the family, and pointed out that never once was there
any allegation...of parental alienation...[76]

9.11 Joint Custody—Increasing Time in Care of Rejected Parent

Although the courts generally accept that joint custody should not be ordered
unless there is a history of cooperation between the parents,[77] in some cases
of alienation judges are prepared to make an order of joint custody or shared
parental responsibility as a way to "send a message" to the custodial parent and
child that further resistance to the child's relationship with the other parent
may result in a reversal of custody. This approach is less intrusive than ordering
a change in residence but signals to the alienating parent and third parties that
they should respect the roles of both parents. In a study of reported Canadian
cases in the 1989 to 2009 period (Bala et al., 2010), the court ordered joint custody 29 out of 168 cases (17%) where the court found parental alienation.

Further, ordering joint custody should help the rejected parent obtain
access to health and education–related information, often withheld by alienating parents or by the professionals who mistakenly believe they are prohibited from providing information to noncustodial parents.[78] In *Cox v. Stephen*,
the Ontario Court of Appeal affirmed a lower court decision that made such
a joint custody order, commenting: "[the lower court judge] fashioned a remedy...that took appropriate account of the risk of alienation by awarding
joint custody to [the father], yet protecting the child's sense of stability by not
requiring him to leave his lifelong home and family."[79]

In another Ontario case, *Mikan v. Mikan*, the parties' 11-year-old daughter refused to see the father. The mother had armor-coated tinting placed on

---

[76] Cal: Court of Appeals, 2nd Appellate Dist., 8th Div. 2010.
[77] See *Roy v. Roy* (2006), 27 R.F.L. (6th) 44 (Ont. C.A.); and *Lawson v. Lawson*
(2006), 81 O.R. (3d) 321(C.A.).
[78] Complicating this further, it is not uncommon on the basis of privacy legislation
for an alienated adolescent to refuse to allow the rejected parent medical or
educational information.
[79] [2003] O.J. 371 at para. 3, 47 R.F.L. (5th) 1 (C.A.) and *Zacconi v. Mahdavi*,
[2010] O.J. 2513, 2010 ONSC 3294.

the windows of the matrimonial home, changed the locks, and installed a security apparatus and surveillance cameras. The court found that the father was not a threat to the safety of the child or mother, and concluded that the mother's conduct sent a clear but misguided message to the child that she should fear and reject her father. Justice Langdon observed that in light of her failure to support a relationship with the father, the mother "scarcely qualifies as a suitable sole custody parent" and that "prompt, decisive and perhaps radical steps" need to be taken to "put a stop to this alienation."[80] Accordingly, the court made an interim order of "week-about" joint custody, with an authorization for the father to use "reasonable force" to have the daughter comply, including a direction for police assistance if requested.

In the Washington D.C. case of *Jordan v. Jordan*, the Domestic Relations Court concluded that the custodial mother had been alienating the couple's two daughters, aged 5 and 12 years, from their father. Although there had been a couple of incidents before separation in which the father had assaulted the mother, the court accepted that they were "situational" incidents and that there was no longer a risk of reoccurrence of domestic violence. The court concluded that it was appropriate to award joint physical and legal custody to both of the parents, with care to each parent in alternating weeks, and appointed a parenting coordinator. The Court of Appeal affirmed this decision and explained that the incidents of domestic violence did not preclude a joint custody order:

> And the court stated ... that it had given due consideration to the "emotional damage that [the girls] are suffering, combined with the efforts that Mr. Jordan has taken to rectify the conduct that led to that inappropriate behavior on his part," apparently giving Mr. Jordan credit for his voluntary participation in individual therapy and his attempts to make amends with E.J. [the 12-year-old daughter.] Thus, the court's determination that joint custody was in the children's best interests obviously reflected its judgment that Mr. Jordan was not a danger, and that the emotional damage to the children due to parental alienation would be worse than the difficulties they would face in attempting to salvage their relationship with their father. The court essentially found that the children's emotional development would be significantly impaired if it did not award joint custody to Mr. Jordan.[81]

The 2009 New York case of *Burola v. Meek* involved a same-sex couple who had a daughter, born to one woman (conceived by artificial insemination) and adopted by the other. The couple separated when the girl was 9 years of age; they made an agreement that they were to share legal custody, with the primary residence with the biological mother and significant time with

---

[80] *Mikan v. Mikan*, [2004] O.J. No.740 (Sup. Ct.) at paras. 21–22.
[81] *See*, e.g., *Jordan v. Jordan*, 14 A.3d 1136 (DC 2011), 1995.

her adoptive mother. By the time the girl was 12, she was resisting contact with her adoptive mother, and unwilling to have overnight contact with her. The Family Court found that the biological mother had engaged in alienating conduct. The Court ordered an increase in the time the girl was to spend with the adoptive mother to strengthen the relationship with her, with alternating weeks in the physical care of each parent. The appeal court affirmed this decision, writing:

> Examples abound of petitioner [biological mother], either personally or through surrogates, engaging in such conduct and establish that she is either unable or unwilling to do what is needed and necessary to facilitate a parental relationship between respondent [adoptive mother] and their child, even though such a relationship is clearly in the child's best interests. For example, petitioner, despite her obvious love for the child, systematically engages in conduct that increases, rather than diminishes, the trauma and anxiety that the child routinely experiences whenever she leaves petitioner and is placed in respondent's care. She refuses to use respondent's name whenever she refers to the child and has encouraged the child to abandon respondent's surname as well. She routinely fails to keep respondent informed of the child's ongoing activities and has not kept her advised concerning important details involving the child's medical care.
>
> Here, Family Court concluded that respondent was able to provide a stable and suitable home environment for the child that would promote a healthy relationship between the child and her entire family. It noted that respondent allowed the child, when in her care, to maintain daily contact with petitioner, as well as other members of petitioner's extended family. Respondent also had photographs of petitioner and her family placed throughout her home so as to ease the adjustment that the child had to make when she had left petitioner's home and was placed in respondent's care. Petitioner…has not reciprocated in this effort and seems determined not to allow respondent to enjoy a normal relationship with the child. In that regard, petitioner will not allow respondent in her home and has promoted a belief in the child that respondent is not her mother. Petitioner has communicated with the child regarding ongoing court proceedings and appears to have suggested to the child that if respondent prevails, such a determination will adversely affect her. This evidence…supports Family Court's determination that the child would only enjoy a wholesome relationship with both of her parents—something that was clearly in her best interests—if her time with respondent was significantly increased.[82]

---

[82] *Burola v. Meek*, 64 AD 3d 962, 882 N.Y.S.2d 560 (3d Dept., 2009).

These cases illustrate the willingness of courts to increase the time a resistant child spends with a rejected parent in order to strengthen the parent–child relationship. While this may be effective and is less disruptive than awarding sole custody to the rejected parent, it is not likely to be successful in restoring a relationship if the alienation is severe and the child is unwilling to have relationship with that parent. In these circumstances, the alienating parent will still have ample opportunity to undermine efforts to restore the relationship with the rejected parent.

9.12 Custody Reversal: An Option for Severe Cases

9.12.1 The "Stark Dilemma"

The most dramatic judicial response to alienation is the transfer of custody from the alienating parent to the rejected parent, often with a temporary suspension of contact with the alienating parent. It is *one* option for severe cases of alienation, typically used only after other less intrusive interventions have been attempted and failed. It should never be lightly undertaken and has inherent risks. A variation in custody is sometimes referred to as a "last resort," but if courts wait too long to respond in this way, it may be ineffective. In the most severe cases, a timely decision to vary custody may be the only way to effectively address the alienation, and in some cases it will be the least detrimental alternative for the child. In other cases, however, despite severe alienation and the failure of other interventions, the court may conclude that a change in custody is not appropriate and recognize that there is no effective way for a court order to allow the reestablishment a child's relationship with a rejected parent.

Although some scholars, therapists, and advocates argue that the courts should *never* vary custody as a response to alienation, most judges, professionals, and commentators believe that the question is not whether there should ever be a custody reversal, but rather, in which circumstances it is the most appropriate remedy, and how it should be implemented. When asked which cases are severe enough to justify more extreme remedies like custody reversal, Toronto lawyer Philip Epstein stated:

> ...when you have identified alienation, have taken a number
> of progressive steps to try to change the behavior, and where it
> becomes clear that these kinds of steps—increasingly punitive—are
> not going to have any effect. And then you start to think about
> custody reversal.[83]

Several important questions surface when considering for a specific case the option of reversing custody to the rejected parent, often while suspending,

---

[83] Interview, August 15, 2010.

at least temporarily, the child's contact with the favored parent: Is the alienation emotionally abusive? How good are the parenting capacity and the emotional health of the alienating parent? Stated differently, which risk is greater: separation from an unhealthy or enmeshed relationship or remaining in that relationship? What are the parenting capacities of the rejected parent, and perhaps of a stepparent? What supports and resources are likely to be required to facilitate a successful custody change? In sum, is custody reversal likely to cause more harm than good; that is, do the short- or long-term benefits of placing the child with the once loved, now rejected parent outweigh the risks (trauma or harm) of temporarily separating the child from the alienating parent?

More general questions also arise in these severe cases, such as whether older children have sufficient maturity to make decisions about attending counseling or severing ties with a rejected parent, and most broadly, does custody reversal work?

If an application is made to vary custody, the court must first be satisfied that a "material change of circumstances" has occurred since the original custody arrangement was made. Second, the court must determine that such action is in the "best interests" of the child(ren). It is usually necessary for the parent seeking the variation in custody to provide expert testimony to establish that the child has been alienated, and that any emotional distress to the child from the change is likely to be limited in duration. While the courts are reluctant to vary custody, as it can be very disruptive to children, this option is becoming an increasingly common judicial response to severe alienation. When such action is taken, it is because the alienating parent has proven resistant to less intrusive responses, and the judge has concluded that a change in custody is the only effective way to end the emotional harm caused by the alienating custodial parent.

Decisions to transfer custody in cases of alienation invariably recognize the immediate negative effect such a step is likely to have on the child(ren). However, a common theme is that this concern should be subordinated to the longer term objective of maintaining healthy relationships between the child(ren) and both parents. In the British Columbia case of *A.A. v. S.N.A.*, the trial judge recognized that he faced a "stark dilemma" in whether to leave the child with a "highly manipulative" and "intransigent" mother who would never permit her child to have any sort of relationship with her father, or to transfer custody to the father, who had little contact with the child for over a year. Despite the finding of alienation, Preston J. chose not to award custody to the father due to a concern that "the immediate effect of that change will be extremely traumatic."[84] In reversing this decision and awarding custody to the father, the British Columbia Court of Appeal observed:

> the trial judge wrongly focused on the likely difficulties of a change
> in custody—which the only evidence on the subject indicates will be

---

[84] *A.A. v. S.N.A.*, [2007] B.C.J. 870 para. 75, 77, 84–85, (C.A.) Preston J.

short-term and not "devastating"—and failed to give paramountcy to M.'s long-term interests. Instead, damage which is long-term and almost certain was preferred over what may be a risk, but a risk that seems necessary if M is to have a chance to develop normally in her adolescent years.[85]

The negative short-term and long-term effects of alienation, including intrusive parenting by the alienating parent, have been reasonably well documented (e.g., Baker, 2007a; Barber, 2002; Johnston, 2005a; Johnston, Roseby, & Kuehnle, 2009; Johnston, Walters, & Olesen, 2005c). While there is general recognition that a reversal of custody may be warranted in severe cases (Friedlander & Walters, 2010; Gardner, 1998a; Johnston & Goldman, 2010; Johnston et al., 2009; Sullivan & Kelly, 2001; Warshak, 2010b), debate continues with respect to identifying which cases are, in fact, severe enough to warrant this response.

There may also be differing opinions about the capacity of a rejected parent to assume the care of an alienated child, one who, at least initially, may be quite resistant to the change. It is important to recognize that while a custody reversal may be necessary, it may not in itself be enough to resolve the parent–child contact problem. As Elizabeth McCarty of the Ontario Office of the Children's Lawyer, stated:

> There are cases where a change in custody may be necessary.
> However, the change in custody doesn't simply "fix" the problem.
> It addresses some concerns but can raise others as well. You still
> need to have other services in place to assist the family and, most
> importantly, the children. Someone needs to monitor the children's
> reaction to the change, their coping mechanisms, and the parent's
> ability to respond to the child's reactions.[86]

In speaking about custody reversal as a solution, psychologist Leslie Drozd stated:

> We all need to try every other remedy possible prior to [changing
> custody], which would include legal remedies as well as therapy.
> But if you have an absolutely noncompliant parent who continues
> to engage in some sort of sabotaging or alienating behavior,
> I think that there may not be much of a choice other than to switch
> custody. But I don't think you do the switching of the custody just
> by having one parent pick up the child. I think that probably...that
> is where programs like Richard Warshak's program or the Rachel

---

[85] *A.A. v. S.N.A.*, [2007] B.C.J. 1474 (C.A.) para. 27. The courts ultimately decided that the variation in custody would only be effective if all contact with the mother was suspended for a year; see *A.A. v. S.N.A.*, [2009] B.C.J. 558 (B.C.S.C.).

[86] Interview, July 15, 2010.

Foundation probably come in, where they can help in that transition from the custodial parent to the other parent. There is no doubt that there are going to be short-term problems, even if you have those outside treatment programs that are used to help out with that. I think you can ameliorate some of the short-term trauma by using programs like those, and therefore, I don't think you just willy-nilly switch custody, which I think happens more than it should. I think the responsibility lies with all of those people or parts of the system for not having properly assessed these families and/or treated them prior to that. And now to look for what is a relatively simplistic "solution." I think it's just too simplistic an answer in most instances. I do think that there are instances in which it is absolutely appropriate, but I don't think the number is huge.[87]

This comment emphasizes the importance of considering *how* a transfer in custody is to occur, as well as the question of *whether* it is to occur.

9.12.2 Perspectives Against and For the Option of Court-Ordered Custody Reversal

Bruch (2001) and Wallerstein et al. (2000) maintain that children who are rejecting or strongly resisting a parent are likely to eventually "come around," and further argue that there is no evidence that ordering contact or expensive treatment is effective in restoring a relationship with a rejected parent.[88] Indeed, these writers and others have questioned the benefits to children involved in high-conflict parental separation of having relationships with both parents. These writers argue that enforced parenting time, court-ordered treatment, and custody reversal are counterproductive, as such measures only reinforce the child's hatred for the rejected parent, adding further stress to the already vulnerable child. Further concerns include that a custody reversal may place the child at risk for running away or self-destructive behavior (Jaffe, Ashbourne, & Mamo, 2010; Johnston et al., 2009). Opponents to custody reversal argue that an abrupt, even if temporary, separation from a primary attachment figure (referred to by some as a "parentectomy"), even when, or especially when, the attachment is enmeshed or pathological, places the child at greater risk than losing contact with a rejected parent (Garber, 2004a; Jaffe et al., 2010).

---

[87] Interview, June 23, 2010.

[88] To support her claim, Bruch cites a newspaper report and telephone conversation with Judith Wallerstein on her follow-up of 25 young adults (Wallerstein et al., 2000). Also, see Warshak (2003a, and endnote 29 in 2010b) for a citation of Wallerstein's work that supports an alternative position.

In discussing whether a separation from the favored parent is potentially traumatic for a child, psychologist Robert Marvin also emphasizes the importance of the child's relationship to the primary attachment figure:

> If you have a high-conflict divorce, and one parent is incredibly afraid of what is going to happen to the child when he or she is with the nonfavored parent, and especially in situations where there is some justification for that, we need to focus on what is in the child's best interests, both in the short and long term, and the first priority should be about protecting the primary attachment. There is going to be a risk that the favored parent's fear will disorganize his or her parenting, which will impact their ability to sensitively receive and interpret and respond to the child's signals and needs.[89]

The prominent American psychologist, Joan Kelly, expresses a different view about the importance of attachment in alienation cases:

> There are clinicians and judges who say, no we can't take this child away from this parent because they have this really close relationship. Let's assume that the rejected parent is not neglectful or not a poor parent because you are considering transferring custody to that parent. Leaving the child with a parent with serious psychological problems who is fostering an alienation, and whose child's allegations exactly mirror that parent's (they use the same language, same words)...this child is not being served by staying with the parent who has psychological problems who has difficulty separating from their child or adolescent who may benefit by change of custody. We focus too much on "this child won't survive the change of custody"—most of them do apparently—and not enough time on really evaluating this as an option.[90]

Quebec psychologist and researcher Francine Cyr also suggests the need to balance the emotional effect of a change in custody with the effect of staying with an alienating, and often compromised, parent:

> I think [that custody reversal]...could be traumatic, but we have a moral decision to make here. In order to not traumatize children, are we going to collude with an emotionally sick parent who is damaging these children by depriving them of...at least a good enough parent...are we going to collude with that in order to not traumatize these poor children because they are so attached to this very ill parent who is making them emotionally unhealthy by stopping them from developing normally, as they should be?

---

[89] Interview, April 20, 2010.
[90] Interview, April 21, 2010.

When a child's development is compromised like here, there is an obligation to protect the child from being damaged by taking action. Removing the child from the toxic or damaging environment to stop emotional abuse seems indicated in these severe cases. I heard a lot of my colleagues who are experts in these cases where there was a reversal of custody, and it proved to be extremely useful in the long run.[91]

Some mental health professionals and lawyers are extremely cautious about custody reversal and are likely to argue that alienating conduct in any specific case is not sufficiently emotionally abusive to warrant this response or that the apparent alienating parental behavior arises out of an intention, misguided or not, to protect the child. Concerns are expressed about custody reversal being a punitive action against a well-meaning and protective, albeit misguided, parent. Other legal and mental health professionals are more likely in specific cases to maintain that custody reversal may be justified, not as a punitive measure, but rather to protect a child from the unrelenting emotional abuse by the alienating parent, even when parents may not be conscious of their attempts to turn the child against other parent (just as termination of parental custody is appropriate in child protection cases that raise serious abuse or neglect issues).[92] In these cases, there is clear psychopathology in the favored parent, and the child is demonstrating significant social, behavioral, emotional, or academic problems, not only difficulties in terms of his or her relationship with the rejected parent. Further, while this may not be evident initially and before a comprehensive custody evaluation, typically significant problems are evident in the child's relationship with the favored parent relating to age-appropriate autonomy, boundaries (Johnston et al., 2009), and infantilization, parentification, or adultification (Garber, 2011).

A custody reversal is appropriate in cases where the concerns are not only about the alienated child not having a relationship with the rejected parent, and often the entire extended family, but also about the alienating parent's intrusive and overprotective parenting and the emotional exploitation, indoctrination, induction of fear and hatred (the teaching of prejudice), and, in some cases, paranoia, in children.

Important distinctions need to be made between the *strength* and *quality* of an attachment; a strong bond with an alienating parent is not necessarily a healthy attachment. In fact, strong bonds may be indicative of unhealthy attachments, as can occur between an abusive parent and his or her fearful child, or with an overprotective or intrusive parent and his or her parentified or placating child (Garber, 2004a). Writers also note that attachment is only one element of the parent–child relationship (Arredondo & Edwards, 2000; Byrne,

---

[91] Interview, May 27, 2010.
[92] This view is supported by the majority of our key informants during interviews, including judges, lawyers, and mental health professionals.

O'Connor, Marvin, & Whelan, 2005; Lamb, 2012; Pruett, Cowan, Cowan, & Diamond, 2012) and a child's adjustment. Other factors that are predictive of a child's adjustment include the parent's own attachment style arising out of his or her own parent–child relationships, the parent's ability to meet the child's instrumental needs, parenting capacity and style (authoritarian, authoritative, or permissive), and role modeling. Consequently, many factors, not only the quality or strength of the attachment with the aligned parent, must be considered when making evaluator's recommendations or judicial determinations in child custody disputes (Birnbaum, Fidler, & Kavassalis, 2008).

Proponents of custody reversal may, in specific cases, conclude that in the more severe cases, an alienating parent's parenting is not only compromised but emotionally abusive, and consequently, the risks associated with not separating the child from the aligned parent are greater than any potential risks of changing custody, provided that the rejected parent is an at least adequate parent and the child once had a reasonably good relationship with that parent. While opponents of custody reversal generally acknowledge that it is preferable for a child to have good relationships with both parents and their extended families, they are likely to argue that despite alienating conduct by the "primary" caregiver, severing ties with a rejected "nonprimary" parent and the extended family is preferable to separating the child from the alienating primary parent.

Opponents of custody reversal tend to assume that in severe alienation cases, children will be traumatized or go into crisis if separated from the alienating parent. American advocate for abused women, Joan Meier, for example, stated that "[a child] need[s] a primary secure attachment and that losing that is the most destructive thing short of abuse that can be done to a child. Now, I understand the alienation people are saying, an alienating parent is not a secure attachment, but they are claiming it, there is no evidence of that."[93]

Moreover, there are no good longitudinal studies that use random assignment to compare outcomes for alienated children who were separated from their favored parent and placed with their previously loved parent, and those who are left in the care of the alienating parent. However, preliminary research from retrospective studies and clinical anecdotes reported by many seasoned clinicians suggest that for at least some children, a separation from the favored parent is liberating because the child is able to resume what was a positive relationship with the parent he or she has not been free to love in the presence of the favored parent. Amy Baker's research (supported by that of Clawar & Rivlin, 1991), indicating that many of the adults in her study, who as children had expressly rejected a parent (in her study almost always the father), reported secretly wishing that someone "called their bluff" as children and insisted they have a relationship with the parent they claimed to fear or hate, is an important consideration when making these extremely difficult decisions.

---

[93] Interview, April, 21, 2010.

Further, many of the experts interviewed for this book, both legal and mental health professionals, note that they have repeatedly observed that once out of the orbit of the preferred parent, an alienated child can transform very well, sometimes very quickly, from staunchly resisting the rejected parent, to being able to show and receive love from that parent. This transformation is sometimes followed by an equally swift shift back to the alienated position as soon as the child returns to the favored parent, or even before a return in anticipation of the reunion. The child's need and ability to vacillate between denying and accepting parts of him or herself so quickly and visibly suggests a compromised adjustment and development of self.

Mental health professionals, especially custody evaluators, and the courts need to carefully consider what poses the greatest risk to a *particular* child in a *particular* set of family circumstances, considering the likely short- *and* long-term detrimental effects of living in a distorted reality where the child is not free to be emotionally autonomous. In some cases, the least detrimental long-term option is to place the child with the parent more likely to promote overall healthy psychological development and adjustment, including but not limited to a healthy relationship with the other parent. For others, the reverse is the case. It is important to recognize that a healthy relationship with a parent is not without challenges or complaints; there is no perfect parent–child relationship. Rather, a functional relationship will include the child's ability to accept and integrate both good and bad qualities of the parent, coupled with flexible thinking, the capacity for multiple perspective taking, good communication and problem solving skills, and so on, all of which are indices of mature interpersonal skills and relationships.

Ethical issues related to coercion, children's rights, and civil liberties are also important and debated considerations. As previously mentioned, these concerns are relevant not only to custody reversal, but to all of the interventions typically recommended and used in alienation cases, such as family-focused therapy, parenting coordination, and some parent education programs. The issue may be less about coercion per se and more about the nature and degree of the coercion, and further, determining for which cases it is appropriate. One needs to ask not only about the ethical issues of intervening when children protest, but also about the ethical issues when intervention is not provided to protect children from alienating abusive parenting (Warshak, 2010a). Warshak elaborates on the ethical issues and notes that it will be up to the individual professional to determine "where they stand when it comes to the ethics of recommending or providing services to children who are referred against their will."

When to heed and not heed a child's wishes about custody arrangements is another area of considerable discussion and debate. For example, Bruch (2001) and Wallerstein and Tanke (2006) emphasize the importance of respecting a child's wishes not to see a parent. Some writers vociferously object to the court's involvement in mandating treatment, parenting time enforcement, and custody reversal (see also Faller, 1997; Walker et al., 2004a, 2004b), though most of those who oppose custody reversal do not adequately address the studies of young adults who report a longing to have had more time with their noncustodial fathers (see for example, Ahrons & Tanner, 2003; Fabricius, 2003; Fabricius & Hall, 2000; Hetherington & Kelly, 2002; Laumann-Billings & Emery, 2000; Parkinson, Cashmore, & Single, 2005; Parkinson & Smyth, 2004; Schwartz & Finley, 2009).

Proponents of custody reversal in severe cases of alienation note that children's feelings and ideas are indeed important to consider, but they should not be determinative. As discussed more fully in Chapter 8, a child's views and preferences must be independent to be given weight. Children should always have a feeling of "being heard" when decisions are being made about their lives, but it should also be made clear to them that they do not have the responsibility for making decisions (Warshak, 2003b). Warshak stated:

> Naturally, older children are more likely to have the intellectual capacity to understand long-term consequences, but at the same time older children are quite vulnerable to external influence. Teenagers are notorious for allowing others to influence their ideas and behavior. So I think what is important to look at is whether the preference being expressed is in the child's best interests or not, and I don't think that the courts should abdicate that responsibility merely because the child has reached a certain age.[94]

The need for ultimate adult responsibility applies not only to children, but also to adolescents whose brains and executive functioning (e.g., coordinating information, judgment, planning, weighing alternatives, analysis, cognitive flexibility, problem solving, etc.), are still developing rapidly in important ways. The adolescent brain is in effect "under construction," hence the greater risk-taking behavior, poor judgment, and problems with impulse control often observed in adolescence. To make fully informed decisions, one has to be able to anticipate and understand the future consequences of different options. It is not until the early 20s that the brain completes the maturation process. By law, younger adolescents are not permitted to vote, consume alcohol, drive, obtain tattoos, or not attend school. Typically, parents do not permit their children and adolescents to refuse to go to school or receive medical treatment. Logically then, proponents of custody reversal maintain that alienated children should not be permitted to make a life-altering decision, such as severing ties with one parent or their grandparents and other relatives. Rather, custodial parents should "require," not force, their children to work toward resolving the conflicts with the other parent and resuming contact, unless there is a determination that such contact is not in the child's

---

[94] Interview, April 15, 2010.

best interests.[95] However, as discussed in Chapter 8, as children grow older, both legal theory and practical constraints require that more weight be given to their views, even if they are not making decisions that will promote their long-term well-being.

Another important consideration is the efficacy of treatment with severe cases. Qualitative case studies and experienced clinicians supporting recommendations and orders to reverse custody maintain that therapy, as the primary intervention, simply does not work in severe and even in some moderate alienation cases (Clawar & Rivlin, 1991; Dunne & Hedrick, 1994; Gardner 2001a; Kopetski, 1998a, 1998b, 2006; Lampel, 1996; Lowenstein, 2006; Lund, 1995; Rand, 1997b; Rand et al., 2005). This is not unexpected given that by definition, severe cases involve significant parental psychopathology or personality disorders, which may include paranoia, severe mental illness, disordered thinking, lack of insight capacity, or even sociopathy of the alienating parent. When therapy is indicated, in the less severe cases, it requires a competent mental health professional, specifically trained in high-conflict separation and divorce and alienation; otherwise, the therapy may actually increase the problems with contact enforcement (Rand, 1997b), resulting in the alienated child and favored parent further entrenching their distorted views (Fidler et al., 2008).

The option of custody reversal is one that the courts are prepared to seriously consider in alienation cases. In a Canadian study of reported decisions between 1989 and 2009 (Bala et al., 2010), the court awarded sole custody to the alienated parent, in 69 out of the 168 cases (41%) where alienation was found.[96] In one case, custody was transferred to a foster parent to facilitate eventual transition to the care of the alienated parent. In a study of reported Australian court decisions where alienation was found by the court, the judge ordered a change in residence in 19 out of 36 cases (53%) (Bala, 2012).

9.12.3 Research on Enforced Parenting Time and Custody Reversal

To date, there has been little well-controlled research on outcomes, either positive or negative, of ordering parenting time or reversing custody in alienation cases. It is important to recognize that this lack of research on the effect of these interventions to remedy alienation exists in a context of a growing body

---

[95] See, e.g., *S. V. v. C.T.I.*, [2009] O.J. 816, per Reilly J. where the judge makes the important distinction between a parent "forcing" and "requiring" certain behavior from a child, including such conduct as attending school and visiting with a noncustodial parent.

[96] In one case involving split custody, the judge found that both parents alienated the child in their custody from the other parent; there was no variation of custody in that case.

of research about the long-term harmful effects of alienating parental con-duct on children, but only very limited research on effects (or outcomes) of *any type* of judicial decision making related to court interventions in custody and contact cases in general. There is actually more literature and research on the effects of custody reversal on children in alienation cases than on most other interventions that are ordered in these cases, such as family-focused or reunification therapy, parenting coordination, a finding of contempt of court, or, perhaps most significantly, a judicial decision not to deal with alienation because of a concern about the potential trauma of a change in custody or the limitations of the rejected parent.

Experienced clinicians and those reporting on their qualitative research using case studies have reported on the benefits of changing custody or enforced parenting time in severe alienation cases (Clawar & Rivlin, 1991; Dunne & Hedrick, 1994; Gardner 2001b; Lampel, 1996; Rand et al., 2005; Warshak, 2010a). For example, Clawar & Rivlin (1991) reported an improvement in 90% of cases in children's relationships with rejected par-ents and in other areas of their functioning in 400 cases where an increase in the child's contact with the parent was court ordered, with half of these orders made over the objection of the children. They further reported that children interviewed after the imposed parenting time expressed relief, say-ing they could not have reestablished the relationship on their own, indi-cating the need to be able to save face and lay blame for seeing the parent on someone else. In their case analysis of 26 alienation cases, 16 of these meeting Gardner's eight criteria for severe alienation, Dunne and Hedrick (1994) reported that alienation was eliminated in 4 of the 26 children, for 3 of whom the court ordered a custody reversal and restricted contact with the alienating parent. In the remaining 22 cases, where there was no change in custody, improvements in the relationship with the rejected parent did not occur, even with therapy.

Gardner (2001b) conducted a qualitative follow-up of 99 children from 52 families whom he had previously "diagnosed" with PAS. He concluded:

> The court chose to either restrict the children's access to the alienator or change custody in 22 of the children. There was a significant reduction or even elimination of PAS symptomatology in all 22 of these cases. This represents a 100 percent success rate. The court chose not to transfer custody or reduce access to the alienator in 77 cases. In these cases there was an increase in PAS symptomatology in 70 (90.9 percent). In only 7 cases (9.1 per cent) of the non-transferred was there spontaneous improvement. Custodial change and/or reduction of the alienator's access to the children was found to be associated with a reduction in PAS symptomatology. (Gardner, 2001b, p. 39)

He reported a spontaneous reconciliation in only four cases, and no reduction in PAS symptoms in the seven children for whom contact with the rejected parent was not increased. However, in all of the 22 instances in which custody was changed or the alienating parent's contact was restricted, PAS was eliminated or reduced. Limitations to Gardner's follow-up include that the same individual who formulated the hypotheses and diagnoses (Gardner) also conducted the follow-up interviews, and only the rejected parents and not the children or the alienating parents were interviewed. While Gardner's development and use of the "parental alienation *syndrome*" (PAS) is controversial, this study remains one of the few pieces of longitudinal research on the effects of different types of judicial response to alienation, and the findings have been replicated in other studies.

Rand et al. (2005) reported similar findings on the value of custody reversal in their follow-up study of the 45 children from 25 families Kopetski had studied for over 20 years starting in 1976. A range of moderate to severe PAS characterized these cases. Alienation was interrupted by judicial action for 20 children from 12 families where there was enforced parenting time or a change of custody. For those in the treatment group, where there were orders for therapy with the objective of gradually increased parenting time, alienation remained uninterrupted and in some cases became worse. Those who were subject to court orders maintained better relationships with both parents unless the alienating parent was too disturbed; this group included children subject to both court-enforced contact and custody reversal, and consequently, it remains unclear the extent to which each of these factors was successful in alleviating the alienation. These follow-up results, however, are consistent with other previously mentioned studies reporting on various interventions.

Clearly, it would be desirable to have well-designed research, including longitudinal, randomly assigned designs, comparing children who change custody with those who do not. Conducting such research, however, is very difficult, and results would not be known for many years. Custody reversal (or not reversing custody) in an alienation case can only be the result of a judicial decision, and a judicial determination (or prediction) that this will be in the best interests of the particular child whose case is being decided. The judicial involvement would confound any research results.

Aggregate data derived from quantitative studies can provide a framework for using evidence to guide practice and to help determine what may or may not work in specific cases. Awareness of the current literature provides indicators of the potential consequences of case-based decisions. Despite the limitations of existing research, judges and policymakers need to make decisions. Further, an integrated approach using the best available evidence to guide practice is required in child custody determinations since decisions for a child should be based on the circumstances of the specific case and professional wisdom and should not be based solely on aggregate data. Consequently, a careful investigation and risk–benefit analysis of each case is required, as would be the case even if better research were available.

The need for decision making in the face of uncertainty was specifically acknowledged by Chief Judge Peter Boshier of the New Zealand Family Court in an interview:

> I think that you have to be extremely careful in changing care...but this is a challenge that judges have to be prepared to take. A judge shouldn't, I think, be risk averse and not reverse primary care in a case just because there are possible risks. In the one case that I have just done where the child seemed to be suicidal, reinforces my view that judges should follow their instinct. Based on reasonable psychological evidence, everything seemed to point to me that the risks that I was taking were proper, manageable risks. Since the child was moved [3 months before this report], the child is flourishing. All sorts of disorders that the child seemed to have had started to disappear...I acknowledge the risks, but I don't think that we should get too obsessed with the fact that separating from a parent that has an unhealthy, close dependency relationship with a child will necessarily ruin a child.[97]

This pragmatic judicial approach recognizes that just as there may be risks to a child in reversing custody, there are risks in leaving the child with an emotionally disturbed, alienating parent.

Proponents and, with few exceptions, opponents of custody reversal agree that it is preferable for children to have good relationships with both parents. In addition, they agree that it is preferable to identify alienation cases early and implement interventions such as education, coaching, counseling, and court monitoring to prevent the escalation of parent–child contact problems and the need for custody reversal. Competent assessment in the early stages will assist to differentiate the mild and moderate cases from the more severe ones. Education and counseling are more appropriate for the less severe cases. A more extreme intervention may be necessary for the more severe cases, and even for some of those where education and counseling have yet to be attempted. With few exceptions, most commentators agree that in the severest of cases, which are a minority and may present as such at the outset or later after various efforts to intervene have failed, custody reversal may be the least detrimental alternative for the child. Recognizing that these cases are unlikely to settle, an evaluator's recommendations and subsequent court decisions can make a difference between interrupted and completed alienation in more severe cases.

9.12.4 Judicial Decisions Changing Custody in Alienation Cases

Courts now are prepared to order a reversal of custody as a response to alienation. This will generally only be done if there is evidence from a custody

---

[97] Interview, May 24, 2010.

evaluator or other mental health expert that there has been alienation, that the alienated parent is capable of caring for the child, and that the benefits of the change in custody outweigh any emotional distress that the child may experience from such a change in living arrangements. Although the courts recognize that a change in custody may be very disruptive to the children involved, and accordingly are cautious about this, judges are increasingly aware that in severe alienation cases this may be the only effective way of dealing with the emotional and psychological harm caused by an alienating parent (Epstein, 2007). This recognition of the need for custody reversal in some alienation cases was shared by the judges from the United States, Canada, New Zealand, Australia, and Israel who were interviewed for this book.

In speaking about progressive judicial remedies, Toronto lawyer Philip Epstein stated:

> [As an initial response to alienation] there should be very, very specific orders for access. These may also be coupled with therapy or counseling. And the judge should closely monitor to see whether the access occurred and what occurred during the access. There should be reporting back on a regular occasion, and the order needs to be very multidirectional; it directs how the parties communicate, how the pickup and drop-off work, and thus the order leaves no opportunity for disagreement and argument. And if the access order is breached, the judge should cite for contempt, suspend the sentence for contempt, and give parties another chance to comply. The judge should bend over backwards to make very specific orders and encourage compliance. But if compliance cannot be achieved at an early stage in an alienation case with relatively young children, the judge should consider custody reversal.[98]

One of the first cases in Canada to reverse custody in response to a custodial parent undermining children's relationship with the other parent was the 1991 Quebec case of *P.S.-M v. LJ-A.C.*[99] The judge, in transferring custody of the two youngest children from their alienating father to the rejected mother, also ordered that there was to be no contact with the father and two older children for a period of 6 months. Justice Gomery found that this case represented an extreme example of parental alienation. "Hatred," he stated, "is not an emotion that comes naturally to a child. It has to be taught. The person who taught [these] ... children to hate [their mother] is their father. They would be better off if he were removed totally as an influence upon their development until they are able to withstand and reject his negative attitudes."[100]

The 1999 New York Family Court case of *J.F. v. L.F.* provides another early illustration of judicial willingness to transfer custody to respond to severe

---

[98] Interview, August 15, 2010.
[99] Unreported, [1991], SCM 500–12-184613895 (Que. Sup.Ct.).
[100] Unreported, [1991], SCM 500–12-184613895 (Que. Sup.Ct.) at p. 21.

alienation.[101] The parties were married, had two children, and separated when the children were 2 and 4 years of age. In the initial proceedings, the court awarded joint legal custody with primary residence to mother and unsupervised contact with the father at specified times. The separation was acrimonious, and the order included a provision that the police were to assist in "procuring" the father's contact, if required. The court also warned the parties that there was the prospect of an award of sole custody if there was an "interference with the parental rights" of the other party. The mother did not comply with the terms of the contact order; the father obtained court orders finding the mother in contempt and suspending child support for this.

When the children were 11 and 13 years old, the father brought an application awarding him sole custody, introducing expert evidence to establish that the mother had alienated the children from him, as well as evidence of such maternal conduct as telling the children that the father was "disowning them" by requesting a religious annulment from her to allow him to remarry within his faith, making the children return to their father's home mementos of trips and presents that the father gave to them, and creating unfounded fears in the children before a vacation trip with their father to Europe. More generally, she did nothing to support the children's relationship with their father.

The judge had the opportunity to meet with the children alone and observed:

> They are both highly intelligent and articulate and, in many ways, engaging and charming. They also show a resilience and ability to adapt to situations. Yet, particularly when discussing their father and his family, they present themselves at times in a surreal way with a pseudo-maturity which is unnatural and, even, strange. They seem like "little adults." This court finds that they live a somewhat sheltered, cloistered existence with their mother, emotionally and socially. They do not have friends to their home on a regular basis, and they do not go to other children's homes with any frequency. They do not have friends in their mother's neighborhood.
>
> The loving way in which the children perceive their mother, and the way in which they uncritically describe her as being perfect, stands in stark contrast to their descriptions of their father. Their opinions about their father are unrealistic, misshapen and cruel. They speak about and to him in a way which seems, at times, to be malicious in its quality. Nothing in the father's behavior warranted that treatment…
>
> Their negative view of their father is out of all proportion to reality. The children, by their conduct, have demonstrated that they do not wish to visit with their father.[102]

---

[101] 181 Misc.2d 722,694 N.Y.S.2d 592 (1999).
[102] 181 Misc.2d 722, at 725 694 N.Y.S.2d 592 (1999).

The mother's position was that she had not contributed in any way to the children's negative views of their father, that she had encouraged them to have a good relationship with him, and that the poor relationship was due to the father's lack of concern, inattention, insensitivity, and poor parenting. The court rejected her evidence and concluded:

> the mother's interference with the relationship between the children and the father is not an outright denial of visitation by making the children physically unavailable at the appointed time. Rather, the mother's interference here "involves a more subtle and insidious form of interference, a form of interference which, in many respects, has the potential for greater and more permanent damage to the emotional psyche of a young child than other forms of interference; namely, the psychological poisoning of a young person's mind to turn him or her away from the noncustodial parent."
>
> ... if the children were to be left with the mother "the children would have no relationship with their father given the mother's constant and consistent single-minded teaching of the children that their father is dangerous. She has demonstrated that she is unable and unwilling to support the father's visitation."
>
> In the instant case, the children do not want to visit with their father. With the passage of time, these children have become "staunch corroborators" of their mother's ill opinion of the father. They call their father names, they make fun of his personal appearance, they treat him as though he were incompetent, and they speak of and treat his wife similarly.[103]

After reviewing the evidence, the judge concluded that a variation in custody was necessary to promote the children's well-being:

> The children in this case have always resided with the mother. This court is mindful that although stability is an important consideration and has been found to be in children's best interests, it cannot be the decisive factor. "That a change in custody may prove temporarily disruptive to the children is not determinative, for all changes in custody are disruptive." In this case, the children's emotional stability will benefit from a change of custody, despite the fact that they have always resided with their mother...
>
> This court is faced with unanimous conclusions on the part of the three forensic evaluators... that these children have been alienated from their father by their mother. Where the opinions diverge is whether or not to change custody. This court accepts and adopts the reports and testimony of the mental health professionals to the extent that they indicate that the mother alienated the children

---

[103] 181 Misc.2d 722, at 729–30, 694 N.Y.S.2d 592 (1999).

from the father. She psychologically poisoned their minds, despite her love for and devotion to them. The court finds that the children will have no relationship with the father if left in the custody of their mother. The court finds, further, that they will continue to be psychologically damaged if they remain living with the mother. She is apparently unwilling or unable to control her behaviors.

The court has struggled mightily with this decision, balancing the short-term consequences to the children of a change of custody, including foreseeable emotional upset and possible trauma, against the long-term consequences of allowing physical custody to remain with the mother, which likely will result in the children having pathological personality traits which would interfere with their ability to establish whole relationships not only with their father but also with peers, future spouses or significant others, with extended family members, with employers and co-workers, and with the risk of their passing down a jaundiced and paranoid view of life to their own children. The mother has "poisoned" their childhood. The poison must be purged to restore them to a healthy state. This court seeks to restore normalcy to their lives and give them a chance to have a better childhood and a healthy adolescence and adulthood.[104]

The court ordered the transfer of sole custody of the two children to the father, a suspension of the children's contact with their mother, until otherwise recommended by the children's therapist, and that the father was to expeditiously enroll the children in therapy with a therapist experienced in treating families with parental interference or alienation.

There are a number of appeal cases that have affirmed trial decisions to transfer of custody from an alienating parent. For example, in 2005 in *J. W. v. D. W.*,[105] the Nova Scotia Court of Appeal affirmed a trial judge's finding that the mother had "demonized" the father to the children, and that they were emotionally abused. The boys told the custody evaluator that they wished to stay with their mother, and the trial judge expected that they would suffer "some immediate trauma and grief" as a result of the custody variation. Nevertheless, the judge concluded that this was "one of those rare and exceptional cases where drastic action [was] required to meet the best interests of the children,"[106] and transferred custody to the father. He remarked that it was

---

[104] 181 Misc.2d 722, at 730–31, 694 N.Y.S.2d 592 (1999).

[105] *J. W. v. D. W.*, [2005] N.S.J. 8 para. 64 (S.C. Fam. Div.), aff'd [2005] NSCA 102. See also *C.M.B.E v. D.J.E.*, [2006] N.B.J. 364 (C.A.), where the New Brunswick Court of Appeal, at para. 9, accepted the trial judge's determination that the custodial mother had been "waging marital warfare," which resulted in a denial of parenting time to the father, and accepted that this was "sufficient to trigger a fresh inquiry into the issue of custody" and to justify transferring custody to the father.

[106] *J. W. v. D. W.*, [2005] N.S.J. 8 (S.C.) aff'd. [2005] N.S.J. 275 (C.A) at para. 64.

"unfortunate for the parents that things have gotten so bad that the court is left with such limited options."[107] To limit the possibility of the alienating parent undermining the new custodial arrangement, the judge denied the mother contact with the boys for 4 weeks after the change in custody and also retained jurisdiction to deal with parenting time thereafter.

In 2006 in *Rogerson v. Tessaro*,[108] the Ontario Court of Appeal upheld a lower court's decision to transfer custody of twin boys, aged 5 years at the time of trial, to their father based on evidence that the mother was persistently attempting to undermine the relationship between the children and father. The court acknowledged that the remedy of changing custody was a "drastic one," but it approved the trial judge's structuring of the order as it was gradual, and thus likely to "cause as little disruption as possible for the children."[109]

A change of custody in alienation cases is often accompanied by suspended or restricted contact, at least initially, with an alienating parent, because restoring the relationship with the rejected parent and reeducating the child require separation from the source of influence (Baker, 2006; Gardner, 1999, 2001b; Rand, 1997b; Rand & Warshak, 2008). The order should include precise specification of the parenting time for the alienating parent after the moratorium, which in some cases may be supervised. Interestingly, many alienation cases at supervised visitation centers involve alienating parents and their children. In other cases, where the alienating parent continues to pose a threat to the emotional well-being of the child, the least detrimental option for the child may be an indefinite suspension of contact. In cases that require monitoring, it is highly desirable for the same judge to remain seized of the case.

In the 2008 Ontario case of *J.K.L. v. N.C.S.*,[110] the alienation of the parties' 13-year-old son from his mother was the result of the father's conduct and attitudes. Justice Turnbull quoted from the reasons of the judge who made a finding of contempt in an earlier proceeding in the same case, who had observed:

> …contact with even a flawed parent ... is better for a child than no contact at all. To cut off contact is a devastating thing for a child and can have serious long-term consequences."[111]

Justice Turnbull took a different view of the situation, concluding that this was a blatant and severe case of alienation, where the alienating father had been in breach of many court orders. The 13-year-old boy, who had previously testified against the mother at a criminal hearing (where she was found not guilty of assault of the father), was refusing all contact with her. The court

---

[107] Ibid. para. 62.
[108] [2006] O.J. 1825 (C.A.).
[109] Ibid., at para. 8.
[110] 2008 CarswellOnt 2903 (S.C.J.)
[111] Ibid. at para 64.

relied heavily on a comprehensive court-ordered evaluation as well as expert testimony from a local psychiatrist, and from an alienation expert, Dr. Richard Warshak. The court ordered a reversal of custody to the mother, whose contact for the previous few years was limited to observing her son occasionally at his sport events. As the sole custody parent, the mother then had the responsibility for making all health care decisions. The judge suggested that the mother might want to take the boy to an intensive alienation-directed program, like that operated by Dr. Warshak, since the court heard evidence about that program, but the court indicated that this decision was to be made by the custodial mother. A restraining order was put in place, and the father was to have no contact with his son for the next 4 months. The order also included terms for the police to enforce the court's order that the immediate transfer of custody occur at the court house in the absence of the father, and for the judge to remain seized of the matter with a return to court in 4 months.

As this case illustrates, if there is severe alienation and a custody reversal is being contemplated, those involved, including lawyers, mental health professionals, judges, and rejected parents, need to carefully plan for the transition. Factors to consider in planning include the age and attitude of the children, the attitude of the alienating parent, whether any travel is involved, and, of course, the resources available to support the transition. In some cases, for example, where contact with the alienating parent is to continue, it may be appropriate for the court to simply set a date in the near future when a change in residence is to occur; even in these cases, judicial monitoring and counseling support for all concerned will be helpful.

In the most severe cases where a child has been refusing all contact with the rejected parent and there is a prospect that the child might run away (inevitably with at least the tacit support and often with the covert aid of the alienating parent), there must be more planning and detailed judicial control over the transition process. The alienating parent may be required to bring the child along with possessions and clothing to the courthouse or another place within hours, or at most a day or so, of the judgment being rendered. Perhaps a person other than the alienating parent should bring the child to the transition location, and the initial meeting with the rejected parent should be supervised. It may be advisable that prior to the date on which judgment is to be rendered the alienating parent be ordered to bring the children to the courthouse on that date, in the event that a custody transition is ordered; plans then need to be made for their supervision at the courthouse, for telling the children what the judge has ordered, and supporting their transition. In some cases, a child's lawyer or therapist may be engaged to tell the child about the decision. As discussed in Chapter 8, in some cases the judge will want to meet the children to explain the decision. Children should always be permitted to say good-bye to the favored parent, but in severe cases, this may need to be supervised. Even if contact with an alienating parent is being suspended, children should be reassured that this is not intended to be permanent and that once certain requirements are in place they will see that parent again.

It will be very important for the rejected parent and advisors involved to plan for the possible use of support services, as children's attitudes and behavior at the time of the transition and immediately following may be difficult to handle. In severe cases where children refuse contact and threaten to run away or harm themselves or someone else, a transitional support program such as Family Bridges, discussed in Chapter 7, may help the family safely adjust to the court orders. In other cases, transfer to a transitional site may be indicated before the rejected parent and child are united for further intervention (Gardner, 1998b, 2001b; Gottlieb, 2006). Here the child is separated from both parents for a short time—generally a few days—before reintegrating with the rejected parent. While the child is at the transition site, supervised visits with the rejected parent should be undertaken. Sites vary in degree of control required, ranging from placement with a friend or relative to being placed in a foster home or treatment center.

If contact with the alienating parent has been suspended, after the child has spent some time living with the previously rejected parent and reestablished a relationship, a gradual reintroduction with alienating parent should be considered. Preferably, that parent will have had some counseling to gain insight into his or her behavior and its effects on the children, and demonstrated some behavior change. Initial contacts should be carefully monitored to ensure that the parental alienating behavior does not resume.

9.12.5 Judicial Decisions Against Custody Reversal Despite Severe Alienation

In some cases, the courts conclude that despite severe alienating behavior by the custodial parent and the child's resulting rejection of a parent, the child should not be removed from the care of the alienating parent as, on balance, it is not in the best interests of the child. Even if the courts conclude that there has been severe alienation that will continue without a change in custody, they may decide not to vary custody, as the rejected parent may lack the capacity to adequately care for the child. In some cases, a court is faced with a difficult situation in which an older child is steadfastly refusing contact with one parent, and the court is concerned that the child will "vote with his feet," regardless of what order is made. It must also be appreciated that a reversal of custody is only a viable option if requested by the rejected parent, who has the emotional energy and resources to deal with a transition process that may be challenging.

In the Nova Scotia case of *Corkum v. Corkum*,[112] the court had to decide the appropriate custodial arrangements for a 14-year-old girl who was unwilling to see her father. The father had had little contact with his daughter in the

---

[112] 2005 CarswellNS 235 (N.S.S.C.)

preceding 3 years, and in the 2 years immediately prior had no contact with her despite several findings of contempt against the mother. A custody evaluator found that although the child was thriving academically and socially in the care of her alienating mother, her emotional and psychological needs were not being adequately met in the mother's home. The expert concluded that if the child continued to remain with her mother, she was at risk of mental health difficulties and continued emotional harm. It was recommended that she be placed in the care of the child welfare authorities, who declined to intervene, leaving the trial judge to decide between placing the girl with a father of whom she was terrified (without good reason), or leaving her with a mother who was causing her emotional harm. In making the decision, the judge stated:

> I cannot find that it is [the child]'s best interest to take her from a place she feels safe and put her with someone which will cause her great fear and anxiety. She is fourteen years old and I doubt she would go or stay if I made such an order. The option proposed by [a mental health clinic where the girl had received treatment that she should be] allowed to feel safe in a neutral place while she received counseling to deal with her mother's mental health and to reunite her with her father. This is the option that I find would be in [the child]'s best interest. However, it is not available to me [because the child welfare authorities declined to be involved].[113]

The judge ordered that the parents have joint legal custody of the child with primary residence to remain with the mother but all legal decision-making authority resting in the hands of the father. The mother could obtain emergency medical treatment for the child, but all other consents were to be signed by the father. The child was to have counseling, and the father's parenting time was to be as recommended by the counselor in the interim. Lastly, the court ordered the parties to return to court in 6 months, sending a clear message to the mother that the progress was to be monitored.

Similarly, in the Ontario case of *Korwin v. Potworowski*,[114] the court reluctantly concluded it had no alternative but to allow a 13-year-old to remain with his mother, despite finding she would not promote the relationship between the child and his father. In allowing the 13-year-old boy to remain with his mother, Justice Gauthier stated: "There is no means of forcing this thirteen-year-old boy to remain in his father's home, short of locking him up. He is now of an age where, even if he may be too immature to appreciate what is best for him, he cannot be physically forced to remain where he does not want to be."[115] The two younger children were placed in their father's custody with parenting time granted to their mother. The judge had envisioned a situation where the children would be together every weekend, but left the oldest boy's

---

[113] Ibid. at para. 19.
[114] (2006), 31 R.F.L. (6th) 164 (Ont. S.C.J.).
[115] Ibid. at para. 145.

contact subject to his wishes, given that parenting time to a child of that age and in that situation is virtually unenforceable.

In the New York appellate decision of *Lew v. Sobel*, the court affirmed the decision of the trial judge that custody was not to be varied, despite the mother's violation of the provisions of the court-ordered visitation and her alienating behavior. Relying on the evidence of the independent custody evaluator, the court concluded:

> A change of custody should be made only if the totality of the
> circumstances warrants a change that is in the best interests of
> the child...While one parent's alienation of a child from the
> other parent is an act inconsistent with the best interests of the
> child...here, the children's bond to the alienating parent is so strong
> that a change of custody would be harmful to the children without
> extraordinary efforts by both parents and extensive therapeutic,
> psychological intervention. [116]

However, in accordance with New York law, the court ordered a reduction in child support until the mother could establish that she was in compliance with the previously ordered parenting time regime, and required her to pay 75% of the costs of the therapeutic contact facilitator, the Law Guardian, and the forensic evaluator employed during the course of the proceedings.

9.12.6 The Saga of Re S: A Cautionary Tale on the Need for Timely Judicial Decision

While it would be wrong to place too much weight on any single case, consideration of the English case of *Re S* is instructive as an illustration of the financial and emotional costs of failing to have a clear and timely response to a severe alienation case, as well as providing an interesting example of interaction of controversies within the mental health profession and the courts about alienation. The judge with the most involvement in the case characterized it as one in which "a wholly deserving father left my court in tears having been driven to abandon his battle to implement" the court order for a change in residence.

The child, S, was born in 1998. His parents were both professionals (his mother, a psychologist) who separated before his birth. For the first 7 years of the boy's life, he resided with his mother but had a good relationship with his father, who had remarried and had two more children. The mother had considerable anger toward the father, but when he was young, the boy had overnight parenting time with the father's family and traveled with them on vacations. However, by the time he was 8, the boy was refusing all contact. During the next 4 years, "immense energy and resources were invested in trying to reinstate a meaningful relationship between father and son."

---

[116] 46 A.D.3d 893, 849 N.Y.S.2d 586 (2007).

Initially, in response to the boy's resistance to contact with his father, the mother and father agreed to use voluntary therapeutic interventions to restore the relationship. After more than a year of trying, these therapeutic efforts failed to restore the contact. The father commenced court proceedings to secure contact when the boy was 9 years old. There was judicial case management with numerous court appearances. By the time of the trial, the boy was 11 years of age; a number of mental health professionals were involved, though most had little experience with alienation. The trial judge, HHJ Bellamy, concluded that the boy had been "profoundly alienated" by his mother and decided that the care of the boy should be transferred to his father, a decision affirmed by the English Court of Appeal.[117] Litigation then commenced over how the transfer of custody should be arranged. A psychiatrist with considerable experience with alienation cases recommended an immediate transfer, if necessary involving the court staff and the use of force. The boy, who had legal representation, continued to say he wanted to live with his mother and asserted that he would feel like a "criminal" if force were used to make him live with his father. Child protection authorities had become involved in the case and preferred use of transitional foster care and counseling to provide a "stepping stone" for a change in residence.

The psychiatrist testified that further therapy at that stage would be "fruitless" and recommended against the use of foster care, opining:

> The delay allows a period when attitudes can become entrenched, behaving badly, and further risk of harm occurring... at the end after the work and negotiation there will still be the same situation where we have to force him to live with his father. Even if he is willing to go into foster care, which is a good thing because it avoids a scene at the time, the bad thing is that we are not dealing immediately with what is ultimately necessary, that is, to make him to go live with his father.[118]

The trial judge ordered that there was to be a change in residence within a week, stating that the time had "come to grasp the nettle." [119] The judge hoped that the mother would take the boy to live with his father, but if not, ordered that court staff should transport the boy to this father. Before the change in residence occurred, the mother appealed, and the Court of Appeal ordered the use of foster care and counseling to ease the transition rather than an immediate change in residence.[120] The boy was placed in foster care but was allowed telephone contact with his mother. When his father came to the foster home, supervised by a therapist, the boy refused to speak to his father and sat with

---

[117] *Re S (Transfer of Residence)*, [2010] 1 FLR 1785, affirmed *Re S (A Child)*, [2010] EWCA Civ 219.

[118] *Re S (Transfer of Residence)*, [2010] 1 FLR 1785, at para. 34.

[119] *Re S (A Child)*, [2010] EWHC B2 Fam.

[120] *Re S (A Child)* [2010] EWCA Civ 325.

his head in his lap and his hands over his ears. These contacts lasted as long as 3 hours, during which time the boy also refused to eat or drink. Intensive therapy sessions were tried, including sessions with both parents present. The last reunification therapist involved concluded that after 24 hours of sessions spread over 13 weeks, there had been "tiny progress," and suggested that after another 6 to 12 months of therapy it might be possible for the boy to have unsupervised contact with his father. As well as having therapy aimed at reunifying the boy with his father, the child protection authorities arranged for mental health counseling, during which it was concluded that the boy was showing "numerous clinical symptoms of depressive illness" and starting to express suicidal ideation.

The final reported court decision in this saga records the history and the father's agreement for his son to reside with his mother and to have no direct contact with him.[121] The order included provision for a final supervised meeting for the boy and his father and held out the faint hope that the continued involvement of the child protection agency over the next year might achieve some degree of reconciliation between the boy and his father. In this decision, HHJ Bellamy recognized that "alienation is now a mainstream concept," though acknowledging the uncertainty in the research literature about the most effective response. The judge commented:

> I am bound to say that, for my part, I am in no doubt that in
> determining any high conflict case involving an alienated child it is
> essential that the court has the benefit of professional evidence from
> an expert who has personal experience of working with alienated
> children.[122]

It should be noted that while there are reports of cases where transitional foster care has been used to effect a successful transfer from an alienating parent to a rejected parent,[123] there is no research to support the "stepping stone" foster care approach that the English Court of Appeal tried, and the clinical literature does not support the relatively long period of transitional foster care. While the child protection agency planned for 3 months or more of transitional foster care, that agency admitted that it lacked expertise in dealing with alienation cases.

Although HHJ Bellamy correctly emphasized that "one size does not fit all" in alienation cases (or any other cases involving children), this case suggests that in severe alienation cases, there is real value in "grasping the nettle," and either ordering an immediate transfer of custody, or abandoning legal efforts to enforce contact. For a severely alienated child who is in or approaching

---

[121] *Re S*, [2010] EWHC B19 Fam.
[122] *Re S*, [2010] EWHC B19 Fam, at para. 59.
[123] See, e.g., *Re M (Intractable Contact Dispute)*, [2003] 2 FLR 636. In that case, the order for interim foster care was actually made before a final determination had been made about whether there would be a change in residence.

adolescence, any significant period in therapy or "stepping stone" foster care is only likely to lead to an entrenchment of the child's resistance and a deterioration in the child's mental health, with an escalating risk of physical self-harm as the "transition" continues. Severe alienation cases require judicial continuity and management of the case by a judge who has experience in dealing with high-conflict family cases, and decisive legal action; any appeals should be expedited, or alternatively there should not be a stay of the order pending an appeal. Delay can both undermine the effectiveness of any legal intervention tried and negatively affect the child's well-being while the uncertainty and litigation continue.

9.13 Suspension of Contact with the Alienating Parent

As discussed in the preceding section, when there is a change in custody, the court may determine that there must also be a suspension of contact with the alienating parent, at least for a period of time, to prevent undermining of the relationship with the rejected parent.

In a study of reported Canadian alienation cases between 1998 and 2009, the court withheld access in 17 cases where parental alienation was found. In 14 of those 17 cases, custody was transferred to the previously rejected parent, and the alienating parent lost both custody and contact. Thus, in 14 out of the 83 cases (17%), where there was a change in custody, there was also a suspension of contact (Bala et al., 2010). In 12 of the 95 cases (13%) in the 1989 to 2009 period where the court found that there had been an unsubstantiated claim of alienation, the court declined to order parenting time to the rejected parent. These included cases of justified rejection where there were concerns about the safety or welfare of the child in the care of that parent.

9.14 Deciding Not to Enforce Contact Despite Alienation

In some cases, children are very resistant to any efforts to change their attitudes toward seeing an alienated parent, whether by counseling or by using judicial sanctions imposed on a custodial parent to enforce contact. In some cases, the child's resistance is a reaction to a high level of conflict between the parents and reflects a desire to avoid a loyalty conflict. In other cases, however, the child's contact refusal may be the result of alienating conduct by the custodial parent and occurs despite the absence of fault on the part of the noncustodial parent. It can be very difficult for the noncustodial parent to come to terms with this type of rejection, but in some of these cases, the rejected parent may decide to give up the effort to seek to enforce contact rights. The decision may reflect the emotional or financial exhaustion of the rejected parent, or an assessment that not to seek to enforce an access order is better for the child.

In some cases a judge may decide that it is not appropriate to order or enforce access,[124] or may make comments suggesting that continuing efforts to enforce contact may not be in the child's best interests,[125] despite (or because of) the alienating conduct of the custodial parent. In *El-Murr v. Kiameh*,[126] Katarynch J. decided not to take steps to require a 10-year-old boy to see his father after 4 years without contact, commenting:

> Perhaps this boy is best served at this time in his life by being left in peace. He has been given opportunity to open himself to a reunion with his father. He has declined the opportunity... There is no benefit for the father at this time—just a faint hope. It is cruel to keep alive hope that is faint, when there is no indication on the evidence that this child is likely to open himself to his father in the near future.
>
> Whatever the benefit, it is no more than a potential. At this point in this child's life, his actuality is that he has moved on to establish a father-and-son relationship with his stepfather. From his perspective, he does not need any other father-and-son relationship.

In the 2010 English case of *Re Children B*,[127] the father engaged in contested proceedings stretching over 4 years concerning his two sons, aged 8 and 9 years by the conclusion of the proceedings. The court characterized this as "a very sad case in which an entirely deserving father has been alienated from these two boys and a substantial responsibility for that alienation must lie with their mother." Three independent experts testified, providing evidence that the mother is "unable to contain her strong emotions, highly critical of the father and paternal family [and the] children have been exposed to all these feelings and they have been adversely affected in their emotional development." One expert testified that the children were "parentified: acting like adults in control of the mother." Nevertheless, the experts concluded that a transfer of residence to the father would be "too risky in terms of the children's development" because the mother was the children's sole attachment figure. Meetings with father and children supervised by the experts had not gone well. The trial judge ordered that the children continue to reside with the mother and have only "indirect contact" with the father, such as with letters through the Office of the Law Guardian. There was also an order for the children to receive

---

[124] See, e.g., *Bailey v. Bailey* [1996] O.J. No. 4891; *Roda v. Roda* [2000] O.J. No. 3786 (S.C.J.).

[125] See, e.g., *P. (J.E.) v. W. (H.J.)*(1987), 11 R.F.L. (3d) 136 (Sask. Q.B (Sask. Q.B.) where a 6-year-old girl had an aversion toward her father because of the mother's hostility to him. The mother was opposed to parenting time, despite mediation efforts. The court refused to order contact, at least until "the child is considerably older."

[126] [2006] O.J. 1521 (Ont. Ct. J.).

[127] [2010] EWCA1045.

counseling to repair their relationship with their father. However, 6 months after the decision the mother had failed to comply with the order, and there was no practical way to enforce this order. In affirming the decision to leave the children in the care of their mother with no effective steps to secure a relationship with their father, Thorpe LJ wrote:

> It is an extremely sad case where any judge at trial must have almost shrunk from his role in a situation which offered so little opportunity for judicial intervention, so little hope for the future. The judge was choosing between very poor alternatives, and that is a tragic situation not just for the family but for the judge who has to carry out his role, and this court has very limited powers of principled intervention.[128]

The appeal judge referred to the order for counseling as offering "slender" hope for the father.

If a court determines that a child's rejection of a parent is due to alienation (and not justified rejection), it may nevertheless conclude that it would be contrary to a child's best interests to force a child to have a relationship with the parent; in these situations, it may be appropriate for the noncustodial parent to have a "final" meeting with the child, even if the child seems reluctant to attend. That meeting might be attended by a mental health professional or the child's lawyer, with the intent of allowing the parent to tell the child why the legal process is being discontinued, and to express the hope that a relationship may be resumed at some point in the future.[129] These sentiments may also be put in a letter to the child. In some cases, the judge might also consider it appropriate to meet with the child or write the child a letter (copying the parents and lawyers involved in the case) to explain the decision. The noncustodial parent may also be permitted to continue to correspond with the child and send gifts at special occasions, which the custodial parent should be required to share with the child. Leaving the lines of communication open in whatever manner possible, such as occasional letters, cards, gifts, e-mail or use of social media, and so on, will demonstrate the parent did not abandon the children and may permit positive memories that may pave the way for a future reconciliation, a better alternative than providing no trail of resolution for the grown child (Baker, 2005b; Cartwright 2006).

While a decision not to enforce parenting time may relieve the child of the immediate pressure of being caught between two parents, the child may well still feel abandoned under such circumstances, notwithstanding any stated

---

[128] [2010] EWCA1045, at para. 8.
[129] See Warshak, (2003a), at 282; and Sullivan & Kelly (2001), at 311.

wishes and protestations of hate and rejection. In some cases, children do resume a relationship with a rejected noncustodial parent after a long period without contact, though sometimes only in adulthood. In other cases a relationship may never be reestablished.

9.15 Financial Penalties

As discussed above, in most jurisdictions the courts may order a party to a family case who has caused unnecessary legal proceedings to pay compensation for all, or a portion, of the legal fees and other litigation expenses incurred by the other party. Thus, a parent in contempt of a contact or parenting time order may be required to reimburse the parent enforcing the order, or a parent who makes an unfounded allegation of alienation may be required to pay the legal fees of a parent who has been justified in withholding contact due to abuse or who has made reasonable efforts to comply with the order.

In some American states, in cases where a custodial parent is willfully violating a visitation order, the courts may also suspend child or spousal support, as a means of sanctioning the alienating parent and encouraging compliance. When the courts suspend the payment of support, they stipulate that when parenting time is restored, support will resume. New York is one state where courts may suspend support obligations in alienation cases: an example of the judicial approach to this issue in that jurisdiction is the statement in *Usack v. Usack*:

> While alteration of...[father's] child support obligations may be an imperfect remedy with which to address...[custodial mother's] harmful, unfair conduct, there is no proof that suspending [the father's support] obligations temporarily would result in the children becoming public charges. Accordingly,...[the father's] support obligations are suspended pending further court order upon a showing that...[the mother] has made good faith efforts to actively encourage and restore [the father's]...relationship with the children....[130]

In most jurisdictions, however, courts follow a traditional approach and refuse to link contact denial to support enforcement.[131] Even in jurisdictions that follow this approach, in cases of clear alienation by the custodial parent, a few judges have been prepared to threaten suspension of child or spousal support if the problems continue or actually make such an order,[132] especially

---

[130] 17 AD 3d 736 (NY: App. Div., 3rd Dept. 2005).
[131] *Lee v. Lee* (1990), 29 R.F.L. (3d) 417 (B.C.C.A.).163.
[132] See, e.g., *Ungerer v. Ungerer*, [1998] B.C.J. 698 at para. 42, 158 D.L.R. (4th) (C.A.) where the wife's alienating conduct was considered "sufficiently egregious to disentitle her to continued [spousal] support." See also *Bruni v. Bruni*, 2010 ONSC 6568 where Quinn J. terminated spousal support in response to the mother's alienating conduct.

where the custodial parent has sufficient resources that the child would not suffer harm.[133]

In some jurisdictions the law may allow for orders to be made to requires parents to provide financial support for young adult children who are continuing their education. In some cases in these jurisdictions,[134] the courts may be more willing to consider unjustified rejection of a payer parent as a reason for terminating child support; in these cases the payer is usually paying support to allow the child to pursue postsecondary education, and the child may be refusing to even tell the parent about the progress of his or her studies. Even in cases involving adult children who are refusing to communicate with a parent who is paying support, there is a reluctance to penalize the child, and it is more common for judges to threaten termination in an attempt to pressure the children to become more engaged with the rejected parent, for example, by at least requiring the child to provide the payer reports on his or her academic progress than to actually terminate the support.[135]

9.16 Case Management—The Need for Judicial Control

Almost all of the experts, and all of the judges, interviewed for this book, were strong supporters of judicial case management. They recognize the importance of early, effective judicial control for cases where alienation is an issue by a single judge who can get to know the parties and their situation and set clear limits for the parents. Justice Philip Marcus of the Israeli Family Court, for example, commented on the value of judicial continuity for cases where alienation is an issue:

> It is exceptionally important to know the parties. As I say, in many cases I know the parties better than their lawyers do. In particular, litigants with personality disorders will fire their lawyers frequently, so that a lawyer will come into the case not knowing the background and the client's personal problems. I may have been dealing with the family for several years, so that I have learned what each litigant is like.[136]

Ontario Superior Court Justice, George Czutrin observed:

> I think that we should try to identify these cases, whatever we are calling them, as early as possible…I really do believe very strongly that there should be one judge who absolutely manages the case. And then…look for a new approach to managing and bringing the

---

[133] *Welstead v. Bainbridge* (1994), 2 R.F.L. (4th) 419 (Ont. Ct. J. (Prov. Div.)); see also James G. McLeod, "Annotation to *Lee v. Lee*" (1990), 29 R.F.L. (3d) 417.

[134] See, e.g., *Lampron v. Lampron* (2006), 29 R.F.L. (6th) 307 (Ont. Sup. Ct.); *Webb v. Stropple*, 2006 BCSC 294; and *Moore-Orlowski v. Johnston*, 2006 SKQB 279, 27 R.F.L. (6th) 396.

[135] *Morgan v. Morgan*, 2006 SKQB 76; and *Caterini v. Zaccaria*, 2010 ONSC 6473.

[136] Interview, June 2, 2010.

matter to conclusion in a timely manner. We may need to consider/
study a team management approach involving other professionals.[137]

In response to the argument that the judge may "get it wrong," Toronto
lawyer Philip Epstein said:

> The judge is supposed to be the case manager, not to be the trial
> judge. So the judge is supposed to move it along, and if the judge
> can't resolve it, then at least some other judge would try it. So there
> is always a risk that the judge will get it wrong, and there is always a
> risk that the judge will get it wrong at trial. But, you know, judges do
> the best they can with the evidence they have. And the idea that one
> judge might get it wrong and therefore we should try a host of other
> judges is ludicrous.
>
> Further, without case management, you are more likely to
> have a number of judges getting it wrong because of inadequate
> information, compounded if they are not specialist judges.[138]

Case management—one knowledgeable family law judge for one family—
is especially valuable for cases where alienation is alleged (Martinson, 2010).
Judicial continuity allows the judge to gain an appreciation of the complex
nature of the case and to set clear expectations for the parents (and in some
cases, the children). Although contempt of court orders, reversal of custody,
and temporary suspension of contact with an alienating parent are important
weapons in the judicial arsenal for dealing with alienation, their use is clearly
not optimal. The primary judicial role, in all but the most intractable cases,
should be educational—an authoritative figure making clear to both parents
how their behavior is negatively affecting their children. The exhortations
of a judge—setting out clear expectations and consequences for failures to
comply—can move many parents and children, who may also be interviewed
by the judge, to alter their behaviors, especially if combined with directions
for educational or therapeutic interventions (Brownstone, 2008; Darnall &
Steinberg, 2008a). Only the most personality-disordered or psychotic parents
are likely to defy a judge who has set out clear expectations and consequences.
When this defiance occurs, it may be necessary to resort to remedies more
suitable for the severe cases of alienation.

Judicial continuity and short adjournments (or conditional adjournments
if the parenting time ordered does not occur) are especially valuable in cases
where there are parent–child contact problems and noncompliance with previous orders (Bala, Fidler, et al., 2007; Epstein, 2002). Judicial exhortations
and threats, in particular, are more likely to be effective when the parents
know that they will have to return to the judge who has had the opportunity
to get to know them and their issues. While there will always be exceptions,

---

[137] Interview, April 19, 2010.
[138] Interview, August 15, 2010.

many (but not all) alienating parents will heed the advice and warnings of the judge who has control over their case (Bala & Bailey, 2004).

In some jurisdictions, having effective case management will require some administrative restructuring in the court system, but case management not only promotes the interests of children; it should also result in more efficient use of resources in the justice system, with less judicial time spent on high-conflict cases and fewer lengthy trials (Bala, Birnbaum, & Martinson, 2011). Even where there is no case management system, a judge may rule that he or she "remains seized of the matter" (responsible for the case) to address future problems (Bala et al., 2011.) This may be especially useful in a contempt proceeding in order to enable judicial monitoring of a parent's willingness and ability to comply with the existing order (Epstein, 2002).

9.17 Child Protection Agency Involvement

Child protection agencies are increasingly being involved in high-conflict separations. In some cases the agency is involved because there have been repeated allegations by one parent that the other parent is abusing the child; often in alienation cases these are unfounded allegations of child sexual abuse.

In almost every jurisdiction, child protection legislation specifies that emotional abuse is a form of child abuse that must be reported to child protection authorities. This includes emotional abuse, if sufficiently severe, arising from parental conflict. Judges and other professionals may be obliged to report severe alienation cases to child protection authorities for investigation.

While involvement of child protection authorities can be intrusive for children and parents alike, in some cases the agency can provide a needed independent source of evidence for the court about the validity of allegations of alienation, abuse, or domestic violence. When parents have limited resources, a child protection agency may also provide counseling and support services for the children and parents that may otherwise be unavailable. The child protection agency may also be able to provide foster care for an alienated child; usually this is expected to be "transitional," but in some cases it may need to be long term, if the alienating parent is offering an emotionally toxic home and the rejected parent is unable to provide adequate care.

Although child protection agencies can have a positive role in alienation cases, at present too few child protection workers have the necessary education, training, and experience to deal with them effectively. As a result, there continue to be cases where the courts have been critical of insensitive and inappropriate involvement by agency workers in alienation cases, for example, if they are too quick to "blindly accept" the allegations of abuse from an alienating parent and erroneously conclude that the child's rejection of a parent is justified.[139]

---

[139] See, e.g., *W.C. v. C.E.*, 2010 ONSC 3575.

While it would be desirable for child protection agencies to have more involvement in severe alienation cases as these almost inevitably involve "emotional abuse," these agencies have heavy caseloads and limited resources, and in many jurisdictions give low priority to these cases. Although in some places judges dealing with family cases have the jurisdiction to order the local child protection agency to provide services in an alienation case, in most jurisdictions judges lack the legal authority to mandate agency involvement.[140]

9.18 The Importance of Timely Legal Intervention

The literature and all of the interviews conducted for this book consistently stress the value of prevention and early identification by the courts, followed by appropriate judicial, educational, and clinical intervention in cases involving parent–child contact problems. A majority of researchers now reject the view advanced by a few commentators in the past (see Bruch, 2001; Faller, 1997; Wallerstein & Blakeslee, 1989) that rejection of a parent—especially for the older child—is a "normal" part of divorce and that it is best to leave well enough alone, as the child will "come around." An important consideration is that it may not be known in the early stages which seemingly mild or justified contact resistance or refusal may develop into more severe alienation.

Most writers agree that alienating parental behavior and strategies are a form of emotional abuse that should be addressed. The results of research on the long-term negative effects of alienation of a child from a parent are sobering (Baker, 2005a, 2005b, 2006a). Janet Johnston writes that "alienating behavior by parents is a malignant form of emotional abuse of children that needs to be corrected, whether a parent agrees or not" (Johnston, 2005a, p. 770). She and other researchers point to the growing body of literature documenting the negative effects of psychological control and intrusive parenting on children (see, for example, Barber, 2002).

A child's negative attitudes toward a rejected parent and resistance to contact may become more serious as legal proceedings drag on. While it is important to try less intrusive interventions, including voluntary responses, before more intrusive interventions are attempted, if there are not fairly quick changes in attitudes and responses to the less intrusive responses, there needs to be a timely decision to either have a more intrusive response or abandon the ineffective efforts. While therapy for children and their parents can be an effective response to alienation in some cases, it can take 9 months to 2 years to build sustainable relationships. However, the clinical literature and experience of seasoned practitioners indicate that if signs of some progress are not

---

[140] For a rare example of an Ontario case where a Superior Court judge concluded that he had the "inherent authority" to require a child protection agency to provide services in an alienation case in order to address emotional abuse concerns, see *Fiorito v. Wiggins,* 2011 ONSC 1868, per Harper J.

evident within a reasonable length of time, in the range of 3 to 6 months, it is unlikely that more therapy will have a positive effect. Moreover, inappropriate or unrelenting, ineffective therapeutic interventions can actually entrench a child's negative attitudes toward a rejected parent. Although judicial responses like imprisonment for contempt or a reversal of custody may be viewed as a "last resort," delaying invoking these for years in the face of intransigent behavior by an alienating parent only allows the situation to worsen. Similarly, while a judicial decision that there is no effective means to enforce contact is deeply frustrating to an unjustifiably rejected parent, needless delay of this decision merely increases the frustration and expense and prolongs the period in which the child experiences the emotional stress of the legal process.

9.19 Conclusion: The Law as a Blunt but Necessary Instrument

Alienation is a complex problem that the family courts are facing with increasing frequency. These cases present unique challenges for legal and mental health professionals. Judges in particular are placed in a difficult position, often faced with conflicting testimony and allegations, competing theories underlying the phenomenon, conflicting expert evidence, a limited range of resources and possible judicial approaches to managing the problem, and ultimately, the dilemma of trying to promote the best interests of the child while upholding the administration of justice.

In some instances, early cooperation between parents, lawyers, and mental health professionals may avoid judicial intervention completely, a result that is clearly in the interests of all parties and their children. In some milder alienation cases, referral to group or individual parent education, if available, will suffice to help parents understand the effects of their conduct and attitudes on their children. A lawyer may also influence parental behavior by providing information and advice to their client. While lawyers representing alienating parents may face an unreceptive audience, a clear description of the negative consequences of alienation for children may have the effect of curtailing damaging parental conduct.[141] Similarly, a lawyer for a rejected parent may need to

---

[141] For example, the *Rules of Professional Conduct* of Ontario's Law Society state that counsel for parents have an obligation to advise those clients about the effect of their conduct on their children, with the Commentary to Rule 4.01 providing:

In adversary proceedings that will likely affect the health, welfare, or security of a child, a lawyer should advise the client to take into account the best interests of the child, where this can be done without prejudicing the legitimate interests of the client.

See also Waldron and Joanis (1996), p. 130.

provide information and give advice about different kinds of strained relationships, pointing out that not all are the result of parental alienating behaviors. Drawing on social science literature, lawyers can provide parents with information about the negative effects of parental conflict and alienating conduct on their children's emotional well-being.

Where alienation is claimed, independent evidence tendered through a court-ordered evaluation by an independent mental health professional is generally necessary if the court and the parents are to understand the context in which events are taking place. Although the final determination of how to respond to cases involving alienation ultimately lies with the judge, lawyers play an important role in providing the court with clear evidence of the issues demanding intervention, as well as in supporting an approach that will best reflect the needs of the child. A custody evaluation should inform any therapeutic intervention that may follow.[142]

It is important for judges to take control of these cases to the greatest extent possible, to limit the possibility of manipulation and delay of the court process by the parents or lawyers, and to ensure that there is a firm and timely response to violations of court orders. These are cases for which judicial case management is especially appropriate.

Although, in general, diversion of family law cases from the courts and nonadversarial approaches are to be strongly supported, judges should be prepared to be involved and take firm approaches when the circumstances warrant. Having an effective, early legal response to parents who are alienating their children from their former partners, wittingly or not, will both tend to encourage compliance with court orders and promote the interests of children. If there is no effective legal response to violation of court orders, custodial parents may feel encouraged to thwart them, dispiriting the rejected parent and emotionally harming the children. Having case management for high-conflict cases can help to reduce the possibility of parents manipulating the court. If judges make more detailed and explicit orders, this can also reduce the temptation of parents to manipulate the courts.

In the immediate postseparation period, when feelings of anger, betrayal, and distrust between the parents are likely to be at their highest, there is often value in giving separating parents a little time to gain perspective on their situation and "cool down" before trying to negotiate a settlement. However, there are different considerations where there are allegations of abuse or alienation, especially if resistance to contact develops after a period in which postseparation parenting time has been going reasonably well. A significant concern in alienation cases is that prolonged periods of no contact or litigation without remedial efforts being applied will likely serve to only further entrench the alienation, inappropriately empowering both the alienating parent and the alienated child.

---

[142] Johnston (2005a), p. 757, and Baker (2005b).

Family law lawyers and judges who ordinarily contemplate "cooling-off" periods in family cases must be aware that in these types of high-conflict cases, skilled and early intervention is usually required. Indeed, in one severe alienation case, the judge stated:

> ...[P]rompt, decisive and perhaps radical steps must be taken to put a stop to this alienation. Those steps are to be put in place immediately...[143]

Alienation cases need to be understood and treated differently than most other types of family disputes. Delaying intervention for many months after the child has become alienated to allow for voluntary counseling, mediation, or a custody evaluation is likely to make court-ordered response more difficult or impossible. Mental health professionals, lawyers, and judges need to be cognizant that their decisions not only need to address the immediate problem in the case before them, but also need to consider the long-term interests of children who have a right to have a healthy relationship with both parents.

These cases must be carefully assessed and responded to on an individual basis, premised on the promotion of the interests of children, and the recognition that they are the ones who suffer the most. It must be recognized that in many high-conflict separation cases, the courts are really left to make a choice about the least detrimental alternative, but this does not make their role any less important.

---

[143] *Mikan v. Mikan* [2004] O.J. 740 (Ont. Sup. Ct.).

10

Recommendations for Practice, Policy, and Research

In this concluding chapter, we synthesize and summarize a dozen of the central ideas that we have discussed in this book for change and reform in the understanding and response to cases in which children are resisting contact with a parent in the context of separation or divorce. A detailed discussion of the reforms for practice, policy, and legislation is beyond the scope of this book, and in any event, these types of reforms must always be addressed within the context of the specific legal, cultural, and institutional framework of a specific jurisdiction. However, a discussion of themes for reform should be of value for those working for change within their own jurisdictions, and many of the issues have both local and transnational applications.

10.1. Prevention

Educational programs are helpful before people decide to have children together and when raising children, and are especially valuable if they find themselves having relationship difficulties or are in the early stages of separation. Educational programs directed at parents who are separating can assist them in developing effective communication, problem-solving, and conflict resolution skills, and effective parenting and coparenting, including learning about the importance for their children of maintaining positive relationships with both parents, and about the harms for children of spousal abuse and parental alienating behaviors. Programs explaining the various methods of nonadversarial dispute resolution and the negative effects of parental conflict and litigation are imperative. While such programs may not prevent the most severe cases of alienation from occurring, they have positive value for many parents and thus benefit their children.

With so many children experiencing parental conflict and divorce, schools are starting to establish divorce-specific psychoeducational programs for children relating to communication and relations with parents. Such programs and related support groups can have real value for children, and more are needed.

10.2. Interprofessional Education and Standards for Best Practices

Mental health professionals, mediators, child protection workers, lawyers, and judges in the family justice system require a sound understanding of the specialized issues involved in high-conflict cases (including the systemic problems related to "negative advocates," family relationships, domestic violence, and alienation) (Fidler, Bala, Birnbaum, & Kavassalis, 2008; Martinson, 2010; J. McIntosh, interview, 2010). Developing this understanding should be a focus of their initial professional formation, as well as the subject of ongoing professional education and training. Cross-disciplinary training and collaboration are imperative (Beck, Holtzworth-Munroe, D'Onofrio, Fee, & Hill, 2009).

In some cases, lawyers and mental health professionals become inappropriately enmeshed with their clients, ultimately doing the children and their parents a disservice; education and training can help professionals to be aware of this dynamic and avoid it.

Best practice guidelines for the services and professionals who work with high-conflict cases (e.g., mediation, custody evaluation, expert testimony consultation, parent–child contact problem family therapy, reintegration therapy or therapeutic access, parenting coordination, divorce coaching, etc.) are being developed by multidisciplinary groups (Fidnick et al., 2011). These efforts should continue and will be helpful for improving future responses.

Better education, training, and protocols are also needed for child protection workers and police, especially for those who undertake investigations of allegations of abuse in high-conflict separations.[1]

10.3. Improving Professional Collaboration

The need for collaboration between professional groups and agencies is clear. Legal and mental health professionals need to remain open-minded

---

[1] See comments about the need for better training and protocols for police and child protection workers involved in alienation cases by MacPherson, J., in the Ontario case of *W.C. v C.E.*, 2010 ONSC 3575.

about each other's ideas and perspectives. Improved collaboration is imperative if the needs of children are to be properly identified and addressed. Given the systemic nature of this problem, the efforts and models used by mental health professionals cannot stand in isolation from those used by the judicial system (Beck et al., 2009). Improved interventions require both better collaboration in the research and the development of interdisciplinary professional standards of practice and local task forces to coordinate service provision.[2]

For mild and some moderate cases involving parent–child contact problems, including alienation, the most effective response is likely to be court-directed and monitored family therapy, with the therapist keeping the court informed of the progress (or sabotaging) of therapy. This approach requires a higher degree of interdisciplinary collaboration than exists in most locales at present.

10.4. Early Identification, Screening, Triage, and Expedited Process

There is continuing debate on some important issues regarding responses to children resisting or refusing contact with one parent. However, there is unanimous agreement among experienced legal and mental health practitioners and commentators that there is a need for early identification and screening of high-conflict cases, including recognition and responses to intimate partner violence *and* parent–child contact problems (Salem, Kulack, & Deutsch, 2007). The need for early identification and response applies irrespective of whether the cause of the contact problems is parental abuse, justified rejection, alienation, or some combination of reasons. While not all high-conflict cases involve parent–child contact problems, alienation cases all involve high conflict.

About the importance of early, effective legal responses, Toronto lawyer Phil Epstein emphasized that

> There should be a triage system that allows for early identification of high-conflict cases of all kinds, gives specific attention to alienation cases, pulls them out of the system and deals with them on a streamlined basis.[3]

Effective early identification of high-conflict cases will be assisted by the development of validated screening instruments (Birnbaum & Bala, 2010a; Birnbaum & Saini, 2007), and efforts are being made to develop such instruments. For example, Ontario social work professor Rachel Birnbaum and her

---

[2] See the July 2009 *Family Court Review*, Volume 47(3), for several articles that discuss models for multidisciplinary training and collaboration.

[3] Interview, August 15, 2010.

colleagues are piloting the Dimensions of Conflict in Separated Families Scale[4] in multiple clinical, child welfare, and court sites in Ontario, Quebec,[5] and Florida[6] to empirically validate and test an instrument to differentiate families based on levels of conflict. The goal of this research is to provide: 1) timely and accurate identification of disputing families to allow for early intervention, thereby reducing the associated risks to children; 2) a common language associated with high conflict to reduce the extent to which multiple services (i.e., adult and children's mental health, child welfare, medical, police, legal, and education) are provided to no avail; 3) an empirically validated instrument that identifies different levels of conflict to assist mental health practitioners in targeting specific interventions; and 4) assistance for further practice, research, and policy decision making with families postseparation (Birnbaum & Bala, 2010a; Birnbaum & Saini, 2007; Saini & Birnbaum, 2007). Although not specific to alienation, early identification of high-conflict families can help to provide early interventions to change the trajectory of high-conflict families, before acrimonious family interactions and situations of alienation become entrenched.

Another example of early screening is the Supervised Visitation Checklist (SVC) developed by Saini and Newman (2010)[7]. The SVC, currently being pilot tested in Ontario with judges, lawyers, and mental health professionals, is intended to assist professionals in making decisions regarding the suitability for parents and children to use supervised access services to help protect the safety of children while promoting maximum contact between children and their parents.

Early assessment by a court-appointed mental health professional with specialized knowledge in alienation, abuse, and intimate partner violence is highly desirable. The key questions in any assessment should be: Is it in the best interest of this particular child in this particular circumstance to have contact with the rejected parent? If so, how, when, and where should this be achieved? Parent–child contact problems, including alienation, generally become more difficult to address with the passage of time, as children and parents are more likely to become entrenched in their positions, further exacerbated by the litigation over parenting and financial matters. Later, ineffective

---

[4] This scale was originally developed as a clinical tool by a subcommittee of the High Conflict Forum in Toronto, Canada. The Forum is made up of 30–40 social service agencies (child welfare, counseling, children's mental health, and other assessment services) chaired by Howard Hurwitz (Clinical Director, Jewish Family and Child Services).

[5] With the assistance of collaborators, Dr. Francine Cyr (University of Montreal) and Lorraine Filion, Director at the Palais de Justice, Montreal, Canada.

[6] With the assistance of The Advocate Program, Inc., in connection with Bridging Families & Communities, Miami, Florida.

[7] SVC was developed based on a grounded theory study of 127 legal summations and the integration of social science evidence regarding supervised access within the context of custody disputes.

interventions are not only a waste of resources but can result in escalating polarization (Schepard, 2001).

If the parents are able to agree that there are problems with a child's relationship with one parent and that it is indeed in the child's best interest to have a good relationship with both parents, the parties themselves may decide to have counseling for themselves and their children; such a voluntary intervention may be based on a written agreement or consent order, with detailed terms concerning the provision of services that are intended to improve the child's overall adjustment, including repairing the family relationships. A voluntary response is often best for all involved and most likely to be effective, provided both parents truly intend to engage. The fact that the parties agree to take some action may be itself an important predictor of positive outcomes. However, there are also cases in which an alienating or abusive parent will agree to some form of voluntary intervention as a delaying tactic without any real intention of following through on commitments.

If voluntary therapy is undertaken, a clinical assessment for the purposes of the therapy is needed to develop a treatment/intervention plan. If the parents do not accept the plan, they are free to return to court. The therapist may decide to recommend a court-ordered comprehensive custody evaluation, and mandatory reporting of abuse or neglect would be required, thereby addressing cases suspected to involve pure or even primarily justified rejection (realistic estrangement) at the outset. If it becomes apparent that a parent is not meaningfully engaging in therapy, having only agreed to the process as a stalling tactic or in the expectation that the therapy would fail, it is important that the therapist terminate the process and indicate that one party is not engaging. The agreement to undertake a voluntary response should provide for this type of reporting.

If an evaluation is required by a court-appointed mental health professional, the assessment (Bala, Fidler, Goldberg, & Houston, 2007) and settlement process and trial (Martinson, 2010), if necessary, should be expedited. While recognizing the challenges this may pose, custody evaluations in these cases should be completed as quickly as possible, preferably in no more than 6 to 8 weeks. Mental health professionals should be canvassed before an order is made as to their expected completion date. Those clinicians who are unable to comply with an expedited process should not agree to undertake the assessment.

In addition, consideration needs to be given to how, when, and where to best disseminate the evaluation findings or report to the parents. Some parents in high-conflict cases misuse these reports, sharing their contents with their children, resulting in the ill-advised and premature involvement of the children leading to an exacerbation of the alienation and what can become the child's phobic reaction to the recommendations for therapy or custody reversal. Initially, and before it is clear if there is going to be a settlement on the basis of the recommendations, it is preferable for evaluation reports to be shared with the parents under the supervision of the court and their lawyers, with the evaluator providing guidance in understanding the report and recommendations as well as how to discuss these with the children. The parents should be required by the court not to share the report or its contents with the children until a time when it is appropriate to do so, and even then, the conditions for doing this need to be clarified (Trussler, 2008).

Delays and ineffective intervention are likely to entrench the alienation, making it more difficult to remedy. Sometimes, the attempted solution exacerbates problems in the family. Those determining the intervention should carefully consider any previous efforts that were unsuccessful so that similar approaches are not repeated, thereby reinforcing the alienation and the child's negative reaction to the failed efforts.

10.5. Detailed and Unambiguous Parenting Plan Orders

In high-conflict cases where the parents cannot agree on a voluntary plan that will adequately address concerns about postseparation relationships with both parents, a detailed court order is needed to govern parenting arrangements. That order should address both issues of day-to-day care and major child-related decisions, as well as treatment, where relevant. In high-conflict cases, detailed and comprehensive parenting plans, including all aspects of parenting arrangements (parenting time, location and manner of transitions, decision making, parental communication and sharing of information), will assist toward disengagement and parallel coparenting, thereby protecting children from the damaging effects of unremitting parental conflict (Birnbaum, Fidler, & Kavassalis, 2008, Chapter 6). These orders should be "multidirectional," with provisions dealing with relations with third parties such as doctors, therapists, and schools (Epstein, 2007)[8]

10.6. Early and Effective Case Management by One Judge

The practice of case management is reflected in the slogan "One judge for one family." This involves having every appearance in a family case before the same judge, and it is distinguished for the common practice where every time a case appears in court prior to trial, it is dealt with by a "duty judge." This traditional model of justice administration may result in a high-conflict case being dealt with by a half-dozen or more judges as it proceeds through various hearings for interim orders, procedural rulings, and judicial conferences, to at least narrow the issues in dispute and move the case toward a trial. There is growing recognition of the value of judicial continuity and active case management in high-conflict family cases, with a focus on attempting to facilitate

---

[8] Interview, August 15, 2010.

a settlement or, if that is not possible, moving the case more quickly to a trial (Altobelli, 2011; Martinson, 2010).

The best resolution for mild and moderate alienation cases is often through judicial exhortation, education, and encouragement of parents toward settlement and adoption of more child-focused parenting by the parents; this will often require undertaking parenting education or counseling. Resolution through judicially encouraged settlement requires early identification of high-conflict cases and judicial case management by a knowledgeable family law judge at the preresolution, resolution, and enforcement stages (Bala, Birnbaum, & Martinson, 2011; Martinson, 2010). More severe alienation cases are also better addressed by having case management by a single judge. Litigating parents need to know from the start that there will be accountability for their behavior and that there will be clear consequences for failing to comply with court orders or for undermining the child's relationship with the other parent; this accountability is greatly facilitated by having judicial case management. In some cases when court-monitored counseling is ordered or recommended, the judge may also need to include a warning that if there is noncompliance, the court may consider specific sanctions or a custody reversal.

At present, in many locales, there is only limited use of case management for family cases. In many jurisdictions case management occurs only if an individual judge is willing to do this, often in effect undertaking extra responsibilities and an increased workload. More extensive use of case management will require some administrative restructuring in family court systems. However, case management not only promotes the interests of children, but it also results in more efficient use of resources in the justice system, with less judicial time spent on high-conflict cases, fewer lengthy trials, and less delay.

As Elizabeth McCarty from the Ontario Children's Lawyer emphasized,

> Delay has a very negative impact on these cases. These cases, more than any others can get out of hand without structure and strict management. To achieve this you need a Judge who knows and understands the details of a case and the personalities involved. Case management for these cases is essential also to ensure a consistency in the message to the parties. Receiving mixed messages from different perspectives can also have an impact on your ability to work with the parties and can cause further delay. Consistency, expediency and structure can be much more difficult to achieve without the benefit of case management.[9]

Establishing family courts with a comprehensive and specialized jurisdiction will facilitate case management by knowledgeable family law judges.

---

[9] Interview, July 14, 2010. Also emphasized in interviews with Justices George Czutrin (April 19, 2010) and June Maresca (April 12, 2010), and Toronto lawyer Philip Epstein, August 15, 2010.

More broadly, the issue of the judicial role in the family litigation process requires more study and discussion. In Australia, there are ongoing reforms that are seeing family judges take a more active role in these cases—"the less adversarial trial process." While research on the effectiveness of these reforms has yet to be completed, there are promising signs that these changes in judicial role and powers may help to bring high-conflict cases to more expeditious and child-focused resolutions.[10]

10.7. Effective Enforcement of All Court Orders

Recognizing that many alienating parents have personality disorders or exhibit characteristics consistent with these disorders, the judiciary must follow through on violations of their orders with appropriate responses to failure to comply (Bala, Hunt, & McCarney, 2010; Epstein, 2007; Kelly, 2010; Martinson, 2010). Ineffective enforcement of court orders only reinforces the alienating parent's narcissism and disregard for authority and rules, characteristics also frequently observed in alienated children. In more severe, intractable cases, there may need to be a change in custody and quite possibly also temporary suspension of, or supervised contact with, the alienating parent.

10.8. Judicial Control After a Trial

In many alienation cases, it will be important for the judge who has heard the evidence and rendered a decision to remain in control of a case (or "seized") after trial in order to review compliance with the court orders, and make adjustments if needed. In some cases the judge may decide to schedule a review date to monitor progress, while in other cases it may be appropriate to leave it to the parties to decide whether to return to court, but make clear that if the matter comes back to court it will be to the same judge. This judge will know the parents and dynamics of the case and, perhaps more importantly, be known by the parents. Knowing that they will return to the judge who made the order should encourage compliance, and if counseling has been directed, it may encourage engagement with the counselor.

10.9. Hearing the Voice of the Child

The stated wishes of children are not determinative of their best interests, and, especially in alienation cases, there are concerns that children may be

---

[10] T. Altobelli, *Less adversarial trial processes: Their role in cases where a child has rejected a parent*, AFCC 47th Annual Conference, Denver, CO, June 2–5, 2010. A similar approach is advocated by Principal Family Court Judge Peter Boshier of New Zealand (Interview, May 24, 2010; Boshier, Taylor, & Seymour, 2011).

manipulated by parents into having inappropriate involvement in decision making. However, children have a "right to be heard," and a right to know that they have been heard. Allowing decision makers to hear from children may improve the quality of decisions and outcomes for children. It should be made clear to children, and their parents, that "children have a voice, but not a choice." If the parents are unable to agree on a plan of care, it is the responsibility of the court to make a final decision about the child based on an assessment of the child's best interests, not the child's wishes.

There are a range of methods that can be used to ensure that the child's views are brought before the court, including custody evaluations by court-appointed mental health professionals, counsel for children, "voice of the child reports," and meetings with a judge. There are advantages and disadvantages to each of these methods, and selecting one will depend on such factors as the age of the child, the stage of the proceedings, and the institutional resources available. It is often appropriate to consult with the children about whether and how they want to be involved in the process. The most thorough approach to determining the child's perspectives and preferences is through a report prepared by a court-appointed mental health professional, who has training in interviewing children and can meet the child on a number of occasions and can put the child's views in context for the court. The practice of judicial interviewing of children is controversial, but there seems to be growing interest in having judges meet with children, in appropriate cases, recognizing that judges are not in a position to make factual determinations or accurately assess a child's true feelings based on such an interview. Judicial interviews with children may occur more frequently in the future, though there is a need for judicial education and planning if such meetings are to become common.

It is also important for judges to ensure that their decisions about children are communicated to them in an appropriate fashion. In high-conflict cases this will often require that the judge ensure that a neutral professional or the judge communicate the decision to the children.

10.10. Further Development of Interventions

Notwithstanding the recent professional and media attention, alienation is not a new phenomenon; professionals, parents, and children have been struggling with these difficult high-conflict cases for decades. There has been a significant increase in research and understanding in the past few years both about the nature of parental rejection cases, and the types of interventions that may be effective and those that may be less effective. Recently, there has been a growing interest in many countries regarding alienation in legal and mental health writings and presentations at professional and academic conferences. However, far too few interventions have been subject to systematic research study. There is a need for further international and interdisciplinary collaborative efforts to develop educational, treatment, prevention, and legal intervention models and strategies, including evaluation components for interventions that are being developed.

10.11. Better and More Focused Access to Services

Resources are limited. A small percent of the divorcing population uses a disproportionate amount of court time and court-connected resources. While some families may benefit from multiple services and professionals, not infrequently too many are involved, sometimes working, albeit unintentionally, at cross-purposes. There is a need to further develop "triaged," as opposed to "tiered," approaches[11] to access to services connected to the family justice process (Bala et al., 2011; Salem, 2009). A triaged approach will facilitate coordination of services for complex and varied high-conflict families, including those experiencing parent–child contact problems, irrespective of sole or primary cause. Services are expensive and not available in many areas. Efforts need to hone the best service for the particular family and to make these readily and equally available to all families in need.

In some jurisdictions, such as Israel, the children's mental health system has residential facilities that can treat children in the most severe alienation cases and in some cases facilitate a gradual transition in custody. In most countries the mental health system needs to be able to better recognize and treat the effects of alienation and, in the most severe cases, be prepared to support a change in custody.

10.12. More and Better Research

Well-designed, methodologically sound research into the efficacy of different legal, educational, and clinical responses to mild, moderate, and severe alienation is needed to know whether these interventions "do no harm," and also to be confident that they have positive effects. Given the complexity of the causes and dynamics of resistance to parent contact, conducting such research poses significant fiscal, practical, and ethical challenges.[12] Family life, and high-conflict families in particular, are complex; the dynamic interplay of many factors

---

[11] A triaged approach involves a screening and identification process that is then linked to a particular intervention, such as education, therapy, mediation, or assessment, while a tiered approach tends to start with the least intrusive intervention, which in the case of failure will then be augmented with another intervention, such as assessment followed by mediation.

[12] See the article by Kelly and Ramsey (2009) and the reply by Austin (2009) both in the *Family Court Review* for an important discussion of these issues with respect to custody evaluations. Much of the same can be said for research applied to the problem of and remedies for alienation.

will impact our understanding of what interventions work and what does not work. Large samples are needed to capture the complexity of these situations, but doing research with large populations is expensive, and it is often not realistic to expect it to occur.

Ethical as well as fiscal realities prohibit certain types of research, especially challenging in these more difficult economic times. Further, we are in a catch-22 to the extent that children and families need to participate in these options for us to study their relative efficacy. Cross-sectional retrospective studies, qualitative research, case analyses, and preexperimental designs are more realistic to expect; these studies can be informative and instructive, especially when similarities are found across these studies. At best, data from these studies need to be treated as preliminary and a basis upon which to develop hypotheses for further research and for work with individual families. The results from any one study, especially a smaller study, need replication before interventions can be widely adopted. Without a large sample, longitudinal designs, and random assignment, we can never be certain that the effects are due to the intervention and not due to other factors.

Longitudinal research with randomized control groups on both clinical and judicial interventions for high conflict and alienation are needed. There is, however, also a pressing reality for practitioners, parents, and children. While longitudinal research is vitally important, legal and mental health professionals cannot wait for science to catch up to their ongoing cases, as recommendations and decisions need to be made before we have the results of better research. Nevertheless, we must be vigilant that such recommendations and decisions made without sound evidence do not create further harm to children and their families.

There is a growing body of evidence that can inform clinical and legal decisions. For example, emerging research suggests that therapy and education, at least the methods and programs currently available, are ineffective for the severe cases of alienation. In addition, there is good research available on the impact of separation, high conflict, and intimate partner violence on children and adolescents and on related matters that can inform responses to alienation cases. Further, even when more and better designed research is available, decisions for any individual child and family cannot be based solely on aggregate data. By using the best available research and our experience as legal and mental health practitioners, a careful investigation and risk–benefit analysis of each case is required.

In conclusion, as we have discussed, a child may resist or reject a parent for many reasons. Parent–child contact problems of any type, be it an affinity, alignment, justified rejection, or alienation, or some combination of these, will range in severity. The reasons for the contact problem and the behavior of each parent and child will inform legal and mental health responses. However, the focus must be on whether or not restoring contact is in the child's best interests, not on the rights of the parents. Irrespective of the type of contact problem, education and clinical intervention are indicated for the less severe cases. In some more severe cases of alienation, the best interests of the child may require very significant legal interventions, including custody reversal. Once a case is before the courts, not intervening and leaving the child alienated and in the care of a disturbed parent—that is, a decision to take no action—is also a decision that needs to be researched and justified.

References

Ackerman, M. (2006). *Clinician's guide to child custody evaluations* (3rd ed.). Hoboken, NJ: John Wiley & Sons, Inc.

Ahrons, C. R., & Tanner, J. L. (2003). Adult children and their fathers: Relationship changes 20 years after parental divorce. *Family Relations, 52,* 340–351.

Ainsworth, M. D. S., Blehar, M., Waters, E., & Wall, S. (1978). *Patterns of attachment: A psychological study of the strange situation.* Hillsdale, NJ: Lawrence Erlbaum.

Altobelli, T. (2011). When a child rejects a parent: Why children resist contact. *Australian Journal of Family Law, 25,* 185–209.

American Psychiatric Association (1994). *Diagnostic and statistical manual of mental health disorders* (4th ed). Washington, DC: American Psychiatric Association.

Andre, K., & Baker, A. J. L. (2009). *I don't want to choose: How middle school kids can avoid choosing one parent over the other.* New York: Kindred Spirits.

Anonymous (February 9, 2010). Coercion adds to trauma. Editorial in *Globe & Mail.* Retrieved October 31, 2010, from http://www.theglobeandmail.com/news/opinions/editorials/coercion-adds-to-trauma/article1460817/

Arredondo, D. E., & Edwards, L. P. (2000). Attachment, bonding and reciprocal connectedness: Limitations of attachment theory in the juvenile and family court. *Journal of the Center for Families, Children and the Courts, 2,* 109–127.

AFCC Task Force on Parenting Coordination (2003). Parenting coordination: Implementation issues. *Family Court Review, 41*(4), 533–564.

Association of Family and Conciliation Courts (2005). *Guidelines for parenting coordination.* Retrieved April 21, 2012 from http://www.afccnet.org/ResourceCentre/PracticeGuidelinesandStandards

Association of Family and Conciliation Courts (2010). *Guidelines for court involved therapy*. Retrieved October 18, 2010 from http://www.afccnet.org/ResourceCenter/PracticeGuidelinesandStandards

Austin, W. G. (2009). Responding to the call for child custody evaluators to justify the reason for their professional existence: Some thoughts on Kelly and Ramsey. *Family Court Review, 47,* 544–551.

Bacon, B. L., & McKenzie, B. (2004). Parent education after separation/divorce. *Family Court Review, 42,* 85–98.

Bagby, R. M., Nicholson, R. A., Buis, T., Radovanovic, H., & Fidler, B. J. (1999). Defensive responding on the MMPI-2 in family custody and access evaluations. *Psychological Assessment, 11,* 24–28.

Bailey, R. (n.d.) *Reunification therapy for complex case scenarios: A solution-focused, case specific response to support and unify families in conflict.* Retrieved on November 3, 2010 from www.transitioningfamilies.com/images/pdf/reunificationwhitepaper-6.pdf

Baker, A. (2005a). Parent alienation strategies: A qualitative study of adults who experienced parental alienation as a child. *American Journal of Forensic Psychology, 23*(4), 41–63.

Baker, A. (2005b). The long-term effects of parental alienation on adult children: A qualitative research study. *American Journal of Family Therapy, 33*(4), 289–302.

Baker, A. (2005c). The cult of parenthood: A qualitative study of parental alienation. *Cultic Studies Review,* 4(1), 1–20.

Baker, A. (2006). Patterns of parental alienation syndrome: A qualitative study of adults who were alienated from a parent as a child. *The American Journal of Family Therapy, 34,* 63–78.

Baker, A. (2007a). *Adult children of parental alienation syndrome: Breaking the ties that bind.* New York: W. W. Norton.

Baker, A. (2007b). Knowledge and attitudes about the parental alienation syndrome: A survey of custody evaluators. *American Journal of Family Therapy, 35*(1), 1–19.

Baker, A. (2010). Adult recall of Parental Alienation in a community sample: Prevalence and associations with psychological maltreatment. *Journal of Divorce & Remarriage, 51*(1), 16–35.

Baker, A., Bernet, W., Elrod, L., Jaffe, P. G., & Johnston, J. R. (2010, June). *Opening session—Parental alienation and the DSM-V* [mp3 file]. Paper presented at the Association of Family and Conciliation Courts (AFCC) 47th Annual Conference, Denver, CO.

Baker, J. L., & Andre, K. (2008). Working with alienated children and their targeted parents: Suggestions for sound practices for mental health professionals. *Annals of Psychotherapy and Integrative Health, 11,* 10–17.

Baker, A., & Fine, P. (2008). *Beyond the highroad: Responding to 17 parental alienation strategies without compromising your morals or harming your child.* Retrieved October 27, 2010 from htpp://www.amyjlbaker.com/index.php

Baker, A., Jaffe, P., Bernet, W., & Johnston, J. (2011). Brief report on parental alienation survey. Retrieved November 4, 2010 from http://www.afccnet.org/members/2011-05-MAY-survey.asp.

Bala N. (2011, July). *Parental alienation & the child's voice in family proceedings.* Presentation at the Nuffield Foundation, London.

Bala, N. (2012, February). *Parental alienation, contact problems and the family justice system.* Presentation at Australian Institute of Family Studies, Melbourne, Australia.

Bala, N., & Bailey, N. (2004). Enforcement of access and alienation of children: Conflict reduction strategies and legal responses. *Canadian Family Law Quarterly, 23,* 1–61.

Bala, N., Birnbaum, R., & Martinson, D. (2011). Differentiated case management for family cases: "One judge for one family." *Canadian Journal of Family Law, 26,* 339–394.

Bala, N., Fidler, B. J., Goldberg, D., & Houston, C. (2007). Alienated children and parental separation: Legal responses in Canada's family courts. *Queen's Law Journal, 3333,* 79–138.

Bala, N., Hunt, S., & McCarney, C. (2010). Parental alienation: Canadian court cases 1989–2008. *Family Court, 48,* 164–179.

Bala, N., Mitnick, M., Trocmé, N., & Houston, C. (2007). Sexual abuse allegations and parental separation: Smokescreen or fire? *Journal of Family Studies, 13,* 26–56.

Bala, N., Talwar V., & Harris, J. (2005). The voice of the children in family law cases. *Canadian Family Law Quarterly, 24,* 221–274.

Barber, B. K. (2002). Reintroducing parental psychological control. In B. K. Barber (Ed.), *Intrusive parenting* (pp. 33–14). Washington, DC: American Psychological Association.

Baris, M. A., Coates, C. A., Duvall, B. B., Garrity, C. B., Johnson, E. T., & LaCrosse, R. R. (2000). *Working with high-conflict families of divorce: A guide for professionals.* Northvale, NJ: Jason Aronson Publishers.

Bathurst, K., Gottfried, A. W., & Gottfried, A. E. (1997). Normative data for the MMPI-2 in child custody litigation. *Psychological Assessment, 9,* 205–211.

Beck, C. J. A., Holtzworth-Munroe, A., D'Onofrio, B. M., Fee, W. C., & Hill, F. G. (2009). Collaboration between judges and social science researchers in family law. *Family Court Review, 47,* 451–467.

Berg, I. (1994). *Family based services: A solution-focused approach.* New York: Norton.

Bernet, W. (Ed.) (2010). *Parental alienation DSM-5, and ICD-11.* Springfield, IL: Charles C Thomas Publisher, Ltd.

Bernet, W., von Boch-Galhau, W., Baker, A. J. L., and Morrison, S. L. (2010). Parental Alienation, DSM-V, and ICD-11. *The American Journal of Family Therapy,* 38(2), 76–187.

Bernstein, A. C. (2007). Re-visioning, restructuring, and reconciliation: Clinical practice with complex post divorce families. *Family Process,* 46(1), 67–78.

Birnbaum, R., & Bala, N. (2010a). Towards a differentiation of high conflict families: An analysis of social science and Canadian case law. *Family Court Review,* 48(3), 403–416.

Birnbaum, R., & Bala, N. (2010b). Judicial interviews with children in custody and access cases: Comparing experiences in Ontario and Ohio. *International Journal of Law, Policy and the Family,* 24(3), 1–38.

Birnbaum, R., & Chipeur, S. (2010). Supervised visitation in custody and access disputes: Finding legal solutions for complex family problems. *Family Law Quarterly,* 29(1), 79–94.

Birnbaum, R., Fidler, B., & Kavassalis, K. (2008). *Child custody assessments—A resource guide for legal and mental health professionals.* Toronto, Canada: Thomson Canada Limited.

Birnbaum, R., & Saini, M. (2007). A pilot study to establish reliability and validity. *OACAS Journal, 51*(2), 23–31.

Bone, M. J. (2003). The parental alienation syndrome: Examining the validity amid controversy. *Family Law Section Commentator, 20*(1), 24–27.

Boshier, P., Taylor, N., & Seymour, F. (2011). Early intervention in New Zealand family court cases. *Family Court Review, 49*(4), 818–830.

Bow, J. N., Gould, J. W., & Flens, J. R. (2006, October). *Examining parental alienation in child custody cases: A survey of mental health and legal professionals* [mp3 file]. Presented at the Association of Family and Conciliation Courts (AFCC) 7th Annual International Symposium on Child Custody Evaluations, Atlanta, GA.

Bow, J. N., Gould, J. W., & Flens J. R. (2009). Examining parental alienation in child custody cases: A survey of mental health and legal professionals. *American Journal of Family Therapy, 37*(2), 127–145.

Boyan, S. M., & Termini, A. (2004). *The psychotherapist as parent coordinator in high conflict divorce: Strategies and techniques.* New York: The Haworth Clinical Practice Press.

Brandon, D. J. (2006). Can four hours make a difference? Evaluation of a parent education program for divorcing parents. *Journal of Divorce & Remarriage, 45*(1/2), 171–185.

Braver, S. L., Coatsworth, D., & Peralta, K. (2006, July). *Alienating behavior within divorced and intact families: Matched parents' and now-young adult children's reports.* Paper presented at the International Conference on Children and Divorce, University of East Anglia, Norwich, UK.

Braver, S. L., Griffin, W. A., & Cookston, J. T. (2005). Prevention programs for divorced nonresident fathers. *Family Court Review, 43*(1), 81–96.

Bricklin, B., & Elliot, G. (2006). Psychological test-assisted detection of parental alienation syndrome. In R. A. Gardner, S. R. Sauber, & D. Lorandos (Eds.), *The international handbook of parental alienation syndrome: Conceptual, clinical and legal considerations* (pp. 264–275). Springfield, IL: Charles C Thomas.

Brody, B. (2006). The misdiagnosis of PAS. In R. A. Gardner, S. R. Sauber, & D. Lorandos (Eds.), *The international handbook of parental alienation syndrome: Conceptual, clinical and legal considerations* (pp. 209–227). Springfield, IL: Charles C Thomas.

Brown, C. (1995, November). *Involving children in decision making without making them the decision makers.* Paper presented at the Association of Family and Conciliation Courts Northwest Regional Conference, Skamania Lodge, WA. Available online at http://familylawcourts.gov.au/wps/wcm/resources/file/eb9da00247423b4/Involving_children_in_decisions.pdf (last accessed Sept. 3, 2011)

Brownstone, H. (2008). *Tug of war.* Toronto, Canada: ECW Press.

Bruch, C. (2001). Parental alienation syndrome and parental alienation: Getting it wrong in child custody cases. *Family Law Quarterly, 35*, 527–552.

Burrill, J. (2006a). Descriptive statistics of the mild, moderate, and severe characteristics of parental alienation. In R. A. Gardner, S. R. Sauber, & D. Lorandos (Eds.), *The international handbook of parental alienation syndrome:*

Conceptual, clinical and legal considerations (pp. 49–55). Springfield, IL: Charles C Thomas.

Burrill, J. (2006b). *Reluctance to verify PAS as a legitimate syndrome.* In R. A. Gardner, S. R. Sauber, & D. Lorandos (Eds.), *The international handbook of parental alienation syndrome: Conceptual, clinical and legal considerations* (pp. 323–330). Springfield, IL: Charles C Thomas.

Butcher, J. N., Dahlstrom, W. G., Graham, J. R., Tellegen, A., & Kaemmer, B. (1989). *The Minnesota Multiphasic Personality Inventory-2 (MMPI-2): Manual for administration and scoring.* Minneapolis, MN: University of Minnesota Press.

Butler, A. C., Chapman J. E., Forman E. M., & Beck A. T. (2006). The empirical status of cognitive-behavioral therapy: A review of meta-analyses. *Clinical Psychology Review, 26*(1), 17–31.

Byrne, J. G, O'Connor, T. G, Marvin, R. S., & Whelan, W. F. (2005). Practitioner review: The contribution of attachment theory to child custody assessments. *Journal of Child Psychology and Psychiatry, 46,* 115–127.

Caldwell, J. (2011). Common law judges and judicial interviewing. *Child and Family Law Quarterly, 23,* 41–62.

Campbell, T. (2005). Why doesn't parental alienation occur more frequently? The significance of role discrimination. *American Journal of Family Therapy, 33*(5), 365–377.

Carl, E., & Karl, M. (2011, June). *Interviewing children: Challenging for the judge, but is it a burden or relieve for the child?* Workshop presented at the 48th Annual Conference, AFCC, Orlando, FL.

Carter, S. (2011). *Family restructuring therapy: Interventions with high conflict separations and divorces.* Arizona: HCI Press.

Carter, S., Haave, B., & Vandersteen, S. (2006a). *Family restructuring therapy.* Unpublished manuscript.

Carter, S., Haave, B., & Vandersteen, S. (2006b, June). *Workshop 53: Family restructuring therapy for high conflict families and estranged children* [mp3 file]. Workshop presented at the Association of Family and Conciliation Courts (AFCC) 43rd Annual Conference, Tampa Bay, FL.

Carter, S., Haave, B., & Vandersteen, S. (2009a, May). *Family restructuring therapy for high conflict families* [mp3 file]. Workshop presented at the Association of Family and Conciliation Courts (AFCC) 46th Annual Conference, New Orleans, LA. Available from http://www.afccnet.org/conferences/afcc_conference_history.asp

Carter, S., Haave, B., & Vandersteen, S. (2009b, May). *Institute 3: Family restructuring therapy for high conflict families* [mp3 file]. Pre-conference Institute presented at the Association of Family and Conciliation Courts (AFCC) 46th Annual Conference, New Orleans, LA. Available from http://www.afccnet.org/conferences/afcc_conference_history.asp

Carter, S., Vandersteen, S., Haave, B., Trussler, M., & Bateman, J. (2008, May). *Workshop 52: Family restructuring therapy: Working with high conflict parents and angry children* [mp3 file]. Workshop presented at the Association of Family and Conciliation Courts (AFCC) 45th Annual Conference, Vancouver, Canada. Available from http://www.afccnet.org/conferences/afcc_conference_history.asp

Cartwright, G. F. (1993). Expanding the parameters of parental alienation syndrome. *American Journal of Family Therapy, 21*(3), 205–215.

Cartwright, G. F. (2006). Beyond the parental alienation syndrome: Reconciling the alienated child and the lost parent. In R. A. Gardner, D. Lorandos, & S. R. Sauber (Eds.), *The international handbook of parental alienation syndrome: Conceptual, clinical, and legal considerations* (pp. 286–291). Springfield, IL: Charles C Thomas.

Cashmore, J. (2003). Children's participation in family law matters. In C. Hallett & A. Prout (Eds.), *Hearing the voices of children: Social policy for a new century.* New York: Routeledge Falmer.

Cashmore, J., & Parkinson, P. (2009). Children's participation in family law disputes: The views of children, parents, lawyers, and counsellors. *Family Matters, 82*, 15–21.

Clawar, S. S., & Rivlin, B. V. (1991). *Children held hostage: Dealing with programmed and brainwashed children.* Chicago: American Bar Association Press.

Coates, C. (2003). Parenting coordination: Implementation issues. *Family Court Review, 41*(4), 533–564.

Coates, C., Deutsch, R., Starnes, H., Sullivan, M. J., & Sydlik, B. (2004). Parenting coordination for high conflict families. *Family Court Review, 42*(2), 246–262.

Conger, K. J., Stocker, C., & McGuire, S. (2009). Sibling socialization: The effects of stressful life events and experiences. In L. Kramer & K. J. Conger (Eds.), *Siblings as agents of socialization. New directions for child and adolescent development*, Vol. 126 (pp. 45–60). San Francisco: Jossey-Bass.

Cookston, J. T., & Fung, W. W. (2011). The kids' turn program evaluation: Probing change within a community-based intervention for separating families. *Family Court Review, 49*(2), 348–363.

Crary, D. (2010, October 1). Is Parental Alienation a mental disorder? *The Washington Times.* Retrieved November 1, 2010 from http://www.washingtontimes.com/news/2010/Oct1/psychiatric-experts-assess-parental-alienation.

Criddle, Jr., M. N., Allgood, S. M., & Piercy, K. W. (2003). The relationship between mandatory divorce education and level of post-divorce parental conflict. *Journal of Divorce & Remarriage, 39*(3/4), 99–113.

Darnall, D. (1997). *New Definition of Parental Alienation – What is the difference between Parental Alienation (PA) and Parental Alienation Syndrome (PAS)?* Retrieved October 22, 2010 from http://www.parentalalienation.com/articles/parental-alienation-defined.html

Darnall, D. (1998). *Divorce casualties: Protecting your children from parental alienation.* Lanham, MD: Taylor Publishing Co.

Darnall, D. (2010). *Beyond divorce casualties—Reunifying the alienated family.* New York: Taylor Trade Publishing.

Darnall, D., & Steinberg, B. F. (2008a). Motivational models for spontaneous reunification with the alienated. *The American Journal of Family Therapy, 36*, 107–115.

Darnall, D., & Steinberg, B. F. (2008b). Motivational models for spontaneous reunification with the alienated Part II. *The American Journal of Family Therapy, 36*(3), 253–261.

De Shazer, S. (1988). *Clues: Investigating solutions in brief therapy.* New York: W.W. Norton & Co.

Dimeff, L. A., & Koerner, K. (2007). *Dialectical behavior therapy in clinical practice: Applications across disorders and settings.* New York: Guilford Publications, Inc.

Dobson, K. S., & Dozois, D. J. A. (2001). Historical and philosophical bases of the cognitive-behavioral therapies. In K. Dobson (Ed.), *Handbook of cognitive-behavioral therapies* (2nd ed.) (pp. 3–39). New York: Guilford Press.

Drozd, L. M., Kuehnle, K., & Olesen, N. W. (2011, June). *Rethinking the evaluation of abuse and alienation with gatekeeping in mind* [mp3 file]. Workshop presented at the Association of Family and Conciliation Courts (AFCC) 48th Annual Conference, Orlando, FL. Available from http://www.afccnet.org/ConferencesTraining/AFCCConferences

Drozd, L. M., & Olesen, N. W. (2004). Is it abuse, alienation, and/or estrangement? A decision tree. *Journal of Child Custody, 1*(3), 65–106.

Drozd, L. M., & Olesen, N. W. (2009, May). *When a child rejects a parent* [mp3 file]. Workshop presented at the Association of Family and Conciliation Courts (AFCC) 46th Annual Conference, New Orleans, LA. Available from http://www.afccnet.org/ConferencesTraining/AFCCConferences

Drozd, L. M., & Olesen, N. W. (2010). Abuse and alienation are each real: A response to a critique by Joan Meier. *Journal of Child Custody, 7*(4), 253–265.

Dunne, J., & Hedrick, M. (1994). The parental alienation syndrome: An analysis of sixteen selected cases. *Journal of Divorce & Remarriage, 21*(3/4), 21–38.

Eddy, B. (2009). *New ways for families in separation and divorce: Professional guidebook for judicial officers, lawyers and therapists.* Scottsdale, AZ: High Conflict Institute, LLC.

Eddy, B. (2010). *Don't alienate the kids! Raising resilient children while avoiding high conflict divorce.* Scottsdale, AZ: High Conflict Institute, LLC.

Eekelaar, J. (1992). The importance of thinking that children have rights. In P. Alston, S. Parker, & J. Seymour (Eds.), *Children, rights and the law* (pp. 221–235). New York: Oxford University Press.

Ellis, E. (2007). A stepwise approach to evaluating children for parental alienation syndrome. *Journal of Child Custody, 4*(1/2), 55–78, Taylor & Francis, Ltd.

Emery, R. E. (2003). Children's voices: Listening—And deciding—Is an adult responsibility. *Arizona Law Review, 45*, 621–627.

Emery, R. E. (2005). Parental alienation syndrome: Proponents bear the burden of proof. *Family Court Review, 43*, 8–13.

Epstein, P. (2002, December). *Enforcement of access: Judicial management of interference with access.* Paper presented to the Law Society of Upper Canada 6-Minute Lawyer Lecture Series, Toronto, Canada.

Epstein, P. (2007, November). *Judicial management of interference with access.* Paper presented at the Trials Lawyers Association Fall Conference: Gaining an Edge. Regina, Canada.

Everett, C. A. (2006). Family therapy for parental alienation syndrome: Understanding the interlocking pathologies. In R. A. Gardner, S. R. Sauber, & D. Lorandos (Eds.), *The international handbook of parental alienation syndrome: Conceptual, clinical and legal considerations* (pp. 228–241). Springfield, IL: Charles C Thomas.

Fabricius, W. V. (2003). Listening to children of divorce: New findings that diverge from Wallerstein, Lewis & Blakeslee. *Family Relations, 52*, 385–396.

Fabricius, W. V., & Hall, J. A. (2000). Young adults' perspectives on divorce: Living arrangements. *Family & Conciliation Courts Review, 38*, 446–461.

Fackrell, T. A., Hawkins, A. J., & Kay, N. M. (2011). How effective are court-affiliated divorcing parents education programs? A meta-analytic study. *Family Court Review, 49*(1), 107–119.

Faircloth, W., & Cummings, E. (2008). Evaluating a parent education program for preventing the negative effects of marital conflict. *Journal of Applied Developmental Psychology, 29*, 114–156.

Faller, K. C. (1997). The parental alienation syndrome: What is it and what data support it? *Child Maltreatment, 3*(2), 100–115.

Fasser, R. L., & Duchen, R. (2010, June). *Descriptions of rigid family patterns: A challenge to the alienation label* [mp3 file]. Workshop presented at the Association of Family and Conciliation Courts (AFCC) 47th Annual Conference, Denver, CO. Available from http://www.afccnet.org/ConferencesTraining/AFCCConferences

Feinberg, R., & Greene, J. T. (1997). The intractable client: Guidelines for working with personality disorders in family law. *Family and Conciliation Court Review, 35*, 351–365.

Fernando, M. (2009). Conversations between judges and children: An argument in favour of judicial conferences in contested children's matters. *Australian Journal of Family Law, 23*, 48–70.

Fidler, B. J. (2007). Developing parenting time schedules: Conundrums and considerations. In Martha Shaffer (Ed.), *Contemporary issues in family law: Engaging with the legacy of James G. McLeod* (pp. 351–392). Toronto, Canada: Thomson Carswell.

Fidler, B. J. (2011). *Children and divorce: The voice of the child and interventions when children resist parental contact.* Chicago: Loyola University Chicago School of Law's Civitas ChildLaw Center and Association of Family and Concilation Courts (AFCC).

Fidler, B. J., & Bala, N. (2010). Children resisting post separation contact with a parent: Concepts, controversies, and conundrums. *Family Court Review, 48*(1), 10–47.

Fidler, B. J., and Bala, N. (Eds.) (2010). Special Issue: Alienated children in divorce and separation: Emergency approaches for families and courts. *Family Court Review, 48*(1), 1–245.

Fidler, B. J, Bala, N., Birnbaum, R., & Kavassalis, K. (2008). *Challenging issues in child custody disputes.* Toronto, Canada: Carswell Thomson.

Fidler, B. J., Chodos, L., Nelson, C. S., & Vanbetlehem, J. (2009, May). *Alienation: Clinical and legal interventions* [mp3 file]. Workshop presented at the Association of Family and Conciliation Courts (AFCC) 46th Annual Conference, New Orleans, LA. Available from http://www.afccnet.org/ConferencesTraining/AFCCConferences

Fidler, B. J., & Epstein, P. (2008). Parenting coordination in Canada: An overview of legal and practice issues. *Journal of Child Custody, 5*, 53–87.

Fidler, B. J., & Vanbetlehem, J. (June, 2011). *Family interventions when children resist post-separation contact* [mp3 file]. Workshop presented at the Association of Family and Conciliation Courts (AFCC) 48th Annual Conference, Orlando, FL. Available from http://www.afccnet.org/ConferencesTraining/AFCCConferences

Fidnick, L. S., Koch, K. A., Greenberg, L. R., Sullivan, M. (2011) Association of Family and Conciliation Courts, white paper guidelines for court-involved therapy: A best practice approach for mental health professionals. *Family Court Review, 49*(3), 557–563.

Forgatch, M. S., & DeGarmo, D. (1999). Parenting through change: An effective prevention program for single mothers. *Journal of Consulting & Clinical Psychology, 67*, 711–724.

Freeman, R. (2008). Children and absent parents: A model for reconnection. In L. B. Fieldstone & C. A. Coates (Eds.), *Innovations in interventions with high conflict families* (pp. 41–81). Madison, WI: Association of Family and Conciliation Courts.

Freeman, R., Abel, D., Cowper-Smith, M., & Stein, L. (2004). Reconnecting children with absent parents: A model for intervention. *Family Court Review, 42*, 439–459.

Friedlander, S., & Walters, M. G. (2010). When a child rejects a parent: Tailoring the intervention to fit the problem. *Family Court Review, 48*, 97–110.

Garber, B. (2004a). Parental Alienation in light of attachment theory: Considerations of the broader implications for child development, clinical practice, and forensic process. *Journal of Child Custody, 1*(4), 49–76.

Garber, B. (2004b). Directed co-parenting intervention: Conducting child centered interventions in parallel with highly conflicted co-parents. *Professional Psychology: Research and Practice, 35*(1), 55–64.

Garber, B. (2007). Conceptualizing visitation resistance and refusal in the context of parental conflict, separation, divorce. *Family Court Review, 45*(4), 588–599.

Garber, B. D. (2011). Parental alienation and the dynamics of the enmeshed dyad: Adultification, parentification and infantilization. *Family Court Review, 49*(2), 322–335.

Gardner, R. A. (1985). Recent trends in divorce and custody litigation. *Academy Forum, 29*(2), 3–7.

Gardner, R. A. (1992a). *The parental alienation syndrome: A guide for mental health and legal professionals.* Cresskill, NJ: Creative Therapeutics, Inc. (with updated addenda in 1994 and 1996).

Gardner, R. A. (1992b). *True and false allegations of child sex abuse.* Cresskill, NJ: Creative Therapeutics, Inc.

Gardner, R. A. (1998a). Recommendations for dealing with parents who induce a parental alienation syndrome in their children. *Journal of Divorce and Remarriage, 28*, 1–21.

Gardner, R. A. (1998b). *The parental alienation syndrome* (2nd ed.). Cresskill, NJ: Creative Therapeutics Inc.

Gardner, R. A. (1999). Family therapy of the moderate type of Parental Alienation Syndrome. *The American Journal of Family Therapy, 27*, 195–212.

Gardner, R. A. (2001a). Should courts order PAS children to visit/reside with the alienated parent? A follow-up study. *American Journal of Forensic Psychology, 19*(3), 61–106.

Gardner, R. A. (2001b). *Therapeutic interventions for children and parental alienation syndrome.* Cresskill, NJ: Creative Therapeutic, Inc.

Gardner, R. A. (2002a). The empowerment of children in the development of parental alienation syndrome. *The American Journal of Forensic Psychology, 20*(2), 5–29.

Gardner, R. A. (2002b). Denial of the parental alienation syndrome also harms women. *The American Journal of Family Therapy, 30*, 191–202.

Gardner, R. A. (2004). Commentary on Kelly and Johnston's "The Alienated Child": A reformulation of parental alienation syndrome. *Family Court Review, 42*(4), 611–621.

Garrity, C., & Baris, M. (1994). *Caught in the middle: Protecting the children of high-conflict divorce.* Toronto, Canada: Maxwell Macmillan Canada, Inc.

Garvin, V., Leber, D., & Kalter, N. (1991). Children of divorce: Predictors of change following preventive intervention. *American Journal of Orthopsychiatry, 61*, 438–447.

George, C., Kaplan, N., & Main, M. (1985). *Adult attachment interview* (3rd ed.). Berkeley, CA: University of California at Berkeley, Department of Psychology.

Goodman, M., Bonds, D., Sandler, I., & Braver, S. (2004). Parent psycho educational programs and reducing the negative effects of interparental conflict following divorce. *Family Court Review, 42*(2), 263–279.

Gordon, R. M., Stoffey, R., & Bottinelli, J. (2008). MMPI-2 findings of primitive defenses in alienating parents. *American Journal of Family Therapy, 36*(3), 211–228.

Gottlieb, D. S. (2006). Parental alienation syndrome—An Israeli perspective: Reflections and recommendations. In R. A. Gardner, S. R. Sauber, & D. Lorandos (Eds.), *The international handbook of parental alienation syndrome: Conceptual, clinical and legal considerations* (pp. 9090–9107). Springfield, IL: Charles C Thomas.

Gould, J. (2006). *Conducting scientifically crafted child custody evaluations* (2nd ed.). Sarasota, FL: Professional Resource Press.

Gould, J., & Martindale, D. (2007). *The art and science of child custody evaluations.* New York: The Guilford Press.

Greenberg, L., Fick, L. D., Perlman, G., & Barrows, C. (2010, June). *Keeping the developmental frame: Child-centered conjoint therapy in high conflict cases* [mp3 file]. Paper presented at the Association of Family and Conciliation Courts (AFCC) 47th Annual Conference, Denver, CO. Available from http://www.afccnet.org/ConferencesTraining/AFCCConferences

Greenberg, L. R., Gould, J. W., Schnider, R. A., Gould-Saltman, D. J., & Martindale, D. A. (2003). Effective intervention with high-conflict families: How judges can promote and recognize competent treatment in family court. *Journal of the Centre for Families, Children and the Courts, 4*, 49–65.

Grych, J. H. (2005). Interparental conflict as a risk factor for child maladjustment: Implications for the development of prevention programs. *Family Court Review, 43*, 97–108.

Grych, J., & Fincham, F. (1999). Marital conflict and children's adjustment: A cognitive contextual framework. *Psychological Bulletin, 108*, 267–290.

Haley, J., & Hoffman, L. (1994). *Techniques of family therapy.* Northvale, NJ: Aronson.

Herschell, A. D., & McNeil, C. B. (2005). Theoretical and empirical underpinnings of parent-child interaction therapy with child physical abuse populations. *Education and Treatment of Children, 28*(2), 142–162.

Hesse, E. (1999). The adult attachment interview: Historical and current perspectives. In J. Cassidy & P. R. Save (Eds.), *Handbook of attachment: Theory, research and clinical applications* (pp. 395–433). New York: Guildford Press.

Hetherington, E. M., & Kelly, J. B. (2002). *For better or for worse: Divorce reconsidered.* New York: W. W. Norton & Company, Inc.

Hetherington, E. M., Stanley-Hagan, M., & Anderson, E. R. (1989). Marital transitions: A child's perspective. *American Psychologist, 44,* 303–312.

Hoppe, C., & Kenney, L. (1994, August). *A Rorschach study of the psychological characteristics of parents engaged in child custody/visitation disputes.* Paper presented at the 102nd Annual Convention of the American Psychological Association, Los Angeles.

Jaffe, P., Ashbourne, D., & Mamo, A. (2010). Early identification and prevention of parent-child alienation: A framework for balancing risks and benefits of intervention. *Family Court Review, 48,* 136–152.

Jaffe, P., Ashbourne, D., Mamo, A., & Martinson, D. (2010, June). *Assessment and differential interventions for alienating allegations: Punishing parents or helping children* [mp3 file]? Paper presented at the Association of Family and Conciliation Courts (AFCC) 47th Annual Conference, Denver, CO. Available from http://www.afccnet.org/ConferencesTraining/ AFCCConferences

Jaffe, P. G., Johnston, J. R., Crooks, C. V., & Bala, N. (2008). Custody dispute involving allegations of domestic violence: Toward a differentiated approach to parenting plans. *Family Court Review, 46*(3), 500–522.

Jenuwine, M. J., & Cohler, B. J. (1999). Major parental psychopathology and child custody. In R. Galatzer-Lary & L. Kraus (Eds.), *The scientific basis of child custody decisions* (pp. 285–318). New York: Wiley.

Johnston, J. R. (1993). Children of divorce who refuse visitation. In C. Depner & J. Bray (Eds.), *Non-residential parenting: New vistas in family living* (pp. 109–135). Newbury Park, CA: Sage Publications.

Johnston, J. R. (2001, July). *Rethinking parental alienation and redesigning parent-child access services for children who resist or refuse visitation.* Paper presented at the International Conference on Supervised Visitation, Munich, Germany.

Johnston, J. R. (2003). Parental alignments and rejection: An empirical study of alienation in children of divorce. *Journal of the American Academy of Psychiatry and Law, 31,* 158–170.

Johnston, J. R. (2004). *Coding manual. Child alienation project: Guidelines for clinical coding and psychometric properties of scales.* Unpublished manuscript.

Johnston, J. R. (2004). Alienating Parenting and Supportive (Co) Parenting Scale. Unpublished manuscript.

Johnston, J. R. (2011). *Alienating Parenting and Supportive (Co) Parenting Scale.* Unpublished manuscript.

Johnston, J. R. (2005a). Children of divorce who reject a parent and refuse visitation: Recent research and social policy implications for the alienated child. *Family Law Quarterly, 38,* 757–775.

Johnston, J. R. (2005b). Clinical work with parents in entrenched custody disputes. In L. Gunsberg & P. Hymowitz (Eds.), *A handbook of divorce and custody: Forensic, developmental, and clinical perspectives* (pp. 343–364). Hillsdale, NJ: The Analytic Press.

Johnston, J. R. (2010) *Revised coding manual. Child alienation project: Guidelines for clinical coding and psychometric properties of scales.* Unpublished manuscript.

Johnston, J. R., & Campbell, L. E. (1988). *Impasses of divorce: The dynamics and resolution of family conflict.* New York: The Free Press.

Johnston, J. R., & Campbell, L. E. (1993). Parent-child relationships in domestic violence families disputing custody. *Family and Conciliation Courts Review, 31*(3), 252–298.

Johnston, J. R., & Goldman, J. R. (2010). Outcomes of family counseling interventions with children who resist visitation: An addendum to Friedlander and Walters. *Family Court Review, 48,* 112–115.

Johnston, J. R., & Kelly, J. B. (2004). Rejoinder to Gardner's "Commentary on Kelly and Johnston's 'The alienated child': A reformulation of parental alienation syndrome." *Family Court Review, 42*(4), 622–628.

Johnston, J. R., Lee, S., Oleson, N. W., & Walters, M. G. (2005). Allegations and substantiations of abuse in custody-disputing families. *Family Court Review, 43*(2), 283–294.

Johnston, J. R., & Roseby, V. (1997). *In the name of the child: A developmental approach to understanding and helping children of conflicted and violence divorce.* New York: The Free Press.

Johnston, J. R., Roseby, V., & Kuehnle, K. (2009). Parental alignments and alienation: Differential assessment and therapeutic interventions. In *In the name of the child: A developmental approach to understanding and helping children of conflicted and violent divorce* (2nd ed.) (pp. 361–389). New York: Springer Publishing Company.

Johnston, J. R, Walters, M. G., & Friedlander, S. (2001). Therapeutic work with alienated children and their families. *Family Court Review. Special issue: Alienated children of divorce, 39,* 316–333.

Johnston, J. R, Walters, M. G., & Olesen, N. W. (2005a). Clinical ratings of parenting capacity and Rorschach protocols of custody-disputing parents: An exploratory study. *Journal of Child Custody, 2,* 159–178.

Johnston, J. R, Walters, M. G., & Olesen, N. W. (2005b). Is it alienating parenting, role reversal or child abuse? A study of children's rejection of a parent in child custody disputes. *Journal of Emotional Abuse, 5*(4), 191–218.

Johnston, J. R, Walters, M. G., & Olesen, N. W. (2005c). The psychological functioning of alienated children in custody disputing families: An exploratory study. *American Journal of Forensic Psychology, 23*(3), 39–64.

Kelly, J. B. (2002). Psychological and legal interventions for parents and children in custody and access disputes: Current research and practice. *Virginia Journal of Social Policy & The Law, 10*(1), 129–163.

Kelly, J. B. (2010). Commentary on Family Bridges: Using insights from social science to reconnect parents and alienated children (Warshak, 2010). *Family Court Review, 48,* 81–90.

Kelly, J. B., & Johnson, M. P. (2008). Differentiation among types of intimate partner violence: Research update and implications for interventions. *Family Court Review, 46*(3), 476–499.

Kelly, J. R., & Johnston, J. R. (2001). The alienated child: A reformulation of parental alienation syndrome. *Family Court Review. Special issue: Alienated children in divorce, 39*(3), 249–266.

Kelly, J. R., & Johnston, J. R. (2004). Rejoinder to Gardner's "Commentary on Kelly and Johnston's 'The alienated child': A reformulation of parental alienation syndrome." *Family Court Review, 42*(4), 622–628.

Kelly, R. F., & Ramsey, S. H. (2009). Child custody evaluations: The need for systems-level outcome assessment. *Family Court Review, 47,* 286–303.

Kendall, P. C., Ed. (2005). *Child and adolescent therapy: Cognitive-behavioral procedures* (3rd ed.). New York: Guilford Press.

Kendler, K. S., Kupfer, D., Narrow, W., Phillips, K., & Fawcett, J. (2009). *Guidelines for making changes to DSM-V.* Retrieved November 5, 2010 from www.dsm5.org

Kierstead, S. (2011). Parent education programs in family courts: Balancing autonomy and state intervention. *Family Court Review, 49*(1), 140–154.

Kirkland, K. (2008). Parenting Coordination (PC) laws, rules, and regulations: A jurisdictional comparison. *Journal of Child Custody, 5*(1/2), 25–52.

Kirkland, K., & Kirkland K. E. (2006). Risk Management and aspirational ethics for Parenting Coordinators. *Journal of Child Custody, 3*(2), 23–43.

Klass, J. L., & Klass, J. V. (2005). Threatened Mother Syndrome (TMS): A diverging concept of Parental Alienation Syndrome (PAS). *American Journal of Family Law, 18*(4), 189–191.

Kopetski, L. (1998a). Identifying cases of parent alienation syndrome: Part I. *The Colorado Lawyer, 29*(2), 65–68.

Kopetski, L. (1998b). Identifying cases of parent alienation syndrome: Part II. *The Colorado Lawyer, 29*(3), 63–66.

Kopetski, L. (2006). Commentary: Parental alienation syndrome. In R. A. Gardner, S. R. Sauber, & D. Lorandos (Eds.), *The international handbook of parental alienation syndrome: Conceptual, clinical and legal considerations* (pp. 378–390). Springfield, IL: Charles C Thomas.

Kopetski, L. M., Rand, D. C., & Rand, R. (2006). Incidence, gender, and false allegations of child abuse: Data on 84 parental alienation syndrome cases. In R. A. Gardner, R. S. Sauber, & D. Lorandos (Eds.), *The international handbook of parental alienation syndrome: Conceptual, clinical and legal considerations* (pp. 65–70). Springfield, IL: Charles C Thomas.

Lamb, M. (2012). Critical analysis of research on parenting plans and children's well-being. In K. Kuehnle & L. Drods (Eds), *Parenting plan evaluations: Applied research for the family court* (pp. 214–246). New York: Oxford University Press.

Lampel, A. K. (1996). Children's alignment with parents in highly conflicted custody cases. *Family & Conciliation Courts Review, 34*(2), 229–239.

Laumann-Billings, L., & Emery, R. E. (2000). Distress among young adults in divorced families. *Journal of Family Psychology, 14,* 671–687.

Lebow, J., & Rekart, K. N. (2007). Integrative family therapy for high-conflict divorce with disputes over child custody and visitation. [Case Reports]. *Family Process, 46*(1), 79–91.

Lee, M., Calloway, G., Nachlis, L., & Marvin, R. (2010, June). *Attachment relationships in the courtroom* [mp3 file]. Paper presented at the Association of Family and Conciliation Courts (AFCC) 47th Annual Conference, Denver, CO. Available from http://www.afccnet.org/ConferencesTraining/AFCCConferences

Lee, S. M., & Olesen, N. W. (2001). Assessing for alienation in child custody and access evaluations. *Family Court Review, 39*(3), 282–298.

Leonoff, A., & Montague, R. (1996). *Guide to child custody assessments.* Scarborough, Canada: Carswell Publishing.

Leving, J. M. (2006). The parental alienation syndrome and gender bias in the courts. In R. A. Gardner, S. R. Sauber, & D. Lorandos (Eds.), *The international handbook of parental alienation syndrome: Conceptual, clinical and legal considerations* (pp. 391–396). Springfield, IL: Charles C Thomas.

Linehan, M. (1993). *Cognitive-behavioral treatment of Borderline Personality Disorder.* New York: Guilford Press.

Lorandos, D. (2006a). Parental alienation syndrome: Detractors and the junk science vacuum. In R. A. Gardner, S. R. Sauber, & D. Lorandos (Eds.), *The international handbook of parental alienation syndrome: Conceptual, clinical and legal considerations* (pp. 397–418). Springfield, IL: Charles C Thomas.

Lowenstein, L. F. (1998). Parent alienation syndrome: A two step approach toward a solution. *Contemporary Family Therapy, 20,* 505–520.

Lowenstein, L. F. (2005). *Attempting to solve child contact disputes (Recent Research).* Retrieved November 17, 2010 from http://www.parental-alienation. info/publications/36-atttosolchicondisrecres.htm

Lowenstein, L. F. (2006). The psychological effects and treatment of the parental alienation syndrome worldwide. In R. A. Gardner, S. R. Sauber, & D. Lorandos (Eds.), *The international handbook of parental alienation syndrome: Conceptual, clinical and legal considerations* (pp. 292–301). Springfield, IL: Charles C Thomas.

Ludolph, P. S., & Bow, J. N. (2010, June). *Buffeted in the eye of the storm: Helping young children in families with alienation dynamics* [mp3 file]. Paper presented at the Association of Family and Conciliation Courts (AFCC) 47th Annual Conference, Denver, CO. Available from http://www.afccnet.org/ ConferencesTraining/AFCCConferences

Lund, M. A. (1995). A therapist's view of parental alienation syndrome. *Family & Conciliation Courts Review, 33*(3), 308–316.

Maccoby, E. E., & Mnookin, R. H. (1992). *Dividing the child: Social and legal dilemmas of Custody.* Cambridge, MA: Harvard University Press.

Main, M., & Goldwyn, R. (1998). *Adult attachment scoring and classification system.* Unpublished manuscript, Department of Psychology, University of California at Berkeley.

Marcus, P., & Lehmann, S. (2010, June). *High conflict families and alienation: Judicial and therapeutic intervention in Israel Family Court* [m3p file]. Paper presented at the Association of Family and Conciliation Courts (AFCC) 47th Annual Conference, Denver, CO. Available from http://www.afccnet.org/ ConferencesTraining/AFCCConferences

Martinson, D. J. (2010). One case - one specialized judge: Why courts have a duty to manage alienation and other high-conflict cases. *Family Court Review, 48,* 178–187.

Marvin, R., Cooper, G., Hoffman, K., & Powell, B. (2000). The circle of security project: Attachment-based intervention with caregiver-preschool dyads. *Attachment & Human Development, 4*(1), 107–124.

McIntosh, J. E., & Long, C. M. (2006). Children beyond dispute: A prospective study of outcomes from child focused and child inclusive post-secondary family dispute resolution, Final Report. *Family Relationships Quarterly,*

3. Retrieved November 22, 2011 from http://www.aifs.gov.au/afrc/pubs/
newsletter/n3pdf/n3.pdf

McIntosh, J. E., Wells, Y. D., Smyth, B. M., & Long C. M. (2008). Child-focused
and child-inclusive divorce mediation: Comparative outcomes from a
prospective study of post separation adjustment. *Family Court Review, 46*(1),
105–124.

McSweeney, L., & Leach, C. (2011, May). Children's *participation in family law
decision-making: Considerations for striking the balance.* Presented to the
Ontario Association of Family Mediators, Toronto.

Meier, J. S. (2009). A historical perspective on parental alienation syndrome and
parental alienation. *Journal of Child Custody, 6*, 232–257.

Meier, J. S. (2010). Getting real about abuse and alienation: A critique of Drozd and
Olesen's decision tree. *Journal of Child Custody, 7*(4), 219–252.

Minuchin, S. (1974). *Families and family therapy.* Cambridge, MA: Harvard
University Press.

Minuchin, S., Rosman, B. L., & Baker, L. (1978). Psychosomatic familes: Anorexia
nervosa in context. Cambridge, MA: Harvard University Press.

Mnookin, R. H., & Kornhauser, L. (1979). Bargaining in the shadow of the law. *Yale
Law Journal, 88*, 950–997.

Moné, J. (2010, June). *Narratives on divorce and interparental conflict: Study
findings and ethical considerations for research* [mp3 file]. Paper presented
at the Association of Family and Conciliation Courts (AFCC) 47th
Annual Conference, Denver, CO. Available from http://www.afccnet.org/
ConferencesTraining/AFCCConferences

Moné, J. G., & Biringen, Z. (2006). Perceived parent-child alienation: Empirical
assessment of parent-child relationships within divorced and intact families.
Journal of Divorce and Remarriage, 45(3/4), 131–156.

Neale, B. (2002). Dialogues with children: Children, divorce and citizenship,
Childhood, 9(4), 455–475.

Neff, R., & Cooper, K. (2004). Parental conflict resolution. *Family Court Review, 42*,
99–114.

Otis, M. R., & Warshak, R. A. (2009, May). *Family Bridges: Principles, procedures
and ethical considerations in reconnecting severely alienated children with
their parents* [mp3 file]. Paper presented at the Association of Family and
Conciliation Courts (AFCC) 46th Annual Conference, New Orleans,
LA. Available from http://www.afccnet.org/ConferencesTraining/
AFCCConferences

Otis, M. R., & Warshak, R. A. (2010, June). *Family Bridges: Principles, procedures
and ethical considerations in reconnecting severely alienated children
with their parents* [mp3 file]. Workshop presented at the Association
of Family and Conciliation Courts (AFCC) 46th Annual Conference,
Denver, CO. Available from http://www.afccnet.org/ConferencesTraining/
AFCCConferences

Paetsch, J. J., Bertrand, L. D., Walker, J., MacRae, L. D., & Bala, N. (2009).
*Consultation on the Voice of the Child at the 5th World Congress on Family
Law and Children's Rights.* National Judicial Institute and Canadian
Research Institute for Law and the Family, Department of Justice Canada.
Retrieved November 30, 2010 from http://www.lawrights.asn.au/index.
php?option=com_wrapper&view=wrapper&Itemid=118

Parkes, A. (2009). The right of the child to be heard in family law proceedings: Article 12 UNCRC. *International Family Law,* 238–244.

Parkinson, P., Cashmore, J., & Single, J. (2005). Adolescents' views on the fairness of parenting and financial arrangements after separation. *Family Court Review, 43,* 429–444.

Parkinson, P., & Smyth, B. (2004). Satisfaction and dissatisfaction with father-child contact arrangements in Australia. *Child and Family Law Quarterly, 16,* 289–304.

Pedro-Carroll, J. (1997). The children of divorce intervention program: Fostering resilient outcomes for school-aged children. In G. W. Albee & T. P. Gullotta (Eds.), *Primary prevention works* (pp. 213–238). Thousand Oaks, CA: Sage.

Pedro-Carroll, J. (2005). Fostering resilience in the aftermath of divorce: The role of evidence-based programs for children. *Family Court Review, 43,* 52–64.

Pedro-Carroll, J. (2010). *Putting children first: Proven parenting strategies for helping children thrive through divorce.* New York: Avery/Penguin.

Pedro-Carroll, J., & Alpert-Gillis, L. J. (1997). Preventative interventions for children of divorce: A developmental model for 5 and 6 year old children. *The Journal of Primary Prevention, 18*(1), 5–23.

Pedro-Carroll, J., Alpert-Gillis, L. J., & Cowen, E. L. (1992). An evaluation of the efficacy of a preventative intervention for 4th-6th grade urban children of divorce. *The Journal of Primary Prevention, 13,* 115–129.

Pedro-Carroll, J., & Cowen, E. (1985). The children of divorce intervention program: An investigation of the efficacy of a school-based prevention program. *Journal of Consulting and Clinical Psychology, 53,* 603–611.

Pedro-Carroll, J. L., Sutton, S. E., & Wyman, P. A. (1999). A two-year follow-up evaluation of a preventive intervention for young children of divorce. *School Psychology Review, 28*(3), 467–476.

Pollet, S. L. (2009). A nationwide survey of programs for children of divorcing and separating parents. *Family Court Review, 47,* 523–543.

Pruett, M., Cowan, C. P., Cowan, P., & Diamond, J. (2012). Supporting father involvement in the context of separation and divorce. In K. Kuehnle & L. Drozds (Eds.), *Parenting plan evaluations: Applied research for the family court* (pp. 123–151). New York: Oxford University Press.

Racusin, R., & Copans, S. (1994). Characteristics of families of children who refuse post-divorce visits. *Journal of Clinical Psychology, 50,* 792–801.

Rand, D. (1997a). The spectrum of parental alienation syndrome, part I. *American Journal of Forensic Psychology, 15*(3), 23–52.

Rand, D. (1997b). The spectrum of parental alienation syndrome. Part II. *American Journal of Psychology, 15*(4), 39–92.

Rand, D. (2011). Parental alienation critics and the politics of science. *The American Journal of Family Therapy, 39,* 48–71.

Rand, D., & Rand, R. (2006). Factors affecting reconciliation. In R. A. Gardner, S. R. Sauber, & D. Lorandos (Eds.), *The international handbook of parental alienation syndrome: Conceptual, clinical and legal considerations* (pp. 195–208). Springfield, IL: Charles C Thomas.

Rand, D., Rand, R., & Kopetski, L. (2005). Spectrum of parental alienation syndrome part III: The Kopetski follow-up study. *American Journal of Forensic Psychology, 23*(1), 15–43.

Rand, R., & Warshak, R. (2008). *Overview of the family workshop—2.2.* Unpublished manuscript.

Reich, W. (1949). Character analysis (3rd ed.). (T. P. Wolfe, Trans.). New York: Orgone Institute Press.

Ripple, C. (2004). What is…prevention? *Voice, 5*(1), 27–28.

Saini, M., & Birnbaum, R. (2007). Unraveling the label of high conflict: What factors really count in separated and divorced families? Part 1. *Ontario Association of Children's Aid Society Journal, 51*(1), 14–20.

Saini, M. A., Johnston, J., Fidler, B. J., & Bala, N. (2012). Empirical studies of alienation . In K. F. Kuehnle & L. M. Drozd (Eds.), *Parenting plan evaluations: Applied research for the family court* (pp. 339–441). New York: Oxford Press.

Saini, M., & Newman, J. (2010). *Supervised visitation checklist (SVC).* Unpublished manuscript.

Salem, P. (2009). The emergence of triage in family court services: The beginning of the end for mandatory mediation? *Family Court Review, 47,* 371–388.

Salem, P., Kulack, D., & Deutsch, R. (2007). Triaging family court services: The Connecticut judicial branch's family civil intake screen. *Pace Law Review, 27*(4), 101–146.

Schepard, A. (2001). *Children, courts, and custody: Interdisciplinary models for divorcing families.* New York: Cambridge University Press.

Schirm, S., & Vallant, P. (2004). *La représentation des enfants en matière famille: Leur droits, leur avenir.* Cowansville, Canada: Yvonne Blais.

Schmidt, F., Cuttress, L. J., Lang. J., Lewandowski, M., & Rawana, J. S. (2007). Assessing the parent-child relationship in parenting capacity evaluations: Clinical applications of attachment research. *Family Court Review, 45*(2), 247–259.

Schutz, B., Dixon, E., Lindenberger, J., & Rutter, N. (1989). *Solomon's sword—A practical guide to conducting child custody evaluations.* San Francisco, CA: Jossey-Bass Publishers.

Schwartz, S. J., & Finley, G. E. (2009). Mothering, fathering and divorce: The influence of divorce on reports of and desires for maternal and paternal involvement. *Family Court Review, 47,* 506–522.

Semple, N. (2010). The silent child: A quantitative analysis of children's evidence in Canadian custody and access cases. *Canadian Family Law Quarterly, 29,* 7–43.

Shear, L. E. (2008). In search of statutory authority for parenting coordinator orders in California: Using a grass-roots hybrid model without an enabling statute. *Journal of Child Custody, 5*(1/2), 88–100.

Shifflett, K., & Cummings, E.M. (1999). A program for educating parents about the effects of divorce and conflict on children: An initial evaluation. *Family Relations, 48,* 79–89.

Siegel, J. (1996). Traditional MMPI-2 validity indicators and initial presentation in custody evaluations. *American Journal of Forensic Psychology, 13*(3), 55–63.

Siegel, J., & Langford, J. (1998). MMPI-2 validity scales and suspected parental alienation syndrome. *American Journal of Forensic Psychologist, 16*(4), 5–14.

Sigal, A., Sandler, I., Wolchik, S., & Braver, S. (2011). Do parent education programs promote healthy postdivorce parenting? Critical distinctions and a review of the evidence. *Family Court Review, 49*(1), 120–139.

Silverman, W. K., Pina, A. A., & Viswesvaran, C. (2008). Evidence-based psychosocial treatments for phobic and anxiety disorders in children and adolescents. *Journal of Clinical Child and Adolescent Psychology, 37*(1), 105–130.

Smart, C. (2002). From children's shoes to children's voices. *Family Court Review, 40*(3), 307–319.

Stahl, P. (1994). *Conducting child custody evaluations—A comprehensive guide.* Thousand Oaks, CA: Sage Publications.

Stahl, P. (1999). *Complex issues in child custody evaluation.* New York: Sage Publications.

Steinberger, C. (2006a). Father? What father? Parental alienation and its effect on children. *NYSBA Family Law Review, 38(1), 10–24.*

Steinberger, C. (2006b). Father? What father? Parental alienation and its effect on children. Part II. *Family Law Review, 38*(2), 9–14.

Stolberg, A.L., & Mahler, J. (1994). Enhancing treatment gains in a school-based intervention for children of divorce through skill training, parental involvement, and transfer procedures. *Journal of Consulting and Clinical Psychology, 62*(1), 147–156.

Stoltz, J. A. M., & Ney, T. (2002). Resistance to visitation: Rethinking parental and child alienation. *Family Court Review, 40*(2), 220–231.

Sullivan, M. J. (2004). Ethical, legal and professional practice issues involved in acting as a psychologist coordinator in child custody cases. *Family Court Review, 42*(3), 576–582.

Sullivan, M. J., & Kelly, J. B. (2001). Legal and psychological management of cases with an alienated child. *Family Court Review, 39,* 299–315.

Sullivan, M. J., Ward, P. A., & Deutsch, R. M. (2010). Overcoming barriers family camp: A program for high-conflict divorced families where a child is resisting contact with a parent. *Family Court Review, 48,* 115–134.

Timmer, S. G., Urquiza, A. J., Zebell, N. M., & McGrath, J. M. (2005). Parent-child interaction therapy: Application to maltreating parent-child dyads. *Child Abuse and Neglect, 29,* 825–842.

Timms, J. E. (2003). The silent majority—The position of children involved in the divorce and separation of their parents. *Child Care in Practice, 9*(2), 162–175.

Trahan, A. (2008). Le jude et l'enfant. In B. Morre, C. Bideau-Caye, & V. Lemay (Eds.), *La Représentation de l'enfant devant les tribineaux* (pp. 276–286). Montreal, Canada: Les Éditions Thémis.

Trussler, M. (2008). Managing high conflict family law cases for the sake of the children. *Canadian Bar Review, 86,* 515–538.

Tucker, A. (2006, October). *Parental alienation and rejection: Effects on children.* Paper presented at Independent Children's Lawyer Training Program, Law Council of Australia, Melbourne.

Turkat, I. D. (1994). Child visitation interference in divorce. *Clinical Psychology Review, 14,* 737–742.

Turkat, I. D. (1999). Divorce-related malicious parent syndrome. *Journal of Family Violence, 14,* 95–97.

Turkat, I. D. (2002). Parental alienation syndrome: A review of critical issues. *Journal of the American Academy of Matrimonial Lawyers, 18,* 131–176.

Vanbetlehem, J., Chodos, L., Geraldo, L., & Mingorance, J. (2010, June). *Alienation intervention: Hands-on work in the trenches* [mp3 file]. Paper presented at the Association of Family and Conciliation Courts (AFCC) 47th Annual Conference, Denver, CO. Available from http://www.afccnet.org/ ConferencesTraining/AFCCConferences

van IJzendoorn, M. H. (1995). Adult attachment representations, parental responsiveness, and infant attachment. A meta-analysis on the predictive validity of the Adult Attachment Interview. *Psychological Bulletin, 117,* 387–403.

Vassiliou, D., & Cartwright, G. (2001). The lost parents' perspective on parental alienation syndrome. *American Journal of Family Therapy, 29*(3), 181–191.

Velez, C. E., Wolchik, S. A., & Sander, I.N. Interventions to help parents and children through separation and divorce. In R. E. Tremblay, M. Boivin, & R. DeV. Peters (Eds.), *Encyclopedia on early childhood development* (online). Montreal, Candada: Centre of Excellence for Early Children Development; 2011:1–7. Available at http://www.child-encyclopedia.com/pages/PDF/ Velez-Wolchik-SandlerANGxp1.pdf. Accessed July 20, 2011.

Waldron, K. H., & Joanis, D. E. (1996). Understanding and collaboratively treating parental alienation syndrome. *American Journal of Family Law, 10,* 121–133.

Wallerstein, J. S., & Blakeslee, S. (1989). *Second chances: Men, women, and children a decade after divorce.* New York: Ticknore & Fields.

Wallerstein, J., & Kelly, J. (1976). The effects of parental divorce: Experiences of the child in later latency. *American Journal of Orthopsychiatry, 46*(2). Reprinted in *The anatomy of loneliness,* Hartog (Ed.), International Universities Press, New York, 1979.

Wallerstein, J. S., & Kelly, J. B. (1980). *Surviving the breakup: How children and parents cope with divorce.* New York: Basic Books.

Wallerstein, J., Lewis, J., & Blakeslee, S. (2000). *The unexpected legacy of divorce: A 25-year landmark study.* New York: Hyperion.

Wallerstein, J. S., & Tanke, T. (2006). To move or not to move. *Family Law Quarterly, 30*(4), 1–18.

Walker, L. E., & Shapirio, D. L. (2010). Parental Alienation Disorder: Why label children with a mental diagnosis? *Journal of Child Custody, 7*(4), 266–286.

Walker, L. E. A., Brantley, K. L., & Rigsbee, J. A. (2004a). A critical analysis of parental alienation syndrome and its admissibility in the family court. *Journal of Child Custody, 1*(2), 47–74.

Walker, L. E. A., Brantley, K. L., & Rigsbee, J. A. (2004b). Response to Johnston and Kelly critique of PAS Article. *Journal of Child Custody, 1*(4), 91–97.

Walsh, R., & Bone, M. (1997). Parental alienation syndrome: An age-old custody problem. *The Florida Bar Journal, 71*(6), 93–96.

Walters, M., & Friedlander, S. (2010). Finding a tenable middle space: Understanding the role of clinical interventions when a child refuses contact with a parent. *Journal of Child Custody, 7,* 287–328.

Walters, M. G., Friedlander, S. N., & Harper, J. R. (2010, June). *Interventions for hybrid cases involving alienation: Case studies.* Paper presented at the Association of Family and Conciliation Courts (AFCC) 46th Annual Conference, New Orleans, LA. Available from http://www.afccnet.org/ ConferencesTraining/AFCCConferences

Ward, P., Deutsch, R. M., & Sullivan, M. (2010, June). *Group weekend retreat for alienated and estranged families: An intensive model.* Paper presented at the Association of Family and Conciliation Courts (AFCC) 47th

Annual Conference, Denver, CO. Available from http://www.afccnet.org/ ConferencesTraining/AFCCConferences

Ward, P., & Harvey, J. (1993). Family wars: The alienation of children. *New Hampshire Bar Journal, 34*(1), 30–40.

Warshak, R. A. (2000). Remarriage as a trigger of parental alienation syndrome. *American Journal of Family Therapy, 28*(3), 229–241.

Warshak, R. A. (2001). Current controversies regarding parental alienation syndrome. *American Journal of Forensic Psychology, 19*(3), 29–59.

Warshak, R. A. (2002). Misdiagnosis of parental alienation syndrome. *American Journal of Forensic Psychology, 20*(2), 31–52.

Warshak, R. A. (2003a). Bringing sense to parental alienation: A look at the disputes and the evidence. *Family Law Quarterly, 37*(2), 273–301.

Warshak, R. A. (2003b). Payoffs and pitfalls of listening to children. *Family Relations, 52*(4), 373–384.

Warshak, R. A. (2006). Social science and parental alienation: Examining the disputes and the evidence. In R. A. Gardner, S. R. Sauber, & D. Lorandos (Eds.), *The international handbook of parental alienation syndrome: Conceptual, clinical and legal considerations* (pp. 352–371). Springfield, IL: Charles C Thomas.

Warshak, R. A. (2010a). Family Bridges: Using insights from social science to reconnect parents and alienated children. *Family Court Review, 48*, 48–80.

Warshak, R. A. (2010b). *Divorce poison: How to protect your family from badmouthing and brainwashing.* New York: Harper.

Weir, K. (2011). High-conflict contact disputes: Evidence of the extreme unreliability of some children's ascertainable wishes and feelings. *Family Court Review, 49*, 788–800.

Weitzman, J. (2004). Use of the one-way mirror in child custody reunification cases. *Journal of Child Custody, 1*(4), 27–48.

White, M., & Epston, D. (1990). *Narrative means to therapeutic ends.* New York: WW Norton.

Whitworth, J. D., Capshew, T. F., & Abell, N. (2002). Children caught in the conflict: Are court endorsed divorce-parenting education programs effective? *Journal of Divorce & Remarriage, 37*(3/4), 1–18.

Williams, J., & Van Dorn, R. (1999). Delinquency, gangs, and youth violence. In J. Jenson & Howard, M. (Eds.), *Youth violence: Current research and recent practice innovations* (pp. 199–228). Washington, DC: NASW Press.

Williams, R. J. (2001). Should judges close the gate on PAS and PA? *Family Court Review- Special issue: Alienated children in divorce, 39*(3), 267–281.

Wolchik, S. A., Sandler, I. N., Millsap, R. E., Plummer, B. A., Greene, S. M., Anderson, E. R., et al. (2002). Six-year follow-up of a randomized, controlled trial of preventive interventions for children of divorce. *Journal of the American Medical Association, 288*, 1874–1881.

Wolchik, S., Sandler, I. N., Weiss, L., & Winslow, E. (2007). New Beginnings: An empirically-based intervention program for divorced mothers to promote resilience in their children. In J. Briesmeister & C. Schaefer (Eds.), *Handbook of parent training: Helping parents prevent and solve problem behaviors* (pp. 25–62). Hoboken, NJ: John Wiley & Sons.

Wolchik, S. A., Sandler, I. N., Winslow, E., & Smith-Daniels, V. (2005). Programs for promoting parenting of residential parents: Moving from efficacy to effectiveness. *Family Court Review, 42,* 65–80.

Wolchik, S. A., West, S. G., Westover, S., Sandler, I. N., Martin, A., Lustig, J., et al. (1993). The children of divorce parenting intervention: Outcome evaluation of an empirically-based program. *American Journal of Community Psychology, 21,* 293–331.

Wood, J., Nezworski, M., Lilenfeld, S., & Garb, H. (2009). Projective techniques in the courtroom. In J. Skeem, K. Douglas, & S. Lilenfeld (Eds.), *Psychological science in the courtroom—Consensus and controversy.* New York: The Guilford Press.

Yankeelov, P. A., Bledsoe, L. K., Brown, J., & Cambron, M. L. (2003). Transition or not? A theory based quantitative evaluation of families in transition. *Family Court Review, 41*(2), 242–256.

Zeanah, C. H., & Benoit, D. (1994). Clinical applications of parent perception interview in infant mental health. *Child and Adolescent Psychiatric Clinics of North America, 4,* 439–554.

Zervopoulous, J. (2008). *Confronting mental health evidence: A practical guide to reliability and experts in family law.* USA: American Bar Association.

Zirogiannis, L. (2001). Evidentiary issues with parental alienation syndrome. *Family Court Review, 39*(3), 334–343.

Index

Note: Page numbers followed by *t, f* and *n* refer to tables and figures.